Contents

UFV Physics 083

Welcome to UFV Physics 083

UFV Physics 083 is a print and digital resource for classroom and independent study, aligned 100% with the curriculum. You, the student, have two core components — this write-in textbook or WorkText and, to provide mobile functionality, an interactive Online Study Guide.

UFV Physics 083 WorkText

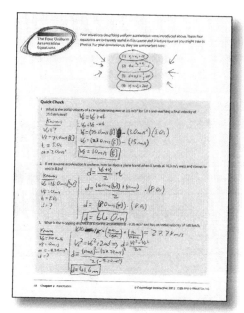

What is a WorkText?

A WorkText is a write-in textbook. Not just a workbook, a write-in **textbook**.

Like the vast majority of students, you will read for content, underline, highlight, take notes, answer the questions — all in this book. **Your book**.

Use it as a textbook, workbook, notebook, AND study guide. It's also a great reference book for post secondary studies.

Make it your own personal WorkText.

Why a write-in textbook?

Reading is an extremely active and personal process.

Research has shown that physically interacting with your text by writing margin notes and highlighting key passages results in better comprehension and retention.

Use your own experiences and prior knowledge to make meaning, not take meaning, from text.

How to make this book work for you:

1. Scan each section and check out the shaded areas and bolded terms.

2. Do the Warm Ups to activate prior knowledge.

3. Take notes as required by highlights and adding teacher comments and notes.

4. Use Quick Check sections to find out where you are in your learning.

5. Do the Review Questions and write down the answers. Scan the **QR codes** or go to the **Online Study Guide** to see YouTube-like video worked solutions by *UFV Physics 083* authors.

6. Try the **Online Study Guide** for online quizzes, PowerPoints, and more videos.

7. Follow the six steps above to be successful.

8. Need extra support? ASK AN AUTHOR!

For more information on how to purchase your own personal copy or if you'd like to ASK AN AUTHOR a question — info@edvantageinteractive.com

PHYS 083

University of the Fraser Valley

Authors

Dr. Gordon Gore
BIG Little Science Centre (Kamloops)

Lionel Sandner
Edvantage Interactive

Advisory Group

Oksana Makarenko
J.N. Burnett Secondary School
School District 38 Richmond

Peter Vogel
Notre Dame Regional Secondary School
Vancouver, British Columbia

Lui Zucchetto
Garibaldi Secondary School
School District 42 Maple Ridge

EDVANTAGE
● ●● INTERACTIVE

COPIES OF THIS BOOK MAY BE
OBTAINED BY CONTACTING:

Edvantage Interactive

E-MAIL:
info@edvantageinteractive.com

TOLL-FREE FAX:
866.275.0564

TOLL-FREE CALL:
866.422.7310

OR BY MAILING YOUR ORDER TO:

P.O. Box 20001
9839 Fifth Street
Sidney, BC V8L 2X4

BC Science Physics 11
Copyright © 2012, Edvantage Interactive

ISBN 978-1-77249-350-4

PHYS 083: University of the Fraser Valley – Reprint January 2017

Care has been taken to trace ownership of copyright material contained
in this text. The publishers will gladly accept any information that will
enable them to rectify any reference or credit in subsequent printings.

Vice-President of Marketing: *Don Franklin*
Director of Publishing: *Yvonne Van Ruskenveld*
Design/Illustration/Production: *Donna Lindenberg*
Proofreading: *Eva van Emden*
Glossary: *Rhys Sandner*
Index: *Noeline Bridge*
Photos: *p. 10, K. Jung; p. 11, Bureau international des poids et
mesures (BIPM)*

QR Code — What Is This?

The image to the right is called a QR code. It's similar to bar
codes on various products and contains information that
can be useful to you. Each QR code in this book provides you
with online support to help you learn the course material.
For example, find a question with a QR code beside it. If
you scan that code, you'll see the answer to the question
explained in a video created by an author of this book.

You can scan a QR code using an Internet-enabled mobile device. The program
to scan QR codes is free and available at your phone's app store. Scanning the
QR code above will give you a short overview of how to use the codes in the
book to help you study.

Note: We recommend that you scan QR codes only when your phone is
connected to a WiFi network. Depending on your mobile data plan, charges
may apply if you access the information over the cellular network. If you are
not sure how to do this, please contact your phone provider or us at
info@edvantageinteractive.com

UFV Physics 083 Online Study Guide (OSG)

What is an Online Study Guide?

It's an interactive, personalized, digital, mobile study guide to support the WorkText.

The **Online Study Guide** or OSG, provides access to online quizzes, PowerPoint notes, and video worked solutions.

Need extra questions, sample tests, a summary of your notes, worked solutions to some of the review questions? It's all here!

Access it where you want, when you want.

Make it your own personal mobile study guide.

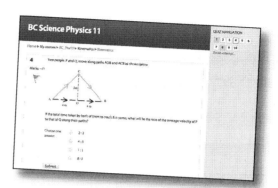

What's in the Online Study Guide?

- Online quizzes, multiple choice questions, provincial exam-like tests with instant feedback

- PowerPoint notes: Key idea summary and student study notes from the textbook

- Video worked solutions: Select video worked solutions from the WorkText

Scan this code for a quick tour of the OSG

If you have a smart phone or tablet, scan the QR code to the right to find out more. Colour e-reader WorkText version available.

Where is the Online Study Guide located?

edvantagescience.com

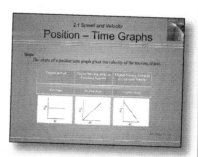

Should I use the Online Study Guide?

YES... if you want to do your best in this course.

The OSG is directly LINKED to the activities and content in the WorkText.

The OSG helps you learn what is taught in class.

If your school does not have access to the Online Study Guide and you'd like more information — info@edvantageinteractive.com

1 Skills, Methods, and the Nature of Physics

By the end of this chapter, you should be able to do the following:

- Describe the nature of physics
- Apply the skills and methods of physics including:
  - conduct appropriate experiments
  - systematically gather and organize data from experiments
  - produce and interpret graphs
  - verify relationships (e.g., linear, inverse, square, and inverse square) between variables
  - use models (e.g., physics formulae, diagrams, graphs) to solve a variety of problems
  - use appropriate units and metric prefixes

By the end of this chapter, you should know the meaning to these key terms:

- accuracy
- dependent variable
- experimental error
- independent variable
- law
- linear function
- model
- precision
- scalar quantities
- scientific method
- scientific notation
- slope
- uncertainty
- vector quantities
- y-intercept

In this chapter, you'll learn about the tools, skills, and techniques you'll be using as you study physics and about the nature of physics itself.

1.1 What is Physics?

Warm Up

This is probably your first formal physics course. In the space below, describe your definition of physics.

_____

_____

_____

Physics Explains the World

We live in an amazing place in our universe. In what scientists call the Goldilocks principle, we live on a planet that is just the right distance from the Sun, with just the right amount of water and just the right amount of atmosphere. Like Goldilocks in the fairy tale eating, sitting, and sleeping in the three little bears' home, Earth is just right to support life.

Yet there is much that we don't know about our planet. To study science is to be part of the enterprise of observing and collecting evidence of the world around us. The study of physics is part of this global activity. In fact, from the time you were a baby, you have been a physicist. Dropping food or a spoon from your baby chair was one of your first attempts to understand gravity. You probably also figured out how to get attention from an adult when you did this too, but let's focus on you being a little scientist. Now that you are a teenager you are beginning the process of formalizing your understanding of the world. Hopefully, this learning will never stop as there are many questions we do not have answers to and the wonder of discovering why things happen the way they do never gets boring. That is part of the excitement of physics — you are always asking why things happen.

Physics 11 will give you many opportunities to ask, "Why did that happen?" To find the answers to this and other questions, you will learn skills and processes to help you better understand concepts such as acceleration, force, waves, and special relativity. You will learn how to apply what you have learned in math class to solve problems or write clear, coherent explanations using the skills from English class. In physics class, you can apply the skills and concepts you have learned in other classes. Let's begin by looking at one method used to investigate and explain natural phenomena: the scientific method.

The Scientific Method

How do you approach the problems you encounter in everyday life? Think about beginning a new class at the start of the school year, for example. The first few days you make observations and collect data. You might not think of it this way, but when you observe your classmates, the classroom, and your teachers, you are making observations and collecting data. This process will inevitably lead you to make some decisions as you consider the best way to interact with this new environment. Who would you like for a partner in this class? Where do you want to sit? Are you likely to interact well with this particular teacher? You are drawing conclusions. This method of solving problems is called the **scientific method**. In future courses you may have an opportunity to discuss how the scientific method varies depending on the situation and the type of research being undertaken. For this course, an introduction to the scientific method is provided to give you a foundation to develop habits of thinking scientifically as you explore our world.

Figure 1.1.1 *Galileo (top) and Newton*

Four hundred years ago, scientists were very interested in understanding the world around them. There were hypotheses about why the Sun came up each day or why objects fell to the ground, but they were not based on evidence. Two physicists who used the scientific method to support their hypotheses were the Italian Galileo Galilei (1564–1642) and the Englishman Sir Isaac Newton (1642–1727).

Both Galileo and Newton provided insights into how our universe works on some fundamental principles. Galileo used evidence from his observations of planetary movement to support the idea that Earth revolved around the Sun. However, he was forced to deny this conclusion when put on trial. Eventually, his evidence was accepted as correct and we now consider Galileo one of the fathers of modern physics. Sir Isaac Newton, also considered one of the fathers of modern physics, was the first to describe motion and gravity. In this course, you will be introduced to his three laws of motion and the universal law of gravitation. Both ideas form a foundation for classical physics. Like many others that followed, both Galileo and Newton made their discoveries through careful observation, the collection of evidence, and interpretations based on that evidence.

Different groups of scientists outline the parts of the scientific method in different ways. Here is one example, illustrating its steps.

Steps of the Scientific Method

1. **Observation**: Collection of data. **Quantitative** observation has numbers or quantities associated with it. **Qualitative** observation describes qualities or changes in the quality of matter including, for example, a substance's colour, odour, or physical state.

2. **Statement of a hypothesis**: Formulation of a statement in an "if…then…" format that explains the observations.

3. **Experimentation**: Design and carry out a procedure to determine whether the hypothesis accurately explains the observations. After making a set of observations and formulating a hypothesis, scientists devise an experiment. During the experiment they carefully record additional observations. Depending on the results of the experiment, the hypothesis may be adjusted and experiments repeated to collect new observations many times.

   Sometimes the results of an experiment differ from what was expected. There are a variety of reasons this might happen. Things that contribute to such differences are called **sources of error**. They can include random errors over which the experimenter has no control and processes or equipment that can be adjusted, such as inaccurate measuring instruments. You will learn more about sources of error in experiments in section 1.3.

4. **Statement of a Theory**: Statement of an explanation for the hypotheses being investigated. Once enough information has been collected from a series of experiments, a reasoned and coherent explanation called a theory may be deduced. This theory may lead to a **model** that helps us understand the theory. A model is usually a simplified description or representation of a theory or phenomenon that can help us study it. Sometimes the scientific method leads to a **law**, which is a general statement of fact, without an accompanying set of explanations.

Quick Check

1. What is the difference between a law and a theory?

   _____

2. What are the fundamental steps of the scientific method?

   _____

   _____

   _____

   _____

3. Classify the following observations as quantitative or qualitative by placing a checkmark in the correct column. **Hint:** Look at each syllable of those words: quantitative and qualitative. What do they seem to mean?

Observation	Quantitative	Qualitative
Acceleration due to gravity is 9.8 m/s^2.		
A rocket travels faster than fighter jet.		
The density of scandium metal is 2.989 g/cm^3.		
Copper metal can be used for wire to conduct electricity.		
Mass and velocity determine the momentum in an object.		
Zinc has a specific heat capacity of 388 J/(kg·K).		
The force applied to the soccer ball was 50 N.		

4. Use the steps of the scientific method to design a test for the following hypotheses:
   (a) If cardboard is used to insulate a cup, it will keep a hot drink warmer.

   _____

   _____

   (b) If vegetable oil is used to grease a wheel, the wheel will turn faster.

   _____

   _____

   (c) If hot water is placed in ice cube trays, the water will freeze faster.

   _____

   _____

The Many Faces of Physics

There are many different areas of study in the field of physics. Figure 1.1.2 gives an overview of the four main areas. Notice how the areas of study can be classified by two factors: size and speed. These two factors loosely describe the general themes studied in each field. For example, this course focusses mainly classical mechanics, which involves relatively large objects and slow speeds.

A quick Internet search will show you many different ways to classify the areas of study within physics. The search will also show a new trend in the study of sciences, a trend that can have an impact on your future. Rather than working in one area of study or even within one discipline such as physics, biology, or chemistry, inter-disciplinary studies are becoming common. For example, an understanding of physics and biology might allow you to work in the area of biomechanics, which is the study of how the human muscles and bones work. Or maybe you will combine biology and physics to study exobiology, the study of life beyond the Earth's atmosphere and on other planets.

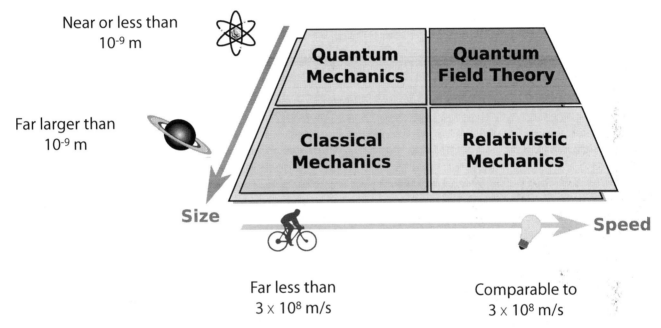

Figure 1.1.2 *The four main areas of physics. (Credit: Yassine Mrabet)*

1.2 Equipment Essentials

Warm Up

Your teacher will give you a pendulum made from some string and a washer. One swing of the pendulum back and forth is called a period and measured in seconds. Work with a partner to determine the period of your pendulum. Outline your procedure and results below. When you are done, identify one thing you would change in your procedure to improve your answer.

Using a Calculator

A calculator is a tool that helps you perform calculations during investigations and solving problems. You'll have your calculator with you for every class. At the same time, however, you are not to rely on it exclusively. You need to understand what the question is asking and what formula or calculation you need to use before you use your calculator. If you find yourself just pushing buttons to find an answer without understanding the question, you need to talk to your teacher or a classmate to figure it out. Many times you'll just need one concept clarified and then you can solve the problem.

Every calculator is different in terms of what order of buttons you need to push to find your answer. Use the Quick Check below to ensure you can find trigonometric functions and enter and manipulate exponents. If you cannot find the answers for these questions, check with your teacher immediately.

Quick Check

Using your calculator, what are the answers to the following mathematical statements?

1. $\sin 30°$ _____

2. $\tan^{-1} .345$ _____

3. 34^2 _____

4. $(3.2 \times 10^{-4}) \times (2.5 \times 10^6)$ _____

5. $pi - \cos 60°$ _____

Measuring Time

For objects that have a regularly repeated motion, each complete movement is called a **cycle**. The time during which the cycle is completed is called the **period** of the cycle. The number of cycles completed in one unit of time is called the **frequency** (f) of the moving object. You may be familiar with the frequencies of several everyday objects. For example, a car engine may have a frequency of several thousand rpm (revolutions per minute).

The turntable of an old phonograph record player may have frequencies of 33 rpm, 45 rpm, or 78 rpm. A pendulum 24.85 cm long has a frequency of one cycle per second. Tuning forks may have frequencies such as 256 vibrations per second, 510 vibrations per second, and so on.

Any measurement of time involves some sort of event that repeats itself at regular intervals. For example, a year is the time it takes Earth to revolve around the Sun; a day is the time it takes Earth to rotate on its axis; a month is approximately the time it takes the Moon to revolve around Earth. Perhaps *moonth* would be a better name for this time interval.

All devices used to measure time contain some sort of regularly vibrating object such as a pendulum, a quartz crystal, a tuning fork, a metronome, or even vibrating electrons. With a pendulum you can experiment with the properties to make it a useful timing device. When a pendulum undergoes regularly repeated movements, each complete movement is called a cycle, and the time required for each cycle is called its period.

A frequency of one cycle per second is called a **hertz (Hz)**. Higher frequencies (such as radio signal frequencies) may be expressed in kilohertz (kHz) or even megahertz (MHz), where 1 kHz is 1000 Hz, and 1 MHz is 1 000 000 Hz.

The Recording Timer

In Investigation 1-1, you will use a device called a recording timer like the one in Figure 1.2.1. The timer is a modified electric buzzer. A moving arm driven by an electromagnet

vibrates with a constant frequency, and each time it vibrates, it strikes a piece of carbon paper. The carbon paper makes a small dot on a moving piece of ticker tape. The small dots are a record of both time and distance. If you know the frequency of vibration of the timer, you can figure out the period of time between the dots, because period (T) and frequency (f) are reciprocals of one another.

$$T = 1/f, \text{ and } f = 1/T$$

If you measure the distance between the dots, this will tell you how far the object attached to the tape has moved. Knowing both distance and time, you can also calculate speed, since the speed of an object is the distance travelled divided by the time.

Figure 1.2.1 *A recording timer that uses ticker tape to record time and distance*

Using a Motion Probe

Another method for recording motion is a motion probe. There are several different models that can be used, but they all follow the same basic principles. Using a computer or graphing calculator, the probe is plugged in and run via a software program. The software program collects data on the motion you are studying and represents them as a graph on your computer screen.

Using the data collected, you can analyze the motion. Your teacher will demonstrate how to use the motion probe in your lab.

Investigation 1-1   Measuring the Frequency of a Recording Timer

Purpose
To measure the frequency of a recording timer and calculate its period

Procedure
1. Load the recording timer with a fresh piece of carbon paper. Pass a piece of ticker tape through the guiding staples, so that the carbon side of the paper faces the ticker tape. When the timer arm vibrates, it should leave a black mark on the tape.
2. To measure the frequency of the recording timer, you must determine how many times the arm swings in 1 s. Since it is difficult to time 1 s with any reasonable accuracy, let the timer run for 5 s, as precisely as you can measure it, then count the number of carbon dots made on the tape and divide by 5. Practise moving the tape through the timer until you find a suitable speed that will spread the dots out for easy counting, but do not waste ticker tape.
3. When you are ready, start the tape moving through the timer. Have your partner start the timer and the stopwatch simultaneously. Stop the timer when 5 s have elapsed. Count the number of dots made in 5 s and then calculate the frequency of your timer in hertz (Hz).

Concluding Questions
1. What was the frequency of your recording timer in Hz?
2. Estimate the possible error in the timing of your experiment. (It might be 0.10 s, 0.20 s, or whatever you think is likely.) Calculate the percent possible error in your timing. To do this, simply divide your estimate of the possible error in timing by 5.0 s and then multiply by 100.

   Example: If you estimate your timing error to be 0.50 s, then

   $$\text{percent possible error in timing} = \frac{0.50 \text{ s}}{5.0 \text{ s}} \times 100\% = 10\%$$

3. Your calculated frequency will have the same percent possible error as you calculated for your timing error. Calculate the range within which your timer's frequency probably falls.

   Example: If you calculate the frequency to be 57 Hz, and the possible error is 10%, then the range is 57 Hz $\pm$ 5.7 Hz, or between 51.3 Hz and 62.7 Hz. Rounded off, the range is between 51 Hz and 63 Hz. You might therefore conclude that the frequency of your timer is 57 $\pm$ 6 Hz.

4. If your timer operates on household voltage, its frequency (in North America) should be 60 Hz. Is 60 Hz within your estimated range for your timer?
5. (a) What is the period of your timer?
   (b) How many dots on the ticker tape represent
   (i)   1.0 s?
   (ii) 0.10 s?

1.3 Physics Essentials

Significant Digits

Imagine you are planning to paint a room in your house. To estimate how much paint you need to buy, you must know only the approximate dimensions of the walls. The rough estimate for one wall might be 8 m × 3 m. If, however, you are going to paste wallpaper on your wall and you require a neat, precise fit, you will probably make your measurements to the nearest millimetre. A proper measurement made for this purpose might look like this: 7.685 m × 2.856 m.

Significant digits ("sig digs") are the number of digits in the written value used to indicate the **precision** of a measurement. They are also called significant figures ("sig figs"). In the estimate of the wall size for determining how much paint is needed to cover a wall, the measurements (8 m × 3 m) have only one significant digit each. They are accurate to the nearest metre. In the measurements used to install wallpaper, the measurements had four significant digits. They were accurate to the nearest millimetre. They were more precise.

If you are planning to buy a very old used car, the salesman may ask you how much you want to spend. You might reply by giving him a rough estimate of around $600. This figure of $600 has one significant digit. You might write it as $600, but the zeros in this case are used simply to place the decimal point. When you buy the car and write a cheque for the full amount, you have to be more precise. For example, you might pay $589.96. This "measurement" has five significant digits. Of course, if you really did pay exactly $600, you would write the check for $600.00. In this case, all the zeros are measured digits, and this measurement has five significant digits!

You can see that zeros are sometimes significant digits (measured zeros) and sometimes not. The measurer should make it clear whether the zeros are significant digits or just decimal-placing zeros. For example, you measure the length of a ticker tape to be 7 cm, 3 mm, and around ½ mm long. How do you write down this measurement? You could write it several ways, and _all_ are correct:

7.35 cm, 73.5 mm, or 0.0735 m.

Each of these measurements is the same. Only the measuring _units_ differ. Each measurement has _three significant digits_. The zeros in 0.0735 m are used only to place the decimal.

In another example, the volume of a liquid is said to be 600 mL. How precise is this measurement? Did the measurer mean it was "around 600 mL"? Or was it 600 mL to the nearest millilitre? Perhaps the volume was measured to the nearest tenth of a millilitre. Only the measurer really knows. Writing the volume as 600 mL is somewhat ambiguous. To be unambiguous, such a measurement might be expressed in **scientific notation**. To do this, the measurement is converted to the product of a number containing the intended number of significant digits (using one digit to the left of the decimal point) and a power of 10. For example, if you write 6×10^2 mL, you are estimating to the nearest 100 mL. If you write 6.0×10^2 mL, you are estimating to the nearest 10 mL. A measurement to the nearest millilitre would be 6.00×10^2 mL. The zeros here are measured zeros, not just decimal-placing zeros. They are significant digits.

If it is not convenient to use scientific notation, you must indicate in some other way that a zero is a measured zero. For example, if the volume of a liquid is measured to the nearest mL to be "600." mL, the decimal point will tell the reader that you measured to the nearest mL, and that both zeros are measured zeros. "600. mL" means the same as 6.00×10^2 mL.

The number of significant digits used to express the result of a measurement indicates how precise the measurement was. A person's height measurement of 1.895 m is more precise than a measurement of 1.9 m.

Accuracy and Precision

Measured values are determined using a variety of different measuring devices. There are devices designed to measure all sorts of different quantities. The collection pictured in Figure 1.3.1 measures temperature, length, and volume. In addition, there are a variety of precisions (exactnesses) associated with different devices. The micrometer (also called a caliper) is more precise than the ruler while the burette and pipette are more precise than the graduated cylinder.

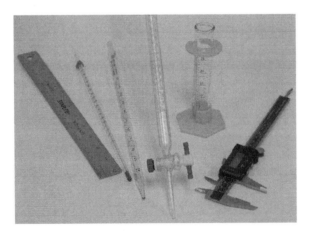

Figure 1.3.1 *A selection of measuring devices with different levels of precision*

Despite the fact that some measuring devices are more precise than others, it is impossible to design a measuring device that gives perfectly exact measurements. All measuring devices have some degree of **uncertainty** associated with them.

The 1-kg mass shown in Figure 1.3.2 is kept in a helium-filled bell jar at the BIPM in Sèvres France. It is the only exact mass on the planet. All other masses are measured relative to this and therefore have some degree of uncertainty associated with them.

Figure 1.3.2 *This kilogram mass was made in the 1880s. In 1889, it was accepted as the international prototype of the kilogram. (©BIPM — Reproduced with permission)*

Accuracy refers to the agreement of a particular value with the *true value*.

Accurate measurements depend on careful design and calibration to ensure a measuring device is in proper working order. The term **precision** can actually have two different meanings.

Precision refers to the reproducibility of a measurement or the agreement among several measurements of the same quantity.

– or –

Precision refers to the exactness of a measurement. This relates to uncertainty: the lower the uncertainty of a measurement, the higher the precision.

A measurement can be very precise, yet very inaccurate. In 1895, a scientist estimated the time it takes planet Venus to rotate on its axis to be 23 h, 57 min, 36.2396 s. This is a very precise measurement! Unfortunately, it was found out later that the period of rotation of Venus is closer to 243 days! The latter measurement is much less precise, but probably a good deal more accurate!

Experimental Error

There is no such thing as a perfectly accurate measurement. Measurements are always subject to some uncertainty. Consider the following sources of experimental error.

Systematic Errors

Systematic errors may result from using an instrument that is in some way inaccurate. For example, if a wooden metre stick is worn at one end and you measure from this end, every reading will be too high. If an ammeter needle is not properly "zeroed," all the readings taken with the meter will be too high or too low. Thermometers must be regularly checked for accuracy and corrections made to eliminate systematic errors in temperature readings.

Random Errors

Random errors occur in almost any measurement. For example, imagine you make five different readings of the length of a laboratory bench. You might obtain results such as: 1.626 m, 1.628 m, 1.624 m, 1.626 m, and 1.625 m. You might average these measurements and express the length of the bench in this way: 1.626 ± 0.002 m. This is a way of saying that your average measurement was 1.626 m, but the measurements, due to random errors, range between 1.624 m and 1.628 m.

Quick Check

Four groups of Earth Science students use their global positioning systems (GPS) to do some geocaching. The diagrams below show the students' results relative to where the actual caches were located.

1. Comment on the precision of the students in each of the groups. (In this case, we are using the "reproducibility" definition of precision.)

    _____

2. What about the accuracy of each group?

    _____

3. Which groups were making systematic errors?

    _____

4. Which groups made errors that were more random?

    _____

Other Errors

Regardless of the accuracy and precision of the measuring instrument, errors may arise when you, the experimenter, interact with the instrument. For example, if you measure the thickness of a piece of plastic using a micrometre caliper, your reading will be very precise but inaccurate if you tighten the caliper so much that you crush the plastic with the caliper!

A common personal error made by inexperienced experimenters is failing to read scales with eye(s) in the proper position. In Figure 1.3.3, for example, only observer C will obtain the correct measurement for the length of the block.

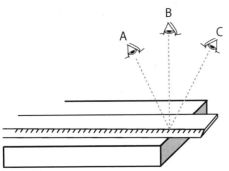

Figure 1.3.3 *Observers A and C will make incorrect readings because of their positions relative to the ruler.*

Imagine that you have a laboratory bench that is 1.75**6** m long. The last digit (in italics) is an estimate to the nearest millimetre. You might call it an uncertain digit. Perhaps a truer measure might be 1.75**5** m or 1.75**7** m. Often you must estimate the last digit in a measurement when you guess what a reading is between the smallest divisions on the measuring scale. This is true whether you are using a metre stick, a graduated cylinder, a chemical balance, or an ammeter.

Adding or Subtracting Measurements

Now imagine that you decide to add some thin plastic trim to the two ends of your bench. The trim has a width of 2.**2** mm, which is 0.002**2** m. What is the total length of the bench with the new trim added?

You add the widths of the two trimmed edges to the original length of the bench, like this:

```
1.756     m
0.0022    m
0.0022    m
1.7604    m = 1.760  m
```

There is no point in carrying the last digit in the total. Since the **6** in 1.75**6** is uncertain, this makes the **0** in 1.76**0**4 also uncertain, and the **4** following it a meaningless number. The proper way to write the total width of the bench is with just one uncertain digit, 1.76**0** m.

Now imagine you have a graduated cylinder containing 12.0**0** mL of water. You carefully lower a glass marble into the graduated cylinder, and observe that the water level rises to 14.2**0** mL. What is the volume of the glass marble? To find out, you subtract the two measurements:

```
 14.20    mL
−12.00    mL
  2.20    mL
```

Notice that when the two measurements are subtracted, you lose a significant digit in this particular situation. What if the object added to the water was a small lead pellet and the volume increased from 12.0**0** mL to 12.2**0** mL? The volume of the pellet would be 0.2**0** mL. This measurement has only two significant digits. When measurements are subtracted, there is often a loss of precision.

Here is a common sense rule for adding or subtracting measurements:

> When adding or subtracting measurements, the sum or difference will have as many digits after the decimal point as the single measurement with the least number of digits after the decimal point.

Sample Problem 1.3.1 — Addition and Subtraction

1. Add 4021.7 cm + 0.089 cm.
2. Subtract 5643.92 m – 5643.7 m.

What to Think About	How to Do It
1. Addition	
1. Determine uncertain digits to be added. Indicated in bold italic type.	$\begin{aligned} 4021.\boldsymbol{7} &\ cm \\ +\ \underline{0.0\boldsymbol{89}} &\ cm \end{aligned}$
2. Solve and report with the correct number of digits after decimal the point.	$\cong 4021.8\ cm$
1. Subtraction	
1. Determine uncertain digits to be added. Indicated in bold.	$\begin{aligned} 5643.9\boldsymbol{2} &\ m \\ -\ \underline{5643.\boldsymbol{7}} &\ m \end{aligned}$
2. Solve and report with the correct number of digits after the decimal point.	$\cong\quad 0.2\ m$
3. Notice that the subtraction of two precise measurements has produced a very imprecise difference.	

Practice Problems 1.3.1 — Addition and Subtraction

Complete the following operations, using the rules for adding or subtracting measurements.

1. 12.678 mm + 0.25 mm

2. 45.987 m³ + 2.1 m³ → $45.987\ m^3 + 2.1\ m^3$

3. 12.345 mL – 0.34 mL

4. 1.0001 mm – 0.1 mm

5. 12.5 g + 0.0005 g

6. 16.768 kg – 1.0 g

Multiplying or Dividing Measurements

You measure the dimensions of a wall to be 8.53 m × 2.74 m. What is the area of the wall? Imagine your calculator battery is dead, and you have to multiply the old-fashioned way. In the two measurements, the last digit is uncertain, so any product involving either of these two digits will also be uncertain.

$$
\begin{array}{r}
8.5\mathbf{3} \text{ m} \\
\times\ \ 2.7\mathbf{4} \text{ m} \\
\hline
\mathbf{3412} \\
597\mathbf{1}\ \ \ \\
170\mathbf{6}\ \ \ \ \ \ \ \\
\hline
23.\mathbf{3722}\ \ \text{m}^2 \cong 23.\mathbf{4}\ \text{m}^2
\end{array}
$$

Since the **3** following the decimal is an uncertain digit, all digits following it are meaningless. Round off the **.3722** to **.4**, and write 23.**4** m^2 for the area of the wall.

Use the following common sense rule when multiplying or dividing measurements:

> When multiplying or dividing measurements, the product or quotient must have no more significant digits than the single measurement with the fewest significant digits. In other words, the least precise single measurement determines the precision of the final product or quotient.

Sample Problem 1.3.2 — Multiplication and Division

1. Multiply 2.5**4** cm × 5.0**8** cm.
2. Divide 56.**8** m^2 by 2.**3** m.

What to Think About	How to Do It
1. Multiplication	
1. Determine uncertain digits. Indicated in bold.	2.54 cm × 5.08 cm
2. Multiple with calculator.	12.9032 cm^2
3. Answer is not to correct number of significant digits.	
4. Solve and report with correct number of digits after decimal point. Remember to multiple units as well.	12.9 cm^2
2. Division	
1. Determine uncertain digits. Indicated in bold.	56.8 m^2 by 2.3 m
2. Divide with calculator.	24.695652
3. Answer is not to correct number of significant digits.	
4. Solve and report with correct number of digits after decimal point. Remember to divide units as well.	25 m

---

Practice Problems 1.3.2 — Multiplication and Division

Perform the following operations, using the rule for multiplying and dividing measurements. Express answers in proper measuring units.

1. $1.25 \text{ m} \times 0.25 \text{ m}$

2. $3.987654 \text{ cm} \times 1.3 \text{ cm}$

3. $14.0 \text{ cm}^2 \div 2.1 \text{ cm}$

4. $5.646 \text{ mL} \times 13.6 \text{ g/mL}$

5. $\dfrac{98.45 \text{ g/mL} \ \ 5.762 \text{ mL}}{1.4 \text{ mL}}$

Scientific Notation

Scientific notation is a convenient way to express numbers that are very large or very small. For example, one ampere of electric current is a measurement of 6 240 000 000 000 000 000 electrons passing a point in a wire in 1 s. This same number can be written, in scientific notation, as 6.24×10^{18} electrons/second. This means 624 followed by 16 zeros.

Any number can be expressed in scientific notation. Here are some examples:

$$0.10 = 1.0 \times 10^{-1}$$
$$1.0 = 1.0 \times 10^{0}$$
$$10.0 = 1.00 \times 10^{1}$$
$$100.0 = 1.000 \times 10^{2}$$
$$1\,000.0 = 1.0000 \times 10^{3}$$

Quick Check

1. Write the following measurements in scientific notation.

   (a) 0.00572 kg _____

   (b) 520 000 000 000 km _____

   (c) 300 000 000 m/s _____

   (d) 0.000 000 000 000 000 000 16 C _____

   (e) 118.70004 g _____

2. Simplify.

   (a) $10^3 \times 10^7 \times 10^{12}$ _____

   (b) $10^{23} \div 10^5$ _____

   (c) $10^{12} \times 10^{-13}$ _____

   (d) $10^{-8} \times 10^{-12}$ _____

   (e) $10^5 \div 10^{-7}$ _____

   (f) $10^{-2} \div 10^{-9}$ _____

3. Do the following calculations, and express your answers in scientific notation with the correct number of significant digits.

   (a) $(6.25 \times 10^{-7}) \div (0.25 \times 10^4)$

   (b) $\dfrac{(93.8 \times 10^5)(6.1 \times 10^1)}{(7.6 \times 10^{11})(1.22 \times 10^7)}$

   (c) $4.10 \times 10^7 + 5.9 \times 10^6$

   (d) $(4.536 \times 10^{-3}) - (0.347 \times 10^{-4})$

4. A room has dimensions 13.48 m × 8.35 m × 3.18 m. What is its volume? Express your answer in scientific notation, with the correct number of significant digits.

5. The volume of water in a graduated cylinder is 5.00 mL. A small lead sphere is gently lowered into the graduated cylinder, and the volume rises to 5.10 mL. The mass of the lead sphere is 1.10 g. What is the density of the lead? (Density = mass/volume)

Review of Basic Rules for Handling Exponents

Power of 10 Notation

$$0.000001 = 10^{-6} \qquad 1 = 10^{0}$$
$$0.00001 = 10^{-5} \qquad 10 = 10^{1}$$
$$0.0001 = 10^{-4} \qquad 100 = 10^{2}$$
$$0.001 = 10^{-3} \qquad 1\,000 = 10^{3}$$
$$0.01 = 10^{-2} \qquad 10\,000 = 10^{4}$$
$$0.1 = 10^{-1} \qquad 100\,000 = 10^{5}$$
$$1 = 10^{0} \qquad 1\,000\,000 = 10^{6}$$

Multiplying Powers of 10

Law of Exponents: $a^{m} \cdot a^{n} = a^{m+n}$

(When multiplying, **add** exponents.)

Examples: $100 \times 1\,000 = 10^{2} \cdot 10^{3} = 10^{5}$

$$\frac{1}{100} \times 1\,000 = 10^{-2} \times 10^{3} = 10^{1}$$

$$2500 \times 4000 = 2.5 \times 10^{3} \times 4.0 \times 10^{3} = 10 \times 10^{6} = 1.0 \times 10^{7}$$

Dividing Powers of 10

Law of Exponents: $a^{m} \div a^{n} = a^{m-n}$

(When dividing, **subtract** exponents.)

Examples: $\dfrac{10^{5}}{10} = 10^{5-1} = 10^{4}$

$$\frac{100}{1000} = \frac{10^{2}}{10^{3}} = 10^{-1}$$

$$\frac{1.00}{100\,000} = \frac{10^{0}}{10^{5}} = 10^{-5}$$

1.4 Analysis of Units and Conversions in Physics

Warm Up

Place a check by the larger quantity in each row of the table.

Metric Quantity		Imperial Quantity	
A kilogram of butter		A pound of butter	
A five-kilometre hiking trail		A five-mile mountain bike trail	
One litre of milk		One quart of milk	
A twelve-centimetre ruler		A twelve-inch ruler	
A fifteen-gram piece of chocolate		A fifteen-ounce chocolate bar	
A temperature of 22°C		A temperature of 22°F	

Measurement Through History

Units of measurement were originally based on nature and everyday activities. The grain was derived from the mass of one grain of wheat or barley a farmer produced. The fathom was the distance between the tips of a sailor's fingers when his arms were extended on either side. The origin of units of length like the foot and the hand leave little to the imagination.

The inconvenient aspect of units such as these was, of course, their glaring lack of consistency. One "Viking's embrace" might produce a fathom much shorter than another. These inconsistencies were so important to traders and travellers that over the years most of the commonly used units were standardized. Eventually, they were incorporated into what was known as the English units of measurement. Following the Battle of Hastings in 1066, Roman measures were added to the primarily Anglo-Saxon ones that made up this system. These units were standardized by the Magna Carta of 1215 and were studied and updated periodically until the UK *Weights and Measures Act* of 1824 resulted in a major review and a renaming to the **Imperial system of measurement**. It is interesting to note that the United States had become independent prior to this and did not adopt the Imperial system, but continued to use the older English units of measure.

Despite the standardization, development of this system from ancient agriculture and trade has led to a vast set of units that are quite complicated. For example, there are eight different definitions for the amount of matter in a ton. The need for a simpler system, a system based on decimals, or multiples of 10, was recognized as early 1585 when Flemish mathematician Simon Stevin (1548–1620) published a book called *The Tenth*. However, most authorities credit Frenchman Gabriel Mouton (1618–1694) as the originator of the metric system nearly 100 years later. Another 100 years would pass before the final development and adoption of the metric system in France in 1795.

The International Bureau of Weights and Measures (BIPM) was established in Sévres, France, in 1825. The BIPM has governed the metric system ever since. Since 1960, the metric system has become the International System of Units, known as the SI system. SI is from the French *Système International*. The SI system's use and acceptance has grown to the point that only three countries in the entire world have not adopted it: Burma, Liberia, and the United States (Figure 1.4.1).

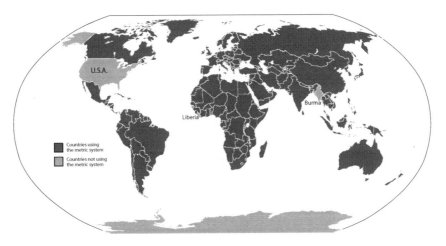

Figure 1.4.1 *Map of the world showing countries that have adopted the SI/metric system*

Dimensional Analysis

Dimensional analysis is a method that allows you to easily solve problems by converting from one unit to another through the use of conversion factors. The dimensional analysis method is sometimes called the factor label method. It may occasionally be referred to as the use of unitary rates.

> A **conversion factor** is a fraction or factor written so that the denominator and numerator are equivalent values with different units.

One of the most useful conversion factors allows the user to convert from the metric to the imperial system and vice versa. Since 1 inch is exactly the same length as 2.54 cm, the factor may be expressed as:

$$\frac{1 \text{ inch}}{2.54 \text{ cm}} \quad \text{or} \quad \frac{2.54 \text{ cm}}{1 \text{ inch}}$$

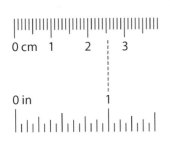

Figure 1.4.2 *A ruler with both imperial and metric scales shows that 1 inch = 2.54 cm.*

These two lengths are identical so multiplication of a given length by the conversion factor will not change the length. It will simply express it in a different unit (Figure 1.4.2).

Now if you wish to determine how many centimetres are in a yard, you have two things to consider. First, which of the two forms of the conversion factor will allow you to *cancel* the imperial unit, converting it to a metric unit? Second, what other conversion factors will you need to complete the task?

Assuming you know, or can access, these equivalencies: 1 yard = 3 feet and 1 foot = 12 inches, your approach would be as follows:

$$1.00 \; \text{yards} \times \frac{3 \; \text{feet}}{1 \; \text{yard}} \times \frac{12 \; \text{inches}}{1 \; \text{foot}} \times \frac{2.54 \; \text{cm}}{1 \; \text{inch}} = 91.4 \; \text{cm}$$

Notice that as with the multiplication of any fractions, it is possible to cancel anything that appears in both the numerator and the denominator. We've simply followed a numerator-to-denominator pattern to convert yards to feet to inches to cm.

The number of feet in a yard and inches in a foot are defined values. They are not things we measured. Thus they do not affect the number of significant digits in our answer. This will be the case for any conversion factor in which the numerator and denominator are in the same system (both metric or both imperial). Interestingly enough, the BIPM has indicated that 2.54 cm will be exactly 1 inch. So it is the only multiple-system conversion factor that will not influence the number of significant digits in the answer to a calculation. As all three of the conversion factors we used are defined, only the original value of 1.00 yards influences the significant digits in our answer. Hence we round the answer to three sig digs.

Converting Within the Metric System

The metric system is based on powers of 10. The power of 10 is indicated by a simple prefix. Table 1.4.1 is a list of SI prefixes. Your teacher will indicate those that you need to commit to memory. You may wish to highlight them.

Metric conversions require either one or two steps. You will recognize a one-step metric conversion by the presence of a *base unit* in the question. The common base units in the metric system are shown in Table 1.4.2.

Table 1.4.1 *SI Prefixes*

Prefix	Symbol	10^n
yotta	Y	10^{24}
zetta	Z	10^{21}
exa	E	10^{18}
peta	P	10^{15}
tera	T	10^{12}
giga	G	10^9
mega	M	10^6
kilo	k	10^3
hecto	h	10^2
deca	da	10^1
deci	d	10^{-1}
centi	c	10^{-2}
milli	m	10^{-3}
micro	μ	10^{-6}
nano	n	10^{-9}
pico	p	10^{-12}
femto	f	10^{-15}
atto	a	10^{-18}
zepto	z	10^{-21}
yocto	y	10^{-24}

Table 1.4.2 *Common Metric Base Units*

Measures	Unit Name	Symbol
length	metre	m
mass	gram	g
volume	litre	L
time	second	s

One-step metric conversions involve a base unit (metres, litres, grams, or seconds) being converted to a prefixed unit or a prefixed unit being converted to a base unit.

Two-step metric conversions require the use of two conversion factors. Two factors will be required any time there are two prefixed units in the question. In a two-step metric conversion, you must always convert to the base unit first.

Sample Problems 1.4.1— One- and Two-Step Metric Conversions

1. Convert 9.4 nm into m.   2. Convert 6.32 μm into km.

What to Think About	How to Do It
Question 1	
1. In any metric conversion, you must decide whether you need one step or two. There is a base unit in the question and only one prefix. This problem requires only one step. Set the units up to convert nm into m. Let the units lead you through the problem. You are given 9.4 nm, so the conversion factor must have nm in the denominator so it will cancel.	$9.4 \text{ nm} \times \dfrac{m}{nm} = m$
2. Now determine the value of nano and fill it in appropriately. **1 nm = 10^{-9} m** Give the answer with the appropriate number of significant digits and the correct unit. Because the conversion factor is a defined equality, only the given value affects the number of sig figs in the answer.	$9.4 \text{ nm} \times \dfrac{10^{-9} m}{1 \text{ nm}} = 9.4 \times 10^{-9} m$
Question 2	
1. This problem presents with two prefixes so there must be two steps. The first step in such a problem is always to convert to the base unit. Set up the units to convert from μm to m and then to km.	$6.32 \text{ μm} \times \dfrac{m}{μm} \times \dfrac{km}{m} = km$
2. Insert the values for 1 μm and 1 km. 1 μm = 10^{-6} m 1 km = 10^3 m	$6.32 \text{ μm} \times \dfrac{10^{-6} m}{1 \text{ μm}} \times \dfrac{1 km}{10^3 m} = 6.32 \times 10^{-9} km$
3. Give the answer with the correct number of significant digits and the correct unit.	

Practice Problems 1.4.1 — One- and Two-Step Metric Conversions

1. Convert 16 s into ks.

2. Convert 75 000 mL into L.

3. Convert 457 ks into ms.

4. Convert 5.6×10^{-4} Mm into dm.

Derived Unit Conversions

A **derived unit** is composed of more than one unit.

Units like those used to express rate (km/h) or density (g/mL) are good examples of derived units.

Derived unit conversions require cancellations in two directions (from numerator to denominator as usual AND from denominator to numerator).

Sample Problem 1.4.2 — Derived Unit Conversions

Convert 55.0 km/h into m/s.

What to Think About	How to Do It
1. The numerator requires conversion of a prefixed metric unit to a base metric unit. This portion involves one step only and is similar to sample problem one above.	$\dfrac{55.0 \ km}{h} \times \dfrac{m}{km} \times \dfrac{h}{min} \times \dfrac{min}{s}$
2. The denominator involves a time conversion from hours to minutes to seconds. The denominator conversion usually follows the numerator. Always begin by putting all conversion factors in place using *units only*. Now that this has been done, insert the appropriate numerical values for each conversion factor.	$= \dfrac{m}{s}$ $\dfrac{55.0 \ \cancel{km}}{\cancel{h}} \times \dfrac{10^3 \ m}{1 \ \cancel{km}} \times \dfrac{1 \ \cancel{h}}{60 \ \cancel{min}} \times \dfrac{1 \ \cancel{min}}{60 \ s}$
3. As always, state the answer with units and round to the correct number of significant digits (in this case, three).	$= 15.3 \ \dfrac{m}{s}$ The answer is 15.3 m/s.

Practice Problems 1.4.2 — Derived Unit Conversions

1. Convert 2.67 g/mL into kg/L. Why has the numerical value remained unchanged?

2. Convert the density of neon gas from 8.9994×10^{-4} mg/mL into kg/L.

3. Convert 35 mi/h (just over the speed limit in a U.S. city) into m/s. (Given: 5280 feet = 1 mile)

Use of a Value with a Derived Unit as a Conversion Factor

A quantity expressed with a derived unit may be used to convert a unit that measures one thing into a unit that measures something else completely. The most common examples are the use of rate to convert between distance and time and the use of density to convert between mass and volume. These are challenging! The keys to this type of problem are determining which form of the conversion factor to use and where to start.

Suppose we wish to use the speed of sound (330 m/s) to determine the time (in hours) required for an explosion to be heard 5.0 km away. It is always a good idea to begin any conversion problem by considering what we are trying to find. Begin with the end in mind. This allows us to decide where to begin. Do we start with 5.0 km or 330 m/s?

First, consider: are you attempting to convert a unit → unit, or a $\frac{unit}{unit} \rightarrow \frac{unit}{unit}$?

As the answer is unit → unit, begin with the single unit: km. The derived unit will serve as the conversion factor.

Second, which of the two possible forms of the conversion factor will allow conversion of a distance in km into a time in h? Do we require $\frac{330 \text{ m}}{1 \text{ s}}$ or $\frac{1 \text{ s}}{330 \text{ m}}$? As the distance unit must cancel, the second form is the one we require. Hence, the correct approach is

$$5.0 \text{ km} \times \frac{10^3 \text{ m}}{1 \text{ km}} \times \frac{1 \text{ s}}{330 \text{ m}} \times \frac{1 \text{ min}}{60 \text{ s}} \times \frac{1 \text{ h}}{60 \text{ min}} = 4.2 \times 10^{-3} \text{ h}$$

Sample Problem 1.4.3 — Use of Density as a Conversion Factor

What is the volume in L of a 15.0 kg piece of zinc metal? (Density of Zn = 7.13 g/mL)

What to Think About	How to Do It
1. Decide what form of the conversion factor to use: g/mL or the reciprocal, mL/g. Always begin by arranging the factors using *units* only. As the answer will contain one unit, begin with one unit, in this case, kg.	$$15.0 \text{ kg} \times \frac{g}{kg} \times \frac{mL}{g} \times \frac{L}{mL} = \underline{\quad} \text{ L}$$
2. Insert the appropriate numerical values for each conversion factor. In order to cancel a mass and convert to a volume, use the reciprocal of the density: $\dfrac{1 \text{ mL}}{7.13 \text{ g}}$	$$15.0 \text{ kg} \times \frac{10^3 \text{ g}}{1 \text{ kg}} \times \frac{1 \text{ mL}}{7.13 \text{ g}} \times \frac{10^{-3} \text{ L}}{1 \text{ mL}} = 2.10 \text{ L}$$
3. Calculate the answer with correct unit and number of significant digits.	

Practice Problems 1.4.3 — Use of Rate and Density as Conversion Factors

1. The density of mercury metal is 13.6 g/mL. What is the mass of 2.5 L?

2. The density of lead is 11.2 g/cm^3. The volumes 1 cm^3 and 1 mL are exactly equivalent. What is the volume in litres of a 16.5 kg piece of lead?

3. The speed of light is 3.0×10^{10} cm/s. Sunlight takes 8.29 min to travel from the photosphere (light-producing region) of the Sun to Earth. How many kilometres is Earth from the Sun?

Conversions Involving Units with Exponents (Another Kind of Derived Unit)

If a unit is squared or cubed, it may be cancelled in one of two ways. It may be written more than once to convey that it is being multiplied by itself *or* it may be placed in brackets with the exponent applied to the *number* inside the brackets as well as to the *unit*. Hence, the use of the equivalency 1 L = 1 dm^3 to convert 1 m^3 to L might appear in either of these formats:

$$1 \text{ m}^3 \times \frac{1 \text{ dm}}{10^{-1} \text{ m}} \times \frac{1 \text{ dm}}{10^{-1} \text{ m}} \times \frac{1 \text{ dm}}{10^{-1} \text{ m}} \times \frac{1 \text{ L}}{1 \text{ dm}^3} = 1 \text{ m}^3 \times \left(\frac{1 \text{ dm}}{10^{-1} \text{ m}}\right)^3 \times \frac{1 \text{ L}}{1 \text{ dm}^3} = 1000 \text{ L}$$

Chapter 1 Skills, Methods, and the Nature of Physics

Sample Problem 1.4.4 — Use of Conversion Factors Containing Exponents

Convert 0.35 m³ (cubic metres) into mL. (1 mL = 1 cm³)

What to Think About	How to Do It
1. The unit cm must be cancelled three times. Do this by multiplying the conversion factor by itself three times or through the use of brackets.	$0.35 \ m^3 \times \dfrac{cm}{m} \times \dfrac{cm}{m} \times \dfrac{cm}{m} \times \dfrac{mL}{cm^3}$ $= \underline{\hspace{2cm}} \ mL$ or $0.35 \ m^3 \times \left(\dfrac{cm}{m}\right)^3 \times \dfrac{mL}{cm^3}$ $= \underline{\hspace{2cm}} \ mL$
2. Once the units have been aligned correctly, insert the appropriate numerical values.	$0.35 \ m^3 \times \dfrac{1 \ cm}{10^{-2} \ m} \times \dfrac{1 \ cm}{10^{-2} \ m} \times \dfrac{1 \ cm}{10^{-2} \ m} \times \dfrac{1 \ mL}{1 \ cm^3}$ $= 3.5 \times 10^5 \ mL$
3. Calculate the answer with the correct unit and number of significant digits.	or $0.35 \ m^3 \times \left(\dfrac{1 \ cm}{10^{-2} \ m}\right)^3 \times \dfrac{1 \ mL}{1 \ cm^3} = 3.5 \times 10^5 \ mL$

Practice Problems 1.4.4 — Use of Conversion Factors Containing Exponents

1. Convert 4.3 dm³ into cm³.

2. Atmospheric pressure is 14.7 lb/in². Convert this to the metric unit, g/cm². (Given 454 g = 1.00 lb)

3. Convert a density of 8.2 kg/m³ to lb/ft³ using factors provided in this section.

Graphing

In Figure 1.4.3, a variable y is plotted against a variable x. Variable y is the **dependent** variable and variable x is the **independent** variable. In this particular situation, the graph is a straight line. (You might say that variable y is a **linear function** of the variable x.)

The Equation for a Straight Line

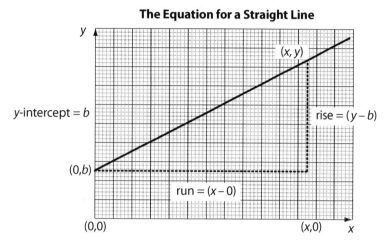

Figure 1.4.3 *In a straight line graph like this one, the variable y is a linear function of the variable x*

The **slope** of the graph is given the symbol m, where $m = \dfrac{\text{rise}}{\text{run}}$.

To find the value of the slope, the two points with coordinates $(0,b)$ and (x, y) will be used. The value of y where the graph intercepts the y-axis is called the **y-intercept**, and it is given the symbol b.

$$\text{Since } m = \frac{\text{rise}}{\text{run}} = \frac{(y - b)}{(x - 0)},$$

$$\text{Therefore, } mx = y - b, \text{ or}$$

$$y = mx + b$$

This is a general equation for any straight line. The slope of the line is m and the y-intercept is b.

To write an equation for any straight-line graph, you need only determine the value of the y-intercept by inspection and the slope by calculation. You can then substitute these values into the general equation.

For the linear graph in Figure 1.4.4, the y-intercept, by inspection, is 1.4. ($b = 1.4$) The **slope** is calculated using the two points with coordinates $(0, 1.4)$ and $(10.0, 4.4)$.

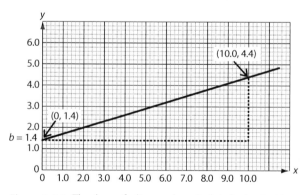

Figure 1.4.4 *The slope of a line can be calculated using just two points.*

$$m = \frac{(4.4 - 1.4)}{(10.0 - 0)} = \frac{3.0}{10.0} = 0.30$$

The equation for this straight line is therefore: $y = 0.30\,x + 1.4$

In these examples, the units of measure of the variables have not been included, in order to simplify the explanation. In experiments, the observations you make are frequently summarized in graphical form. When graphing experimental data, always include the measuring units and the specific symbols of the variables being graphed.

The three most common types of graphic relationships are shown in Figure 1.4.5.

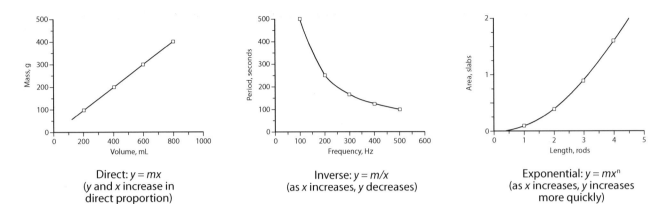

Direct: $y = mx$
(y and x increase in
direct proportion)

Inverse: $y = m/x$
(as x increases, y decreases)

Exponential: $y = mx^n$
(as x increases, y increases
more quickly)

Figure 1.4.5 *Three common types of graphic relationships*

Sample Problem 1.4.5 — Determination of a Relationship from Data

Find the relationship for the graphed data below:

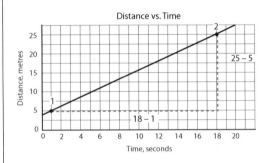

What to Think About

1. Determine the slope for the straight line. To do this, select two points on the line of best fit. These should be points whose values are easy to determine on both axes. *Do not use data points* to determine the constant.
   Determine the change in y (Δy) and the change in x (Δx) including the units.
   The constant is $\Delta y / \Delta x$.

2. Determine the relationship by subbing the *variable names* and the constant into the general equation, $y = mx + b$.

   Often, a straight line graph passes through the origin, in which case, $y = mx$.

How to Do It

Δy is $25-5 = 20$ m
Δx is $18 - 1 = 17$ s

$\dfrac{20 \text{ m}}{17 \text{ s}} = 1.18$ m/s

distance $= (1.18$ m/s$)$time $+ 4.0$ m/s.

Practice Problems 1.4.5 — Determination of a Relationship from Data

1. Examine the following graphs. What type of relationship does each represent? Give the full relationship described by graph (c).

(a)

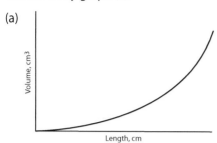

(b)

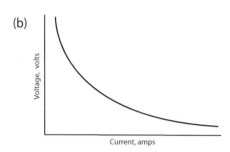

(c)

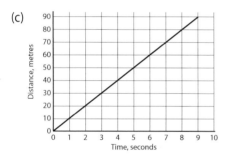

2. A beaker full of water is placed on a hotplate and heated over a period of time. The temperature is recorded at regular intervals. The following data was collected. Use the following grid to plot a graph of temperature against time. (Time goes on the x-axis.)

Temperature (°C)	Time (min)
22	0
30	2
38	4
46	6
54	8
62	10
70	12

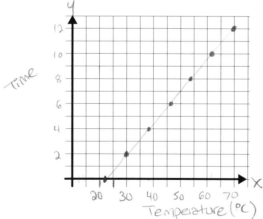

Continued on the next page

Practice Problems 1.4.5 — Determination of a Relationship from Data (Continued)

(a) What type of relationship was studied during this investigation?

The relationship between time and water temperature °C

(b) What is the constant (be sure to include the units)?

Time

(c) What temperature was reached at 5 min?

43°C

(d) Use the graph to determine the relationship between temperature and time.

It's direct, the longer time (x) the higher the temp (y)

(e) How long would it take the temperature to reach 80°C?

$y = mx$

(f) What does the *y*-intercept represent?

(g) Give a source of error that might cause your graph to vary from that expected.

Investigation 1-4   Making a Pendulum Clock

Purpose
To learn how a pendulum can be used as a clock

Procedure
1. Prepare a simple pendulum by tying a string to a pendulum bob, either a large washer, as in Figure 1.4.6, or a drilled metal ball. Feed the string through the opening of the pendulum support. Avoid winding the string around the support rod. If you do this, the length of the pendulum changes during a swing.

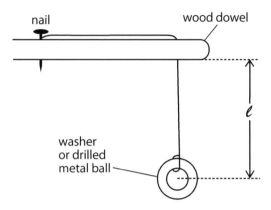

Figure 1.4.6 *Setup for Investigation 1-4*

2. Start by adjusting the length *l* of the pendulum so that it is as close to being 10.00 cm as you can make it. Measure *l* from the bottom of the pendulum clamp to the centre of the bob, as shown in Figure 1.4.6.
3. Push the bob a small distance, about 2 cm, to one side and let it swing freely. To get a rough idea of how long the pendulum takes to make one swing, use a stopwatch to measure the time it takes for the bob to swing from the highest point on one side of the swing to the highest point on the other side, then back to its starting position. The time it takes the pendulum bob to complete a full swing like this is called the period (*T*) of the pendulum. Try measuring the period of one swing several times with your stopwatch. Why do you think your measurements are so inconsistent?
4. To obtain a more reliable measurement of the period of the pendulum, you will now measure the time for a large number of swings (50) and find the average time for one swing by dividing by 50. Set your 10.00 cm pendulum swinging through a small arc, as before. Start counting backward (3, 2, 1, 0, 1, 2, 3, 4, etc.) and start your stopwatch at 0. Stop your watch after 50 swings and record the time your pendulum took to complete 50 swings.
5. To figure out the period of the pendulum, divide the time for 50 swings by 50.0. Record the period, *T*, in a table like Table 1.4.3. Check your result by repeating the measurement. If necessary, repeat a third time.

6. Measure the period of your pendulum for each of the lengths in Table 1.4.3. Record all your results in Table 1.4.3.
7. Prepare a graph with headings and labels like those in Figure 1.4.7. In this experiment, the period of the pendulum depends on its length, so the period is called the **dependent variable.** The dependent variable goes on the *y*-axis. Length is the **independent variable.** We chose what its values would be. Length is on the *x*-axis. Plot period against length using all your data from Table 1.4.3. Use a small dot with a circle around it to make each position more visible. See Figure 1.4.7 for a sample point. When you have plotted all the points, draw one smooth curve through as many of the points as possible. If one or two points are obvious errors, ignore them when drawing your curve.
8. Make pendulums with the lengths you obtain from your graph for pendulums with periods of 1.0 s and 2.0 s. See if the lengths predicted by the graph actually do produce 1.0 s and 2.0 s "clocks."

Table 1.4.3 *Data Table*

Length of Pendulum, ℓ (cm)	Time for 50 Swings (s)	Time for 1 Swing, Period, T (s)
10.00		
15.00		
20.00		
25.00		
30.00		
40.00		
50.00		
60.00		
70.00		
80.00		
90.00		
100.0		

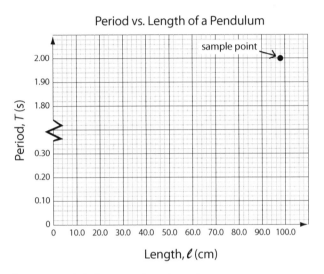

Figure 1.4.7 *Label your graph as shown here.*

Concluding Questions
1. According to your graph of period vs. length, how long must your pendulum be if it is to be used as (a) a "one-second clock"? (b) a "two-second clock"? (Such a pendulum takes 1s to swing one way, and one second to swing back.)
2. To increase the period of your pendulum from 1 s to 2 s, by how many times (to the nearest whole number) must you increase its length?

Challenges
1. Predict what length a 3.0 s pendulum clock would have to be. Test your prediction by experiment.
2. Predict what will happen to the period of a pendulum if you double the mass of the pendulum bob. Test your prediction.
3. Will the period of a pendulum change after it has been swinging for a while? Test your answer by experimenting!

1.5 Vectors

Introduction to Vectors

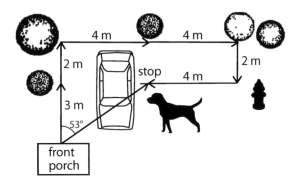

Figure 1.5.1 *Buddy's trip around the front yard*

In Figure 1.5.1, notice a series of arrows drawn on the map of a physics teacher's front lawn. Each arrow shows the *magnitude* (size) and *direction* of a series of successive trips made by Buddy, the teacher's dog. Buddy was "doing his thing" before getting into the car for a trip to school. These arrows, showing both magnitude and direction of each of Buddy's displacements, are called **vectors**.

To identify the direction of vectors, two common conventions are used: numerical and compass. Sometimes compass directions are also called cardinal directions.

Numerical directions use a positive and negative sign to indicate direction. If you think of a graph, the "up" direction on the *y*-axis and the "right" direction on the *x*-axis are positive. "Down" on the *y*-axis and "left" on the *x*-axis is negative. For example, a person walking 2 km right is walking +2 km and a person walking 2 km left is walking –2 km. The sign indicates direction.

Compass or cardinal directions are another way of indicating vector directions. As Figure 1.5.2 shows, there are four main directions on the compass: north, east, south, and west. North and west are usually positive, and east and south are negative. For example, if a person walking north encounters a person walking south, the two people are walking in opposite directions.

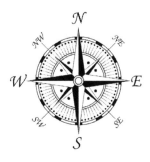

Figure 1.5.2 *The cardinal directions are north, east, south, and west, as shown on this compass.*

To determine the angle θ, you use trigonometric ratios. Three trigonometric ratios are particularly useful for solving vector problems. In the right-angled triangle ABC, consider the angle labelled θ. With reference to θ, AC is the opposite side (o), BC is the adjacent side (a), and AB is the hypotenuse (h). In any right-angled triangle, the hypotenuse is always the side opposite to the right angle.

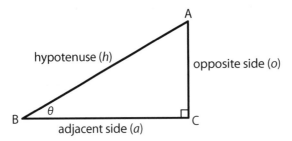

Figure 1.5.3 *The sides of a right-angled triangle are used to define trigonometric ratios.*

The three most commonly used trigonometric ratios are defined as follows:

$$\text{sine } \theta = \frac{\text{opposite side}}{\text{hypotenuse}} = \frac{o}{h}$$

$$\text{cosine } \theta = \frac{\text{adjacent side}}{\text{hypotenuse}} = \frac{a}{h}$$

$$\text{tangent } \theta = \frac{\text{opposite side}}{\text{adjacent side}} = \frac{o}{a}$$

Trigonometric ratios can help you solve vector problems quickly and accurately. Scientific calculators can provide you with the ratios for any angle.

Now, back to Figure 1.5.1. When Buddy reaches his final spot near the car door, how far has he walked since he left the front porch? This question has two answers, depending on what "How far?" means. The distance Buddy has travelled is the arithmetic sum of all the short distances he has travelled between the shrubs, trees, and fire hydrant while he visited them. This is simple to calculate.

total distance = 3.0 m + 2.0 m + 4.0 m + 4.0 m + 2.0 m + 4.0 m = 19.0 m

If, however, you want to know how far Buddy has travelled from the porch, the bold line in Figure 1.1.5, then you want to know Buddy's **displacement**. It turns out that Buddy's displacement from the front porch is 5.0 m. The bold arrow represents the magnitude (5.0 m) and the direction (53° to the right of his starting direction) of Buddy's displacement, and is called the **resultant displacement**. The resultant displacement is not the arithmetic sum, but the vector sum of the individual displacement vectors shown on the diagram.

There are two ways to indicate that a quantity is a vector quantity. The best way is to include a small arrow above the symbol for the vector quantity. For example, $\Delta \vec{d}$ symbolizes a displacement **vector**. If it's not possible to include the arrow when typing, a vector quantity may be typed in *bold italics*. For example, **Δd** also symbolizes a displacement **vector**. If only the magnitude of the vector is of importance, the symbol Δd (no arrow or not bold) is used.

Adding Vectors

Draw the first vector to scale and in the proper direction. Draw the second vector to scale, beginning at the tip of the first vector, and in the proper direction. Add the third vector (if there is one), beginning at the tip of the second vector. Repeat this procedure until all the vectors have been added. The vector sum or resultant of all the vectors is the vector that starts at the tail of the first vector and ends at the tip of the last vector.

This is what was done in Figure 1.5.1. The resultant displacement of Buddy is correctly written as 5.0 m, 53° to the right of his starting direction.

Scalars and Vectors

If you add 3 kg of sugar to 2 kg of sugar, you will have 5 kg of sugar. If you add 3 L of water to 2 L of water, you will have 5 L of water. Masses and volumes are added together by the rules of ordinary arithmetic. Mass and volume are **scalar quantities**. Scalar quantities have magnitude but no direction. Other scalar quantities include: distance, speed, time, energy, and density.

If you add a 3 m displacement to a 2 m displacement, the two displacements together may add up to 5 m, but they may also add up to 1 m or any magnitude between 1 m and 5 m! Figure 1.5.2 shows some of the ways these displacements might add up. In Figure 1.5.4, the two displacement vectors are added by the rule for vector addition. As you can see, the resultant displacement depends on the directions of the two vectors as well as their magnitudes. In addition to displacements, other vector quantities include force, velocity, acceleration, and momentum. These are all quantities you will study in Physics 11.

When you describe displacement, force, velocity, acceleration, or momentum, you must specify not only the magnitude of the quantity but also its direction.

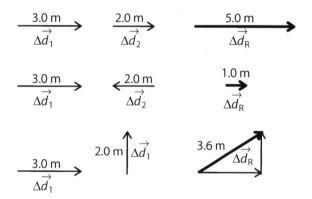

Figure 1.5.4 *Different ways to add up displacements*

Free Body Diagrams

In Figure 1.5.5(a)**,** two basketball players, A and B, are having a tug-of-war for possession of the ball. Neither is winning. What is the resultant of the forces exerted by A and B on the ball? A is pulling with a force of 120.0 N to the left, and B is pulling with a force of 120.0 N to the right. If the two force vectors $\vec{F}_A$ and $\vec{F}_B$ are added by the rule for vector addition, the resultant is zero. (See Figure 1.5.5(b).) This should not surprise anyone, because if there is no acceleration of the ball in either direction, the net force on the ball *should* be zero!

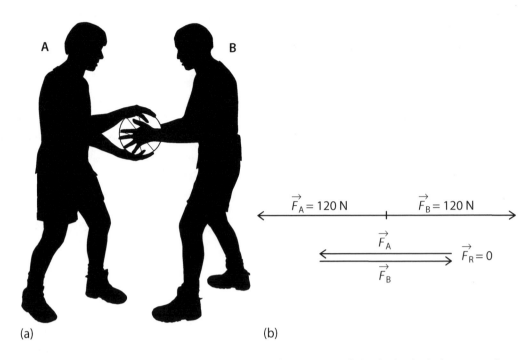

Figure 1.5.5 (a) *The basketball players are both exerting forces on the ball.* **(b)** *The free body diagram on the right shows the forces and work and the resultant force.*

For many problems, it helps to draw a diagram that represents the situation being examined. These diagrams do not have to be a work of art, but rather a clear representation of the vectors being examined. When you sketch a diagram and add vector arrows you have created a **free-body diagram**. Figure 1.5.3(b) is an example of a very simple, but effective diagram. A free-body diagram is a representation used to analyze the forces acting on a body of interest. A free body diagram shows all forces of all types acting on this body. All other information in the problem is not included. While all the vectors may not be exerted on the same point in real life, it is customary to place the tails of the vectors at the centre of the object. You should also include directions indicating what direction is positive and what direction is negative.

2 Kinematics

By the end of this chapter, you should be able to do the following:

➤ Apply knowledge of the relationships between time, displacement, distance, velocity, and speed to situations involving objects in one dimension
- differentiate between scalar and vector quantities
- construct displacement-versus-time graphs, based on data from various sources
- use a displacement-versus-time graph to determine
  - displacement and distance
  - average velocity and speed
  - instantaneous velocity and speed
- solve problems involving
  - displacement
  - time
  - average velocity
- construct velocity-versus-time graphs, based on data from various sources
- use velocity-versus-time graphs to determine
  - velocity
  - displacement
  - average velocity

➤ Apply knowledge of the relationships between time, velocity, displacement, and acceleration to situations involving objects in one dimension
- use velocity-versus-time graphs to determine acceleration, given appropriate data
- solve a range of problems for objects with constant acceleration involving
  - displacement
  - initial velocity
  - final velocity
  - acceleration
  - time
- recognize that a projectile experiences a constant downward acceleration due to gravity if friction is ignored
- solve projectile motion problems involving
  - displacement
  - initial velocity
  - final velocity
  - acceleration due to gravity
  - time

By the end of this chapter, you should know the meaning to these **key terms**:

- acceleration
- average velocity
- constant acceleration
- displacement
- distance
- final velocity
- initial velocity
- instantaneous velocity
- projectile motion
- scalar quantity
- speed
- vector quantity
- velocity

A roller coaster is an exciting example of kinematics in action.

By the end of the chapter, you should be able to use and know when to use the following formulae:

$$v = \frac{\Delta d}{\Delta t} \qquad a = \frac{\Delta v}{\Delta t} \qquad d = \bar{v}t \qquad v = v_0 + at$$

$$\bar{v} = \frac{v + v_0}{2} \qquad d = v_0 t + \frac{1}{2}at^2 \qquad v^2 = v_0^2 + 2ad$$

2.1 Speed and Velocity

The Study of Motion

How far did it travel? How long did it take? How fast did it move? Did it speed up or slow down? These are typical questions one might ask about any object that moves, whether it is a car, a planet, an electron, or a molecule. All of these questions fall under the heading of **kinematics:** the study of the motion of objects, without reference to the cause of the motion. In kinematics, we learn how to describe the motion of objects in terms of measurable variables such as time, distance, speed, and acceleration.

Distance and Displacement

When you take a trip a road sign will tell you the distance you have to travel to reach your destination. This distance is usually measured in kilometres. Other distances you are familiar with include metres, centimeters, and millimetres. Each of these measurement units tells you how far two points are apart. Because magnitude, or amount of distance covered, and not distance is stated, distance is a scalar quantity. The symbol for distance is d.

In the vector section of Chapter 1, two methods for determining direction were described. The first method involved the use of positive (+) and negative (–) signs to indicate direction. Any motion right or up is usually considered positive. Any motion left or down is usually considered negative. The second method uses compass points. North and east are usually considered positive, and west and south are negative. Sometimes this can change depending on the question. For example if all the motion is downward, you may consider using down as positive so the math calculations do not involve negative signs.

When a direction is added to a distance, the position of an object or person is described. For example, if you are 5 km [east] of your home you are describing your position. **Position** is the shortest distance between the origin and where the person or object is located. Position is a vector quantity and includes magnitude and direction. The symbol for position is $\vec{d}$.

If you change your position by moving another position 5 km [east] of your original position, then you have a displacement. **Displacement** is a change in position and is a straight line between initial and final positions. It includes magnitude and direction. The symbol for displacement is $\Delta \vec{d}$. It is calculated by determining the change from one position to another. Or put mathematically:

$$\Delta \vec{d} = \vec{d}_f - \vec{d}_0$$

The Δ sign is important because it indicates a change. In this situation, displacement is defined as the change between the initial position and final position, not the displacement from the origin, which is your home.

Sample Problem 2.1.1 — Calculating Displacement

A person is 2.0 m to the left of a viewpoint sign enjoying the view. She moves 4.5 m to the right of the sign to get a better view. What is the person's displacement?

What to Think About	How to Do It
1. Assume right is positive and identify the positions.	$\vec{d}_o = 2.0 \text{ m [left]} = -2.0 \text{ m}$ $\vec{d}_f = 4.5 \text{ m [right]} = 4.5 \text{ m}$
2. Find the displacement.	$\Delta\vec{d} = \vec{d}_f - \vec{d}_o$ $\Delta\vec{d} = 4.5 \text{ m} - (-2.0 \text{ m})$ $\quad = 6.5 \text{ m}$ The person's displacement is 6.5 m [right]

Practice Problems 2.1.1 — Calculating Displacement

1. A woman walking her dog travels 200 m north, then 400 m west, then 500 m south.
    (a) What was the total distance she travelled?

    (b) What was the magnitude of her displacement for the entire trip?

Continued on the next page

---

2. The diagram below shows the displacements of a golf ball caused by a rookie golfer attempting to reach hole number 7 on Ocean View Golf and Country Club. The golfer requires six shots to put the ball in the hole. The diagram shows the six displacements of the ball.

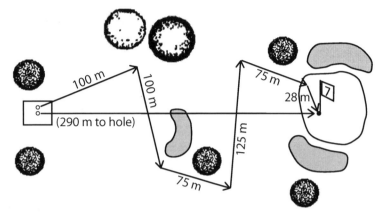

(a) What is the total distance the golf ball travelled while the golfer was playing the seventh hole?

(b) What is the resultant displacement of the ball?

3. What is the total distance and displacement the dog takes after it leaves the front porch?

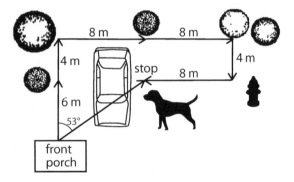

Speed

The **speed** of an object such as a car is defined as the distance it travels in a unit of time. For highway traffic, speeds are measured in kilometres per hour (km/h). Typical highway speed limits are 80 km/h, 100 km/h, and 120 km/h. Within city limits, speed limits may be 60 km/h, 50 km/h, or 30 km/h (school zone or playground). The average speed of an athlete in a 100 m dash might be approximately 9.0 m/s. The speed of sound is 330 m/s, while the speed of light is approximately 300 000 000 m/s or 300 000 km/s.

If you make a long journey by car, you might be interested in calculating your **average speed** for the trip. For example, if you travel a distance of 450 km in a time of 6.0 h, you would calculate your average speed by dividing the total distance by the total time.

$$\text{average speed} = \frac{\text{total distance}}{\text{total time}} = \frac{450 \text{ km}}{6.0 \text{ h}} = 75 \text{ km/h}$$

The symbol used for speed is v, and for average speed, $\bar{v}$. Note that it is a line above the v, not an arrow. The formula for calculating average speed from distance (d) and time (t) is therefore:

$$\bar{v} = \frac{d}{t}$$

If you are driving along the highway and spot a police car parked beside the road with its radar aimed at your car, you will be less interested in your average speed and more concerned with your **instantaneous speed**. That is how fast your car is going at this instant in time! Your speedometer will indicate what your instantaneous speed is.

Quick Check

1. (a) What is the difference between average speed and instantaneous speed?

    (b) Under what condition may average speed and instantaneous speed be the same?

2. A tourist travels 320 km in 3.6 h. What is her average speed for the trip?

3. A trucker travels 65 km at an average speed of 85 km/h. How long does the trip take?

4. If your car averages 92 km/h for a 5.0 h trip, how far will you go?

The Difference Between Speed and Velocity

You learned that speed is distance travelled in a unit of time. Average speed is total distance divided by time, and instantaneous speed is the speed of an object at a particular instant. If an object moves along at the same speed over an extended period of time, we say its speed is uniform or constant.

Uniform speed is uncommon, but it is possible to achieve nearly uniform speed in some situations. For example, a car with "cruise control" may maintain fairly constant speed on the highway. Usually, however, a vehicle is making small changes in speed and direction all the time.

If an object is not travelling in a straight line all the time, then its direction becomes important and must be specified. When both the size and the direction of a speed are specified, we call the two properties (speed and direction) the **velocity** of the object. The symbol for velocity is $\vec{v}$. If you say your car is moving 80 km/h, then you are describing your car's speed. If you say your car is travelling 80 km/h in a northerly direction, then you are describing your car's velocity. The difference between speed and velocity becomes important in situations where direction changes during a trip. For example, when a ball is thrown into the air, both its speed and its direction change throughout its trajectory, therefore velocity is specified in this situation. Velocity is calculated by finding the displacement of an object over a period of time. Mathematically this is represented by:

$$\vec{v} = \frac{\Delta \vec{d}}{\Delta t} = \frac{\vec{d}_f - \vec{d}_0}{\Delta t}$$

Position-Time Graphs

Speed and velocity can be graphically represented. The slope of a position-time graph gives the velocity of the moving object. A positive slope indicates positive velocity. A negative slope indicates negative velocity. When an object is not moving, the position does not change, so the slope is zero. That is, the line is horizontal.

Sometimes it can be confusing to determine the direction and the sign to use. It is important to remember what point of view or frame of reference you are using to observe the action. For example, if you are riding a bike toward your friend at a velocity of 10 km/h [west], your friend sees you coming at 10 km/h [east]. Both of you observe the same situation, it's just the direction that is different. That is why it is important to know which direction is positive and which direction is negative before you start. Usually, if all the motion is in one direction, positive values will be used unless indicated. That will be the case in this book.

The next sample problem describes how the motion of a skateboarder can be solved mathematically and graphically and the velocity of the skateboarder determined.

Sample Problem 2.1.2 — Solving Motion Problems Mathematically

You are on a skateboard and moving to the right covering 0.5 m each second for 10 s. What is your velocity?

What to Think About	How to Do It
1. Motion is uniform so the velocity is the same for each time interval. Right will be positive.	$\vec{d}_o = 0.0 \, m$ $\vec{d}_f = 0.5 \, m$ $\Delta t = 1.0 \, s$
2. Solve for velocity.	$\vec{v} = \dfrac{\Delta \vec{d}}{\Delta t} = \dfrac{\vec{d}_f - \vec{d}_o}{\Delta t}$ $= \dfrac{0.5 \, m - 0.0 \, m}{1.0 \, s}$ $= 0.5 \, m/s$
3. Include direction in the answer, which is right since the answer is positive.	$\vec{v} = 0.5 \, m/s \, [right]$

Sample Problem 2.1.3 — Solving Motion Problems Graphically

You are on a skateboard and moving to the right covering 0.5 m each second for 10 s. What is your velocity?

What to Think About

1. Collect data and record in table. Moving right will be considered positive.

How to Do It

d (m)	0	0.5	1.0	1.5	2.0	2.5	3.0	3.5	4.0	4.5	5.0
t (s)	0	1.0	2.0	3.0	4.0	5.0	6.0	7.0	8.0	9.0	1.0

2. Graph data and draw best fit line.

Position vs time of a skateboarder

3. Find slope as it is equal to the velocity of the skateboarder.

$$slope = \frac{\Delta \vec{d}}{\Delta t} = \frac{\vec{d}_f - \vec{d}_o}{\Delta t} = \vec{v}$$

$$\vec{v} = \frac{5.0 \, m - 0.0 \, m}{10 \, s}$$

$$= 0.5 \, m/s$$

$$\vec{v} = 0.5 \, m/s \, [right]$$

4. The slope is positive, so the direction is to the right.

Practice Problems 2.1.3 —Solving Motion Problems Graphically

1. Describe the motion represented in each of the following position-time graphs.

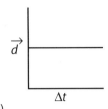

(a)

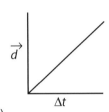

(b)

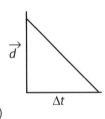

(c)

2. Sketch a graph of each of the following situations.
    (a) A golf ball is rolling towards a cup at 1.5 m/s [west].

    (b) A person is watching from the view of the cup and seeing the ball roll 1.5 m/s [east].

    (c) A person is traveling at 1.5 m/s [west] watching the ball roll towards the cup.

3. (a) Fill in the data table if a car is traveling at 30 km/h through a school zone.

Time (s)	1.0	2.0	3.0	4.0	5.0	6.0	7.0	8.0
Distance (m)								

    (b) Graph this data on a distance vs. time graph.

Investigation 2-1   Measuring the Speed of a Model Car

Purpose

To measure the speed of a model car, such as a radio-controlled vehicle

Procedure

1. Remove a 5.0 m length of ticker tape from a roll. Pass one end of it through a recording timer, and then tape it to a battery-powered toy car. (Figure 2.3)

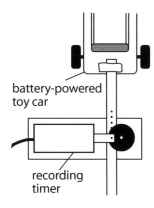

battery-powered
toy car

recording
timer

Figure 2.1.1 *Step 1*

2. Turn on the timer and let the car travel at its full speed until all the tape has passed through the timer.
3. Every six dots is one-tenth of a second. Mark off the time intervals in one-tenth of a second on your tape
4. Measure the distance traveled in each tenth of a second. Record your data in a table similar to Table 2.1.1.

Table 2.1.1 *Data Table for Investigation 2-1*

Time (s)	0.0	0.1	0.2	0.3	0.4	0.5	0.6	0.7	0.8	0.9	1.0	1.0	1.1	...
Distance per interval (cm)														...
Total distance (cm)														...

5. Create a distance vs. time graph. On the *y*-axis, use total distance and on the *x*-axis, use time. Draw a best-fit line on your graph.
6. Find the slope of your graph and record it along with the appropriate units.

Concluding Questions

1. What does the slope of a distance-time graph represent?
2. Find the average speed of the toy car over five 1 s intervals of the trip.
3. Compare your slope of the distance-time graph with your average speed over the five 1 s intervals.
4. Why might the average speed of the car during the first 1 s intervals be less than the average speed later in the trip?

2.1 Review Questions

1. Can objects with the same speed have different velocities? Why or why not?

2. What are two ways of describing the direction of an object's motion?

3. If you run with an average speed of 12.0 km/h, how far will you go in 3.2 min?

4. If the average speed of your private jet is 8.0×10^2 km/h, how long will it take you to travel a distance of 1.8×10^3 km?

5. A red ant travels across a driveway, which is 3.5 m wide, at an average speed of 2.6 cm/s. How long will the ant take to cross the driveway? Express your answer (a) in seconds and (b) in minutes.

6. If your car moves with a steady speed of 122 km/h for 20.0 min, then at a steady speed of 108 km/h for 30.0 min, what is the average speed of your car for the entire trip?

7. A car moves with a steady speed of 84 km/h for 45 min, then 96 km/h for 20 min.
   (a) What was the total distance travelled during the whole trip?

   (b) What is its average speed for the whole trip?

8. After a soccer practice, Gareth and Ben are heading home. They reach the corner, where they go separate ways. Gareth heads south to the bus stop. Ben walks north to his house. After 5.0 min, Gareth is 600 m [S] and Ben is 450 m [N].

   (a) On the same graph (below), graph the position of each boy after 5.0 min and find the velocity of each boy.

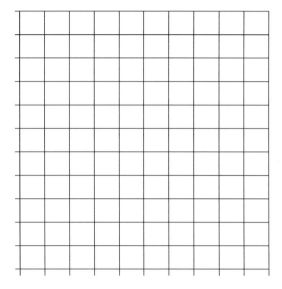

   (b) Find the velocity of each boy using algebra.

2.2 Acceleration

Warm Up

Below are two blank speed-time graphs.
On graph (a), sketch the slope that represents a sports car traveling at constant speed.
On graph (b), sketch the slope of the same car starting from rest and speeding up at a constant rate.

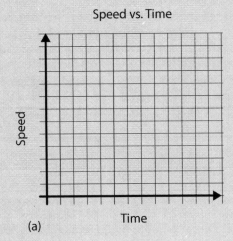

(a)

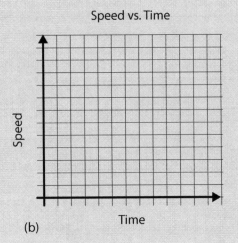

(b)

Changing Velocity

Whenever the velocity of an object changes, the object experiences **acceleration.** Acceleration is a change in velocity over a period of time:

$$\text{acceleration} = \frac{\text{change in velocity}}{\text{change in time}}$$

The symbol for acceleration is a. Velocity has the same symbol as speed, which is v. If the velocity at the start of the time interval is v_0, and at the end of the time interval is v_f, then the change in velocity will be $v_f - v_0$. If the time at the beginning of the time interval is t_0, and the time at the end of the time interval is t_f, then the change in time, the time interval, is $t_f - t_0$. Using these symbols, acceleration can be defined as:

$$a = \frac{v_f - v_0}{t_f - t_0} \text{ or } a = \frac{\Delta v}{\Delta t}$$

where the Δ symbol is shorthand for "change in" or "interval."

Since velocity has two aspects to it, both speed and direction, acceleration can occur under three conditions:
(a) if speed changes,
(b) if direction changes or
(c) if both speed and direction change.

The standard unit for expressing acceleration is m/s^2. An object is accelerating at a rate of 1 m/s^2 if its speed is increasing at a rate of 1 m/s each second.

Sample Problem 2.2.1 — Calculating Acceleration

A runner racing in a 100 m dash accelerates from rest to a speed of 9.0 m/s in 4.5 s. What was his average acceleration during this time interval?

What to Think About	How to Do It
1. Determine the correct formula.	$a = \dfrac{\Delta v}{\Delta t} = \dfrac{v_f - v_o}{t_f - t_o}$
2. Solve for acceleration. Note that runner's average acceleration was 2.0 m/s/s, which is usually written 2.0 m/s^2	$= \dfrac{9.0 \text{ m/s} - 0 \text{ m/s}}{4.5 \text{ s} - 0 \text{ s}}$ $a = 2.0 \text{ m/s}^2$ The runner's average acceleration was 2.0 m/s^2.

Practice Problems 2.2.1 — Calculating Acceleration

1. What is the average acceleration for the following?
   (a) A car speeds up from 0 km/h to 60.0 km/h in 3.00 s.

   (b) A runner accelerates from rest to 9.00 m/s in 3.00 s.

2. What is the average acceleration of a truck that accelerates from 45.0 km/h to 60.0 km/h in 7.50 s?

3. A car travelling 120 km/h brakes hard to avoid hitting a deer on the road, slowing to 60 km/h in 4.0 s. What is its acceleration? Why is it negative?

Negative Acceleration

Sometimes you will find a situation where the acceleration is negative. You may think this implies that an object is slowing down, but that is not always the case. Consider the situations shown in Figure 2.2.1.

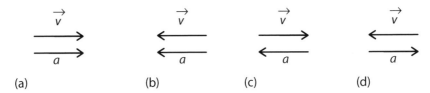

v
a
(a)
v
a
(b)
v
a
(c)
v
a
(d)

Figure 2.2.1 *The vectors represent the velocity and acceleration of a car in different situations.*

In (a) and (b) the velocity of the car and the acceleration are in the same direction. This means the car is speeding up, even though the acceleration is negative in (b). In (c) and (d) the velocity and acceleration are in opposite directions and the car is slowing down. We can summarize that this way:

When the velocity and acceleration are in the same direction, the object is speeding up, even if the acceleration is negative. When the velocity and acceleration are in opposite directions, the object is slowing down.

Graphing Acceleration

In Figure 2.2.2, fictitious data is used to show how your results from Investigation 2-1 might have been graphed. In this figure, the average speed of the cart is plotted on the *y*-axis, since it is the dependent variable. Time is on the *x*-axis, because it is the independent variable.

Notice that in Figure 2.2.2 the speeds are plotted halfway through each time interval. For example, the average speed of 11 cm/s, which occurs in the first time interval of the sample tape, would be plotted at 0.05 s, not at 0.10 s. This is because the average speed during the interval will occur halfway through it, not at the end of the interval. This assumes, of course, that the speed is increasing at a constant rate and therefore acceleration is constant. The average speed for each interval is the same as the instantaneous speed half way through the interval, if acceleration is constant.

The graph you see in Figure 2.2.2 is, in fact, a graph of the instantaneous speed of the cart vs. time, although average speeds were used to obtain it. To write an equation describing the line in this graph, you need to know the *y*-intercept and the slope.

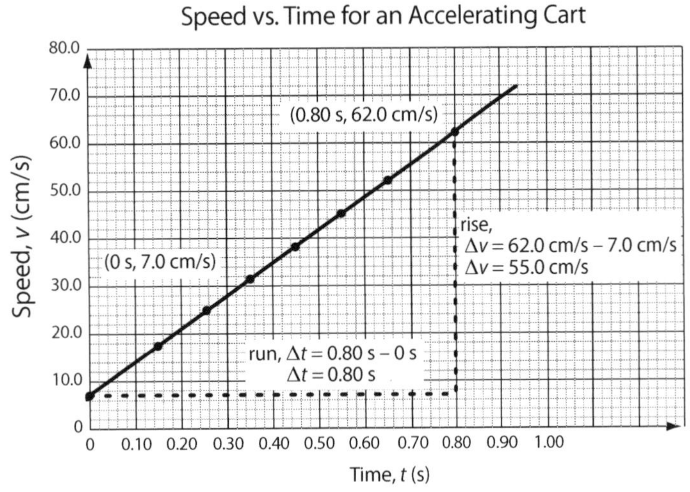

Speed vs. Time for an Accelerating Cart
Speed, v (cm/s)
80.0
70.0
60.0
50.0
40.0
30.0
20.0
10.0
0
(0.80 s, 62.0 cm/s)
(0 s, 7.0 cm/s)
rise,
Δv = 62.0 cm/s – 7.0 cm/s
Δv = 55.0 cm/s
run, Δt = 0.80 s – 0 s
Δt = 0.80 s
0 0.10 0.20 0.30 0.40 0.50 0.60 0.70 0.80 0.90 1.00
Time, t (s)

Figure 2.2.2 *An example of a graph showing acceleration*

By inspection, the y-intercept, b, equals 7.0 cm/s. The slope m is found by using the points (0 s, 7.0 cm/s) and (0.80 s, 62 cm/s). Notice that the "rise" of the line is equal to the change in the speed of the cart, Δv, and $\Delta v = v_f - v_0$. The "run" of the graph is the change in time Δt, and $\Delta t = t_f - t_0$.

$$\text{slope} = m = \frac{\Delta v}{\Delta t} = \frac{v_f - v_0}{t_f - t_0} = \frac{62.0 \text{ cm/s} - 7.0 \text{ cm/s}}{0.80 \text{ s} - 0 \text{ s}} = \frac{55.0 \text{ cm/s}}{0.80 \text{ s}} = 69 \text{ cm/s}^2$$

Notice that the slope has units of acceleration. This is because the slope of the speed-time graph *is* acceleration! Remember that acceleration is equal to the change in speed of the cart per second. The slope $m = \Delta v/\Delta t$, which is the acceleration of the cart.

The equation for the line in Figure 2.2.2 will have the same form as the general equation for a straight line, which is $y = mx + b$. When describing experimental results from a graph, however, we substitute the specific symbols for the variables used in the experiment. We also use the numerical values for the y-intercept and slope, complete with their measuring units. The equation for the line in Figure 2.2.2 is therefore

$$v = (69 \text{ cm/s}^2)t + 7.0 \text{ cm/s}$$

where v is the speed of the cart at any time t.

2.2 Review Questions

1. A policeman travelling 60 km/h spots a speeder ahead, so he accelerates his vehicle at a steady rate of 2.22 m/s^2 for 4.00 s, at which time he catches up with the speeder.

   (a) How fast was the policeman travelling in m/s?

   (b) How fast is the police car travelling after 4.00 s? Give your answer in both m/s and km/h.

2. A motorbike accelerates at a constant rate from a standing start. After 1.2 s, it is travelling 6.0 m/s. How much time will have elapsed (starting from rest) before the bike is moving with a speed of 15.0 m/s?

3. The graph below shows lines representing speed vs. time for an accelerating aircraft, prepared by observers at two different locations on the runway.

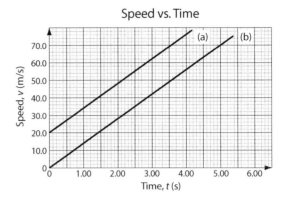

   (a) What is the equation for line (a)?

   (b) What is the equation for line (b)?

   (c) What is the acceleration of the aircraft according to line (a)?

   (d) What is the acceleration of the aircraft according to line (b)?

   (e) Explain why the y-intercept for line (b) is different than the intercept for line (a).

4. A racing motorbike's final velocity is 38 m/s in 5.5 s with an acceleration of 6.0 m/s². What was the initial velocity of the motorbike?

5. While starting your car, which is a standard gearshift, you coast downhill getting to a speed of 2.0 m/s before the engine starts. You accelerate back uphill moving at 5.5 m/s. This takes a total of 3.0 s. If downhill is the positive direction, what is the average acceleration of your car?

6. The graph below describes the motion of a vehicle whose acceleration changes twice. Find the acceleration of the vehicle for the parts of the graph labeled (a), (b) and (c), by finding the slope of each part of the graph.

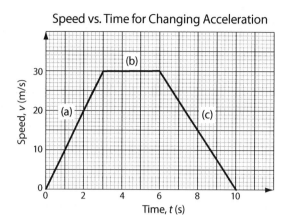

Speed vs. Time for Changing Acceleration

(a)

(b)

(c)

2.3 Uniform Acceleration

Warm Up

In your own words, describe the difference between average velocity, initial velocity, final velocity, and a change in velocity.

_____

_____

_____

_____

Graphing Acceleration

In a situation where the speed of a moving body increases or decreases at a uniform rate the acceleration is considered uniform. This motion can be graphed on a speed vs. time and will be linear (Figure 2.3.1). Since speed is the dependent variable, it is plotted on the y-axis. Time, the independent variable, will be on the x-axis.

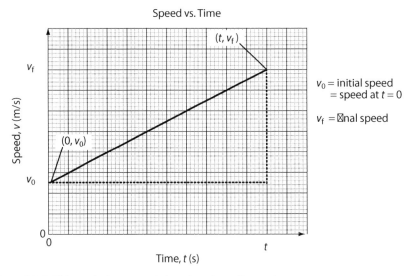

Figure 2.3.1 _This graph shows speed changing at a uniform rate._

The y-intercept for the speed-time graph is $b = v_0$, where v_0 is the speed of the object at time $t = 0$. In Figure 2.3.1, the initial time is zero and the final time is t, so the time interval is simply $\Delta t = t - 0 = t$.

The slope of the graph is $m = \dfrac{\Delta v}{\Delta t} = a$, since acceleration is change in speed divided by change in time.

$$\text{If } a = \frac{v_f - v_0}{t}$$

Then $at = v_f - v_0$ and

$$\boldsymbol{v_f = v_0 + at} \qquad \textbf{(1)}$$

This is a general equation for any object that accelerates at a uniform rate. It says that the final speed of the accelerating object equals the initial speed plus the change in speed (at).

Sample Problem 2.3.1 — Determining Uniform Acceleration

The graph below shows the uniform acceleration of an object, as it was allowed to drop off a cliff.

(a) What was the acceleration of the object?

(b) Write an equation for the graph.

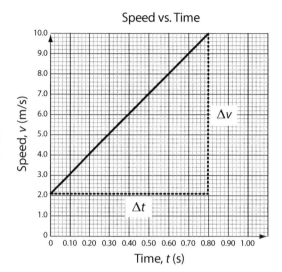

$$\Delta v = v_f - v_0$$

$$\Delta t = t_f - 0$$

What to Think About	How to Do It
(a)	
1. The acceleration is determined by finding the slope of the speed-time graph.	$a = \dfrac{\Delta v}{\Delta t} = \dfrac{v_f - v_0}{t_f - t_0}$
	$= \dfrac{10.0 \text{ m/s} - 2.0 \text{ m/s}}{0.80 \text{ s} - 0 \text{ s}} = \dfrac{8.0 \text{ m/s}}{0.80 \text{ s}}$
	$a = 1.0 \times 10^1 \text{ m/s}^2$
(b)	
1. Determine the general equation for any straight line.	$y = b + mx$
2. For this line, the slope m is the acceleration. Inspection of the graph reveals that the y-intercept, b, is 2.0 m/s.	$m = 1.0 \times 10^1 \text{ m/s}^2$ $b = 2.0 \text{ m/s}$ $x = t$ $y = v_f$
3. Derive the specific equation for this line. Note that the final, specific equation for this graph includes the actual numerical values of the y-intercept and slope, complete with their measuring units. Once this equation is established, it can be used in place of the graph, since it describes every point on the graph.	$v_f = 2.0 \text{ m/s} + (1.0 \times 10^1 \text{ m/s}^2) \cdot t$

Practice Problems 2.3.1 — Determining Uniform Acceleration

Speed vs. Time

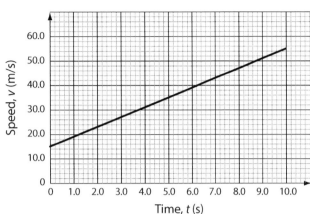

1. (a) What is the *y*-intercept (v_0) for the graph shown above?

   (b) What is the slope of the graph?

   (c) What property of the moving object does this slope measure?

   (d) Write the specific equation for the graph, using symbols *v* for speed and *t* for time.

2. The following equation describes the motion of a ball thrown straight down, by someone leaning out of the window of a tall building:

$$v_f = 5.0 \text{ m/s} + (9.8 \text{ m/s}^2) \cdot t$$

   (a) At what speed was the ball initially thrown out of the window?

   (b) What was the acceleration of the ball?

   (c) How fast was the ball moving after 1.2 s?

Calculating Distance from Uniform Acceleration

Consider an object that is accelerating uniformly from initial speed v_0 to a final speed v_f in time t. as shown in Figure 2.3.2. How would you calculate the distance travelled by the object during this time?

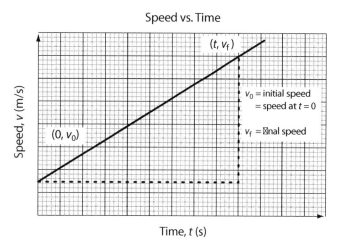

Figure 2.3.2 *This graph represents an object accelerating at a uniform rate.*

The total distance d travelled in time t will equal the average speed $\bar{v}$ multiplied by time t. The average speed $\bar{v}$ is just the average of the initial speed v_0 and the final speed v_f, which is:

$$\bar{v} = \frac{v_0 + v_f}{2}$$

Distance travelled is $d = \bar{v}$ or
$$d = \frac{v_0 + v_f}{2} \cdot t \qquad (2)$$

However, it has already been shown that
$$v_f = v_0 + at \qquad (1)$$

Therefore,
$$d = \frac{v_0 + v_0 + at}{2} \cdot t$$

and
$$d = \frac{2v_0 + at}{2} \cdot t = \frac{2v_0 t + at^2}{2}$$

Finally,
$$d = v_0 t + \frac{1}{2}at^2 \qquad (3)$$

Sometimes you encounter situations involving uniform acceleration where you have no information about the time interval, t, during which the motion occurred. If you know the initial speed v_0 and the final speed v_f, you can still calculate the distance travelled if you know at what rate the object is accelerating.

For uniform acceleration,
$$d = \frac{v_0 + v_f}{2} \cdot t, \text{ and } v_f = v_0 + at$$

Therefore,
$$t = \frac{v_f - v_0}{a}$$

Substituting for t in the first equation,
$$d = \frac{v_0 + v_f}{2} \cdot \frac{v_f - v_0}{a} = \frac{v_f^2 - v_0^2}{2a}$$

Thus,
$$2ad = v_f^2 - v_0^2$$

Therefore,
$$v_f^2 = v_0^2 + 2ad \qquad (4)$$

The Four Uniform Acceleration Equations

Four equations describing uniform acceleration were introduced above. These four equations are extremely useful in this course and in future courses you might take in physics. For your convenience, they are summarized here:

$$(1) \quad v_f = v_0 + at$$

$$(2) \quad d = \frac{v_0 + v_f}{2} \cdot t$$

$$(3) \quad d = v_0 t + \frac{1}{2} at^2$$

$$(4) \quad v_f^2 = v_0^2 + 2ad$$

Quick Check

1. What is the initial velocity of a car accelerating east at 3.0 m/s² for 5.0 s and reaching a final velocity of 25.0 m/s east?

2. If we assume acceleration is uniform, how far does a plane travel when it lands at 16.0 m/s west and comes to rest in 8.00 s?

3. What is the stopping distance of a car if it accelerates at –9.29 m/s² and has an initial velocity of 100 km/h.

Investigation 2-3   Measuring Acceleration

Purpose

To measure the uniform acceleration of an object

Part 1

Procedure

1. Figure 2.3.3 shows one way to produce uniformly accelerated motion. (Your teacher may have a different method and will explain it to you.) Remove a 1-m piece of ticker tape from a roll. Pass the tape through a recording timer and tape it to a laboratory cart, as shown in the diagram. A 500 g mass is attached to the cart by a 1 m string that passes over a pulley. The force of gravity on the mass accelerates both the mass and the cart.

2. For best results in this experiment, there should be no slack in the ticker tape before the cart is released. One partner should place the hanging mass over the pulley, and hold onto the cart so that it does not accelerate prematurely. When all is ready, simultaneously turn on the timer and release the cart.

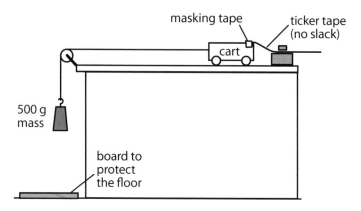

Figure 2.3.3 *Apparatus setup for Part 1*

3. Your finished ticker tape record will look something like the one in Figure 2.3.4. Often there is a smudged grouping of dots at the start, so choose the first clear dot and label it the "0th" dot (Figure 2.3.4). On your tape, mark clearly the 0th dot, 6th dot, 12th dot, 18th dot, 24th dot, and so on until you have at least six time intervals. The timer has a frequency of 60 Hz. This means it makes 60 vibrations each second. The time interval between dots on your tape is 1/60 s. If you use a time interval of six dots, this is 6/60 s or 1/10 s. In other words, an interval of six dots is the same as 0.10 s.

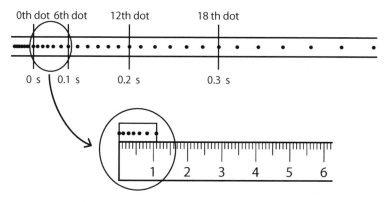

Figure 2.3.4 *The beginning of the tape may have a smudged group of dots.*

4. Carefully measure the distance the cart travelled during each successive 0.10 s time interval. For example, in the sample tape in Figure 2.3.4, the distance travelled during the interval between 0 and 0.10 s was 1.1 cm. Figure 2.3.5 shows how to measure the distance travelled during the second 0.10 s interval between 0.10 s and 0.20 s. In the sample tape, the distance is 1.8 cm. Prepare a table like Table 2.3.1. Record the distances travelled in each of the recorded intervals in your table.

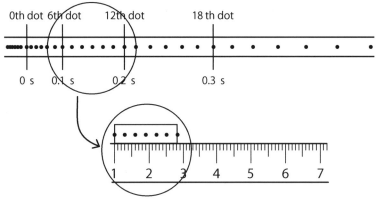

Figure 2.3.5 *How to measure the distance between 0.10 s and 0.20 s*

Table 2.3.1 *Data for an Accelerating Cart*

Time Interval (s)	Distance Travelled (cm)	Average Speed for the Interval (cm/s)
0 to 0.10		
0.10 to 0.20		
0.20 to 0.30		
0.30 to 0.40		
0.40 to 0.50		
0.50 to 0.60		

5. Your next task is to figure out the average speed of the cart during each of the 0.10 s time intervals. Since average speed is just the distance travelled during the time interval divided by the time interval, all you have to do is divide each measured distance by the time interval (0.10 s). During the first time interval on the sample tape, the cart moved a distance of 1.1 cm. The average speed of the cart during the first 0.10 s was therefore

$$\bar{v} = \frac{1.1 \text{ cm}}{0.10 \text{ s}} = 11 \text{ cm/s}$$

During the second time interval (between 0.10 s and 0.20 s), the cart moved a distance of 1.8 cm. Its average speed during the second interval was therefore

$$\bar{v} = \frac{1.8 \text{ cm}}{0.10 \text{ s}} = 18 \text{ cm/s}$$

6. Using your own tape data, calculate the average speed of the cart during each of the time intervals and complete Table 2.3.1.

Concluding Questions

1. (a) What was the average speed of the cart during the first 0.10 s time interval?
   (b) What was the average speed of the cart during the second 0.10 s interval?
   (c) By how much did the average speed of the cart increase between the first interval and the second interval?
   (d) Calculate the acceleration of the cart between the first interval and the second interval by dividing the increase in average speed by the time interval, which was 0.10 s.

   Example: On the sample tape, the average speed increased from 11 cm/s to 18 cm/s between the first and second time intervals. Therefore, the acceleration was:

   $$a = \frac{18\ \text{cm/s} - 11\ \text{cm/s}}{0.10\ \text{s}} = \frac{7\ \text{cm/s}}{0.10\ \text{s}} = 70\ \text{cm/s}^2$$

2. Calculate the acceleration of the cart between the second and third intervals, third and fourth intervals, fourth and fifth intervals, and fifth and sixth intervals. Allowing for slight variations due to experimental errors, is there any pattern to your results?

Part 2

Procedure

1. Using your data table from Investigation 2-1 (Table 2.1.1), plot a graph of speed vs. time for the accelerating cart, like the example shown below in Figure 2.3.6. Remember that the speeds in the table are average speeds for each interval and should be plotted midway through each time interval.

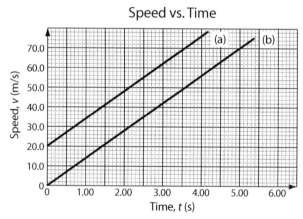

Figure 2.3.6 *This is an example of a speed-time graph like the one you will draw.*

2. Draw a single straight line through all the plotted points. If there are stray points due to experimental error, try to draw a line that leaves as many strays on one side of it as on the other. If a point is an obvious gross error, ignore it when drawing your "best-fit line." If in doubt, ask your teacher for advice.

3. Determine the y-intercept of your line. Also, figure out the slope of the line using the method outlined for Figure 2.2.1 in section 2.2.

Concluding Questions

1. What was the acceleration of your cart according to the slope of your graph?
2. What is the equation for the speed-time graph you plotted for the cart?
3. In Investigation 2-1, you figured out the acceleration of your cart simply by comparing average speeds of the cart in successive time intervals. Compare the acceleration you calculated in Investigation 2-1 with the acceleration you just obtained using the slope of your speed-time graph. Which method of finding the acceleration "averages out" the experimental errors better? Explain.

2.3   Review Questions

1. Use the following graph to answer the questions below.

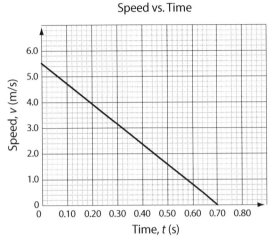

Speed vs. Time

(a) What is the y-intercept (v_0) of the speed-time graph shown above?

(b) What is the acceleration of the moving object?

(c) What is the specific equation for this graph?

2. A cyclist coasting along a road allows her bike to come to rest with the help of a slight upslope in the road. The motion of the bike is described by the equation:

$$v_f = 6.6 \text{ m/s} - (2.2 \text{ m/s}^2) \cdot t$$

(a) What was the initial speed of the bike?

(b) At what rate did the bike accelerate while coming to rest?

(c) How long did the bike take to come to rest?

3. What is the rate of acceleration of a mountain bike, if it slows down from 12.0 m/s to 8.0 m/s in a time of 3.25 s?

4. A truck parked on a down slope slips its brakes and starts to coast downhill, accelerating from rest at a constant rate of 0.80 m/s^2.
   (a) How fast will the truck be moving after 5.0 s?

   (b) How far will the truck coast during the 5.0 s?

5. An aircraft starts from rest and accelerates at a constant rate down the runway.
   (a) After 12.0 s, its speed is 36.0 m/s. What is its acceleration?

   (b) How fast is the plane moving after 15.0 s?

   (c) How far down the runway will the plane be after 15.0 s?

6. A truck is moving along at 80.0 km/h when it hits a gravel patch, which causes it to accelerate at −5.0 km/h/s. How far will the truck travel before it slows to 20.0 km/h?

7. A very frustrated physics student drops a physics textbook off the top of the CN tower. If the tower is 5.3×10^2 m high, how long will the book take to reach the ground, assuming there is no air resistance?

8. If an electron accelerates in a space of 5.0 cm from rest to 1/10 c, (where c is the speed of light, 3.0×10^8 m/s), what is its acceleration?

2.4 Acceleration of Bodies Due to Gravity

Warm Up

Take a piece of paper and book in each hand and raise them to about the height of your shoulder. Predict which one will hit the ground first if they are both dropped at the same time. Drop both and record results. Now crumple the same piece of paper and repeat. Describe and suggest reasons for any differences between the two events.

_____

_____

_____

_____

Free Fall

One of the most common situations involving uniform acceleration is the phenomenon known as **free fall**. For example, if a coin drops out of your pocket, it accelerates toward the ground. If the effects of air resistance are ignored, the acceleration of the coin toward the ground is uniform. The coin starts its downward fall with zero speed, but gains speed as it falls toward Earth. Since gravity is the cause of the acceleration, we call the acceleration during free fall the **acceleration of gravity.** The acceleration of gravity is given a special symbol, g.

The magnitude of g depends on your location. At Earth's surface, g is approximately 9.81 m/s^2. At higher altitudes, g decreases. For our present purposes, g is assumed to be constant at Earth's surface and to be 9.81 m/s^2. On the Moon, the magnitude of g is approximately 1/6 of what it is here on Earth's surface. A body in free fall near the Moon's surface has an acceleration of gravity of only 1.60 m/s^2.

Of course, the four equations for uniform acceleration apply to free fall as well as other uniform acceleration situations. The symbol g may be substituted for a in those equations.

Figure 2.4.1 *These sky divers are in free fall until they open their parachutes to slow their descent.*

Sample Problem 2.4.1 — Free Fall

A golf ball is dropped from the top of the CN tower. Assuming that the ball is in true free fall (negligible air resistance), answer these questions:

(a) How fast will the ball be falling after 1.0 s?

(b) How far down will the ball have fallen after 1.0 s?

What to Think About	How to Do It
(a)	
1. Determine initial conditions in the problem so you can choose the correct formula.	The ball starts from rest, so $v_0 = 0.0$ m/s The rate of acceleration is $g = 9.8$ m/s^2 The time of fall is $t = 1.0$ s
2. Determine which formula to use.	The first uniform acceleration equation (1) applies to this question.
3. Solve.	$v_f = v_0 + at$ $v_f = 0$ m/s $+ (9.8$ m/s$^2) (1.0$ s$)$ $v_f = 9.8$ m/s The ball will be falling 9.8 m/s after 1 s.
(b)	
1. Determine which formula to use.	The third uniform acceleration equation (3) applies to this question.
2. Solve.	$d = v_0 t + \dfrac{1}{2} at^2$ $d = (0$ m/s$)(1.0$ s$) + \dfrac{1}{2}(9.8$ m/s$^2)(1.0$ s$)(1.0$ s$)$ $d = 4.9$ m The ball will have fallen 4.9 m after 1 s.

Practice Problems 2.4.1 — Free Fall

1. (a) How fast will the golf ball in the Sample Problem be moving after it has fallen a distance of 530 m, which is the height of the CN tower? (Assume free fall.)

   (b) Why does the ball not reach this speed when it hits the ground?

Practice Problems 2.4.1 — Free Fall

2. How high is the cliff if you toss a small rock off of it with an initial speed of 5.0 m/s and the rock takes 3.1 s to reach the water?

3. (a) At the Pacific National Exhibition in Vancouver, one of the amusement park rides drops a person in free fall for 1.9 s. What will be the final velocity of the rider at the end of this ride?

   (b) What is the height of this ride?

4. At an air show, a jet car accelerates from rest at a rate of 3g, where g is 9.81 m/s^2. How far does the jet car travel down the runway in a time of 4.0 s?

Projectiles

There are different types of projectile motion. From throwing a ball up and having it land on your hand to a golf ball being hit off a tee to throwing a rock off a cliff. The golf ball and rock examples require analysis of motion using two dimensions and will be studied in later courses. The example of throwing a ball up in the air and having it land back in your hand is an example of projectile motion in one dimension. This type of projectile motion will be studied next.

Recall that acceleration is a vector quantity with both magnitude and direction. In situations where the acceleration is caused by the force of gravity, the direction of acceleration is downward. This is a negative direction. In gravitational acceleration problems, therefore, you use $a = -9.81$ m/s^2.

If a body is thrown into the air, it accelerates downward ($a = -9.81$ m/s^2) at all times during the trajectory, whether the velocity is upward (+), zero, or downward (−).

You throw a baseball straight up. It leaves your hand with an initial velocity of 10.0 m/s. Figure 2.4.2 is a graph showing how the velocity of the ball varies with time, starting when you begin to throw the ball and ending when you finish catching it. At A, the ball has just left your hand. At C, the ball has just reached the glove in which you will catch the ball. Notice that between A and C, the velocity is changing at a uniform rate. If you take the slope of this graph, you will obtain the acceleration of the ball due to gravity alone.

Velocity vs. Time (for a Ball Thrown Straight up)

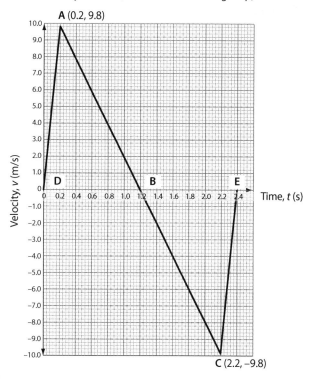

Figure 2.4.2 *This graph represents the velocity of a ball as a function of time, when you throw a ball straight up in the air.*

Quick Check

1. In Figure 2.4.2, what was the acceleration of the ball
   (a) while it was being thrown?

   (b) while it was in free fall?

   (c) while it was being caught?

2. What point on the graph corresponds with the instant when the ball reached the "peak" of its flight? Explain how you know this.

3. What altitude did the ball reach? **Hint:** The distance the ball travels equals the average speed multiplied by the time elapsed when it reaches its "peak" altitude. What property of the graph would give you $d = \bar{v} \cdot t$?

2.4 Review Questions

1. On a certain asteroid, a steel ball drops a distance of 0.80 m in 2.00 s from rest. Assuming uniform acceleration due to gravity on this asteroid, what is the value of g on the asteroid?

2. The graph below represents the velocity of a ball thrown straight up by a strong pitcher as a function of time. In the first part of the graph ending at A, the ball is accelerated to 39.2 m/s in a time of 0.20 s. After the ball leaves the pitcher's hand, it experiences only the acceleration due to gravity until it is caught in a glove and brought to rest in the hand of the catcher.

Velocity vs. Time for a Ball Thrown Straight up

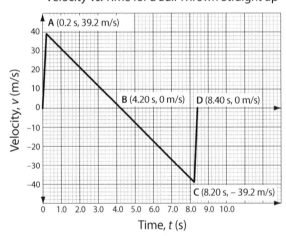

(a) What is the acceleration of the ball while it is being thrown?

(b) What is the acceleration of the ball after it leaves the pitcher's hand? (ABC)

(c) What is the acceleration of the ball while it is being caught? (CD)

(d) What point on the graph (A, B, C, or D) corresponds with the instant when the ball is at the peak of its flight? Explain your answer.

(e) Why is the slope of the graph negative as soon as the ball leaves the pitcher's hand?

(f) Why is the graph labelled velocity rather than speed?

(g) How far up did the ball travel?

(h) How far down did the ball fall?

(i) What is the average velocity of the ball for the whole trip from pitcher's hand to catcher's hand?

3. A body in free fall accelerates at a rate of 9.81 m/s^2 at your latitude. How far does the body fall during (a) the first second? (b) the second second? (Think first!)

Chapter 2   Review Questions

1. What is the difference between velocity and speed?

2. A traveller drives 568 km in 7.2 h. What is the average speed for the trip?

3. The following distances and times, for consecutive parts of a trip made by a red ant, were recorded by different observers. There is considerable variation in the precision of their measurements.

   A. 4.56 m in 12 s   B. 3.4 m in 6.89 s
   C. 12.8 m in 36.235 s

   (a) What total distance did the ant travel?

   (b) What was the total time for the trip?

   (c) What was the average speed of the ant?

4. Light travels with a speed of 3.00×10^5 km/s. How long will it take light from a laser to travel to the Moon (where it is reflected by a mirror) and back to Earth? The Moon is 3.84×10^5 km from Earth.

5. Under what condition can acceleration be calculated simply by dividing change in speed by change in time?

6. A high-powered racing car accelerates from rest at a rate of 7.0 m/s^2. How fast will it be moving after 10.0 s? Convert this speed to km/h.

7. The graph below is a speed-time graph for a vehicle.

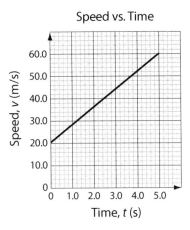

Speed vs. Time

(a) What was the acceleration of the vehicle?

(b) What was the average speed of the vehicle during its 5.00 s trip?

(c) What distance did the vehicle travel during the 5.00 s?

(d) Write a specific equation for this graph.

8. A child on a toboggan slides down a snowy hill, accelerating uniformly at 2.8 m/s². When the toboggan passes the first observer, it is travelling with a speed of 1.4 m/s. How fast will it be moving when it passes a second observer, who is 2.5 m downhill from the first observer?

9. A space vehicle is orbiting the Earth at a speed of 7.58×10^3 m/s. In preparation for a return to Earth, it fires retrorockets, which provide a negative acceleration of 78.4 m/s². Ignoring any change in altitude that might occur, how long will it take the vehicle to slow down to 1.52×10^3 m/s?

10. Snoopy is taking off in his World War I biplane. He coasts down the runway at a speed of 40.0 m/s, then accelerates for 5.2 s at a rate of 1/2 g, where g is the acceleration due to gravity (9.81 m/s²). How fast is the plane moving after 5.2 s?

11. A woman biker (leader of the local chapter of *Heck's Angels*) is driving along the highway at 80.0 km/h, in a 60.0 km/h speed zone. She sees a police car ahead, so she brakes and her bike accelerates at −8.0 km/h/s. How far along the road will she travel before she is at the legal speed limit?

12. Spiderman is crawling up a building at the rate of 0.50 m/s. Seeing Spiderwoman 56 m ahead of him, he accelerates at the rate of 2.3 m/s^2.
    (a) How fast will he be moving when he reaches Spiderwoman?

    (b) How much time will he take to reach Spiderwoman?

    (c) When he reaches Spiderwoman, Spiderman discovers that she is a Black Widow and, as you know, Black Widows consume their mates! He is 200.00 m from the road below. How long will it take him to fall to the safety of the road, if he drops with an acceleration of $g = 9.81$ m/s^2?

13. A stone is dropped from the top of a tall building. It accelerates at a rate of 9.81 m/s^2. How long will the stone take to pass a window that is 2.0 m high, if the top of the window is 20.0 m below the point from which the stone was dropped?

14. An aircraft, preparing for take-off, accelerates uniformly from 0 m/s to 20.0 m/s in a time of 5.00 s.
    (a) What is the acceleration of the aircraft?

    (b) How long will the plane take to reach its take-off speed of 36.0 m/s?

15. At an air show, a jet car accelerates from rest at a rate of $3g$, where g is 9.81 m/s^2. How fast is the jet travelling after 0.25 km?

16. To start a soccer game, the referee flips a coin that travels 50 cm into the air.
    (a) What was the coin's initial speed?

    (b) How long was the coin in the air before landing back in the hand of the referee?

17. A glider on an air track is made to accelerate uniformly by tilting the track at a slight angle. The distance travelled by the glider was measured at the end of each 0.10 s interval, resulting in the following data:

DISTANCE d (cm)	0	0.025	0.100	0.225	0.400	0.625
TIME t (s)	0	0.100	0.200	0.300	0.400	0.500

   (a) Plot a graph with distance d on the y-axis and time t on the x-axis.
   (b) Plot a second graph with distance d on the y-axis and t^2 on the x-axis.
   (c) Use the slope of your second graph to figure out the acceleration of the glider on the air track. HINT: Think about the third equation for uniform acceleration.

Chapter 2   Extra Practice

1. The speed of light in space is 300 000 km/s. How far does light travel in:
    (a) 1 min?
    (b) 1 h?
    (c) 1 d?
    (d) 1 y?

2. A jet aircraft travels a distance of 1867 km in a time of 3.0 h. What is its average speed for the trip?

3. In a certain battery-powered circuit, an electron requires 2.0×10^5 s to travel only 2.0 m. What is the average speed of the electron in the circuit? Express your answer in millimetres per second (mm/s).

4. Light from a laser requires 1.28 s to reach the Moon. If light travels with a speed of 3.00×10^5 km/s, how far is it to the Moon?

5. A tourist averaged 82 km/h for a 6.5 h trip in her car. How far did she go?

6. Use the following graph to answer the questions below.

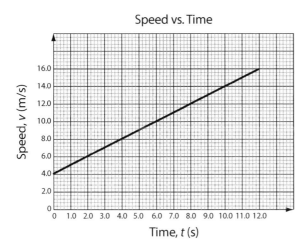

Speed vs. Time

(a) What is the y-intercept of the above graph? (Include units.)
(b) What is the slope of the above graph? (Include units.)
(c) What is the equation for the above graph? (Use symbols v and t in the equation.)

7. A certain airplane has an acceleration of 15.0 m/s^2.
    (a) How fast will it be moving 2.5 s after it starts down the runway?
    (b) How far will it travel during the 2.5 s?
    (c) Minimum take-off speed is 60.0 m/s. What length must the runway be?

8. (a) You are driving along the road at 80 km/h (22 m/s) when you see a moose 50.0 m in front of your car. Your reaction time is 0.40 s, and when you finally hit the brakes, your car accelerates at a rate of –6.4 m/s^2. Will your car stop in time to avoid the moose?
    (b) If the road is wet and your car accelerates at a rate of just –4.8 m/s^2, what will happen? Show your calculations.

9. The CN Tower in Toronto is about 530 m high. If air friction did not slow it down, how long would it take a penny to fall from the top of the tower to the ground below? ($g = 9.81$ m/s^2)

10. A motocross rider is coasting at a speed of 2.00 m/s. He then decides to accelerate his bike at a rate of 3.00 m/s^2 for a distance of 100.0 m.
    (a) How fast is the bike moving, in m/s, at the end of the 100.0 m stretch?
    (b) Convert your answer from m/s to km/h.

11. A mountain bike rider, after coming down a steep hill, loses control of her bike while moving with a speed of 5.00 m/s. Fortunately, she collides with a haystack, which brings her to rest in a distance of 0.625 m. What was the acceleration of the bike and rider while colliding with the haystack?

12. A policeman on a mountain bike is cruising at a speed of 4.00 m/s, when he sees a wanted criminal standing on a corner, 100.0 m ahead of him. If the policeman accelerates at a rate of 2.00 m/s^2, how much time will he take to reach the corner?

13. The graph below shows how the speed of an aging physics teacher varies with time, as he tries to run up a hill.

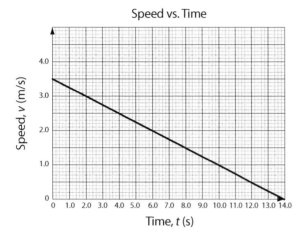

Speed vs. Time

(a) What was the starting speed of the runner?

(b) What was the acceleration of the runner?

(c) What distance did the runner travel?

(d) What is the specific equation for the graph?

14. Equation 4 for uniform acceleration, $v_f^2 = v_0^2 + 2ad$, can be used to show that a body thrown upward with a speed v will return to the same level with the same speed it had when it was thrown upward.

(a) Show mathematically why the magnitude of v_f equals the magnitude of v_0.

(b) Will the ball have the same velocity when it comes down as when it was thrown up in the air? Explain your answer.

15. A skateboarder accelerates uniformly down a hill, starting from rest. During the third 1 s interval from rest, the skateboarder travels 7.5 m. What is the acceleration of the skateboarder?

3 Forces

By the end of this chapter, you should be able to do the following:

- ➤ Solve problems involving the force of gravity
  - recognize the relationship between
    - mass and attractive force due to gravity (e.g., force due to gravity on Earth's surface is proportional to Earth's mass)
    - the force of gravity between two objects and their distance of separation (i.e., the inverse square law)
  - solve a variety of problems involving the relationship between
    - mass
    - gravitational field strength
    - force due to gravity (weight)
  - use Newton's law of universal gravitation to solve problems involving
    - force
    - mass
    - distance of separation
    - universal gravitational constant

- ➤ Analyse situations involving the force due to friction
  - conduct experiments investigating force due to friction, involving
    - normal force
    - various types of material
    - surface area
    - speed
  - recognize the relationship between force due to friction and the strengths of normal force and coefficient of friction
  - solve problems with objects sliding on horizontal surfaces, involving
    - force of friction
    - coefficient of friction
    - normal force

- ➤ Apply Hooke's law to the deformation of materials
  - state Hooke's law
  - use Hooke's law to solve problems that involve
    - force
    - spring constant
    - change in length

By the end of this chapter, you should know the meaning to these **key terms**:

- coefficient of friction
- force
- force due to gravity
- gravitational field strength
- gravity
- Hooke's law
- inverse square law
- kinetic friction
- mass
- Newton's law of universal gravitation
- normal force
- spring constant
- static friction
- universal gravitational constant
- weight

By the end of the chapter, you should be able to use and know when to use the following formulae:

$$F_g = mg$$

$$F_{fr} = \mu F_N$$

$$F_g = G\frac{m_1 m_2}{r^2}$$

$$F = k \Delta x$$

This bungee jumper experiences both the force of gravity and elastic force during her jump.

3.1 Force of Gravity

Warm Up

At shoulder level, hold a sheet of paper in one hand and a book in the other. If you release them at the same time, which will hit the ground first? Test your prediction. Now place the sheet of paper on top of the book. The paper should not extend over the edges of the book. Will the paper fall at the same rate as the book, faster, or slower? Test your prediction. Can you create a rule for falling objects that explains how different masses fall to the Earth?

_____

_____

_____

Force

Every time you push, pull, twist or squeeze something you exert a force on it. Almost every time you exert a force on an object, you change something about that object: its speed, its direction, or its shape. A **force** is a push or a pull.

When a soccer player "heads" the ball the speed of the ball changes, and sometimes its direction does too. When a hockey player is given a solid body check, the force changes his direction and speed. When a golf ball is struck by a golf club, the force of the impact changes the ball's shape during the collision. The force due to air friction alters the shape of a raindrop, from a perfect sphere to something more like a teardrop.

Forces are measured in a unit called the **newton (N)**, named after Sir Isaac Newton.

Gravitational Force

The force of gravity pulls on you all the time. The force of attraction between planet Earth and you keeps you from floating aimlessly off into space! Any two bodies in the universe exert a gravitational force on each other. The amount of force they exert depends upon how massive the bodies are and how far apart they are. Two unique facts about the force of gravity are: (1) it cannot be "shut off"; and (2) it is always an attractive force, never repulsive.

Gravitational force is an example of a force that acts on objects without touching them. This classifies gravity as an action-at-a-distance force. Gravitational force creates a gravitational field around a body. Think of a field as an area where a force is exerted. For example, magnets have a field around them created by the attraction and repulsion between magnetic poles. A gravitational field depends on the mass of an object. The bigger the mass, the bigger the gravitational field. For Earth, this means a small mass like a person is attracted to the centre of Earth because Earth is the larger mass. The gravitational force experienced by the person results mainly from the Earth's gravitational field. The force within the gravitational field is referred to as the gravitational field strength. It is measured as the gravitational force per unit mass or $g = \dfrac{F_g}{m}$. The symbol for gravitational field strength is g. At Earth's surface, g is approximately 9.81 N/kg.

Weight

Regardless of where you are on Earth, near the surface, objects will fall with the same acceleration regardless of their mass. Other forces such as air resistance may slow an object down, but the acceleration due to gravity remains constant. Gravitational force is equal to the product of an object's mass and the acceleration due to gravity.

$$F_g = mg$$

When we calculate the gravitational force acting on an object, we are calculating its **weight**. This is an example of a term that has a specific meaning in science, but has other everyday uses. Many times people use the term *weight* to refer to mass. For example, when someone asks you how much you weigh, they are actually asking you what your mass is. The difference between weight and mass is that weight in measured in newtons and mass is measured in metric units such as grams or kilograms.

Quick Check

1. What is the force of gravity on a 90 kg person? What is the weight of this person?

2. If a person experiences a 637 N force of gravity on Earth's surface, what is the person's mass?

3. A 75 kg person would experience a force of gravity of 127.5 N on the Moon. What is the gravitational field strength on the Moon?

Measuring the Force of Gravity

Gravity causes unsupported objects to fall toward Earth. The usual way to measure the force of gravity is to balance it with another force acting upward. For example, when you stand on a bathroom scale, gravity pulls you downward. A coiled spring inside the scale pushes upward and balances the force of gravity.

The common laboratory spring balance uses a spring that is stretched by the force of gravity acting on the object that is being "weighed" (Figure 3.1.1). If the spring is of good quality, the amount it stretches will depend directly on the force of gravity. That is, if the force of gravity doubles, the stretch will double. If the force of gravity triples, the stretch will triple. In other words, the amount of stretch is directly proportional to the force of gravity on the object.

(a)

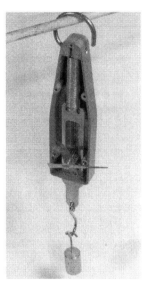
(b)

Figure 3.1.1 *An example of a laboratory spring balance showing the gauge (a) and the spring (b)*

Newton's Law of Universal Gravitation

One of Sir Isaac Newton's many valuable contributions to science is his law of universal gravitation. Newton (1642–1727) realized that the force of gravity, which affects you and everything around you, is a universal force. Any two masses in the universe exert a gravitational force on each other. The force that keeps planets in orbit is the same force that makes an apple fall to the ground. How strong the force is depends on how massive the bodies are. It also depends on the distance between the two bodies.

Like all other forces, gravity is a mutual force. That is, the force with which the Earth pulls on a falling apple is equal to the force with which the apple pulls on the Earth, but in the opposite direction. The Earth pulls on your body with a force of gravity that is commonly referred to as your "weight." Simultaneously, your body exerts a force on planet Earth of the same magnitude but in the opposite direction.

Newton was able to use Kepler's laws of planetary motion as a starting point for developing his own ideas about gravity. Johannes Kepler (1571–1630) was a German astronomer who described the motion of the planets around the Sun now called Kepler's Laws. You will study these laws in future courses. Using Kepler's laws, Newton showed that the force of gravity between the Sun and the planets varied as the inverse of the square of the distance between the Sun and the planets. He was convinced that the inverse square relation would apply to everyday objects near Earth's surface as well. He produced arguments suggesting that the force would depend on the product of the masses of the two bodies attracted to one another. The result was his law of universal gravitation.

Newton's law of universal gravitation can be summarized as follows:

> Every body in the universe attracts every other body with a force that (a) is directly proportional to the product of the masses of the two bodies, and (b) is inversely proportional to the square of the distance between the centres of mass of the two bodies.

The equation for Newton's law of universal gravitation is:

$$F_g = G\frac{m_1 m_2}{r^2}$$

where G is the **universal gravitation constant**, m_1 and m_2 are the masses of the bodies attracting each other, and r is the distance between the centres of the two bodies.

Isaac Newton was unable to measure G, but Henry Cavendish (1731–1810) measured it later in experiments. The modern value for G is 6.67×10^{-11} N•m^2/kg^2.

Cavendish's Experiment to Measure G

You can imagine how difficult it is to measure the gravitational force between two ordinary objects. In 1797, Henry Cavendish performed a very sensitive experiment that was the first Earth-bound confirmation of the law of universal gravitation. Cavendish used two lead spheres mounted at the ends of a rod 2.0 m long. The rod was suspended horizontally from a wire that would *twist* an amount proportional to the gravitational force between the suspended masses and two larger fixed spherical masses placed near each of the suspended spheres. (See Figure 3.1.2.)

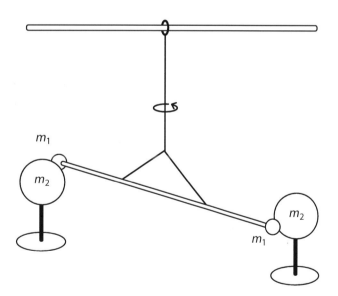

Figure 3.1.2 *Cavendish's apparatus*

The forces involved in this experiment were extremely small (of the order 10^{-6} N), so great care had to be taken to eliminate errors due to air currents and static electricity. Cavendish did manage to provide confirmation of the law of universal gravitation, and he arrived at the first measured value of G.

Earth's Gravitational Field Strength

To calculate the force of gravity on a mass m, you could simply multiply the mass by the gravitational field strength, g ($F = mg$). You could also use the law of universal gravitation:

$$F_g = G\frac{Mm}{r^2}, \text{ where } M \text{ is the mass of Earth.}$$

This means that $mg = G\dfrac{Mm}{r^2}$, and therefore,

$$g = G\frac{M}{r^2}$$

Thus, the gravitational field strength of Earth depends only on the mass of Earth and the distance, r, from the centre of Earth to the centre of mass of the object that has mass m.

Quick Check

1. Given two small, chocolate-centred candies of masses M and m, what will happen to the force of gravity F_g between them in the following situations?

   (a) r is doubled.

   (b) r is tripled.

   (c) r is reduced to 1/2 r.

   (d) r is reduced to 1/3 r.

2. The constant G in the law of universal gravitation has a value of 6.67×10^{-11} N•m^2/kg^2. Calculate the force of gravity between the following objects:

   (a) a 100.0 kg person and Earth. Earth's mass is 5.98×10^{24} kg, and its radius is 6.38×10^6 m.

   (b) a 100.0 kg person and the Moon. The Moon's mass is 7.35×10^{22} kg, and its radius is 1.74×10^6 m.

   (c) two 46 g golf balls whose centres of mass are 10 cm apart.

Investigation 3-1A   The Force of Gravity (Demonstration)

Purpose
To observe some interesting facts about falling bodies

Procedure
1. Two steel balls, one more massive than the other, will be dropped from the same height at the same time. Predict which of the two balls will reach the floor first. Give a reason for your prediction. Now listen when the two balls are dropped to the floor.
2. A piece of tissue paper and a steel ball will be dropped to the floor from the same height at the same time. Predict what will happen and explain your prediction. Observe what happens when the two objects are dropped.
3. Figure 3.1.3 shows a long glass tube from which most of the air can be removed with a vacuum pump. Inside it are two objects: a coin and a feather. Before pumping the air out, let the coin and feather drop the length of the tube and observe which falls faster. Explain. Predict what will happen when the air is removed from the tube. Which will fall faster this time? Now test your prediction.
4. Figure 3.1.4 illustrates an apparatus that can release two identical steel balls at the same time. One ball is projected straight out, while at precisely the same time an identical steel ball is dropped straight down. Predict which ball will hit the floor first. Give a reason for your prediction. Now test your prediction. Listen for the sounds of the balls hitting the floor.

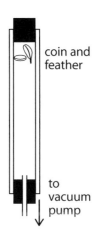

coin and feather

to vacuum pump

Figure 3.1.3 *Force of Gravitation — Step 3*

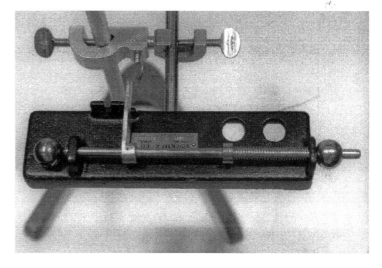

Figure 3.1.4 *Force of Gravitation — Step 4*

Concluding Questions
1. Describe what happened when you dropped two steel balls of different mass simultaneously. Does the mass of the balls affect their rate of fall?
2. (a) Describe what happened when you dropped a piece of tissue paper and a steel ball simultaneously. Explain.
    (b) What would happen if you did this experiment in a vacuum? Explain.
3. What happened when you fired a steel ball straight out horizontally while simultaneously dropping an identical ball? Does horizontal motion affect the rate of vertical fall of a ball?
4. On the Moon, the force of gravity on a given mass is only about 1/6 of what it is on Earth. As a result, there is no atmosphere around the Moon. Explain what you would expect to observe if you did Procedure steps 1 to 4 on the Moon.

Investigation 3-1B How Gravitational Force Depends on Distance

Purpose

To use data to discover the nature of the relationship between gravitational force and distance

Procedure

1. In an imaginary experiment, Superman was hired to measure the force of gravity on a 1 kg mass at different distances from the centre of Earth. He used a precise spring balance to obtain the data in Table 3.1.1. Make a graph with the force of gravity (F_g) on the y-axis and the distance from the centre of Earth (r) on the x-axis.

2. Your first graph will not be a straight line, because the relationship between F_g and r is not linear ($y \neq mx + b$) and is not a direct proportion ($y \neq mx$). The relationship is a **power law** ($y = m \cdot x^n$) where the power n is neither 1 nor 0. How can you find out what the value of n is? If you look at Figure 3.1.6, you will see the shapes of the graphs of several power law relationships. Which of these graphs does your graph most resemble? To find out if your graph is a particular type of relationship, plot force of gravity (F_g) on the y-axis, as before, and your chosen r^n on the x-axis. Plot the following graphs and see which one gives a straight line: (a) F_g vs. r^{-1} (b) F_g vs. r^{-2}

Table 3.1.1 *The Force of Gravity on a Kilogram Mass*

Force of Gravity (N)	Distance from Centre of Earth (Mm*)
9.81	6.37
2.45	12.74
1.09	19.11
0.61	25.48
0.39	31.85

*1 Mm = 1 megametre = 10^6 m

Concluding Questions

1. (a) What variables must you plot to obtain a straight line (through the origin)?

   (b) What is the specific equation for your final straight line?

2. From your equation, calculate the following:

   (a) the distance at which the force of gravity on the kilogram mass is half of what it is at Earth's surface

   (b) the force of gravity on the 1 kg mass at a distance of 10 Earth radii (63.7 Mm)

Graphs of various power law relations

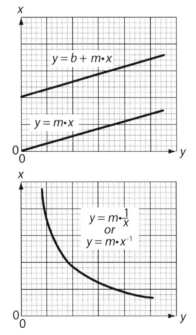

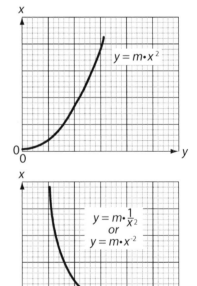

Figure 3.1.6 *Power law graphs*

3.1 Review Questions

1. What is the force of gravity on a 600 N person standing on Earth's surface?

2. Assuming that the sizes of the Sun and Earth stayed the same, how would the force of gravity between them change if the mass of the Sun were three times greater than it is?

3. (a) What is the weight of an 80 kg person?

   (b) What is the weight of an 80 kg astronaut on the Moon where $g = 1.7$ m/s^2?

4. If the force of gravity on a rugby player is 789.5 N in Victoria, what is the mass of the player? Note: The gravitational field strength in Victoria is 9.81 N/kg.

5. The force of gravity on a 5.0 kg mass on Mars is 18.05 N. At what rate will the mass accelerate toward Mars if it is in free fall? What percentage is this acceleration of the acceleration the same mass would have in free fall on Earth?

6. What is the force of gravity on a 14.67 kg mass if the gravitational field strength is 9.790 N/kg?

7. Given two candies with masses M and m a distance d apart, what will the force of gravity F_g between them become in the following situations?
   (a) Only M is doubled.

   (b) Only m is doubled.

   (c) Both M and m are doubled.

   (d) M, m, and d are *all* doubled.

8. What is the force of gravity on a 70.0 kg man standing on Earth's surface, according to the law of universal gravitation? Check your answer using $F = mg$.

9. What is the force of gravitational attraction between a 75 kg boy and a 60.0 kg girl in the following situations?
   (a) when they are 2.0 m apart

   (b) when they are only 1.0 m apart

10. What is the force of gravity exerted on you on Mars, if your mass is 70.0 kg and the mass of Mars is 6.37×10^{23} kg? The radius of Mars is 3.43×10^6 m, and you are standing on its surface, searching for Mars bars.

11. What is the force of gravity exerted on a 70.0 kg person on Jupiter (assuming the person could find a place to stand)? Jupiter has a mass of 1.90×10^{27} kg and a radius of 7.18×10^7 m.

3.2 Friction

Warm Up

Fill a narrow-neck jar to the brim with rice. Poke a pencil into the jar and push the pencil until it can't go any farther. Repeat the poking until you can lift the jar with the pencil in the rice. Why does this happen?

_____

_____

_____

Why We Need Friction

When a body moves, there is almost always a resisting force exerted on it by materials in contact with it. An aircraft moving through the air must overcome the resistance of the air. A submarine encounters resistance from the water. A car experiences resistance from the road surface and from the air. In all cases like this, the force opposing the motion of the body is called **friction**. Engineers attempt to design aircraft, ships, and automobiles so that friction is minimized.

Friction is not always a "bad" thing, of course. You need friction to bring your bike, car, or yourself to a stop. Walking on a frictionless floor would be a major challenge. Friction is desirable when you wish to strike a match or write with a pencil. If you ever have to use a parachute, you will appreciate the resisting force of the air on your parachute.

If you want to push a book along your bench, you know that you have to keep on pushing to keep it moving. This is true in many everyday situations. A skateboarder cannot coast along a level road indefinitely without some force being applied to counter the friction force. Friction is such a normal phenomenon, that for centuries it was believed impossible for an object to keep moving without a constant force being applied. About 400 years ago, Galileo Galilei (1546–1642) suggested that a body, once moving, would continue moving at the same speed and in the same direction indefinitely if friction were eliminated and no other unbalanced forces were present. It is difficult to verify this idea experimentally, and it seems to contradict everyday experiences. For some time, it was a hard concept for people to accept.

Static and Kinetic Friction

Even the smoothest-looking piece of metal, if viewed under a microscope, will have irregular bumps and hollows. Where the bumps come in contact, the electrical attraction between the atoms of the two surfaces produces a small-scale "welding" of the materials at the points of contact (Figure 3.2.1). When one surface is moved over the other, the welded regions must be broken apart. Friction arises from the breaking of these welded regions and from the "plowing" effect as the harder surface moves through the softer one.

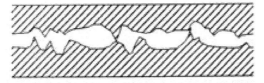

Figure 3.2.1 _An artist's impression of two metal surfaces magnified_

Static friction acts when you have two objects at rest relative to one another. Static friction, for example, keeps a car with its parking brakes on from sliding down a hill. A block of wood will remain stationary on a sloped table until you increase the angle sufficiently that it begins to slide. The force required to overcome static friction is always greater than the force needed to balance **kinetic friction**. Kinetic friction is the friction force between two flat surfaces that exists when one surface slides over the other.

To overcome static friction, you have to break the "welds" before the objects can move relative to one another. When you push a a heavy object, you have probably noticed that the force needed to get the object moving was slightly greater than the force needed to keep it moving at steady speed.

The force of friction F_{fr} is proportional to the force of gravity F_g on the object sliding over a smooth surface. A more general fact about kinetic friction is that the force of friction is proportional to the **normal force** F_N, which is the force acting perpendicular to the surfaces.

If a block slides horizontally across a table as in Figure 3.2.2 (a), the force of gravity is equal in magnitude to the normal force, but if the surfaces are at an angle to the horizontal as in Figure 3.2.2 (b), the normal force does not equal the force of gravity. You will encounter situations like this in future physics courses.

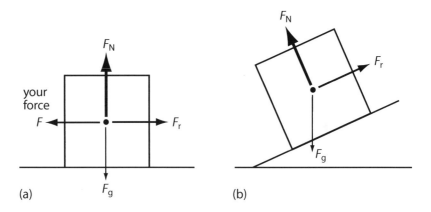

Figure 3.2.2 (a) *For a block sliding horizontally, the force of gravity and the normal force are equal.*
(b) *For block sliding on a slope, these two forces are not equal.*

Coefficients of Friction

In general, for two objects with smooth flat surfaces sliding over one another, the force of friction is proportional to the normal force. The constant of proportionality is called the **coefficient of kinetic friction**. It is given the special symbol μ, which is the Greek letter *mu*.

$$F_{fr} = \mu F_N$$

Table 3.2.1 lists some coefficients of kinetic friction.

Table 3.2.1 *Coefficients of Kinetic Friction**

Surfaces in Contact	Coefficient μ*
wood on wood	0.25
steel on steel	0.50
steel on steel (lubricated)	0.10
rubber on dry asphalt	0.40
rubber on wet asphalt	0.20
rubber on ice	0.005
steel on ice	0.01

* All values are approximate. Precise values vary with conditions such as degree of smoothness.

Surface area does not affect the force of friction appreciably. For example, it will require the same force to slide a building brick on its edge, as it will on its broad side. The two factors that have the greatest effect on friction are:
1. the normal force pushing the surfaces together, and
2. the nature of the surfaces.

Sample Problem 3.2.1 — Kinetic Friction

The coefficient of kinetic friction between a wooden box and a concrete floor is 0.30. With what force must you push to slide the box across the floor at steady speed if the force of gravity on the box is 450 N?

What to Think About	How to Do It
1. If the box is moving at a constant speed, the forces acting on it are balanced. This means the force needed to push the box is equal and opposite to the force of friction. Find the force of friction.	$F_{fr} = \mu F_N$
2. The box is on a flat surface. This means the force of gravity equals the normal force. Find the normal force	$F_N = F_g$ $F_N = 450\ N$
3. Solve.	$F_{fr} = \mu F_g$ $= (0.30)(450\ N)$ $= 135\ N$ $= 1.4 \times 10^2\ N$ You have to push the box with a force of 1.4×10^2 N.

Practice Problems 3.2.1 — Kinetic Friction

1. What is the total force of friction on a wagon's wheels if it takes 30 N to move it at a constant speed across a bumpy path?

2. (a) A 10 kg box of candy rests on a floor with a coefficient of static friction of 0.30. What force is needed to move the box?

   (b) If the coefficient of kinetic friction is 0.25, what force is needed to keep the box moving at a constant speed?

3. What is the coefficient of kinetic friction between a rubber tire and the road if a 2000 kg car needs 1.57×10^4 N to keep the car moving at a constant speed?

Investigation 3-2   Friction Can Be a Real Drag!

Part 1

Purpose

To determine how does the force of friction (F_{fr}) depends on the force of gravity (F_g) on an object when the object slides over a "smooth" horizontal surface

Procedure

1. Use a spring balance to measure the force of gravity on each of four nearly identical wood blocks provided. Write their weights, in N, in pencil on each block.
2. Prepare a data table like Table 3.2.2.

Table 3.2.2 *Data For Investigation 3-2, Part 1*

Number of Blocks	Total Force of Gravity (N)	Force of Friction (N)
1		
2		
3		
4		

3. Adjust your spring balance so that it reads 0 N when it is held in a horizontal position or parallel to the bench top. Attach it to the hook on one of the four blocks. See Figure 3.2.3. Set the wide side of the block on a smooth, clean bench top. To measure the force of sliding friction, measure the smallest force needed to keep the block sliding at a slow, steady speed along the bench top. You will have to give the block a small extra nudge to get it moving. Once it is moving, however, a steady force equal to the force of kinetic friction should keep it moving at a steady speed. Do several trials until you are satisfied you have a meaningful average friction force. Record the force of gravity and the force of sliding friction in your copy of Table 3.2.2.

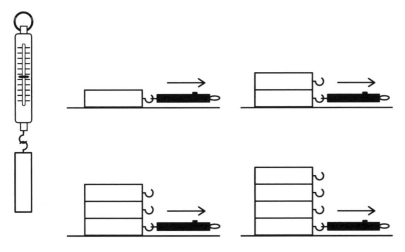

Figure 3.2.3 *Friction — Part 1*

4. Place a second block on top of the first. The total force of gravity will now be the sum of the weights of the two blocks. Measure the force of friction with two blocks.

5. Repeat with three, then four blocks. Record the total force of gravity and force of friction each time in Table 3.2.2.

6. Plot a graph with the force of kinetic friction F_{fr} on the y-axis and force of gravity F_g on the x-axis. Determine the slope of the graph and write a specific equation for your graph. Include the units for the slope, if any.

Concluding Questions

1. When you doubled the force of gravity on the object sliding over your bench, what happened to the force of friction? What happened to the force of friction when the force of gravity was tripled? quadrupled?

2. What is the equation for your graph? (Remember to use the proper symbols and units.)

3. The slope of your graph is the coefficient of kinetic friction. What is the coefficient of kinetic friction between the block and the tabletop you used?

4. Name three situations where you need to have
   (a) a low coefficient of friction, and
   (b) a high coefficient of friction.

Challenge

1. Measure the coefficient of kinetic friction between your blocks and a different horizontal surface.

Part 2

Purpose

To determine how the force of kinetic friction varies with the area of contact between two smooth, flat surfaces, when all other factors are controlled

Procedure

1. Make a prediction: If you double the area of contact between two smooth, flat objects, will the force of friction (a) stay the same, (b) double, (c) be cut in half, or (d) change in some other way?

2. Pile four blocks on top of one another as in Figure 3.2.4(a). Loop a string around the blocks, attach a spring balance, and measure the force of friction as in Part 1.

3. Prepare a table of data like Table 3.2.3. Record your results.

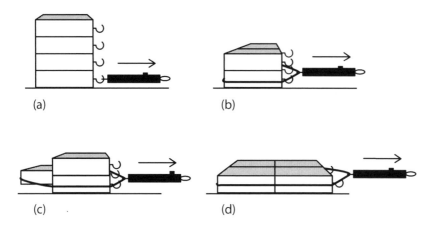

(a)

(b)

(c)

(d)

Figure 3.2.4 *Friction — Part 2*

Table 3.2.3 *Data for Investigation 3-2, Part 2*

Number of Blocks	Area	Total Force of Gravity (N)	Force of Friction (N)
4	1 × A	constant	
4	2 × A	constant	
4	3 × A	constant	
4	4 × A	constant	

4. Double the surface area by arranging the blocks as in Figure 3.2.4(b). Notice that the force of gravity is still the same; only the area has changed. Measure and record the force of friction. Measure it several times until you are satisfied that you have an acceptable average.

5. Arrange the blocks so that the surface area is tripled, then quadrupled without changing the force of gravity. See Figure 3.2.4. Measure and record the force of friction each time.

Concluding Questions

1. After comparing your results for Part 2 with several other groups doing the same experiment, write a conclusion about the effect that varying the surface area has on the amount of friction between a smooth flat object of constant force of gravity and another smooth surface.

2. Discuss sources of error in this experiment.

3.2 Review Questions

1. (a) Where on a bicycle do you want to reduce friction? How is this done?

   (b) Where on a bicycle do you want friction?

2. (a) What is meant by the coefficient of kinetic friction?

   (b) Why are there no units attached to values of μ?

3. A force of 120 N is needed to push a box along a level road at a steady speed. If the force of gravity on the box is 250 N, what is the coefficient of kinetic friction between the box and the road?

4. The coefficient of kinetic friction between a steel block and an ice rink surface is 0.0100. If a force of 24.5 N keeps the steel block moving at a steady speed, what is the force of gravity on the block?

5. A copper block has dimensions 1 cm × 2 cm × 4 cm. A force of 0.10 N will pull the block along a table surface at a steady speed if the 1 cm × 4 cm side is face down on the table. What force will be needed to pull the same block along when its 2 cm × 4 cm side is face down?

6. A 48 N cart is pulled across a concrete path at a constant speed. A 42 N force is required to keep the cart moving. What is the coefficient of kinetic friction between the path and the cart?

3.3 Hooke's Law

Warm Up

Take three different known masses and a rubber band. Measure the length of the rubber band as it hangs from a hook. Add the smallest mass and measure the distance the rubber band stretches. Predict how far the rubber band will stretch with your other two masses. Test each one and record your prediction below.

_____

_____

_____

Spring Constant

Figure 3.3.1 is a graph showing how the stretch of a certain spring varies with the force of gravity acting on it. This is not only a linear graph, but also a direct proportion. When the force of gravity on the spring is 1.0 N, the stretch is 0.75 cm. When the force is doubled to 2.0 N, the stretch doubles to 1.50 cm. If the force is tripled to 3.0 N, the stretch also triples to 2.25 cm.

If a force is exerted on an object, such as a spring or a block of metal, the object will be stretched or compressed. If the amount of stretching or compression, x, is small compared with the length of the object, then x is proportional to the force, F, exerted on the object. Figure 3.3.1 illustrates this proportionality. In Figure 3.3.1, stretch is given the symbol x, and the straight-line graph through (0,0) suggests that $F_g \propto x$ or that $F_g = kx$. The slope of the graph is the **spring constant**, k.

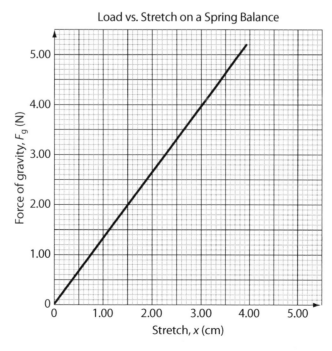

Figure 3.3.1 *The amount of stretch in a spring is proportional to the amount of force exerted on the spring.*

The English scientist Robert Hooke (1635–1703) first noticed the direct proportion between the force exerted on a solid object and the change in length of the object caused by the force. If too much force is applied, and an object is stretched or compressed excessively, the direct proportion breaks down. In that case, the object may be permanently stretched or compressed. **Hooke's law** is written with force as the subject of the equation:

$$F = k\Delta x$$

where F is the applied force, x is the change in length, and k is the spring constant.

Quick Check

1. What is the applied force on a spring when it is stretched 20 cm and the spring constant is 3.2?

2. On Figure 3.3.1, the slope of the line is the spring constant (k). What is k for the spring used in that example?

3. A 2.5 kg mass stretches a spring 10 cm. How far will the spring stretch when it supports 5.0 kg?

Investigation 3-3   Another Way to Weigh

Purpose
To make a "gravity measurer" out of a metre stick

Introduction
In an earlier course, you may have done an experiment where you added known masses to a spring and graphed the stretch of the spring against the force of gravity on the masses. In Investigation 3-3, you will learn how you can measure the force of gravity using a metre stick.

Procedure
1. Set up the apparatus in Figure 3.3.2. Clamp a metre stick horizontally so that 80.0 cm overhangs the edge of your bench. (Use a piece of cardboard to protect the metre stick from damage by the clamp.) Tape a large paper clip to the end of the metre stick and bend the clip so that masses can be hung from it.

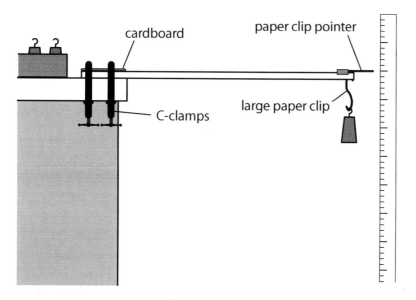

Figure 3.3.2 *Step 1*

2. Mount another metre stick or ruler vertically so that the depression of the horizontal metre stick can be measured. Align the top edge of the horizontal metre stick with a convenient point on the vertical metre stick, such as 0.0 cm. Another paper clip could be used as a pointer.

3. Hang a 50.0 g mass on the paper clip and measure the depression or vertical drop of the end of the horizontal metre stick, estimating to the nearest one-tenth of a millimetre. The force of gravity on a 50.0 g mass is 0.490 N. Record the force of gravity and the depression in a table like Table 3.3.1.

4. Measure the depression caused by each of the forces of gravity listed in Table 3.3.1. When you finish reading the depression for 4.90 N, remove the masses and see whether the depression returns to 0.00 cm. If it does not, check that the metre stick is securely clamped. If it is not, tighten the clamps and repeat your measurements. Do not dismantle your set-up yet.

Table 3.3.1 *Data for Investigation 3-3*

Mass (g)	Depression (y) (cm)	Force of Gravity (F_g) (N)
0		0
50		0.49
100		0.98
150		1.47
200		1.96
250		2.45
300		2.94
350		3.43
400		3.92
450		4.41
500		4.90

5. Prepare a graph of force of gravity (*y*-axis) vs depression (*x*-axis). Find the slope, and write a specific equation for the line you obtain.
6. Hang an object with an unknown force of gravity (such as a small C-clamp) from the metre stick and measure the depression it causes. Find out what the force of gravity on it is (a) by direct reading of your graph and (b) by calculation using the equation for the line.
7. Measure the force of gravity on the object with the unknown force of gravity using a commercial laboratory spring balance.

Concluding Questions

1. (a) What is the equation for the graph you prepared of *F* vs. *x*? Remember to include the numerical value of your slope, with proper units.
   (b) Is the graph linear? Is the relationship between the two variables a direct proportion? Explain.
2. Calculate the percent difference between the unknown force of gravity as determined from the graph and as measured with a laboratory spring balance.

Challenge

1. Make a "letter weigher" using a strip of hacksaw blade instead of a metre stick. Calibrate it in grams instead of newtons. (The gram is a mass unit, but most postal rate scales are based on mass instead of force of gravity.)

3.3   Review Questions

1. What are the units for the spring constant?

2. Using symbols "x" for stretch and "F" for force of gravity, write a specific equation for the line in Figure 3.3.1.

3. (a) Use your equation to solve for the stretch of the spring when a force of gravity of 4.0 N acts on it. Check your solution by looking at the graph in Figure 3.3.1.

    (b) Use your equation to solve for the force of gravity needed to stretch the spring 2.0 cm. Check your solution by looking at the graph in Figure 3.3.1.

4. In a direct proportion graph, the slope of the graph is called the spring constant. At any point on the line, the ratio of the stretch to the force of gravity will equal the constant of proportionality. By looking at the graph on page 93, find the spring constant when $F = 5.0$ N.

5. A wooden beam was clamped horizontally, so that masses could be hung from its free end. The depression x (in cm) caused by the force of gravity F_g (in N) on the masses was measured for loads up to 100 N. The graph below summarizes all the data.

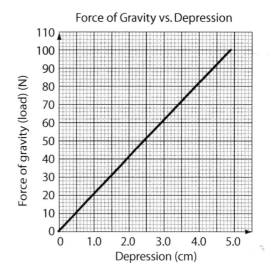

a) What is the slope of the graph, expressed in appropriate units?

(b) Write an equation specifically for this graph.

(c) According to the above graph, how much will the beam be depressed by a load of 80.0 N?

(d) According to the above graph, what load will cause the beam to be depressed by 3.0 cm?

Chapter 3   Review Questions

1. What is the force of gravity on a 70.0 kg man standing on Earth's surface, according to the law of universal gravitation? Check your answer using $F = mg$.

2. The force of gravity on a black bear is 2500 N on Earth's surface. The animal becomes so "unbearable" that it is transported four Earth radii from the *surface* of Earth. What is the force of gravity on it now?

3. Both G and g are constants. Why is G a *universal* constant and not g? Under what conditions is g a constant?

4. (a) Calculate the value of g at each of the locations shown in the table below. Express each answer as a multiple or a decimal fraction of Earth's g.

   (b) Would the force of gravity on you be greatest on the Moon, on Ganymede, or on Mercury?

5. What is the force of gravity exerted on you when standing on the Moon, if your mass is 70.0 kg and the Moon's mass is 7.34×10^{22} kg? The Moon's radius is 1.74×10^6 m.

6. Planet Mars has a mass of 6.4×10^{23} kg, and you have a mass of 5.0×10^1 kg. What force of gravity is exerted between you and Mars, if you are standing on its surface?

	Mass	Radius	Value of g
On the Moon	7.34×10^{22} kg	1.74×10^6 m	
On planet Mercury	3.28×10^{23} kg	2.57×10^6 m	
On Ganymede*	1.54×10^{23} kg	2.64×10^6 m	
On the Sun's surface	1.98×10^{30} kg	6.95×10^8 m	

* One of Jupiter's moons

7. To slide a metal puck across a greased sheet of metal at constant speed requires a force of 0.525 N. If the force of gravity on the puck is 5.00 N, what is the coefficient of friction between the puck and the greased metal?

8. (a) The force of gravity on a wooden crate is 560 N. It can be pushed along a certain floor at steady speed if a horizontal force of 224 N is applied to it. How much horizontal force will be needed to move a stack of two crates at the same steady speed?

   (b) What force will be needed if the two crates are not stacked but tied to one another side by side?

9. The coefficient of kinetic friction between a rubber disc and the ice is 0.0050. If the force of friction is 0.25 N, what is the force of gravity on the rubber disc?

10. A student added masses to the end of a hanging spring, then measured the amount of extension, or stretch, caused by the force of gravity on each mass. The following readings were obtained:

Mass (kg)	0.200	0.400	0.600	0.800	1.000
Force of gravity (N)	1.96	3.92	5.88	7.84	9.80
Extension (cm)	0.47	0.93	1.41	1.89	2.35

(a) Plot a graph with force of gravity (F_g) on the y-axis and extension (x) on the x-axis. Determine the slope of the graph in appropriate units. Write an equation describing how the force of gravity varies with the extension.

(b) Use both your graph and your equation to figure out the force of gravity that would stretch the spring 1.50 cm.

(c) Use both your graph and your equation to figure out how much stretch would occur in the spring when the force of gravity is 6.50 N.

Chapter 3   Extra Practice

1. In what metric unit is mass measured?

2. (a) What is the force of gravity on a 150 kg statue at Earth's surface?

   (b) If the gravitation field strength on the Moon is one-sixth that of Earth, what force of gravity would be exerted on the statue on the Moon's surface?

3. On the Moon, two stowaways on a Moon probe vehicle ran from the vehicle on landing, and fell off a Moon cliff at the same instant. One had a parachute and the other did not. Which stowaway hit the ground at the base of the Moon cliff first?

4. At Earth's surface, a package is a distance of one Earth radius from the centre of Earth. The force of gravity on a particular space payload is 1440 N. If this package is moved to an orbit that is four Earth radii from the centre of Earth, what will the force of gravity on the package be?

5. (a) The mass of the Moon is 7.3×10^{22} kg and its radius is 1 785 000 m. What is the strength of the gravitational field on the surface of the Moon?

   (b) What would be the weight of an 80 kg person on the Moon?

   (c) What would be the mass of the person on the Moon?

6. Two bowling balls each have a mass of 5.8 kg. The centres of the two balls are 35.5 cm apart. What gravitational force do they exert on each other?

7. Two electrons that are 1.0 m apart exert a force of 5.5×10^{-71} N on each other. What is the mass of each electron?

8. Calculate the gravitational force between the Sun and Pluto. The mass of the Sun is 2×10^{30} kg, and the mass of Pluto is 6×10^{23} kg. Pluto is 6×10^{12} m away from the Sun.

9. To slide a 40 N box at steady speed along a smooth bench top, a pulling force of 2.5 N is needed. This force is equal in magnitude to the force of friction. Now an 80 N box is placed on top of the 40 N box. What force must be exerted to slide the *combined* boxes at steady speed across the same bench surface?

10. If the friction force is 2.5 N, when a 40 N object is pulled across a bench, what is the coefficient of kinetic friction?

11. A teacher is moving desks around in the classroom. She pushes one desk with a force of 157 N. The frictional force opposing the motion is 123 N. If the desk has a mass of 5.0 kg, what is the acceleration of the desk?

12. A friend's car has run out of gas and four of you are pushing the car to the gas station at a constant speed of 4.5 km/h. If two of you are pushing with a force of 300 N and the other two are pushing with a force of 425 N, what is the force of friction between the car tires and the road?

13. (a) A wooden block is placed on a table. Using a spring scale you find a force of 16.0 N is required to keep the 45.0 N block moving at a constant speed. What is the coefficient of kinetic friction between the block and the table?

    (b) If a second block of mass 1.8 kg is placed on the first block, what force will be required to keep the two blocks moving at a constant velocity?

14. What happens to the coefficient of friction between a load and the floor if the load is tripled?

15. What single factor has the least effect on the amount of friction between two surfaces sliding over one another?

16. A 2 kg mass stretches a spring 20 cm. What mass will stretch the spring 35 cm?

17. A force of 12 N stretches a spring 3.0 cm. How much stretch will occur with an applied force of 27.0 cm?

18. (a) Create a graph that illustrates a spring constant of 1.5. You have 100 g, 200 g, 400 g, 500 g, and 1000 g masses.

    (b) Using your graph, how much would the spring stretch if you added a 300 g mass?

    (c) Using your graph, how much would the spring stretch if you added a 1200 g mass?

4 Newton's Laws of Motion

By the end of this chapter, you should be able to do the following:

➤ Solve problems that involve the application of Newton's laws of motion in one dimension
  - state Newton's three laws of motion
  - illustrate Newton's first and third laws with examples
  - create free-body diagrams in one dimension for use in solving problems (e.g., elevator problems)
  - use Newton's second law to solve problems that involve
    - net force
    - mass
    - acceleration

➤ Apply the concept of momentum in one dimension
  - solve a variety of problems involving
    - momentum   – impulse
    - mass   – net force
    - velocity   – time
    - momentum (initial and final)
  - state the law of conservation of momentum for isolated, one-dimensional systems
  - solve problems, using the law of conservation of momentum (e.g., collisions and explosions) to determine
    - momentum (initial and final)
    - velocity (initial and final)
    - mass

By the end of this chapter, you should know the meaning to these **key terms**:

- action force
- gravitational mass
- impulse
- inertia
- inertial mass
- law of action and reaction
- law of conservation of momentum
- law of inertia
- momentum
- newton
- Newton's first law of motion
- Newton's second law of motion
- Newton's third law of motion
- reaction force

By the end of this chapter, you should be able to use and know when to use the following formulae:

$$F = ma \qquad p = mv \qquad \Delta p = F\Delta t$$

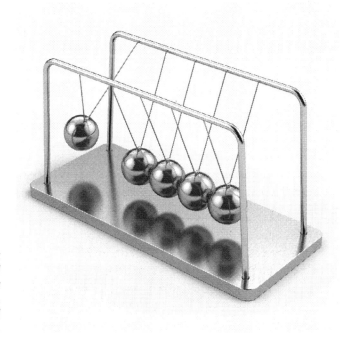

This device is called Newton's cradle, named after Sir Isaac Newton, the British scientist. When a ball at one end is lifted and released, it hits the ball next to it but that ball doesn't move. Only the ball at the end of the row is pushed upward as shown here. In this chapter you'll learn about Newton's laws of motion and momentum, which help to explain how this device works.

4.1 Inertia and Newton's First Law

Warm Up

You are attending a magic show and the magician stands beside a table set with fancy plates, cups, and silverware. Grabbing the edge of the tablecloth she quickly pulls the cloth out, and the plates, cups, and silverware stay in place. Is this magic or just physics in action? Explain your answer.

_____

_____

_____

Inertia

Imagine you are a passenger in a car, and the driver makes a sudden left turn. What sensation do you feel during the left turn? From your own experience, you might recall that you feel as if you are being pushed to the right. Contrary to what you feel, you are not being pushed to the right at all.

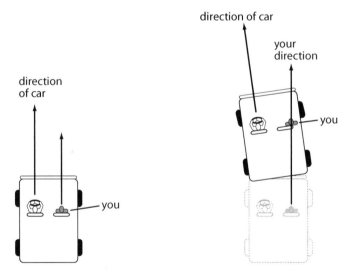

Figure 4.1.1 *As the car turns, your body wants to keep moving straight ahead.*

Figure 4.1.1 illustrates what happens and explains why you feel the force acting on your body. The car starts out by going straight and then the driver steers the car to the left. The car is moving to the left but your body wants to carry on in a straight line. What's stopping you? The door of the car is moving left with the rest of the car so it is pushing you in the direction the car is going. You feel as if you are pushing against the door, but this feeling is not what is happening. What is happening is that your body is trying to continue along its original straight path while the car is turning left. The result is that you are being pulled along with the car rather than continuing in a straight line.

As a general rule, any object tends to continue moving with whatever speed and direction it already has. This can include zero speed. When a driver accelerates a car, a body in the car tends to keep doing what it was already doing. So if the car is stopped, you are stopped. As the car starts to move and speeds up, you feel as if you are being pushed back into your seat.

The tendency that all objects have to resist change in their states of motion is called **inertia**. Every object in the universe that has mass has this property of inertia. Galileo Galilei (1564–1642) was the first person to describe this property of nature, which is called the **law of inertia**.

Some objects have more inertia than others because they have more mass. A logging truck has much more inertia than a mountain bike. Because it has so much more inertia, the logging truck is

(a) more difficult to get moving,

(b) more difficult to stop,

(c) more difficult to turn at a corner.

Measuring Inertia

Is there a way to measure inertia? You have measured it many times in science class. The way to measure inertia is to measure the object's mass. When you measure the mass of an object using a balance, that mass is equal to the object's **inertial mass**.

Strictly speaking, what the balance measures is called **gravitational mass**. This is because the unknown object is placed on one pan, and a standard mass is placed on the other pan. The masses are assumed to be equal when the force of gravity on the unknown mass balances the force of gravity on the standard mass. Gravitational mass is numerically equal to inertial mass, so a balance can be used to measure inertial mass as well.

Quick Check

1. Why does it hurt more to kick a rock shaped like a soccer ball than a soccer ball?

   Inertial mass is more

2. When astronauts are living in the International Space Station (ISS) they are in orbit around Earth at a minimum altitude of 278 km. They live in an environment of apparent weightlessness. Compare the inertial mass of the astronauts when they live on the ISS to their inertial mass when they are on Earth.

   Inertial mass is force of gravity, so where there is no gravity, there is no inertia

Newton's First Law

Isaac Newton (1642–1727) is considered one of the greatest scientists of all time. In any physics class you ever take, you will come across his name at some time. This is impressive, given that all his work was done more than 350 years ago. Newton is probably best known for his laws of motion. Newton's three laws describe motion as we experience it on Earth. They are also the foundation for helping to send humans to the Moon and deep-space vehicles out beyond our solar system.

Newton's first law of motion incorporated Galileo's law of inertia. The first law of motion, or law of inertia, can be stated this way:

> A body will continue to move at the same speed and in the same direction for as long as there are no unbalanced forces acting on it.

Ideal Conditions

Put another way, an object wants to keep doing what it is already doing. This means if a basketball is placed on the floor, it will not move until another force acts on it. Someone picking up the ball is an example of a force acting on the ball.

Sometimes it appears that Newton's first law does not apply. For example, when coasting on your bicycle along a flat part of the road, you have probably noticed that you slow down even though it appears no forces are acting on the bicycle. In fact, the force of friction between the road and tires is responsible for slowing the bicycle. If there were no friction, the bicycle would continue at the same speed until another force acted on it. That is why in many physics problems about motion, you will see the assumption that there is no friction. A situation that is assumed to have no friction is called *ideal conditions*. Using ideal conditions, we can focus on the motion being observed. By specifying ideal conditions, we also show we know that friction would have to be considered under normal conditions.

Quick Check

1. A car you are driving in encounters a patch of ice just as the car enters a corner turn. Using your knowledge of Newton's first law of motion, explain what will happen to the car.

   Friction is decreased, so inertia increases and the car doesn't turn. Inertia causes car to not change path (straight)

2. You are a judge listening to an injury claim from a bus passenger. The passenger claims to have been hurt when the bus driver slammed on the brakes and a suitcase came flying from the front of the bus to hit the passenger. Do you believe the passenger's description of what happened? Explain your answer.

   No, opposite would happen

3. When you receive a drink for a take out order, usually there is a lid on the cup. Use Newton's first law to explain why the lid is necessary to prevent spills.

   Because when movements happen, the liquid stays is original place, and splashes around.

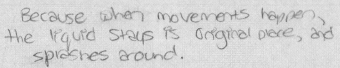

Investigation 4-1 Investigating Inertia

Purpose
To answer problems that will help you develop an understanding of inertia and Newton's first law of motion

Problem 1: How does a seatbelt work?

Figure 4.1.2 *Problem 1*

Procedure
1. Place a small toy human figure on a toy car or truck as shown in Figure 4.1.2. Do not fasten the figure to the vehicle. Let the vehicle move toward an obstruction like another toy vehicle or a brick and collide with it. Observe what happens to the unattached passenger.
2. Repeat step 1, but this time give the toy human figure a "seatbelt" by taping it to the vehicle.

Questions
1. How does this procedure illustrate inertia?
2. How does a seatbelt work?
3. Why are you more likely to survive a collision with a seatbelt than without one?

Problem 2: Does air have inertia?

Procedure
1. Fill a large garbage bag with air, and hold it as shown in Figure 4.1.3.
2. Quickly jerk the bag to one side. What happens to the air in the bag
   (a) when you start moving the bag?
   (b) when you stop moving the bag?

Question
1. What evidence have you observed from this procedure that supports the claim that air has inertia?

Figure 4.1.3 *Problem 2*

Problem 3: Inertia on an air track

Procedure
1. Place a glider on an air track as shown in Figure 4.1.4. Turn on the compressed air supply and check that the track is absolutely level. When the track is level the glider should have no tendency to move in one direction or the other. It should sit still.
2. Place the glider at one end of the track. Give it a slight nudge, and let it go.
3. Observe the motion of the glider.

Questions
1. Are there any unbalanced forces on the glider?
2. Describe its motion.
3. How does this demonstration illustrate Newton's first law?

Figure 4.1.4 *Problem 3*

Problem 4: Get on the right track.

Procedure
1. Place a battery-powered toy train on a circular track, and let it run a few full circles.
2. Predict which way the train will go if one of the sections of curved track is removed. Which one of the following will the train do? Explain your answer.
    (a) continue to move in a circle
    (b) move off along a radius of the circle
    (c) move off in a straight line tangent to the circle
    (d) follow some other path
3. Now test your prediction by setting up a section of track as shown in Figure 4.1.5.

Question
1. What happens to the toy train when it leaves the track? Explain this in terms of inertia.

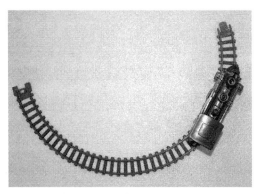

Figure 4.1.5 *Problem 4*

Problem 5: Where will the string break? Getting the "hang" of inertia

Procedure

1. Attach two equal masses, either 500 g or 1 kg, to a supporting rod, as shown in Figure 4.1.6. Use string that is strong enough to support the hanging masses, but not so strong that you cannot break it with a moderate pull with your hand. Add a 50 cm length of the same kind of string to the bottom of each mass.
2. Predict where each string will break, above or below the mass, if you pull on the end of the string first gently and then abruptly. Test your predictions by experiment.

Questions

1. Explain what happened, in terms of inertia.
2. Which action illustrates the weight of the ball and which illustrates the mass of the ball?

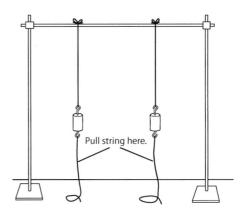

Figure 4.1.6 *Problem 5*

Problem 6: The pop-up coaster

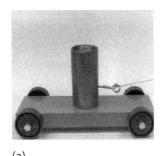 

(a)   (b)

Figure 4.1.7 *Problem 6*

Procedure

1. The cart in Figure 4.1.7 contains a spring that can fire a steel ball straight up in the air. The cart is given a steady horizontal speed when pulled with a string. This also activates the trigger for the spring-loaded cannon. When the cart is moving with a steady speed, giving the string a sudden pull will release the spring and fire the ball up in the air.
2. Predict whether the ball will land ahead of the cannon, behind the cannon, or in the cannon. Explain your prediction.
3. Test your prediction.

Questions

1. What forces are acting on the ball when it is in the air?
2. How does this procedure illustrate Newton's first law of motion?
3. Why does the ball sometimes miss the cart after it is released? Does this mean Newton's first law sometimes does not apply?

Concluding Question

Use your understanding of inertia to explain the following situation: You are carrying a carton of milk with one hand and need to get a section of paper towel off the roll in your kitchen. You can only use one hand to tear off the paper towel. Why does a quick, jerking motion work better than a slow pulling motion when removing the paper towel section from the roll?

4.1 Review Questions

1. In the Warm Up of this section, you were asked to explain why the magician was able to pull the tablecloth out from the under the plates, cups and silverware. Using the concepts of inertia and Newton's first law, explain why this "magic act" succeeds.

2. Does 2 kg of apples have twice the inertia or half the inertia of 1 kg of apples? Explain your answer.

   Twice, inertia is parallel to mass

3. If the pen on your desk is at rest, can you say that no forces are acting on it? Explain your answer.

   gravity, inertia, Normal Force. It is balanced forces

4. If the forces acting on the pen are balanced, is it correct to say that the pen is at rest? Explain your answer.

   Yes

5. If you place a ball in the centre of a wagon and then quickly push the wagon forward, in what direction does the ball appear to go? Why?

   Backwards, because inertia causes ball to stay in original place.

6. Why do headrests in cars help protect a person from head and neck injury in a car accident?

   Because during acceleration, inertia moves head/neck backwards.

7. A hockey puck moving a constant velocity across the ice eventually comes to a stop. Does this prove the Newton's first law does not apply to all situations?

   Yes, because objects are affected by friction.

8. You are travelling in a school bus on a field trip. The driver has to apply the brakes quickly to prevent an accident. Describe how your body would move in response to this rapid braking action.

   move forward

9. While travelling in Africa you are chased by a very large elephant. Would it make more sense to run in a straight line to get away or in a zigzag motion? Explain your answer.

   Zig zag, because its hard for an elephant (high inertia) to change direction.

4.2 Newton's Second Law of Motion

Warm Up

Take an empty spool of thread and wrap a string or thread around it three or four times, leaving the end loose so you can pull on it. Place the spool on the floor and pull on the thread horizontally to make the spool move to the right.

1. Based on your observations, what can you say about the direction of the force applied to the spool and the acceleration of the spool?

    _____

    _____

2. Would the direction of the force or the acceleration of the spool be affected if the thread were wrapped around the spool in the opposite direction? Explain your answer.

    _____

    _____

Defining Newton's Second Law of Motion

In his second law of motion, Newton dealt with the problem of what happens when an unbalanced force acts on a body. **Newton's second law of motion** states: If an unbalanced force acts on a body, the body will accelerate. The rate at which it accelerates depends directly on the unbalanced force and inversely on the mass of the body.

$$a = \frac{F}{m}$$

The direction in which the body accelerates will be the same direction as the unbalanced force. The measuring unit for force is the **newton (N)**. The measuring unit for mass is the kilogram (kg) and for acceleration is m/s^2. Therefore, using $F = ma$, one newton can be defined as the force needed to accelerate one kilogram at a rate of one metre per second per second.

Whenever Newton's second law is used, it is understood that the force F in the equation $F = ma$ is the unbalanced force acting on the body. This unbalanced force is also called the net force. To calculate the unbalanced force acting on a 1.0 kg mass falling due to gravity, you use Newton's second law:

$F = ma = 1.00 \text{ kg} \times 9.81 \text{ m/s}^2 = 9.81 \text{ kg} \cdot \text{m/s}^2 = 9.81 \text{ N}$

To calculate the rate at which the mass accelerates, you rearrange Newton's second law to give:

$a = \dfrac{F}{m} = \dfrac{9.81 \text{ N}}{1.00 \text{ kg}} = \dfrac{9.81 \text{ kg} \cdot \text{m/s}^2}{1.00 \text{ kg}} = 9.81 \text{ m/s}^2$

The acceleration of the mass is g or 9.81 m/s^2.

Quick Check

1. A single engine plane has a mass of 1500 kg and acceleration of 0.400 m/s^2. What is the unbalanced on the plane?

2. What is the mass of a rocket that accelerates at 2.0 m/s^2 and has a net force of 25 000 N?

3. Find the acceleration of a passenger jet that has a mass of 250 000 kg and provides an unbalanced force of 50 000 N.

Multiple Forces

The example and problems in the Quick Check above involve only one unbalanced force. In other situations, like Sample Problem 4.2.1 below, there are more forces to consider.

Remember that, in these problems, it is important to identify the forces that create the unbalanced force. Figure 4.2.1 shows four different forces acting on a block. The two vertical forces are the force of gravity and the normal force (the force exerted by the floor on the block). The two horizontal forces are the applied force and the force of friction.

The two vertical forces balance each other because the force of gravity and the normal force equal each other in size and act in opposite directions. The unbalanced force is the difference between the applied force and the friction force opposing the applied force.

Sample Problem 4.2.1 — Multiple Forces Acting on a Body

A 45.0 N block is being pushed along a floor, where the coefficient of kinetic friction is 0.333. If a force of 25.0 N is applied, at what rate will the block accelerate? The mass of the block is 4.60 kg.

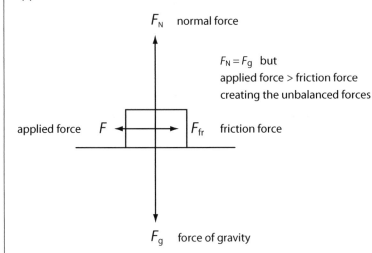

F_N normal force

$F_N = F_g$ but
applied force > friction force
creating the unbalanced forces

applied force F ← → F_{fr} friction force

F_g force of gravity

Figure 4.2.1 *Forces acting on block*

What to Think About	How to Do It
1. Find the force of friction.	$F_{fr} = \mu F_N = \mu F_g = (0.333) \times (45.0 \text{ N}) = 15.0 \text{ N}$
2. Find the unbalanced force.	unbalanced force = applied force − friction force $F = 25.0 \text{ N} - 15.0 \text{ N} = 10.0 \text{ N}$
3. Find the acceleration.	$a = \dfrac{F}{m} = \dfrac{10.0 \text{ N}}{4.60 \text{ kg}} = 2.17 \text{ m/s}^2$

$m \times a$

$\downarrow$

Net force = applied force - Force of friction

Practice Problems 4.2.1 — Multiple Forces Acting on a Body

1. A net force of 20 N is acting on a falling object. The object experiences air resistance of 6.0 N. If acceleration due to gravity is 9.8 m/s², what is the mass of the object?

    $26 N = m(9.8)$

    $m = 2.7 kg$

2. A 900 N person stands on two scales so that one foot is on each scale. What will each scale register in Newtons?

    $450 N$

3. What is the mass of a paratrooper who experiences an air resistance of 400 N and an acceleration of 4.5 m/s² during a parachute jump.

    $4.5 m - 9.8 m = -400 N$

    $\dfrac{-5.3 m}{-5.3} = \dfrac{-400}{-5.3}$

    $m = 75.5 kg$

4. A force of 50 N accelerates a 5.0 kg block at 6.0 m/s² along a horizontal surface.
    (a) What is the frictional force acting on the block?

    $5.0 \times 6.0 = 50 N -$ Force of friction
    Net force

    $30 = 50 -$ Force of friction

    $F_{fr} = 20 N$

    (b) What is the coefficient of friction?

    $M = \dfrac{F_{fr}}{F_N} = \dfrac{20}{5 \times 9.8} = \dfrac{20}{49}$

Investigation 4-2 Newton's Second Law of Motion

Purpose

To investigate how the change in speed of a cart is affected by

(a) the amount of unbalanced force, and (b) the amount of mass in the cart

Procedure

Part 1: Setting up and moving the cart

1. Set up the apparatus as shown in Figure 4.2.2(a). Start with three 200 g masses in the cart. Suspend a mass of 200 g from the end of a string, which passes over a pulley at the end of the bench. The force of gravity on this mass is 1.96 N or approximately 2.0 N.

2. Lift one end of your laboratory table so that the cart rolls toward the pulley at a steady speed. This can be checked with a ticker tape and your recording timer. If your bench cannot be lifted, do the experiment on a length of board, which can be raised at one end. What this lifting does is balance friction with a little help from gravity.

3. The class will now share the task of preparing and analyzing ticker-tape records of speed vs. time for each of the situations in Figure 4.2.2. Each lab group of two students will choose one of the eight set-ups and prepare two tapes or one for each partner. Note that the whole system of cart-plus-string-plus-hanging-mass moves as one unit. The mass of the whole system must be kept constant. This means that once you build your system you must not add any additional masses.

Varying the Unbalanced Force

(a) $F = 2.0$ N

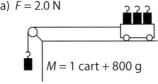

$M = 1$ cart $+ 800$ g

(b) $F = 4.0$ N

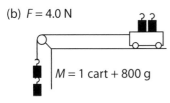

$M = 1$ cart $+ 800$ g

(c) $F = 6.0$ N

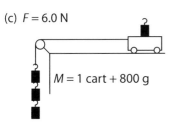

$M = 1$ cart $+ 800$ g

(d) $F = 8.0$ N

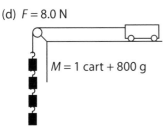

$M = 1$ cart $+ 800$ g

Varying the Mass

(e) $F = 2.0$ N

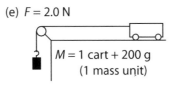

$M = 1$ cart $+ 200$ g
(1 mass unit)

(f) $F = 2.0$ N

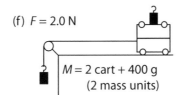

$M = 2$ cart $+ 400$ g
(2 mass units)

(g) $F = 2.0$ N

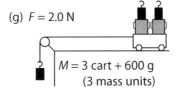

$M = 3$ cart $+ 600$ g
(3 mass units)

(h) $F = 2.0$ N

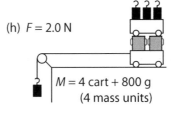

$M = 4$ cart $+ 800$ g
(4 mass units)

Figure 4.2.2 *Cart and mass set-ups*

Part 2: Preparing Your Own Tape

1. The class as a team will prepare and analyze tapes for each of the situations in Figure 4.2.2. If your class is large enough, compare duplicated data for any potential sources of error.
2. Use the technique you used to measure acceleration in an earlier chapter. Remember that a group of six dots represents 0.10 s and that the average speeds for each interval are plotted mid-way through each time interval and not at the end of the interval.
3. Prepare your graph. Label it carefully with the unbalanced force used (2.0 N, 4.0 N, 6.0 N, or 8.0 N) and the mass of the cart system.
4. The most important measurement you need is the acceleration of the cart. You get this from the slope of the graph. Express the acceleration in cm/s^2. You will share this information with the rest of the class.

Part 3: Analyzing Class Data

1. Prepare the following tables of data, summarizing class results.

Table 4.2.1 *Acceleration vs. Unbalanced Force (mass constant)*

Unbalanced Force F (N)	Acceleration a (cm/s²)
0	0
2.0	
4.0	
6.0	
8.0	

Table 4.2.2 *Acceleration vs Mass (unbalanced force constant)*

Mass, m (mass units)	Acceleration, a (cm/s²)	$\frac{1}{mass}$, $\frac{1}{m}$ (mass units⁻¹)
1.0		1.0
2.0		0.50
3.0		0.33
4.0		0.25

2. Plot a graph of acceleration (*y*-axis) against unbalanced force (*x*-axis).
3. Plot a graph of acceleration against mass.
4. Plot a graph of acceleration against the reciprocal of mass (1/*m*).

Concluding Questions

1. Describe how the speed of a cart changes when a constant unbalanced force pulls it.
2. According to your first graph (*a* vs. *F*), how does acceleration depend on unbalanced force? Does your graph suggest that acceleration is directly proportional to unbalanced force? Support your answer with your data.
3. According to your second and third graphs, how does the acceleration of the cart vary when the mass is doubled, tripled, and quadrupled?
4. Write an equation for the third graph, complete with the numerical value and units for the slope.
5. What were some of the experimental difficulties you encountered in this investigation, which would make it difficult to obtain ideal results?

4.2 Review Questions

1. What unbalanced force is needed to accelerate a 5.0 kg cart at 5.0 m/s²?

2. A net force of 7.5×10^4 N acts on a spacecraft of mass 3.0×10^4 kg.
   (a) At what rate will the spacecraft accelerate?

   (b) Assuming constant acceleration is maintained, how fast will the spacecraft be moving after 25 s, if its initial speed was 5.0×10^3 m/s?

3. A model rocket has a mass of 0.12 kg. It accelerates vertically to 60.0 m/s in 1.2 s.
   (a) What is its average acceleration?

   (b) What is the unbalanced force on the rocket?

   (c) If the force of gravity on the rocket is 1.2 N, what is the total thrust of its engine?

4. What is the mass of a rock if a force of 2.4×10^3 N makes it accelerate at a rate of 4.0×10^1 m/s²?

5. A fully loaded military rocket has a mass of 3.0×10^6 kg, and the force of gravity on it at ground level is 2.9×10^7 N.
   (a) At what rate will the rocket accelerate during lift-off, if the engines provide a thrust of 3.3×10^7 N?

   (b) Why will this acceleration not remain constant?

6. A boy and his skateboard have a combined mass of 60.0 kg. After an initial shove, the boy starts coasting at 5.5 m/s along a level driveway. Friction brings him to rest in 5.0 s. The combined force of gravity on the boy and skateboard is 5.9×10^2 N. What is the average coefficient of rolling friction between the driveway and the skateboard wheels?

4.3 Newton's Third Law of Motion

Action and Reaction Forces

Isaac Newton observed that whenever forces exist between two bodies, the forces are mutual. If one body pushes on another, the other body exerts an equal force on the first body, but in the opposite direction. To do push-ups, for example, you push down on the floor. The floor exerts an equal force up on you. The floor lifts you up! Earth exerts a force of gravity on the Moon. What evidence is there that the Moon exerts an equal force on Earth?

Newton studied situations involving forces between pairs of bodies and he stated his conclusions about mutual forces between pairs of bodies as his third law. **Newton's third law of motion** is also called the **law of action and reaction**.

> If two bodies interact, the force the first body exerts on the second body will equal the force the second body exerts on the first body. The two forces will be opposite in direction and will act simultaneously over the same interval of time.

The first force is called the **action force**, and the second force is called the **reaction force**. If we call the first body A and the second body B, then the law of action and reaction can be expressed mathematically like this:

$$F_{A \text{ on } B} = -F_{B \text{ on } A}$$

where the minus sign indicates opposite direction.

It is important to remember that for both forces, each force is exerted on the other body. The forces do not cancel. This is a really important point. For example, imagine a horse pulling a cart. If we just consider the force the horse exerts on the cart, then Newton's third law tells us that the cart exerts an equal and opposite force on the horse. The two forces are illustrated in Figure 4.3.1.

You might look at the picture and say that the horse and cart do not move because the two forces seem to cancel each other out. They are equal and opposite. But remember that the horse is exerting an action force on the cart and the cart is exerting a reaction force on the horse. That is why the horse feels the heavy cart on its harness when it starts pulling.

When applying Newton's third law, always ask yourself what object or thing applies the force and what body or object receives the force. There must be two different bodies or objects.

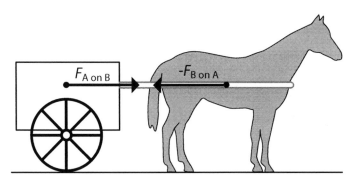

Figure 4.3.1 *Movement occurs when the horse's feet exert a force on Earth's surface and Earth exerts an equal and opposite force back on the horse.*

Quick Check

1. Review your diagrams from the Warm Up activity. In each diagram, label the action force and reaction force.
2. When you are walking, you are producing an action force toward the ground. Why do you move in the opposite direction?

    _____

    _____

3. You see a large dog running along a floating log. If the dog is running to your right, what, if anything, is happening to the log?

    _____

    _____

Investigation 4-3 Newton's Third Law

Purpose

To observe demonstrations of Newton's third law and identify the action and reaction forces

Procedure

Part 1: Exploding Carts

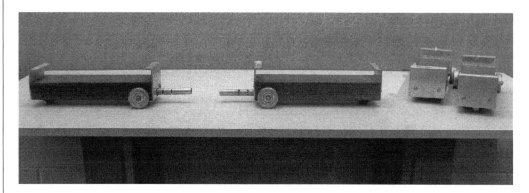

Figure 4.3.2 *Laboratory carts*

1. Push two identical laboratory carts together so that their spring bumpers are compressed. Release the carts on a flat table or floor. Observe as they accelerate away from each other.

   (a) What force makes the carts accelerate?

   (b) Why do the two carts, of identical mass, accelerate at the same rate?

   (c) How does this demonstration illustrate Newton's third law?

2. Predict what will happen if you double the mass of one of the carts by placing an extra cart on top of it. Test your prediction.

   (a) Has the force repelling the carts changed?

   (b) What has changed?

3. Try making the mass of one of the carts much greater than the mass of the other.

   (a) Is the force changed?

   (b) What has changed?

Part 2: Motion from Rest

Figure 4.3.3 Set-up for part 2

1. Place a piece of light plastic insulating Styrofoam board (50 cm × 25 cm × 2.5 cm) at one end of an air table as shown in Figure 4.3.3. Place a wind-up toy car or a radio-controlled car at one end of the board. Turn on the air table and start the car moving. Observe and describe what happens:
   (a) to the car
   (b) to the "road" under the car

2. How does this demonstration illustrate Newton's Third Law?

Part 3: Tug of War

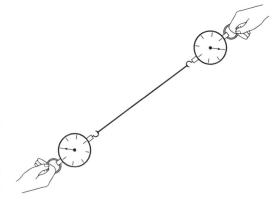

Figure 4.3.4 *Students stretching the string*

1. Tie a string between two 20 N spring balances. Have two students stretch the string between them as shown in Figure 4.3.4. What do the two spring balances read?

2. Try pulling with different forces. Compare the forces on each spring balance each time you pull on the string with a different force. Does it matter who does the pulling?

3. Try adding a third spring balance in the middle of the string. How does this demonstration illustrate Newton's third law?

Concluding Questions

1. When a car moves forward, in which direction do the wheels of the car push on the road? What force actually makes the car move forward?

2. List and discuss three examples of situations from your own everyday experience, that involve Newton's third law.

4.3 Review Questions

1. You are playing softball and your friend throws a ball to you. You catch the ball. The action force is the impact of the ball against your glove. What is the reaction force?

   equal to action force

2. During a golf swing, is the club impacting on the ball the action force or the reaction force? Use a diagram to illustrate your answer.

   Action force

3. If a soccer player kicks a ball with a force of 100 N, what is the magnitude of the reaction force?

   -100N reaction force

4. Spiderman is having a tug of war with a grade 2 student. Both are pulling very hard from opposite ends. Who exerts a greater force on the rope? Explain your answer.

   Same

   Boy would move towards Spiderman

5. In a demolition derby a Hummer SUV collides head-on with a SMART car. Which car experiences a greater impact force? Explain your answer.

   Same

6. During a martial arts demonstration, a black belt uses a karate chop to break a large board with her hand by exerting a force of 2000 N. What force did the board exert on her hand?

   -2000 N

7. A few years from now after much hard work, you are an astronaut and are completing a repair of some solar panels. To do this you have to take a space walk outside the International Space Station. By accident, you find yourself disconnected from the support rope and need to get back to the station. All you have is your tools with you. How can you propel yourself back to safety?

   Throw your tools in opposite direction

4.4 Momentum

Warm Up

Consider the following objects and motion in the two columns below:

feather	fast (10 m/s)
marble	average (5 m/s)
softball	slow (2 m/s)

1. Connect an object in the first column with a motion in the second column for the following situations.

   (a) The combination that will cause the most pain if the object hits your leg

   _____ + _____

   (b) The combination that will cause the least pain if the object hits your leg

   _____ + _____

2. Explain your reasoning for each answer.

   (a) _____

   _____

   (b) _____

   _____

Mass × Velocity = Momentum

One of the most important concepts in physics is that of momentum. Isaac Newton first used the idea when he wrote his second law of motion. In his original version, the second law looks like this:

$$F = \frac{m\Delta v}{\Delta t}$$

Newton called the product of mass and velocity (mv) a quantity of motion. Thus, his second law stated that the unbalanced force on an object is equal to the rate of change of a quantity of motion with respect to time. We now call the product of mass × velocity **momentum** and we give it the symbol p. The unit of measurement for momentum is kg·m/s.

$$p = m\Delta v$$

Newton's second law can be written this way:

$$F = ma = \frac{m\Delta v}{\Delta t} = \frac{\Delta p}{\Delta t}$$

Thus, the unbalanced force equals the rate of change of momentum with respect to time.

Quick Check

1. What is the momentum of a 100 kg motorbike travelling at 10 m/s?

    100 kg m/s

2. What is the mass of plane that is travelling at 200 km/h and has a momentum of 1.1×10^6 kg·m/s?

    2.0×10^4 kg

3. How fast does a 0.01 kg bug have to fly to have a momentum of 0.25 kg·m/s? Is this possible?

    25 m/s , no not possible

Impulse

According to Newton's second law, in its original form $F = \dfrac{m\Delta v}{\Delta t} = \dfrac{\Delta p}{\Delta t}$. This can be rearranged to:

$$\Delta p = F\Delta t = m\Delta v$$

The product of the force and the time interval during which it acts is called the **impulse**. The last equation shows that the impulse is equal to the change in momentum it produces.

This is an important relationship when considering an object that is undergoing a change in momentum. An object's momentum changes because an impulse has been placed on the object. For example, if you are driving down a road at a constant velocity, you and your vehicle have a momentum. When you press on the gas pedal, the velocity of the vehicle increases. The momentum has also increased. This increased momentum was caused by a force being exerted on the vehicle over a period of time. Or put another way, the vehicle experienced an impulse. The amount of impulse equals the change in momentum in the vehicle.

Units for Momentum and Impulse

Momentum is measured in kg·m/s because these units have the dimensions of mass and velocity. Impulse is measured in N·s because these units have the dimensions of force and time. Since impulse is equal to change in momentum, these units must be equivalent. It can easily be shown that this is true:

$$(N{\cdot}s) = (kg{\cdot}m/s^2) \cdot (s) = (kg{\cdot}m/s)$$

Momentum and impulse may be expressed in either unit.

Quick Check

1. (a) What is the momentum of a 112 kg football player running with a velocity of 3.6 m/s?

   4.0×10^2 kg m/s

   (b) What impulse must a tackler impart to the football player to bring him to a stop?

   -4.0×10^2 kg m/s

   (impulse = change in p)

   (c) If the tackle was completed in 0.80 s, what average force did the tackler exert on the other player?

   $\dfrac{-403.2}{0.80} = -504$ N

   (d) Why is the force negative in question 1(c)?

   because its a resisting force

Law of Conservation of Momentum

Any moving body has momentum equal to the product of the body's mass and its velocity. What makes momentum such an important quantity in nature is the fact that in a closed system, momentum is conserved. A closed system is one where no outside forces act on the system. This is the **law of conservation of momentum**. In other words, the total change in momentum within the closed, two-body system is zero. This means that the total momentum is constant, or that momentum is conserved.

Scientists have done many, many experiments with momentum and are convinced that momentum truly is a conserved quantity in nature. At the subatomic level in experiments done with high-energy particle accelerators, physicists rely heavily on the law of conservation of momentum in interpreting the results of collisions of particles.

Conservation of Momentum and Newton's Third Law

Newton's third law is a special case of the law of conservation of momentum. This can be shown by using a proof. A proof is a mathematical solution that logically demonstrates something to be true. The following is a proof showing that Newton's third law is a special case of the law of conservation of momentum.

Consider two bodies interacting such that body A exerts a force on body B, and body B exerts an equal force on body A, but in the opposite direction.

$$F_{A \text{ on } B} = -F_{B \text{ on } A}$$

action force = – reaction force

The minus sign indicates that the direction of the reaction force is opposite to that of the action force. Using Newton's second law, written in terms of momentum:

$$\frac{m_B v_B}{t} = -\frac{m_A v_A}{t}$$

The time intervals on both sides of the equation are the same because both forces act over the same interval of time. So the equation can be simplified to:

$$m_B v_B = - m_A v_A$$

Therefore,

$$m_A v_A + m_B v_B = 0$$

or

$$p_A + p_B = 0$$

Other Examples of the Law of Conservation of Momentum

If you have ever played pool or billiards you will be familiar with the law of conservation of momentum. When the cue ball, or white ball, hits another ball, momentum is conserved. For example, if all the momentum is transferred from the cue ball to the billiard ball, the cue ball will stop and the billiard ball will move.

Sample Problem 4.4.1 — Conservation of Momentum

A railway car of mass 6.0×10^3 kg is coasting along a track with a velocity of 5.5 m/s when suddenly a 3.0×10^3 kg load of sulphur is dumped into the car. What is its new velocity?

What to Think About	How to Do It
1. What do I know about the problem?	The momentum of the railway car will not change because of the law of conservation of momentum. Let initial mass be m_1 and initial velocity be v_1. The final mass of the railway car will be m_2 and the final velocity v_2.
2. What am I trying to solve?	Solve for the final velocity v_2.
3. What formula applies to this situation?	$m_1 v_1 = m_2 v_2$
4. Find the final velocity v_2.	$(6.0 \times 10^3 \text{ kg})(5.5 \text{ m/s}) = (6.0 \times 10^3 \text{ kg} + 3.0 \times 10^3 \text{ kg})(v_2)$ $33 \times 10^3 \text{ kg·m/s} = (9.0 \times 10^3 \text{ kg})(v_2)$ $v_2 = \dfrac{33 \; 10^3 \text{ kg·m/s}}{9.0 \; 10^3 \text{ kg}}$ $= 3.7 \text{ m/s}$ The rail car's new velocity is 3.7 m/s

Practice Problems 4.4.1 — Conservation of Momentum

1. Two identical air track gliders each have a mass of 100 g and are sitting on an air track. One glider is at rest and the other glider is moving toward it at a velocity. When they collide they stick together and move off at 2.0 m/s. What was the initial velocity of the moving glider?

    4.0 m/s

2. A 1.0 kg ball of putty is rolling towards a resting 4.5 kg bowling ball at 1.5 m/s. When they collide and stick together, what is the resulting momentum of the two objects stuck together?

    $$m_1 \times v_1 = m_2 \times v_2$$
    $$1ng \times 1.5m/s + 4.5 \times 0$$
    $$1.5 = P$$

3. A ball rolls at a velocity of 3.5 m/s toward a 5.0 kg ball at rest. They collide and move off at a velocity of 2.5 m/s. What was the mass of the moving ball?

    $$3.5 \times m + 5.0 \times 0 = 2.5 m/s$$
    $$3.5m + 0 = 2.5 (m+5)$$
    $$3.5m - 2.5 = 12.5$$
    $$\boxed{12.5 kg}$$

impulse = Δ momentum

4.4 Review Questions

1. What is the momentum of a 75 g mouse running across the floor with a velocity of 2.6 m/s?

2. What is the impulse of a 55 N force exerted over a time interval of 1.0 ms?

$$55 \times 1 \times 10^{-3}$$
$$= 0.055 \text{ N/s}$$

3. A 0.060 kg rifle bullet leaves the muzzle with a velocity of 6.0×10^2 m/s. If the 3.0 kg rifle is held very loosely, with what velocity will it recoil?

$$V_r = \frac{0.060 \times 6.0 \times 10^2}{3.0}$$
$$= 12 \text{ m/s}$$

4. A 53 kg skateboarder on a 2.0 kg skateboard is coasting along at 1.6 m/s. He collides with a stationary skateboarder of mass 43 kg, also on a 2.0 kg skateboard, and the two skateboarders coast off in the same direction that the first skateboarder was travelling. What velocity will the combined skateboarders now have?

$$55 \times 1.6 + 45 \times 0 = (m+m)V$$
$$88 = \frac{55 \times 1.6 V}{100}$$

$$= .88 \text{ m/s}$$

5. What impulse is needed to change the velocity of a 10.0 kg object from 12.6 m/s to 25.5 m/s in a time of 5.00 s? How much force is needed?

$$10.0 kg (25.5 - 12.6) \frac{m}{s}$$
$$= \frac{129 \text{ kg m/s}}{5 s}$$
$$= 25.8 N$$

6. A 1.5×10^3 kg car travelling at 44 m/s collides head-on with a 1.0×10^3 kg car travelling at 22 m/s in the opposite direction. If the cars stick together on impact, what is the velocity of the wreckage immediately after impact? (Hint: Let the velocity of the second car be –22 m/s, since it is moving in a direction opposite to the first car.)

$$(1.53 \times 10^3 \times 44 m/s) + (1.0 \times 10^3 \times -22 m/s)$$
$$= (5.5 \times 10^3 \times V)$$
$$= 17.6 m/s$$

7. (a) What impulse must be imparted by a baseball bat to a 145 g ball to change its velocity from 40.0 m/s to –50.0 m/s? $I = F \times T$

$$m(V_f - F_i) =$$
$$0.145(-90) = -13.1 \text{ kg/m/s}$$

(b) If the collision between the baseball and the bat lasts 1.00 ms, what force was exerted on the ball? (1 ms = 10^{-3} s)

$$-13.1 = F \times 0.001$$
$$= .131 N$$

Chapter 4 Review Questions

1. A person who does not wear a seatbelt may crash through the windshield if a car makes a sudden stop. Explain what happens to this person in terms of Newton's first law of motion. Explain why it is wise to wear a seatbelt.

   According to Newtons first law, a body will continue to move at same speed as long as there are no unbalenced forces acting on it.

2. In a frame of reference where there are no external, unbalanced forces, show that Newton's second law *includes* the law of inertia.

   It includes inertia because inertia is the resistance to change and the second law states if there are no unbalenced forces it will not accelerate. And if there is, it will accelerate.

3. What unbalanced force is needed to accelerate a 2.0×10^3 kg vehicle at 1.5 m/s^2?

   $$a = \frac{F}{M}$$

   $$1.5 \text{ m/s} = \frac{F}{2.0 \times 10^3}$$

   $$= 3000 \text{ N}$$

4. What is the acceleration of a 5.8×10^3 kg vehicle if an unbalanced force of 1.16×10^2 N acts on it?

   $$a = \frac{1.16 \times 10^2}{5.8 \times 10^3}$$

   $$= 0.02 \text{ m/s}^2$$

5. What is the mass of a space satellite if a thrust of 2.0×10^2 N accelerates it at a rate of 0.40 m/s^2 during a small steering adjustment?

   $$0.40 = \frac{2.0 \times 10^2 \text{ N}}{M}$$

   $$= 500 \text{ kg}$$

6. At what rate will a 5.0 kg object accelerate if a 12.8 N force is applied to it, and the friction force opposing its motion is 2.8 N?

   $$a = \frac{10 \text{ N}}{5.0 \text{ kg}}$$

   $$a = 2 \text{ m/s}^2$$

7. A rope is strong enough to withstand a 750 N force without breaking. If two people pull on opposite ends of the rope, each with a force of 500 N, will it break? Explain.

8. State Newton's third law of motion. Describe an example of a situation involving the law of action and reaction that you have not already used.

9. Two tug-of-war teams are at opposite ends of a rope. Newton's third law says that the force exerted by team A will equal the force that team B exerts on team A. How can either team win the tug-of-war?

10. (a) Define momentum.

    (b) Why is momentum considered a very important quantity in physics?

11. (a) Define impulse.

    (b) What is the impulse due to a force that causes the velocity of a 46 g golf ball to change from 0 m/s to 60.0 m/s in 0.50 ms?

    (c) What force was applied to the ball?

12. A hunter who fails to hold the rifle firmly against a shoulder may be injured when shooting. Explain in terms of Newton's third law.

13. A 4.2 kg rifle shoots a 0.050 kg bullet at a velocity of 3.00×10^2 m/s. At what velocity does the rifle recoil?

14. A 0.250 kg ball of Plasticine moving at 5.0 m/s overtakes and collides with a 0.300 kg ball of Plasticine, travelling in the same direction at 2.0 m/s. The two balls of Plasticine stick together on collision. What is their velocity after the collision?

15. A railroad car of mass 12 000 kg is travelling at a velocity of 6.0 m/s when it collides with an identical car at rest. The two cars lock together. What is their common velocity after the collision?

Chapter 4   Extra Practice

1. What is the difference between inertial mass and gravitational mass?

2. Describe three factors related to inertia that explain why an oil tanker ship is harder to maneuver when it is full than when it is empty.

3. Use Newton's laws to explain why a headrest in a car protects the neck of the person in a car.

4. Some older model trucks did not have headrests. Why could this be a safety hazard for passengers in the truck?

5. How can you use Newton's first law of motion to explain why shooting a hockey puck across a frozen pond will travel a long way?

6. In a car collision seat belts are a safety device to protect you. Should pets in a car wear a seat belt? Use Newton's first law of motion to defend you position.

7. Using only units and Newton's second law of motion, prove that the unit for force can be $kg \cdot m/s^2$.

8. What unbalanced force is needed to push a 35 kg girl in a 20 kg wagon at an acceleration of 1.0 m/s^2?

9. What force is needed to move a 270 N kindergarten student learning to skate at an acceleration of 0.7 m/s^2?

10. Rhys and Gareth are having a tug of war with 1.25 kg of climbing rope. If Rhys pulls with a force of 24 N and the rope accelerates away from him at 1.4 m/s^2, with what force is Gareth pulling the rope?

11 A 70 kg person is standing on a bathroom scale in an elevator purely for scientific purposes. The elevator begins to accelerate upward at 2.25 m/s^2 for 1.75 s and then continues at a constant speed. What is the reading on the scale or weight of the person when the elevator is at rest and when it is accelerating?

12. A 400 g air track glider has an initial velocity of 0.50 m/s. A force of 0.60 N is applied in the opposite direction. How long will it take to bring the glider to a stop?

13. Owen is standing against the boards in a skating rink with his skates on. He pushes against the boards. What direction will he go?

14. If Owen is 40 kg, and pushes with a force of 15 N, what will be his acceleration?

15. A 2100 kg sports car is approaching a stop sign. If the acceleration rate to slow down is −4.5 m/s^2, what is the net force slowing the car down?

16. A plastic bag at a local store can hold a maximum of 275 N before it rips. When lifted, the bag reaches a maximum acceleration of 6.0 m/s^2. What is the maximum mass that can be put into the bag?

17. (a) A racing car can reach a speed of 100 km/h in 1.95 s. If the car is 689 kg and the driver has a weight of 833 N, what is the average acceleration of the car?

    (b) On a drag strip track of 350 m, the racing car completes the distance in 4.67 s. If acceleration is constant, what is the average acceleration and final velocity?

18. What is the acceleration of a 130 g baseball traveling at 25 m/s when it is caught in a glove and brought to rest in 0.05 s?

5 Energy

By the end of this chapter, you should be able to do the following:

- ➤ Perform calculations involving work, force and displacement
  - solve a variety of problems involving:
    - work
    - force
    - displacement
- ➤ Solve problems involving power and efficiency
  - perform calculations involving relationships among:
    - power
    - work
    - time
  - perform calculations involving relationships among:
    - work (input and output)
    - power (input and output)
    - efficiency
  - solve a variety of problems involving:
    - gravitational potential energy
    - mass
    - acceleration due to gravity
    - height above a reference point
- ➤ Solve problems involving different forms of energy
  - solve a variety of problems involving:
    - gravitational potential energy
    - mass
    - acceleration due to gravity
    - height above a reference point
  - solve a variety of problems involving:
    - kinetic energy   – velocity
    - mass
- ➤ Analyse the relationship between work and energy, with reference to the law of conservation of energy
  - relate energy change to work done
  - state the law of conservation of energy
  - solve problems, using the law of conservation of energy to determine:
    - gravitational potential energy
    - total energy
    - kinetic energy
    - thermal energy
  - solve a variety of problems involving:
    - thermal energy   – specific heat capacity
    - mass   – change in temperature

By the end of this chapter, you should know the meaning to these **key terms**:

- conduction
- convection
- efficiency
- energy
- gravitational potential energy

- heat
- kinetic energy
- law of conservation of energy
- power
- radiation

- specific heat capacity
- temperature
- thermal energy
- watt
- work

By the end of the chapter, you should be able to use and know when to use the following formulae:

$$W = Fd$$

$$E_p = mgh$$

$$P = \frac{W}{\Delta t} = \frac{\Delta E}{\Delta t}$$

$$W = \Delta E$$

$$E_k = \frac{1}{2} mv^2$$

$$efficiency = \frac{W_{out}}{W_{in}} = \frac{P_{out}}{P_{in}}$$

An explosion is an example of chemical, sound, light, and thermal energy being released all at the same time.

5.1 Do You Know the Meaning of Work?

Warm Up

Bounce a rubber or tennis ball up and down several times. List all the different forms of energy you observe.

_____

_____

_____

What is Energy?

Energy appears in a variety of forms. Some forms you are familiar with include light, sound, thermal energy, electrical energy, elastic potential energy, gravitational potential energy, chemical potential energy, nuclear energy, and mechanical energy. What is energy? Your experience tells you it is associated with movement or with the potential for motion. Energy is what makes things move. The usual definition of energy says that energy is the capacity to do work.

In physics, **work** has a specific meaning. If work is to be done on an object, two things must happen: (1) a force must act on the object and (2) the object must move through a distance in the direction of the force. The amount of work done is equal to the product of the force exerted and the distance the force causes the object to move, measured in the direction of the force.

$$\text{work} = \text{force} \times \text{distance}$$

$$W = Fd$$

Since force is measured in newtons (N) and distance in metres (m), work can be measured in newton-metres. One newton-metre (N·m) is called a **joule (J)** after James Joule (1818–1889), an English physicist.

$$1\text{ J} = 1\text{ N·m}$$

Sample Problem 5.1.1 — Calculating Work

How much work does a golfer do lifting a 46 g golf ball out of the hole and up to his pocket (0.95 m above the ground)?

What to Think About	How to Do It
1. Find the correct formula.	$W = Fd$
2. Find the force in newtons.	$F = mg = (0.046 \text{ kg})(9.81 \text{ m/s}^2)$ $F = 0.45 \text{ N}$
3. Find work done.	$W = Fd = (0.45 \text{ N})(0.95 \text{ m})$ $= 0.43 \text{ J}$ The golfer does 0.43 J of work lifting the golf ball from the hole to his pocket.

Practice Problems 5.1.1 — Calculating Work

1. How much work will you do if you push a block of concrete 4.3 m along a floor, with a steady force of 25 N?

2. If your mass is 70.0 kg, how much work will you do climbing a flight of stairs 25.0 m high, moving at a steady pace? (g = 9.81 N/kg)

3. Your car is stuck in the mud. You push on it with a force of 300.0 N for 10.0 s, but it will not move. How much work have you done in the 10.0 s?

Power

A machine is powerful if it can do a lot of work in a short time. **Power** is the measure of the amount of work a machine can do in one second.

$$\text{power} = \frac{\text{work}}{\text{time}}$$

$$P = \frac{W}{\Delta t}$$

Power could be measured in joules per second (J/s), but one joule per second is called one **watt (W)**, after James Watt (1736–1819), a Scottish engineer.

$$1\text{ W} = 1\text{ J/s}$$

Power can be measured in kilowatts (kW) or megawatts (MW).

$$1\text{ kW} = 1000\text{ W } (10^3\text{ W})$$
$$1\text{ MW} = 1\ 000\ 000\text{ W } (10^6\text{ W})$$

Sample Problem 5.1.2 — Calculating Power

The power of a small motor in a toy can be calculated by the amount of work it does in a period of time. What is the power rating of a toy motor that does 4200 J of work in 70.0 s?

What to Think About	How to Do It
1. Find the correct formula.	$P = \dfrac{W}{\Delta t}$
2. Calculate the power.	$P = \dfrac{4200\text{ J}}{70.0\text{ s}} = 60\text{ W}$ The power rating of the toy motor is 60 W.

Practice Problems 5.1.2 — Calculating Power

1. An airport baggage handler lifts 42 pieces of luggage, averaging 24 kg each, through a height of 1.6 m onto a baggage cart, in a time of 3.6 min. In this situation, what is the power of the baggage handler?

2. How much work or energy (in J) does a 150 W light bulb convert to heat and light in 1.0 h?

3. A mechanical lifting system is approximately 25% efficient. This means that only 25% of the energy used to lift a mass is converted into useable energy. The rest is mostly lost as heat. If 1.5×10^8 W is used for 2.0 h, how much energy (in J) of useable work is produced? How much heat is produced?

What's Watt?

Power is commonly measured in **horsepower**. Eventually, horsepower may be replaced by the **kilowatt**, which is a metric unit, but the horsepower (non-metric) will persist for some time because it is firmly entrenched in our vocabulary. .

The Scottish engineer James Watt is famous for his improved design of a steam engine, invented earlier by Thomas Newcomen. Watt's new engine was used at first for pumping water out of coal mines, work that previously had been done by horses. Customers wanted to know how many horses Watt's new engines would replace. So that he could answer their questions, Watt did the following:

1. He measured the force, in pounds, exerted by the average horse over a distance, measured in feet.
2. He calculated the amount of work the horse did, in a unit he called foot-pounds.
3. He measured the time it took the horse to do the work.
4. He calculated how much work the horse would do in one second, which is the average power of the horse. He found this to be 550 foot-pounds per second. This was taken to be the average power of one horse equal to one horsepower.

$$1 \text{ horsepower} = 550 \frac{\text{foot-pounds}}{\text{second}}$$

The modern unit for power is the watt (W). One horsepower is equivalent to 746 W, which is almost 3/4 kW. The following example finds the power in an electric motor and them shows how to convert watts to horsepower.

Sample Problem 5.1.3 — Calculating Horsepower

An electric motor is used, with a pulley and a rope, to lift a 650 N load from the road up to a height of 12 m. This job is done in a time of 11 s. What is the power output of the motor?

What to Think About	How to Do It
1. Find the correct formula.	$P = \dfrac{work}{time} = \dfrac{W}{\Delta t}$
2. Calculate the power in watts.	$P = \dfrac{Fd}{\Delta t} = \dfrac{(650 \text{ N})(12 \text{ m})}{11 \text{ s}}$ $= 7.1 \times 10^2 \text{ W}$
3. Calculate the horsepower.	The often-used unit of power, 1 horsepower, is equivalent to 7.5×10^2 W. The motor in this question would have a horsepower of $\dfrac{7.1 \times 10^2 \text{ W}}{7.5 \times 10^2 \text{ W/HP}} = 0.95 \text{ HP}$

Investigation 5-1A   Getting Work Done with Pulleys

Machines such as pulleys are used to get work done, but you must do some work to operate these simple machines.

Purpose
To compare the amount of work that you do using a pulley system with the amount of work the pulley does for you

Procedure
1. Set up the pulley system in Figure 5.1.1. The pulley system will be used to lift a 200 g mass up to a height of 10.0 cm (0.100 m). The force of gravity on the mass is approximately 2.0 N. The work that the pulley system will do is therefore:

    $W = Fd = (2.0 \text{ N})(0.10 \text{ m}) = 0.20 \text{ J}$

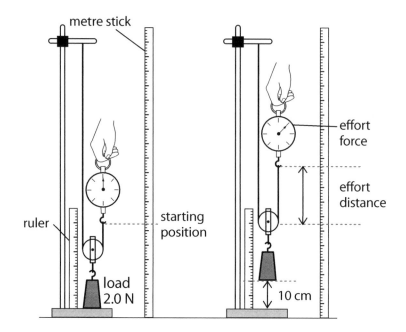

Figure 5.1.1 *Pulleys Step 1*

2. Your task is to see how much work you have to do when you operate the pulley system to do the 0.20 J of work.
    (a) Pull gently on the spring balance until the string is tight and the load is just about to lift. Mark the position of the bottom of the spring balance hook. Pull up on the spring balance until the load has been raised 10.0 cm. Write down the force you had to exert (**effort force**) and the distance through which you had to exert it (**effort distance**).
    (b) Calculate how much work you did by multiplying your effort force by your effort distance. Express your answer in joules (J).
3. Repeat Procedure 2 using each of the pulley arrangements in Figure 5.1.2. In each trial, use the pulley system to lift a 2.0 N load a distance of 10.0 cm (0.100 m), so that the work done by each pulley system is 0.20 J. Measure your effort force and your effort distance with each system. Record all your data in a copy of Table 5.1.1.

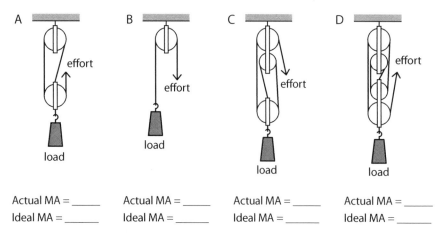

Figure 5.1.2 *Pulleys Step 3*

Table 5.1.1 *Data for Investigation 5-1*

System Used	Load Lifted (N)	Load Lifted This Distance (m)	Work Done By Pulley System (J)	*Your* Effort Force (N)	*Your* Effort Distance (m)	Work Done by You (J)
Fig. 5.1.1	2.0	0.10	0.20			
Fig. 5.1.2A	2.0	0.10	0.20			
Fig. 5.1.2B	2.0	0.10	0.20			
Fig. 5.1.2C	2.0	0.10	0.20			
Fig. 5.1.2D	2.0	0.10	0.20			

Concluding Questions

1. According to your results and those of your classmates, is the work that *you* do operating the pulley systems greater than, equal to, or less than the work done by the pulley systems?
2. Does a pulley system "save" you work? Explain. Why are pulley systems used to lift heavy loads?
3. If a pulley system allows you to lift a load that is twice your effort force, we say that it has a **mechanical advantage (MA)** of 2. Mechanical advantage is equal to the load divided by the effort force:

$$MA = \frac{load}{effort\ force}$$

    Calculate the mechanical advantage of each of the five pulley systems you used.

4. Examine the diagrams in Figures 5.1.1 and 5.1.2. Note the number of sections of rope that are exerting an upward force on the load. Considering that these sections of rope share the load equally, can you figure out a quick and easy way to predict the **ideal mechanical advantage** of each system? Test your prediction against the actual mechanical advantage you calculated for each pulley system.
5. How might the effort distance and the load distance be used to calculate the ideal MA of a pulley system? Write a formula for calculating MA from effort distance and load distance.

Challenges

1. Predict what the mechanical advantage of the pulley system in Figure 5.1.3 will be. Test your prediction by experimenting.
    Hint: Is it really just *one* pulley system?
2. Draw a pulley system that has a mechanical advantage of less than one. For what purpose might it be used?

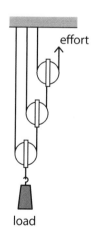

Figure 5.1.3 *Pulleys Challenge 1*

Investigation 5-1B   Measuring the Power of a Small Motor

Purpose
To measure the rate at which a small electric motor does work and thus determine its power output

Procedure

1. Use a small electric motor equipped with a special shaft on which a 2.0 m length of string can be wound. Clamp the motor to a ring stand (Figure 5.1.4).

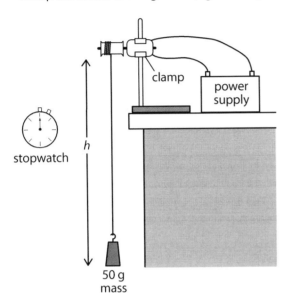

Figure 5.1.4 *Power Step 1*

2. Try different source voltages with the motor to see what you need so that the motor will lift a mass of 50.0 g up from the floor in a time of approximately 2.0–3.0 s.

3. To measure the useful power of the motor, you will need to know the force of gravity on the mass, the height through which the mass will be raised, and the time it takes to lift the mass through that height. (Remember that 1 kg of mass has a force of gravity on it of 9.8 N.)

4. Calculate the power of the motor for at least three different sets of conditions, using

    $power = \dfrac{work}{time}$. Try different loads and/or different source voltages to vary the conditions.

Concluding Questions

1. What is the maximum power output you measured for your motor?
2. What was the maximum power a member of your class achieved with the motor?

5.1 Review Questions

1. How much work is done on a 10.0 kg mass by Earth's gravitational field when the mass drops a distance of 5.0 m?

2. A girl uses a 3.00 m long ramp to push her 110 kg motorbike up to a trailer. The floor of the trailer is 1.20 m above the ground. How much work is done on the motorbike?

3. The force of gravity on a box of apples is 98.0 N. How much work will you do
   (a) if you lift the box from the floor to a height of 1.2 m?

   (b) if you carry the box horizontally a distance of 2.0 m?

4. A hiker carries a 25 kg load up a hill at a steady speed through a vertical height of 350 m. How much work does she do on the load?

5. The force of gravity on a box is 100.0 N. The coefficient of friction between the floor and the box is 0.250. How much work is done when the box is pushed along the floor, at a steady speed, for a distance of 15.0 m?

6. Which of the variables below would improve in your favour if you used a pulley system of MA = 8 to lift a load, compared with a pulley system of MA = 2? Explain your answer.
   (a) effort distance
   (b) effort force
   (c) work done by you
   (d) your power
   (e) work done by the machine

7. Draw a pulley system that has a mechanical advantage of 1/2. For what purpose might you use such a system?

8. How powerful is a motor that can lift a 500.0 kg load through a height of 12.0 m in a time of 12 s?

9. A motor does 25 MJ (megajoules) of work in one hour.

(a) What is the power rating of the motor?

(b) How many horsepower is this motor, if 1 HP = 750 W?

10. How much energy is consumed by a 100.0 W light bulb, if it is left on for 12.0 h?

5.2 Mechanical Energy

Warm Up

Fill a coffee can with three or four handfuls of dry sand. Measure the temperature of the sand. Now shake the can vigorously for three minutes. Take the temperature of the sand. Describe what happened to the temperature and explain why you think it occurred.

_____

_____

_____

Kinetic Energy

A moving object can do work. A falling axe does work to split a log. A moving baseball bat does work to stop a baseball, momentarily compress the ball out of its normal shape, then reverse its direction, and send it off at high speed.

Since a moving object has the ability to do work, it must have energy. We call the energy of a moving object its **kinetic energy.** A body that is at rest can gain kinetic energy if work is done on it by an external force. To get such a body moving at speed v, a net force must be exerted on it to accelerate it from rest up to speed v. The amount of work, W, which must be done can be calculated as follows:

$$W = Fd = (ma)d = m(ad)$$

Remember that for an object accelerating from rest at a uniform rate, $v_f^2 = 2ad$.

Therefore,
$$(ad) = \frac{v_f^2}{2}$$

and

$$W = m(ad) = m\left(\frac{v_f^2}{2}\right) = \frac{1}{2} mv^2$$

The work done on the object to accelerate it up to a speed v results in an amount of energy being transferred to the object, which is equal in magnitude to $\frac{1}{2} mv^2$. This is the object's kinetic energy, E_k.

$$E_k = \frac{1}{2} mv^2$$

Once an object has kinetic energy, it can do work on other objects.

Quick Check

1. A golfer wishes to improve his driving distance. Which would have more effect? Explain your answer.
   (a) doubling the mass of his golf club
   OR
   (b) doubling the speed with which the clubhead strikes the ball

2. How much work must be done to accelerate a 110 kg motorbike and its 60.0 kg rider from 0 to 80 km/h?

3. How much work is needed to accelerate a 1.0 g insect from rest up to 12 m/s?

Gravitational Potential Energy

Figure 5.2.1 shows an extremely simple mechanical system. A basketball player lifts a basketball straight up to a height h. The ball has mass m, so the force of gravity on the ball is mg. In lifting the ball, the basketball player has done work equal to mgh on the ball. He has transferred energy to the ball. Chemical energy in his cell molecules has been changed into gravitational potential energy because of the work he did.

Work is always a measure of energy transferred to a body. When the basketball is held up at height h, it has gravitational potential energy (E_p) equal to mgh.

$$E_p = mgh$$

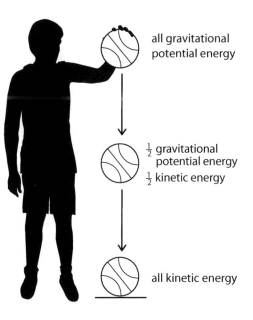

all gravitational potential energy

$\frac{1}{2}$ gravitational potential energy
$\frac{1}{2}$ kinetic energy

all kinetic energy

Figure 5.2.1 *At its highest point, the ball has only gravitational potential energy. Once it starts dropping, it has kinetic energy as well.*

Reference Point

When calculating gravitational potential energy, the height an object moves is always measured from the starting point of the movement. This is called the **reference point**. This is important because it means, the amount of potential energy in an object is relative to where the measurement occurs. For example, a table 1.0 m high has a 1.0 kg book on it. If the book is lifted 0.5 m above the table, how much gravitational potential energy does the book have? If h is measured from the table, it has 4.5 J of potential energy because $h = 0.5$ m or $E_p = (91.0 \text{ kg})(9.8 \text{ m/s}^2)(0.5 \text{ m})$. If h is measured from the ground, the book has 14.7 J of potential energy because $h = 1.5$ m or $E_p = (91.0 \text{ kg})(9.8 \text{ m/s}^2)(1.5 \text{ m})$.

Both answers are correct. What is important that the reference point is identified and only the vertical height is measured when determining the amount of gravitational potential energy in an object.

Quick Check

1. A box of bananas is lifted 5 m and gains a certain amount of potential energy. If the box is lifted another 5 m, describe how the potential energy changes.

2. What is the mass of a television if it takes 620 J to lift it 2.5 m.

3. If it takes 240 J to lift a 4 kg object, how high is the object lifted?

Work Energy Theorem

If a force is applied to an object over a distance, the amount of kinetic energy in the object changes. For example, a car speeds up because the force of the engine turns the wheels faster over a distance. The increased speed of the car represents the increase in the car's kinetic energy. You may have noticed that when the formula for kinetic energy was derived, work equaled the amount of kinetic energy:

$$W = \frac{1}{2} mv^2$$

The work-energy theorem states that the work done on a system equals the energy changes or:

$$W = \Delta E$$

Law of Conservation of Energy

Now consider what happens when the basketball you saw in Figure 5.2.1 is allowed to fall under the influence of the force of gravity. The unbalanced force, ignoring air friction, is equal to the force of gravity on the ball. For any situation where an object of mass m is pulled by an unbalanced force F, there will be an acceleration, a. Newton's second law of motion tells us that $F = ma$.

In our example, the basketball is a free-falling body, and $a = g$. As the ball falls through height h, its speed increases from 0 to v_f. For uniform acceleration,

$$v_f^2 = 2ad$$

For this situation, $v_f^2 = 2gh$. Since the unbalanced force pulling the ball down is mg, the work done on the ball by Earth's gravitational field is mgh.

$$\text{If } v_f^2 = 2gh, \text{ then } gh = \frac{v_f^2}{2}$$

$$\text{Therefore, } mgh = m\left(\frac{v_f^2}{2}\right) = \frac{1}{2}\, mv_f^2$$

When the ball is at the top of its path, all its energy is gravitational potential energy. The ball is not moving. It has energy only because of its position above the floor from which it was lifted. As the ball falls, it loses its potential energy and gains energy of motion, kinetic energy. Just before it collides with the floor, all the energy of the ball is kinetic energy, and the potential energy is zero. The amount of kinetic energy (E_k) at the bottom of its fall is given by:

$$E_k = \frac{1}{2}\, mv_f^2$$

On the way down, the kinetic energy of the ball at any time depends on the speed the ball has reached. For any speed v, kinetic energy $E_k = mv_f^2$. As the ball gains kinetic energy, it loses gravitational potential energy. At all times the sum of the gravitational potential energy and the kinetic energy is constant.

$$E_p + E_k = \text{constant}$$

This is an example of the **law of conservation of energy**, which states:

> The total energy of a mechanical system is constant. Energy can be transformed from one form into another, but the total amount of energy is unchanged.

As the ball falls through positions 1, 2, 3, etc., the sum of the potential energy and the kinetic energy remains constant:

$$mgh_1 + \frac{1}{2}\, mv_1^2 = mgh_2 + \frac{1}{2}\, mv_2^2 = mgh_3 + \frac{1}{2}\, mv_3^2 = \ldots$$

Notice that mechanical energy can be either potential or kinetic. For a mechanical system, the total mechanical energy is constant.

Sample Problem 5.2.1 — The Law of Conservation of Energy

The pendulum bob in Figure 5.2.2 is pulled back far enough that it is raised 0.36 m above its original level. When it is released, how fast will it be moving at the bottom of its swing?

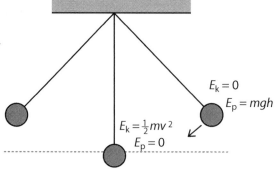

$E_k = 0$
$E_p = mgh$

$E_k = \frac{1}{2}mv^2$
$E_p = 0$

Figure 5.2.2 *Moving pendulum*

What to Think About	**How to Do It**
1. When the pendulum is pulled back, it is also lifted through a height *h*, and work *mgh* is done in lifting the bob against the force of gravity. The bob gains gravitational potential energy equal to the work done on it, so $E_p = mgh$. When the bob is released, its gravitational potential energy is transformed into kinetic energy. At the bottom of the swing, $E_p = 0$, and, $E_k = \dfrac{1}{2}mv^2$ but the kinetic energy at the bottom of the swing must equal the gravitational potential energy at the top according to the law of conservation of energy. 2. Rearrange to find speed. 3. Solve to find the speed of the bob at the bottom of the swing.	$E_p = mgh = \dfrac{1}{2}\ mv^2$ Therefore, $v^2 = 2gh$ and $v = \sqrt{2gh}$ $v = \sqrt{2gh}$ $\quad = \sqrt{2(9.8 \text{ m/s}^2)(0.36 \text{ m})}$ $\quad = 2.7 \text{ m/s}$ The pendulum bob will be moving 2.7 m/s at the bottom of its swing.

Practice Problems 5.2.1 — The Law of Conservation of Energy

1. Spiderman shoots a web line and swings on the end of it, like a pendulum. His starting point is 3.0 m above the lowest point in his swing. How fast is Spiderman moving as he passes through the bottom of the swing?

2. A vehicle moving with a speed of 90 km/h (25 m/s) loses its brakes but sees a runaway hill near the highway. If the driver steers his vehicle into the runaway hill, how far up the hill (vertically) will the vehicle travel before it comes to a stop? (Ignore friction.)

3. A 500 kg roller coaster car is going 10 m/s at the bottom of its run. How high can you build the next hill on the track so that it can get over without any additional work being done on the car? (Ignore friction.) Is your answer reasonable?

5.2 Review Questions

1. How much kinetic energy does the 80.0 kg skier sliding down the frictionless slope shown below have when he is two-thirds of the way down the ramp? The vertical height of the ramp is 60.0 m.

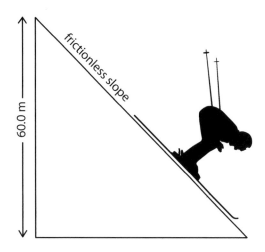

2. (a) How much potential energy is gained when a 75 kg person takes a ski lift up a mountain for 600 m?

   (b) At another ski hill, a 50 kg person gains 3.68×10^5 J when she travels up a ski lift for 1500 m at a 30° angle. What is the vertical height gained by the skier?

3. In a computer simulation, a Moon exploration robot lifted 0.245 kg of Moon rock 60 cm. This action required 0.24 J. What is the acceleration due to gravity on the Moon?

$$PE = mgh$$
$$0.24 = 0.245 \times g \times 0.60$$
$$g = \frac{0.24}{0.245 \times 0.60} = 1.6\ m/s^2$$

4. A physics student lifts his 2.0 kg pet rock 2.8 m straight up. He then lets it drop to the ground. Use the law of conservation of energy to calculate how fast the rock will be moving (a) half way down and (b) just before it hits the ground.

a) 5.2 m/s

b) 7.4 m/s

$$V = \sqrt{2gh}$$
$$V = \sqrt{2 \times 9.81 \times 1.4}$$
$$= 5.2\ m/s$$
$$V = \sqrt{2 \times 9.81 \times 2.8}$$
$$= 7.4\ m/s$$

5. A 65 kg girl is running with a speed of 2.5 m/s.
   (a) How much kinetic energy does she have?

   (b) She grabs onto a rope that is hanging from the ceiling and swings from the end of the rope. How high off the ground will she swing?

$$203 = mgh$$
$$h = \frac{203}{mg} = \frac{203}{65 \times 9.81}$$
$$= .32\ m$$

6. A rubber ball falls from a height of 2.0 m, bounces off the floor and goes back up to a height of 1.6 m.
   (a) What percentage of its initial gravitational potential energy has been lost?

   (b) Where does this energy go? Does this contradict the law of conservation of energy? Why or why not?

7. How much work must be done to increase the speed of a 12 kg bicycle ridden by a 68 kg rider from 8.2 m/s to 12.7 m/s?

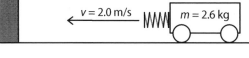

$$mass = 12 + 68$$
$$= 80 kg$$

$$V_i = 8.2 m/s$$
$$V_f = 12.7 m/s$$

$$W = \triangle KE$$

$$W = \triangle KE = \frac{1}{2} m v_f^2 - \frac{1}{2} m v_i^2$$
$$= \frac{1}{2} 80 (12.7)^2 - \frac{1}{2} 80 (8.2)^2$$
$$= \boxed{3.8 \times 10^3 J}$$

8. A 2.6 kg laboratory cart is given a push and moves with a speed of 2.0 m/s toward a solid barrier, where it is momentarily brought to rest by its spring bumper.

$v = 2.0$ m/s $m = 2.6$ kg

   (a) How much elastic potential energy will be stored in the spring at the moment when the spring is fully compressed?

   (b) What is the average force exerted by the spring if it is compressed 0.12 m? Why is it necessary to specify average force in this situation?

5.3 Temperature, Heat, and Thermal Energy

Warm Up

On a hot summer day, you may have noticed that if you walk on concrete with your bare feet, it will be hotter than the grass. If you go inside, a tile floor will feel cooler on your feet than the rest of the house. Why do you experience these differences if the temperature is not changing dramatically?

_____

_____

_____

Kinetic Molecular Theory

According to the **kinetic molecular theory**, all matter is made up of tiny particles that are constantly moving. The particles — molecules or atoms — attract each other to some extent. The particles can move in a number of ways (Figure 5.3.1):

- They can move in straight lines (translational motion between collisions).
- They can rotate.
- They can vibrate.

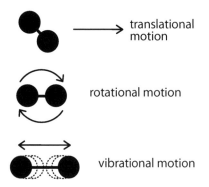

Figure 5.3.1 *Particles in matter can move in three different ways.*

Molecules may have **translational kinetic energy**, which is energy due to motion in straight lines, **rotational kinetic energy** and **vibrational kinetic energy**. They may also have **potential energy**, which arises from attractions between molecules or repulsions at very close range.

The **total energy** of all the molecules in an amount of material is called the **thermal energy** of the material. When thermal energy is transferred from one material to another material, the amount of energy transferred is called **heat**. For a transfer of energy to occur, there must be a difference in temperature between the body from which the thermal energy is being transferred and the body to which the thermal energy is being transferred. Heat is transferred from a hotter body to a cooler body.

The way we describe how hot or cold a body is to use a number we call the body's **temperature** on a standard temperature scale. The **Celsius** scale is named after Anders Celsius (1704–1744), a Swedish astronomer who first suggested its use. In the Celsius scale, 0°C is assigned to the temperature at which ice melts or water freezes, and 100°C is assigned to the temperature at which water boils at standard sea level air pressure. On a typical mercury or alcohol thermometer, the space between 0°C and 100°C is divided into 100 equal divisions called **degrees**.

What does temperature really measure? Temperature depends on the average translational kinetic energy of all the molecules in a material. Imagine a drop of boiling hot water spilled from a large bucket of boiling water. The bucket of boiling water has far more thermal energy in it, and its **total kinetic energy** is far greater than the total kinetic energy in the drop of boiling water. The molecules in the bucket of water and those in the drop of water, however, have the same **average translational kinetic energy**, so both have the same **temperature.**

Absolute Zero

What would happen if a substance were cooled so much that the average translational kinetic energy of its molecules was zero? The substance would have almost no energy to transfer to any other body. If its average translational kinetic energy were zero, its temperature would be the lowest it could possibly be. On the Celsius scale, this temperature would be about –273°C. This temperature is called **absolute zero**.

On another temperature scale called the **Kelvin** scale, after British physicist Lord Kelvin (1824–1907), absolute zero is assigned a value of 0 K. On this scale, the unit for temperature is not called a degree, but instead a kelvin (K). Therefore, 0 K = –273°C. A kelvin is the same size as a Celsius degree. This means that a temperature of 0°C would be equal to 273 K. Water boils at 100°C, or 373 K. To scientists, the Kelvin scale is useful because on this scale, the temperature of an "ideal" gas in kelvins is directly proportional to the average translational kinetic energy of the molecules in the gas. Helium is a gas that behaves like an ideal gas. It is monatomic, which means that its smallest particles consist of just one atom.

Quick Check

1. (a) Explain the difference between temperature, thermal energy, and heat.

thermal energy = total energy
temp = measure of thermal energy
heat = level of energy between 2 bodies

(b) Why is it incorrect to say that a body contains heat?

Because heat is a measure between two bodies, we can say it contains thermal energy.

2. A sample of helium gas has a temperature of 20°C.
   (a) What is its temperature in kelvins (K)?

   (b) In another helium sample, the atoms have twice the average translational kinetic energy. What is the temperature of this sample in
      (i) kelvins?

      (ii) °C?

3. A large pot of near-boiling water has a small, red-hot nail dropped into it.

   (a) Which has more thermal energy to begin with — the pot of water or the nail?

   (b) Which has the higher average kinetic energy to begin with?

   (c) Which will lose heat, and which will gain heat when the nail is dropped into the pot of boiling water?

   (d) After five minutes, which will have
      (i) more thermal energy?

      (ii) higher average kinetic energy?

Heat Transfer by Conduction

Imagine that you hold one end of a glass rod in your hand and heat the other end with the flame of a Bunsen burner (Figure 5.3.2). Molecules near the heated end have thermal energy transferred to them from the flame. These glass molecules gain kinetic energy, collide with their neighbours, and pass the increased kinetic energy on. Eventually, the whole rod will be warmed up and the end you are holding may in time become too hot to hold.

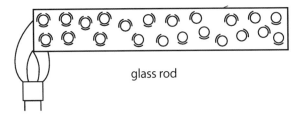

glass rod

Figure 5.3.2 *The heat from the Bunsen burner transfers through the kinetic energy of the glass molecules.*

Heat is transferred through the glass rod slowly by **conduction.** Conduction is the transfer of heat from molecule to molecule or atom to atoms through a material. Glass is not a particularly good conductor. The best **conductors** are metals. Metals conduct heat and electricity well, because atoms of metals have loosely attached electrons, called free electrons. These free electrons can move easily throughout the length of the metal. When these free electrons gain kinetic energy, they can transfer their energy easily to other electrons and atoms with which they collide.

Heat Transfer by Convection

Thermal energy is not easily transferred by conduction through gases and liquids. In conduction, the energy is transferred through collisions of atoms or molecules or electrons with neighbouring particles.

In fluids (gases or liquids), thermal energy can be transferred very efficiently by **convection.** In convection, the thermal energy "flows" with the molecules from one place to another. In convection, the substance being warmed moves, carrying the thermal energy with it. The movement of the substance is called a **convection current.** Investigation 5-3B demonstrates the nature of convection.

Convection in Everyday Life
Different parts of Earth's surface absorb the Sun's heat better than others, so the air near these parts of Earth will be warmed accordingly. Convection currents result from the uneven heating. Small-scale local winds and the larger continental wind patterns are convection currents resulting from uneven heating of air near Earth's surface.

Heat Transfer by Radiation

Our primary source of thermal energy is the Sun. Since the space between the Sun and our planet is for all practical purposes "empty," there is no way heat transfer by conduction or convection can occur. Heat transmission through a vacuum is possible, however, by the process of **radiation.** Any form of energy transmitted by radiation will be in the form of electromagnetic waves and will travel at the speed of light. The various forms of **radiant energy** that originate in the Sun include: radio waves, microwaves, infrared radiation (heat), visible light, ultraviolet light, X-radiation, and gamma radiation. You cannot see infrared radiation, of course, but you can often feel it on your skin. When you sit in front of a fireplace, the warming effect you sense is due to infrared radiation. Infrared radiation can also be detected by photography or by electronic means.

Radiation in Everyday Life
Radiant energy falling on materials may be absorbed or reflected. The absorbed radiation increases the average translational kinetic energy of the molecules in the object, and therefore its temperature. A perfectly black object would absorb all the radiant energy falling on its surface. Light-coloured objects reflect more radiant energy. On a hot, sunny summer day, a good choice of outer-wear would be white, since it will reflect much of the infrared and visible radiation falling on your clothes.

In some parts of the world, radiant energy from the Sun is reflected by well-placed mirrors to receivers in which water is heated and changed into steam. The steam is used to operate a turbine, which runs a generator to produce electricity.

Another way of collecting radiant energy from the Sun is to use a convex lens to focus the radiation to a small area. This type of lens, called a Fresnel lens, can be used to make a solar furnace. On a sunny day, one of these Fresnel lenses can produce a temperature of over 1000°C at its focus. You can find a small-scale example of a Fresnel lens in an overhead projector.

Quick Check

1. Water is a poor conductor, yet water is brought to a boil quickly in a pot or kettle. Explain.

2. The diagram below shows a seashore scene. Water temperature stays quite constant day and night, but the land warms up during the day, so it has a higher temperature than the sea. At night, the land cools rapidly and is cooler than the sea.

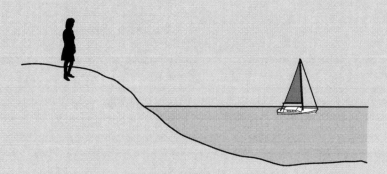

   (a) Sketch the direction of the convection current near the seashore in the daytime.
   (b) Using another colour or dotted arrows, sketch the direction of the convection current near the seashore at night.
   (c) When would you rather launch a sailboat to go out to sea — in the very early morning or in the evening? Why?

4. Carefully dismantle a thermos bottle and examine its construction. Assume it is filled with hot soup. How does the construction of the thermos bottle work to prevent heat loss by conduction, convection, and radiation?

5. Which will melt faster on a bright, sunny day — fresh snow or dirty snow? Why?

Investigation 5-3A Heat Transfer by Conduction

Purpose

To demonstrate conduction and conductors

Procedure

Your teacher may decide to do these activities as a demonstration.

Part 1

1. (a) Obtain a conduction apparatus like the one in Figure 5.3.3 and clamp it above an alcohol burner. Predict which of the metals will conduct heat fastest. Which will be the poorest conductor?

    (b) Test your prediction by heating the rods at the junction. Drops of candle wax have been used to attach small nails or paper clips to the ends of each of the metal rods. Record the order in which the rods drop their nails. Was your prediction correct?

Figure 5.3.3 *Conduction Part 1 — Step 1*

2. Touch the surface of your wooden workbench with the flat of your hand. Now touch the base of a metal ring stand or a sheet of aluminum foil. Which feels warmer to the touch? Is either surface at a different temperature than the other? Why does one surface feel cooler than the other?

Part 2

1. Place some crushed ice in a large test tube and use a few marbles to keep the ice at the bottom of the test tube. Add water to the level shown in Figure 5.3.4.

2. Use a Bunsen burner to carefully heat the test tube near the top. Can you make the water at the top of the test tube boil while the ice remains frozen at the bottom? Do your observations suggest that water is a good conductor or a poor conductor?

Figure 5.3.4 *Conduction Part 2*

Part 3

1. Set up the apparatus shown in Figure 5.3.5. Attach two rings to the same ring stand. Ring A is approximately 15 cm above the top of the Bunsen burner. Cover each ring with a sheet of copper gauze.

2. (a) Turn on the gas and use a match to light the gas at A. Observe what happens. Does the gas initially burn at B and/or C? Turn off the gas.

   (b) Turn on the gas, and light the gas at B. Observe what happens. Turn off the gas.

   (c) Turn on the gas, and light the gas at C. Observe what happens. Turn off the gas.

   (d) Turn on the gas, and light the gas at A and C. Observe, then turn off the gas.

Concluding Questions

1. Of the metals you tested for conductivity in Part 1, list the order in which they conduct heat, from best to worst.

2. List three metals that are used in cooking utensils because they conduct well.

3. Explain the results you observed in Part 3.

Challenge

1. Have a contest to see who can design a container that will keep an ice cube solid for the longest time.

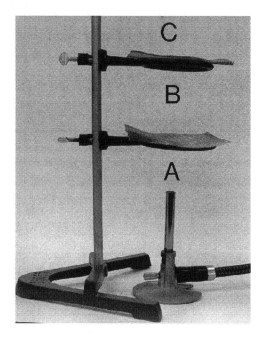

Figure 5.3.5 *Conduction Part 3*

Investigation 5-3B   Convection (Demonstrations)

Purpose
To observe convection currents in fluids

Procedure

Part 1: Convection in a Liquid (Water)
1. Your teacher has filled the ring-shaped glass tube shown in Figure 5.3.6 with water. An alcohol burner or candle is arranged so that its flame will warm a bottom corner of the tube.
2. Predict which way the water in the tube will circulate when the flame is lit and the water is warmed.
3. Your teacher will light the flame. After allowing the water to warm up slightly, your teacher will add one drop of food colouring to the opening at the top of the tube. Sketch the tube and show the direction in which the water flows. The flow you observe is a convection current.

Part 2: Convection in a Gas (Air)
1. Figure 5.3.7 shows a convection box, which has a sliding front window and two glass chimneys. Light the candle and close the front window. Allow the candle to burn for a minute, then light a piece of touch paper (or other source of smoke) and hold the smoking source above each of the two chimneys in turn. Observe the pattern of motion of the air, as shown by the visible smoke carried by the air.

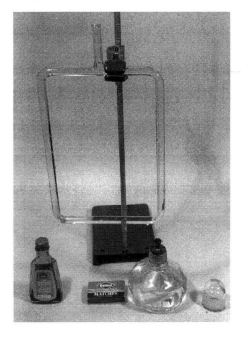

Figure 5.3.6 *Convection Part 1*

Concluding Questions
1. Explain, in terms of molecular motion and density (density = mass/volume), why a convection current in water or air moves in the direction that it does.
2. In Investigation 5-3A, you were able to boil water at the top of a test tube while ice at the bottom of the tube remained frozen. What would happen if you heated the bottom of a test tube that has ice at the top? How would the heat be transferred to the ice?

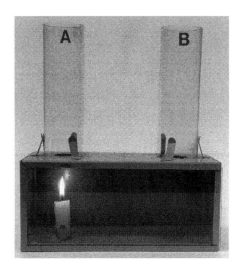

Figure 5.3.7 *Convection Part 2*

Investigation 5-3C   Absorbing Infrared Radiation

Purpose

To find out if a black surface or a shiny surface absorbs more infrared radiation in a given time

Procedure

1. Obtain two used, black plastic film containers. Leave one black, but cover the other container with aluminum foil, as shown in Figure 5.3.8.
2. Fill each container with water, and measure the temperature of the water in each one. Prepare a chart like Table 5.3.1. Enter the starting temperature in the column under 0 min.
3. Set the containers on insulating Styrofoam cups, the same distance (50 cm) from a source of infrared light, such as a 100-W lamp. After 1 min, measure the temperatures of the water in each container. Two students might read the temperatures simultaneously. Record these temperatures in your table.
4. Repeat the measurements after 2, 3, 4, and 5 min. If necessary, continue taking readings until a definite pattern is established.

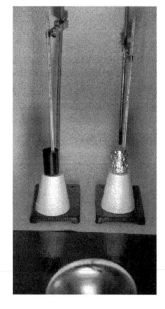

Figure 5.3.8 *Radiation*

Table 5.3.1 *Temperatures of Containers of Water Warmed by a Lamp*

Time (minutes)	0	1	2	3	4	5
Temperature (°C) BLACK						
Temperature (°C) SHINY						

Concluding Questions

1. Which container, if either, warmed up more?
2. Try to explain what you observed.

Challenge

1. A Crooke's radiometer, named after Sir William Crookes (1832–1919), is shown in Figure 5.3.9. Four vanes are connected to a pivot in a glass bulb, which is partially, but not completely, evacuated. There are some air molecules inside the container. One side of each vane is black. The other side may be white or silvered.

    Design an experiment using an infrared light source, a mirror, and a radiometer to test whether infrared radiation reflects from a shiny surface the way visible light does.

Figure 5.3.9 *Crooke's radiometer*

5.3 Review Questions

1. What are the three potential forms of kinetic energy that a molecule could have?

   - translational
   - rotational
   - vibrational

2. If the temperature of an object is 30°C, what is its temperature in kelvins?

   30°C → kelvin

   30°C + 273 = 303 K

3. By what method can heat be transferred without the presence of matter?

   radiation

4. What is the direction of airflow at night in the situation shown below, assuming there are no major weather disturbances?

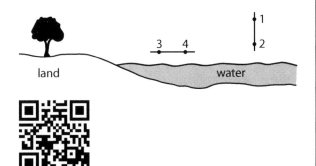

5. A cold weather emergency survival suit is made of a reflecting plastic material with a thin coating of regular plastic. Why is the shiny, reflecting plastic on the *inside* of the suit facing your body? Why is it *not* wise to place this suit on someone who is already suffering from hypothermia?

   To reflect heat back to body.

   Body is already too cold

6. If you are sitting in front of an open fireplace, what is the main method by which heat is transferred to you?

   - radiation

7. When a pot of soup heats up, what is the main method by which heat is transferred within the soup?

   Convection

8. In winter, why do the blades of your skates feel cooler to the touch than your boots do?

   Because metal is a conducter and the cold ice transfers energy to it.

5.4 Measuring Thermal Energy

Warm Up

In the fall when the temperature drops below 0°C many lakes will not freeze over, but smaller puddles will freeze. Why does this happen?

_____

_____

_____

Specific Heat Capacity

The amount of thermal energy in an object depends on several factors. First, it depends on the mass, m, of the object. Second, it depends on the temperature, T, of the object. Third, it depends on the nature of the material in the object. Different materials have different capacities for holding thermal energy. One material that has an exceptionally high capacity for holding thermal energy is water.

It can be shown that to raise the temperature of 1 kg of water by 1°C requires an input of 4200 J. For comparison, it only requires an input of 450 J to raise the temperature of 1 kg of iron by 1°C. The amount of heat required to raise the temperature of 1 kg of a substance by 1°C is called the **specific heat capacity** (c) of the substance. For example, the specific heat capacity of water is written as $c = 4200$ J/kg/°C. For iron, the specific heat capacity is $c = 450$ J/kg/°C.

The joule (J) is an appropriate unit for measuring heat, since the English scientist James Joule did the first experiments to compare the specific heat capacities of different materials. Table 5.4.1 lists some specific heat capacities.

Table 5.4.1 *Specific Heat Capacities*

Substance	J/kg/°C	Substance	J/kg/°C
water	4200	aluminum	920
methyl alcohol	2400	glass	840
ethylene glycol*	2200	iron	450
ice	2100	copper	430
kerosene	2100	lead	130
steam	2100		

*antifreeze

Since the specific heat capacity, c, is the amount of energy that must be transferred to raise the temperature of 1 kg of water by 1°C, then $c = \dfrac{\Delta E}{m\Delta T}$, where ΔE is the energy transferred, m is the mass of material, and ΔT is the change in temperature. This is commonly written as:

$$\Delta E = mc\Delta T$$

Sample Problem 5.4.1 — Working with Specific Heat Capacity

If 25 kJ of heat is transferred to 50.0 kg of water initially at 20.0°C, what will the final temperature of the water be?

What to Think About	How to Do It
1. Find the formula	$\Delta E = mc\Delta T$
2. Identify what you know.	$\Delta E = 25\ kJ$ $m = 50.0\ kg$ $c = 4.2 \times 10^3\ J/kg/°C$ $T_1 = 20.0°C$ $T_2 = ?$
3. To find the final temperature, determine how much the temperature will increase with 25 kJ of heat added.	$T_2 - 20.0°C = \dfrac{2.5 \times 10^4\ J}{(5.0 \times 10^1\ kg)(4.2 \times 10^3\ J/kg/°C)}$ $= 0.12°C$
4. Solve for T_2.	$T_2 = 20.0°C + 0.12°C$ $= 20.1°C$ The final temperature will be 20.1°C.

Practice Problems 5.4.1 — Working with Specific Heat Capacity

1. How much heat is needed to raise the temperature of 90.0 kg of water from 18°C to 80°C?

$M = 90.0 kg$
$T_i = 18°C$
$T_f = 80°C$
$C = 4184 J/kg°C$

$\Delta E = mc\Delta t$
$= 90.0 \times 4184 \times (80-18)$
$\Delta E = 2.3 \times 10^7 J/kg°C = \boxed{2.3 \times 10^4 kJ}$

2. If 1.0 MJ (megajoule) of heat is transferred to 10.0 kg of water initially at 15°C, what will the water's final temperature be?

$m = 10.0 kg$
$T_i = 15.0°C$
$T_f = ?$
$E = 1.0 MJ = 1.0 \times 10^6 J$

$\Delta t = \dfrac{1.0 \times 10^6}{10.0 \times 4184}$
$\boxed{\Delta t = 24}$

$\Delta t = t_f - t_i$
$24 = T_f - 15$
$T_f = 24 + 15$
$= \boxed{39°C}$ T_f

3. If 12 kg of water cools from 100°C down to room temperature (20°C), how much heat will it release to the environment?

$m = 12.0 kg$
$T_i = 100°C$
$T_f = 20°C$
$\Delta E = ?$

$\Delta E = mc\Delta t$
$\Delta E = 12.0 \times 4184 \times (20-100)$
$= -4.0 \times 10^6$

4. Why is water such a desirable material to use as a coolant in a car engine?

Because it keeps the temp from fluxuating (high specific heat) (doesn't catch fire) a lot; it holds heat well.

5. If it takes 1200 J to raise the temperature of 0.500 kg of brass from 20.0°C to 26.2°C, what is the specific heat capacity of brass?

$E = 1200 J$
$M = 0.500 kg$
$T_i = 20.0°C$
$T_f = 26.2°C$
$C = ?$

$\Delta E = mc\Delta t$
$1200 = 0.500 \times C (26.2 - 20.0)$
$1200 = 0.500 \times C (6.2)$
$\dfrac{1200}{3.1} = \dfrac{3.1 C}{3.1}$

$\boxed{C = 387 J/kg°C}$
or
$3.9 \times 10^2 J/kg°C$

Power of a Heat Source

Power is the rate at which energy is produced or consumed (or the rate at which work is done). For our present needs, power is the rate at which heat is transferred.

$$P = \frac{\Delta E}{\Delta t}$$

where P is power, ΔE is the energy transferred, and Δt is the time interval during which the energy is transferred.

Efficiency

For any energy-converting device, a convenient ratio to know is the ratio of the useful energy output of the device to the energy put into the device. This ratio is the **efficiency** of the device.

$$\text{efficiency} = \frac{\text{useful energy out of device}}{\text{energy put into device}}$$

$$\textit{efficiency} = \frac{W_{out}}{W_{in}} = \frac{P_{out}}{P_{in}}$$

The efficiency rating gives us an idea of how much energy a device wastes as heat. One of the least efficient devices is an ordinary incandescent light bulb. Since it converts only 5% of its electrical energy into light and 95% into heat, a light bulb is only 5% efficient. An automobile might be only 10% efficient. Where does all its wasted energy go?

Electric motors may have efficiencies in the range between 60% and 90%, while transformers and generators may be 99% efficient.

Sample Problem 5.4.2 — Calculating Efficiency

To lift a 1200 N motorcycle a vertical height of 1.3 m onto a pickup truck, a motocross rider pushes the bike up a ramp 2.4 m, requiring an effort force up the ramp of 820 N. What is the efficiency of the ramp?

What to Think About	How to Do It
1. Find the useful work done by the ramp.	$W_{out} = (1200 \text{ N})(1.3 \text{ m}) = 1560 \text{ J}$
2. Find the work put into using the ramp.	$W_{in} = (820 \text{ N})(2.4 \text{ m}) = 1968 \text{ J}$
3. Find the efficiency of the ramp.	$efficiency = \frac{1560 \text{ J}}{1968 \text{ J}} \times 100\% = 79\%$ The ramp is 79% efficient.

Practice Problems 5.4.2 — Calculating Efficiency

1. You must do 500 J of work to operate a pulley system that lifts a 150 N load to a height of 3.0 m. How efficient is the pulley system?

$$\frac{W_{out}}{W_{in}} = \frac{P_{out}}{P_{in}} = 150\,N \times 3.0\,m = 450\,J$$

$$= \frac{450}{500} \times 100 = \underline{90\% \text{ efficient}}$$

(450 labeled W_{out}, 500 labeled W_{in})

2. A kettle that is 80% efficient is rated 1200 W. At what rate does the water in the kettle absorb energy (in watts)?

$$80\% = \frac{80}{100} = \frac{W_{out}}{1200\,W} = \boxed{960\,W}$$

3. If a light bulb has an efficiency of 5.0%, at what rate does a 60 W bulb produce light energy?

$$5.0\% = \frac{5}{100} = \frac{60\,W}{W_{in}} = \boxed{3\,W}$$

4. For every megajoule of chemical potential energy in the fuel used to run a certain truck, only 120 kJ of useful work is done by the truck in making itself move. How efficient is the truck? Where are some of the places that the energy from the fuel is wasted?

$$\frac{1\,mJ = 1.0\times10^7\,J = W_i}{120\,kJ = 1.2\times10^5\,J = W_o}$$

$$efficiency = \frac{1.2\times10^5}{1.0\times10^7} \times 100 = \boxed{12\%}$$

Investigation 5-4   Measuring the Power of a Hot Plate

Purpose

To measure the power of a hot plate indirectly, by measuring the heat transferred to a known mass of water in a given time

Procedure

1. Measure out 300 mL of water into a 400 mL beaker using a graduated cylinder. Since water has a density of 1 g/mL, this will give you 300 g or 0.300 kg of water.
2. Arrange the thermometer as in Figure 5.4.1, so that it is not touching the bottom of the beaker.
3. Let the hot plate warm up for a minute or two, and then start your stopwatch and record the temperature of the water as precisely as you can. Record the temperature of the water every half-minute for 10 min. Stop the experiment if the water comes to a boil and use only your data for temperatures less than boiling temperature. Record your data in a table like Table 5.4.2.
4. Plot a graph with temperature on the y-axis and time on the x-axis.
5. Find the slope of your graph, which is $\Delta T/\Delta t$. Units will be °C/s.

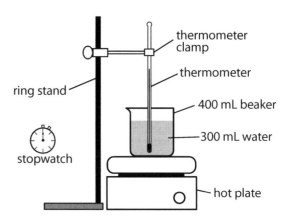

Figure 5.4.1 *Step 2*

Table 5.4.2 *Data for Investigation 5-4*

Time (s)	0	30	60	90	120	150	180	210	240	→
Temperature (°C)										

6. Since the energy transferred to the water from the hot plate is $E = mc\Delta T$, then the power of the hot plate would be:

$$P = \frac{\Delta E}{\Delta t} = \frac{mc\Delta T}{\Delta t} = mc \times (\text{slope})$$

   Calculate the power of your hot plate using $m = 0.300$ kg, $c = 4200$ J/kg/°C, and the slope of your graph.
7. Find a cooled hot plate and read the label on it to see what the manufacturer's power rating is for it.

Concluding Questions

1. What was your calculated power for the hot plate?
2. Calculate the percent difference between your calculated power and the manufacturer's rating, as follows:

$$\% \text{ difference} = \frac{\text{manufacturer's rating} - \text{calculated power rating}}{\text{manufacturer's power rating}} \times 100\%$$

3. Assuming your calculations were correct, and the manufacturer's rating was also correct, what is the ratio of the power you calculated (heat absorbed by the water per second) to the hot plate's rated power (heat given off by the hot plate per second). This ratio is the efficiency of the hot plate. You can convert your decimal fraction to a percent by multiplying by 100.

$$\text{efficiency} = \frac{\text{calculated power rating}}{\text{manufacturer's power rating}} \times 100\%$$

4. Why is the efficiency less than 100%?

5.4 Review Questions

1. How much heat would be needed to warm 1.6 kg of ice from −15°C up to its melting point of 0°C?

$m = 1.6 kg$
$t_i = -15°C$
$v_f = 0°C$
$C = 2100 J/kg°C$

$\Delta E = 1.6 \times 2100 (0 - (-15))$
$= \boxed{5.0 \times 10^4 J}$

2. A 5.0 kg block of lead at 250°C cools down to 20°C. How much heat does it give off in doing so?

$m = 5.0 kg$
$t_i = 250°C$
$t_f = 20°C$
$C = 130 J/kg°C$

$\Delta E = 5.0 \times (130) \times (20 - 250)$
$= \boxed{-1.5 \times 10^5 J}$

3. How much heat must be transferred into 5.0 kg of water to raise its temperature from 20°C up to 97°C?

$M = 5.0 kg$
$V_i = 20°C$
$V_f = 97°C$
$C = 4200$
$\Delta E = 5.0 \times 4200 \times (97 - 20)$
$= \boxed{1.6 \times 10^6 J}$

4. If water has a specific heat capacity of 4200 J/kg/°C, how much heat is needed to warm 50.0 kg of water from 15°C up to 85°C?

$50.0 kg$
$V_i = 15°C$
$V_f = 85°C$
$C = 4200 J/kg°C$

$\Delta E = 50.0 \times 4200 \times (85 - 15)$
$= \boxed{1.5 \times 10^7 J}$

5. If 24.0 kJ of energy will warm 0.600 kg of a metal from 20.0°C up to 220°C, what is the specific heat capacity of the metal?

$E = 24.0 kJ$
$\downarrow$
$2.4 \times 10^4 J$
$m = 0.600 kg$
$V_i = 20.0°C$
$V_f = 220°C$

$2.4 \times 10^4 = 0.600 \times (c) \times (220 - 20)$
$\dfrac{2.4 \times 10^4}{120} = \dfrac{120 (c)}{120}$
$\boxed{C = 200 J/kg°C}$

6. A light bulb is immersed in 0.500 kg of water, which has a specific heat capacity of 4200 J/kg/°C. The apparatus is well insulated, so that essentially all of the radiated heat is used to warm the water. Every 100 s, the temperature of the water is recorded. The graph below summarizes the data.

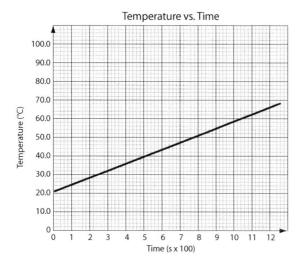

Temperature vs. Time

Temperature (°C)

Time (s x 100)

(a) What is the slope of the above graph, expressed in proper units and in correct significant figures?

(b) Use the slope to calculate the useful heating power of the light bulb.

(c) What is the approximate power rating of the bulb used in this experiment?

7. Why are coastal climates more moderate than inland climates?

8. A 60 W incandescent light bulb is 5% efficient. A 60 W fluorescent bulb is 15% efficient. How much more light will the fluorescent light bulb give off than the incandescent bulb, in the same period of time?

9. A 1500 W kettle warms 1.00 kg of water from 18°C to 88°C in a time of 3.6 min. How efficient is the kettle?

Chapter 5   Review Questions

1. (a) How much work will you do if you lift a 0.67 kg book from a table top up a distance of 1.5 m to a shelf?

   (b) How much work will be done on the book if you lift it and move it 1.5 m sideways to a spot on the same shelf?

2. If you push a 75 N block along a floor a distance of 4.2 m at a steady speed, and the coefficient of kinetic friction is 0.40, how much work will you do on the block?

3. Discuss the scientific accuracy of this statement:
   I used a ramp to get my motorbike up on my truck, and the ramp saved me a lot of work!

4. (a) What is the ideal mechanical advantage of the pulley system shown below??

   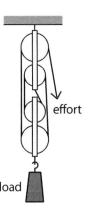

   (b) If the load is 240 N, what will the effort force be, ignoring friction?

   (c) If the load is lifted 2.8 m, how far will you have to pull down on the rope?

   (d) If the load is lifted 2.8 m in 1.6 s, what is the power rating of the pulley system?

5. With a pulley system, a mechanic can lift an 840 N engine using an effort force of only 70.0 N.
   (a) What is the mechanical advantage of the pulley system?

   (b) To lift the engine up 20.0 cm, how far down on the rope will the mechanic pull?

   (c) How much work is done on the 840 N engine when it is lifted a height of 20.0 cm?

   (d) What is the minimum amount of work the mechanic will have to do to lift the engine 20.0 cm?

6. One watt is equivalent to 1 J/s, so a joule is the same as a watt·second. How many joules are there in 1 kW·h?

7. A skier has 60 kJ of gravitational potential energy when at the top of the hill. Assuming no friction, how much kinetic energy does she have when she is one-third of the way down the hill?

8. The head of a golf club transfers a certain amount of kinetic energy to the ball upon impact. Let this be E_k. If the golfer lightens the mass of the club head by 1/3, and increases the club head speed so that it is 3 times it previous speed, how much kinetic energy will be transferred to the ball now?

9. A pendulum bob is moving 1.8 m/s at the bottom of its swing. To what height above the bottom of the swing will the bob travel?

10. The pendulum bob shown here must circle the rod, and the string must remain taut at the top of the swing. How far up must the bob be raised before releasing it to accomplish these goals?

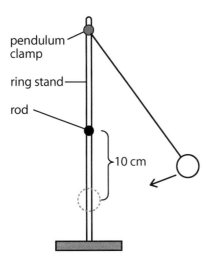

pendulum clamp

ring stand

rod

10 cm

11. Tarzan grabs a vine 12 m long and swings on the end of it, like a pendulum. His starting point is 5.0 m above the lowest point in his swing. How fast is Tarzan moving as he passes through the bottom of the swing?

12. Change 250°C to kelvins.

13. A steel rod is at a temperature of 25°C. To what Celsius temperature must you raise it, in order to double its Kelvin temperature?

14. Why are metals such good conductors?

Because their valence electrons are held loosely and easily transferrable.

15. In your home, what method(s) of heat transfer are involved in the following situations?
(a) Heat is distributed to your rooms from your furnace.

Convection
(radiation)

(b) Heat escapes through the walls of your house.

Conduction

(c) Heat escapes from your roof to the atmosphere.

radiation

16. Why is the water at the top of a hot water tank warmer than the water at the bottom of the tank?

warmer molecules are less dense.

17. A certain metal has a specific heat capacity of 420 J/kg/°C, while water has a specific heat capacity of 4200 J/kg/°C. A kilogram of the metal and a kilogram of water are both at a temperature of 98°C. If both are allowed to cool to 18°C, which will give off more heat to the atmosphere, and how much more will it release?

The water

$metal = \Delta E = m \times C \times \Delta t$
$\Delta E = 420 \times (18 - 98)$
$= -33,600$

$water = 4200 \times (-80)$
$= -336,000$

18. If 10.0 kg of water at 25°C is heated by a 100% efficient 1500 W heater for 5.00 min, what will its final temperature be?

19. How much heat is supplied by a 100% efficient 1200 W kettle in 10.0 min?

20. What is the efficiency of a 1500 W kettle if it supplies heat at the rate of 1400 W to the water in it?

Chapter 5 Extra Practice

1. How much gravitational energy is gained by a 45 kg girl if she climbs 6.0 m up a flight of stairs?

2. (a) A spring in a toy that launches plastic balls requires an average force of 1.2 N to compress it a distance of 3.0 cm. How much elastic potential energy is stored in the spring when it is fully compressed?

   (b) If all the elastic potential energy is transferred to a 10.0 g ball, how fast will the ball move as it leaves the spring?

3. How much kinetic energy does a 1.0×10^3 kg car travelling 90 km/h have?

4. How much gravitational potential energy does a 75 kg skier have when at the top of a hill 2.0×10^3 m high?

5. Predict which of the two students below will move when the rope is pulled. Give a reason for your prediction. Be sure to test your prediction!

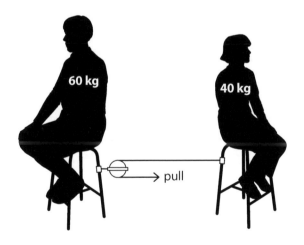

6. The pulley systems shown below may be considered frictionless.

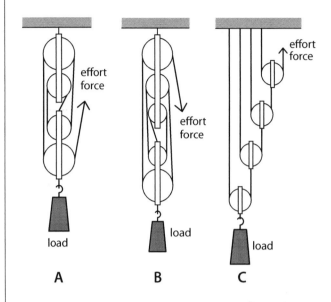

A   **B**   **C**

(a) What is the mechanical advantage of pulley system A?
(b) If the load is 600.0 N, what effort force is needed?
(c) If the load is lifted up a distance of 1.2 m, how much work will be done on the load by the pulley system?
(d) If the load is lifted up 1.2 m, how much rope must you pull? (What is the effort distance?)
(e) How much work will *you* do?

7. (a) What is the mechanical advantage of the pulley system B in question 6? (Assume no friction.)
   (b) If someone pulls on the rope for a distance of 3.5 m, to what height will the load be lifted?

8. (a) What is the ideal mechanical advantage of pulley system C in question 6?
   (b) How heavy a load could you lift with pulley system C in question 6, if your effort force is 300 N?

9. A 75 kg girl runs up a 3.0 m flight of stairs in 2.5 s. What is her "horsepower" in this situation?

10. How much work will a 4.0 HP (3 kW) motor do in half an hour?

11. How much heat does a 1500 W heater give off in one minute?

12. A pendulum is started swinging from a height of 0.3000 m above its rest position, and allowed to swing freely back and forth. If 1.00% of the bob's energy is lost due to friction with each swing, to what maximum height will the bob swing at the end of its fourth swing?

13. The initial speed of a golf ball struck with a driver by professional golfer has been measured to be 285 km/h. From what vertical height would you have to drop a golf ball so that it reaches this same speed as it hits the ground? Assume that air friction can be ignored.

14. Discuss the main forms of heat transfer involved in each of these situations:
    (a) A fireplace warms you as you sit in front of it.
    (b) Heat from the fireplace goes up the chimney.
    (c) Heat is transferred from an electric stove element into a frying pan.
    (d) Soup is heated to near boiling even though it does not conduct well.
    (e) Your house is warmed using a natural gas furnace system.

15. Describe in what direction the vanes of a Crooke's radiometer turn when infrared light falls on them. Suggest a possible reason why they turn in that direction.

16. Why is an igloo warm?

17. Define specific heat capacity.

18. Change 373 kelvins to °C.

19. Why might a metal doorknob feel cold to the touch while the wooden door feels relatively warm, when they are actually both at the same temperature?

20. If 5.00 kg of water at 10°C is heated for 2.00 min by a heater that supplies 1500 W to the water, what will the final temperature of the water be? (c = 4200 J/kg/°C)

21. A 1500 W kettle warms 1.30 kg of water from 25.0°C to 99.0°C in 5.00 min. How efficient is the kettle? (c = 4200 J/kg/°C)

22. A fluorescent lamp is about 15% efficient as a source of light. How much heat does a 40 W fluorescent lamp give off in 1 s?

23. A 1200 W kettle warms 800.0 g of water from 20°C to 99°C in 4.0 min. How efficient is the kettle?

24. A coffee percolator rated at 600 W supplies 500 W to the water in it. What is the efficiency of the kettle?

25. An appliance that consumes electrical energy at the rate of 1500 J/s, accomplishes 1200 J/s of useful work. How efficient is the appliance?

26. How much work is needed to slow down a 1200 kg vehicle from 80 km/h to 50 km/h? What does this work?

6 Wave Motion

By the end of this chapter, you should be able to do the following:

➤ Analyse the behaviour of light and other waves under various conditions, with reference to the properties of waves and using the universal wave equation
- Describe the properties associated with waves, including amplitude, frequency, period, wavelength, phase, speed, and types of waves
- Use the universal wave equation to solve problems involving speed, frequency (period), and wavelength
- Describe and give examples of the following wave phenomena and the conditions that produce them:
    - reflection
    - refraction
    - diffraction
    - interference (superposition principle)
    - Doppler shift

By the end of this chapter, you should know the meaning of these **key terms**:

- amplitude
- constructive interference
- crests
- destructive interference
- diffraction
- Doppler effect
- frequency
- hertz
- longitudinal wave
- nodal lines
- period
- periodic wave
- pulse
- reflection
- refraction
- sonic boom
- sound barrier
- transverse wave
- troughs
- wavelength

By the end of this chapter, you should be able to use and know when to use the following formulae:

$$T = \frac{1}{f} \qquad v = f$$

A tiny drop creates a pattern of circular waves.

6.1 Wave Properties

Good Vibrations

There are many kinds of waves in nature. You have heard of light waves, sound waves, radio waves, earthquake waves, water waves, shock waves, brain waves and the familiar wave created by a cheering crowd at a sports event. Wave motion is an important phenomenon because it is so common and it is one of the major ways in which energy can be transmitted from one place to another.

There are two basic kinds of waves. First, there is the **pulse,** which is a non-repeating wave. A single disturbance sends a pulse from the source outward, but there is no repetition of the event. For example, you may give a garden hose a quick "yank" to one side, causing a pulse to travel the length of the hose.

Second, there is the **periodic wave.** Periodic waves are probably more familiar to you. You have watched water waves moving across a pond. The waves arrive at the shore of the pond at regularly repeated time intervals. Periodic means recurring at regular intervals. Water waves are caused by a disturbance of the water somewhere in the pond.

Whether the wave is a pulse or a periodic wave, a disturbance is spread by the wave, usually through a material substance. An exception is the medium for electromagnetic radiation (light, radio, X-rays, ultraviolet, infrared, gamma radiation, etc.). The medium for electromagnetic radiation is electric and magnetic fields created by charged particles.

To have a regularly repeating wave, there must be regularly repeating vibrations. For example, the regularly repeating sound waves from a tuning fork are caused by the vibrations of the two tines of the fork disturbing the air. Vibrating electrons disturb the electric field around them to create the microwaves that cook your supper or measure the speed of your car in a radar trap.

Describing Waves

Wavelength (λ)

Figure 6.1.1 depicts waves emanating from a vibrating source. They could be water waves. The highest points on the waves are called **crests** and the lowest points are called **troughs**. The distance between successive crests or between successive troughs is called the **wavelength** (λ) of the wave. The symbol λ is the Greek letter lambda. The **amplitude** or height of the wave is measured from its displacement from the horizontal line in the diagram to the crest or trough. The amplitude is shown on the diagram.

Wavelengths may be measured in metres, in the case of water waves, or in nanometres (1 nm = 10^{-9}), in the case of visible light. Microwaves may be measured in centimetres, while the waves produced by AC power lines may be kilometres long. Wavelengths of audible sounds range from millimetres up to metres.

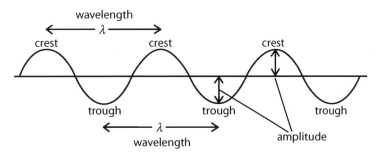

Figure 6.1.1 *Terms used for describing waves*

Frequency (*f*)

Another important aspect of waves is their **frequency**. The frequency of the waves tells you how often or frequently they and their source vibrate. If you are listening to a tuning fork, sound waves reach your ear with the same frequency as the vibrating fork. For example, the fork's tines vibrate back and forth 256 times in 1 s if the frequency of the fork is 256 vibrations per second. Frequency is measured in a unit called the **hertz (Hz)**. The unit is named after Heinrich Hertz (1857–1894), who was the first scientist to detect radio waves. One hertz is one vibration per second: 1 Hz = 1 s^{-1}.

A pendulum 24.8 cm long has a frequency of 1 Hz. Electrons vibrating to and fro in an alternating current circuit have a frequency of 60 Hz. Radio waves may be several kilohertz (kHz), where 1 kHz = 1 000 Hz, or they may be in the megahertz (MHz) range, where 1 MHz is equal to 1 000 000 Hz.

Period (*T*)

Related to the frequency of a vibration is the **period** of the vibration. The period is the time interval between vibrations. For example, if the period of a vibration is 1/2 s, then the frequency must be 2 s^{-1} or 2 Hz. Consider a pendulum with a length of 24.8 cm. It will have a frequency of 1 Hz and a period of 1 s. A pendulum 99.2 cm long will have a frequency of 1/2 Hz and a period of 2 s. A pendulum 223 cm long will have a frequency of 1/3 Hz and a period of 3 s. As you can see, frequency and period are reciprocals of each other.

$$\text{frequency} = \frac{1}{\text{period}}$$

$$f = \frac{1}{T} \text{ or } T = \frac{1}{f}$$

Quick Check

1. A dog's tail wags 50.0 times in 40.0 s.
   (a) What is the frequency of the tail?

   (b) What is the period of vibration of the tail?

2. A certain tuning fork makes 7680 vibrations in 30 s.
   (a) What is the frequency of the tuning fork?

   (b) What is the period of vibration of the tuning fork?

3. Tarzan is swinging back and forth on a vine. If each complete swing takes 4.0 s, what is the frequency of the swings?

Transverse and Longitudinal Waves

Figure 6.1.2 illustrates two ways to send a pulse through a long length of spring or a long Slinky. In method (a), the spring is pulled sideways, so that the disturbance is at right angles to the direction that the pulse will travel. This produces a **transverse wave.** In method (b), several turns of the spring are compressed and let go. The disturbance is in the same direction as the direction the pulse will travel. This produces a **longitudinal wave.** Transverse means *across* and longitudinal means *lengthwise*.

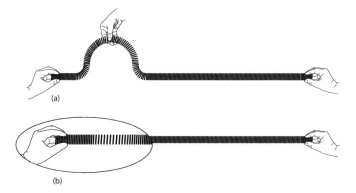

(a)

(b)

Figure 6.1.2 (**a**) A transverse wave; (**b**) A longitudinal wave

---

Wave Reflection and Refraction

When a wave encounters a boundary like a shoreline, wall or another medium, several things can happen. The two most common things are the wave will reflect or refract. **Reflection** occurs when a wave hits an object or another boundary and the wave is reflected back. If you attach or hold one end of a spring and send a wave down the spring, you will see it reflect off the end. Usually not all the wave is reflected back as some can be absorbed or refracted. **Refraction** is a bending of the wave and occurs when the wave hits an object at an angle or the wave enters a new medium. Refraction results from the change in the waves speed. The changing speed causes the wave to bend.

The Wave Equation

The wave shown in Figure 6.1.3 is moving through water in a wave tank. The waves in the wave tank are produced by a wave generator, which vibrates up and down with a frequency f and a period T where $T = 1/f$.

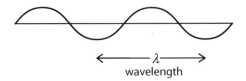

wavelength

Figure 6.1.3 *A wave in a wave tank*

What is the speed of the wave? If you could see the wave tank, you could watch a wave travel its own length, or wavelength λ, and time exactly how long the wave takes to travel its own length. Since the waves are generated once every T seconds by the generator, then this T should be the period of the waves. To calculate the speed v of the waves, all you have to do is divide the wavelength by the period of the wave.

$$v = \lambda / T$$

Since
$$T = 1/f \text{ or } f = 1/T$$

$$\mathbf{v = f\lambda}$$

This relationship is a very important one, because it is true for any kind of wave. This includes sound waves, earthquake waves, waves in the strings of musical instruments or any kind of electromagnetic wave (light, infrared, radio, X-radiation, ultraviolet, gamma radiation, etc.)! In words, the wave equation says

wave speed = wavelength × frequency

Sample Problem 6.1.1 — Calculating Wave Speed

What is the speed of a sound wave if its frequency is 256 Hz and its wavelength is 1.29 m?

What to Think About	How to Do It
1. Determine what you need to find.	speed of sound
2. Select appropriate formula.	$v = \lambda f$
3. Find the speed of sound	$v = (1.29 \text{ m})(256 \text{ s}^{-1}) = 330 \text{ m/s}$

Practice Problems 6.1.1 — Calculating Wave Speed

1. If waves maintain a constant speed, what will happen to their wavelength if the frequency of the waves is
   (a) doubled?

   (b) halved?

2. What is the frequency of a sound wave if its speed is 340 m/s and its wavelength is 1.70 m?

3. Waves of frequency 2.0 Hz are generated at the end of a long steel spring. What is their wavelength if the waves travel along the spring with a speed of 3.0 m/s?

The Wave Tank as a Wave Model

The wave tank is an ingenious device that permits us to study the behaviour of waves using a water wave model. If a series of waves is generated by moving a piece of wood dowelling back and forth in a regularly repeating motion, the waves will look like the ones in Figure 6.1.4 if seen from the side. The actual water waves are transverse in nature.

If light from a point source is allowed to pass through the waves and fall on a large sheet of white paper, the light passing through the waves will form bright lines on the paper underneath the crests of the waves. In Figure 6.1.4, the point source of light is the end of the filament of a straight-filament, clear light bulb. The crests act as convex lenses and make the light from the source converge or come together. The troughs, on the other hand, act as concave lenses and make the light from the source diverge or spread out. The image you see on the white screen consists of a series of bright lines with dark spaces between successive bright lines. The bright lines represent crests and the dark areas represent troughs. The waves you see on the screen are longitudinal waves, whereas the actual water waves were transverse.

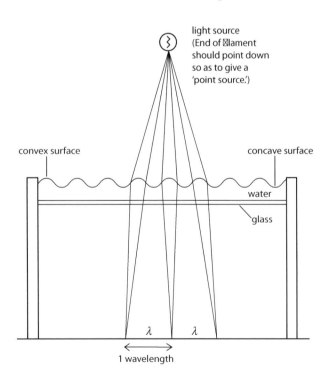

light source
(End of filament should point down so as to give a 'point source.')

convex surface

concave surface

water

glass

λ λ

1 wavelength

Figure 6.1.4 *Using a light source to observe water waves in a wave tank*

Investigation 6-1A Observing Transverse and Longitudinal Waves

Purpose
To observe pulses travelling in springs of different diameters

Procedure
1. With your partner's help, stretch a long spring about 2.5 cm in diameter to a length of 9 or 10 m. Hold on firmly as both you and the spring can be damaged if it is let go carelessly.

2. Create a transverse pulse by pulling a section of the spring to one side and letting it go suddenly. Observe the motion of the pulse and its reflection from your partner's hand.

3. Try increasing the amplitude of the pulse. Does this affect the speed of the wave through the spring?

4. Try tightening the spring. How does increasing the tension affect the speed of the pulse?

5. Observe the pulse as it reflects. Does a crest reflect as a crest or as a trough?

6. Have your partner create a pulse simultaneously with yours. Do the two pulses affect each other as they pass through each other?

7. Repeat Procedure steps 1 to 6 using a long Slinky, which is a spring with a much larger diameter.

8. Try sending a longitudinal pulse through each spring. To do this, bunch up a dozen or so turns of the spring, then let the compressed section go. Do longitudinal waves reflect at your partner's hand?

Concluding Questions
1. In which spring did the transverse waves travel faster — the small diameter spring or the Slinky?

2. In which spring did the longitudinal waves travel faster?

3. Does the amplitude of the waves affect their speed through the spring?

4. Does spring tension affect wave speed? Explain.

5. When a wave travels through the medium, like the spring, does the medium travel or just the disturbance in the medium?

6. When a wave reflects from a fixed end of the medium, does a crest reflect as a crest or is it reflected as a trough? In other words, is the wave inverted?

Investigation 6-1B Wavelength, Frequency, and Speed of Water Waves

Purpose

To investigate the relationship among wavelength, frequency and wave speed

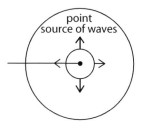
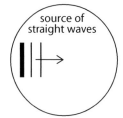

Figure 6.1.5 *Using different types of sources to observe water waves in a wave tank*

Procedure

1. Fill your wave tank with water to a depth of approximately 2 cm. If your tank requires them, make sure the screen dampers are in place.

2. To generate a circular wave, touch the surface of the water at the centre of the tank with the tip of your finger. Is there any evidence that the wave speeds up or slows down as it travels from the centre of the tank to its perimeter?

3. Imagine a single point on one of the crests that you see moving out from the centre of the tank. What path would this point on the crest take?

4. Set up your wave generator so that it generates circular waves at regular intervals. Start with a low frequency. Note the wavelength of the circular waves. This is the distance between successive crests. Increase the frequency of the wave generator and observe how the wavelength changes.

5. Set up your wave generator so that it produces straight waves instead of circular waves. Try different frequencies to see the effect of frequency on wavelength.

Concluding Questions

1. Does a circular wave travel out at the same speed in all directions? How do you know this?

2. Describe what happens to the wavelength of a water wave when the frequency of the wave increases.

6.1 Review Questions

1. What is the source of all wave motion?

2. What kind of wave has no amplitude and no frequency?

3. How many vibrations per second are there from a radio signal from 107.3 MHz?

4. What is the period of a wave that has a frequency of 25 Hz?

5. What is the frequency of a wave that has the period of 2.0 s?

6. When a salmon fishing boat captain describes waves as being 8 m high, what is the approximate amplitude of these waves? Explain your answer.

7. What is the frequency of the second hand on a clock?

8. What is the frequency of the hour hand on a clock?

9. If the frequency of a sound is tripled, what will happen to the period of the sound waves?

11. Some microwaves have a frequency of 3.0×10^{10} Hz. How long is a microwave of this frequency? (Microwave radiation travels at the speed of light.)

10. A student measures the speed of water waves in her tank to be 25 cm/s. If the wavelength is 2.5 cm, what is the frequency of the waves?

12. While fishing, a girl notices the wave crests passing her bob once every 6 s. She thinks the distance between crests is about 12 m. What is the speed of the water waves?

6.2 Wave Phenomena

Warm Up

You and a friend both throw rocks into a lake. The rocks enter the water 1.0 m apart. If you were looking down from above, draw what you think the wave pattern for each of the rocks will look like. Place the letter X at the point or points where the waves would be the highest.

Properties of Waves

You already know several properties of waves. Waves can be reflected and refracted. All waves conform to the wave equation. There are other important properties of waves, such as constructive and destructive interference, that lead to interesting natural phenomena.

Constructive and Destructive Interference

Figure 6.2.1 shows waves coming from two different sources — A and B. What happens if the two sets of waves arrive simultaneously at the same place? The result is shown in the third diagram. The amplitudes of the two sets of waves are additive. Since the waves from source A are in phase with the waves from source B, the resultant waves have twice the amplitude of the individual waves from A or B. This is an example of what is called **constructive interference.** Notice that crests are twice as high and troughs are twice as deep in the combined waves.

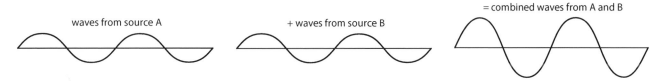

Figure 6.2.1 *Constructive interference*

In Figure 6.2.2, the waves from source A are exactly out of phase with the waves from source B. A crest from source A arrives simultaneously with a trough from source B. The two sets of waves exactly cancel each other. This is an example of **destructive interference.**

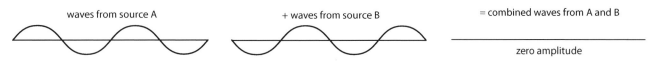

Figure 6.2.2 *Destructive interference*

Interference of waves occurs with all sorts of waves. You may have seen interference of water waves in the wave tank. You can hear interference of sound waves if you simply listen to a tuning fork as you rotate it slowly near your ear. Each tine of the fork produces a set of sound waves. Listen for constructive interference. It's the extra loud sound. Destructive interference is the minimum sound you hear as you slowly rotate the tuning fork.

The interference property of waves was first used to measure the wavelength of light by the English scientist Thomas Young (1773–1829). Young's interference experiment, done in 1801, has great historical importance because it seemed to suggest very strongly that light is a wave phenomenon.

Figure 6.2.3 illustrates how Young's experiment was done. A single slit was illuminated by a source of light of one colour (wavelength). Circular waves spread out from the single slit. When the wave front hit the double slit, each of these two slits acted as a new source of circular waves that travelled toward a vertical screen. On the screen a series of bright and dark bands of light appeared. A sheet of photographic film could be substituted for the screen.

Young's interference experiment can be illustrated very easily now using a classroom laser. The laser automatically produces one single wavelength, and the interference pattern is bright enough to see even in a well-lit room.

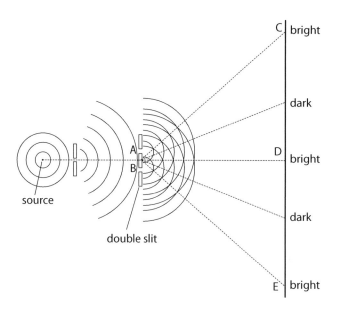

Figure 6.2.3 *Young's experiment*

In Figure 6.2.3, the concentric circles represent successive peaks of light waves coming from the slits. Troughs are midway between the peaks, of course. They are not shown in the diagram because it becomes too cluttered with detail.

On the screen on the right, you would see a series of bright and dark bands, which is an interference pattern. At the bright bands (C, D, and E), crests from the two slits arrive simultaneously, as do troughs. There is constructive interference of the two sets of waves. Notice that waves arriving at D have travelled the same distance from their slits.

Waves arriving at C or at E have travelled distances that differ by exactly one wavelength (λ). Again, the peaks arrive simultaneously and the troughs arrive simultaneously, and there is constructive interference causing the bright bands at C and E.

Figure 6.2.3 is simplified. There will be other bright bands farther out on both sides of the central bright band. These bright bands will occur wherever the difference in distance travelled from slits A and B is an integral number of wavelengths.

At the dark bands, called **nodal lines**, waves from the two sources arrive out of phase. That is, when a crest from slit A is arriving, a trough from slit B is also arriving. The crest cancels the trough. This is destructive interference. The amplitudes of the two arriving waves cancel each other and you see no light.

Figure 6.2.4 shows the geometry of the situation, and how you can use the interference pattern to calculate the wavelength of the light. For simplicity, the first bright band adjacent to the central bright band is used.

CA is the distance from the screen to source (slit) A. CB is the distance from the screen to the second slit B. The difference in these two distances is BF, which is one wavelength.

$$BF = CB - CA = \lambda$$

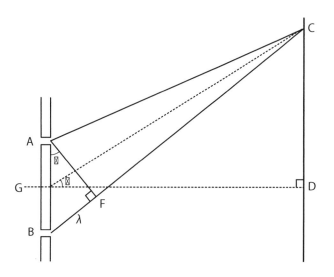

Figure 6.2.4 *Using the interference pattern to calculate the wavelength of light*

In the diagram, GD is the central maximum. A bright band appears on the screen at D. A dashed line, CG, joins the midpoint of the two slits with the bright band at C. You will note that there are similar triangles on this diagram.

Since $\triangle BFA \sim \triangle CDG$, therefore $\dfrac{BF}{CD} = \dfrac{AB}{CG}$

This means that the wavelength BF can be calculated as follows:

$$BF = (CD)\frac{AB}{CG}$$

or $$\lambda = (CD)\frac{AB}{CG}$$

where CD is the distance on the screen between the central bright band and the first bright band to either side of it; AB is the distance between the two slits or sources; and CG is the distance from the midpoint of the two slits to the first bright band on the screen.

For the second bright band, BF = 2λ; for the third bright band, BF = 3λ; and for the nth bright band, BF = $n\lambda$.

In general, for the nth bright band:

$$n\lambda = (CD)\frac{AB}{CG} \text{ and}$$

$$\lambda = \frac{(CD)(AB)}{n(CG)}$$

This relationship can be used to calculate the wavelength of light from an interference pattern. It can also be used to calculate the wavelength of water waves in a wave tank.

If you are familiar with simple trigonometry and you study Figure 6.2.4, you will notice that the ratio of side CD to side CG of triangle CDE is equal to the sine of angle G (which is called θ on the diagram). You will see that the formula for the wavelength can, therefore, be written

$$\lambda = \frac{AB}{n}\sin\theta$$

where θ is the angle between the line GD (central bright band) and the line GC (nth bright band), and n is the number of the bright band. If the symbol d is used for the distance between slits (AB), the formula can be written

$$n\lambda = d\sin\theta$$

Diffraction

You hear someone talking from around a corner. Light leaks through a crack in a closed door. These are both examples of another property of waves called diffraction. **Diffraction** is when a wave spreads out as it passes through narrow openings, around corners or small obstacles.

You have probably seen examples of diffraction many times, perhaps without knowing what it was. If you look out at streetlights through a window screen or a fine mesh curtain, the *starburst* effect you see is due to diffraction of light waves as they pass by the screen. Diffraction is often used in television programs to obtain starburst effects in musical productions. Diffraction is commonplace with sound. Figure 6.2.5 shows the diffraction of red laser light around a razor blade.

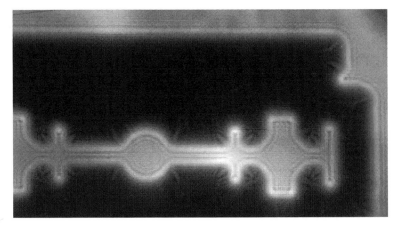

Figure 6.2.5 *Using the interference pattern to calculate the wavelength of light*

The Doppler Effect

When a fast car or motorbike approaches you, the pitch of its sound rises. As the vehicle goes by, the pitch lowers. The effect is quite noticeable if you watch a high-speed automobile race on television. What causes this change in pitch? Austrian physicist C. J. Doppler (1803–1853) was the first to explain the effect in terms of waves, and therefore the effect is called the **Doppler effect**.

Figure 6.2.6 illustrates sound waves coming from a moving source. The vehicle is moving to the left. Sound waves coming from the vehicle are bunched in front of the vehicle, which tends to catch up with its own sound. (This diagram exaggerates the effect.) The wave fronts or compressions are closer together in front of the vehicle and farther apart behind the vehicle.

The observer at A hears a higher pitch than normal, since more compressions and rarefactions pass his ear per second than pass the observer at B. Observer B hears the normal pitch of the vehicle's sound. Behind the vehicle, compressions are spaced out, since the vehicle is travelling away from the sound it sends in that direction. The observer at C hears a lower pitch than normal. Fewer compressions and rarefactions pass his ear per second than if he was at A or B. As the vehicle passes observer A, he will hear the pitch go from high to normal to low in a very short time interval. He will hear the Doppler effect.

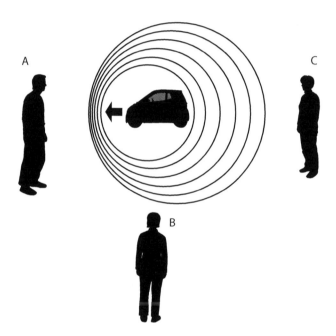

Figure 6.2.6 *The wave fronts are closer together at the front of the moving vehicle as it moves forward and more spread out behind.*

The Sound Barrier

An extreme case of the Doppler effect occurs when an aircraft or bullet travels at the same speed as the sound it is producing. At the leading edges of the aircraft, the compressions it creates tend to bunch up and superimpose on each other (Figure 6.2.7(a)). This creates a wall or barrier of compressed air called the **sound barrier**. Great thrust is needed from the plane's engines to enable the plane to penetrate the sound barrier. Once through the barrier, the plane experiences much less resistance to its movement through the air. The plane, once through the sound barrier, is then supersonic. Its speed is now greater than Mach 1!

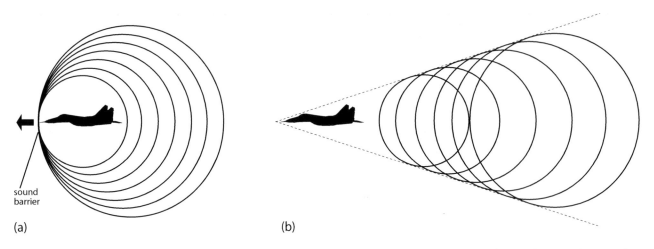

(a)   (b)

Figure 6.2.7 (**a**) *The airplane travelling at the speed of sound creates a wall of compressed called the sound barrier;* (**b**) *An airplane travelling faster than the speed of sound creates a shock wave that you hear as a sonic boom.*

Shock Waves and the Sonic Boom

If a plane travels *faster* than sound, it gets ahead of the compressions and rarefactions it produces. In two dimensions (Figure 6.2.7(b)), overlapping circular waves form a V-shaped bow wave, somewhat like what you see from the air looking down at a speedboat travelling through still water. In three dimensions, there is a cone of compressed air trailing the aircraft. This cone is called a shock wave. When the shock wave passes you, you hear a loud, sharp crack called the **sonic boom.** Aircraft are not the only producers of sonic booms. Cracking whips and rifle bullets causes miniature sonic booms!

Investigation 6-2   Properties of Waves

Purpose
To observe important properties of waves, using water waves in a wave tank as a model

Procedure
This investigation will require several periods to complete. There are six stations where you will observe different wave phenomena. Your teacher will point out any differences in equipment or procedures as required.

Station 1: Reflection of Circular Water Waves

1. Make a solid barrier of two paraffin wax blocks, standing on edge in the middle of the tank. Generate a circular wave by touching the surface of the water in the wave tank at a distance of approximately 10 cm in front of the barrier (Figure 6.2.8). Observe the curvature of the wave as it arrives at the barrier and as it leaves. Is the wave less curved, more curved, or does it have the same curvature after it reflects from the barriers? Sketch what you see.

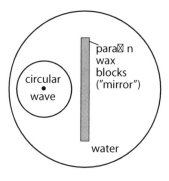

2. From where does the reflected circular wave appear to come? Try generating a circular wave behind the barrier at the same time as you generate one in front of the barrier. Try different distances behind the barrier until you obtain a wave with the same curvature as the one that reflects from the other side of the barrier. The wave from the point behind the barrier will look just as if it is passing through the barrier and joining the reflected wave on the other side.

Figure 6.2.8 *Station 1*

Question
Can you reflect a wave completely? Explain your answer.

Station 2: Reflection of Straight Water Waves

1. Set up the straight-wave generator so that it sends parallel straight waves toward a barrier made of paraffin wax blocks. The angle formed where the incoming or incident waves strike the barrier is called the **angle of incidence** (labeled $\angle i$ in Figure 6.2.9). Measure both the angle of incidence and the **angle of reflection** ($\angle r$). Sketch what you see.

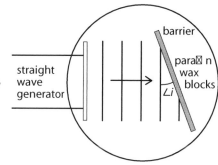

2. Adjust the barrier to change the angle of incidence. Measure the new angle of incidence and the new angle of reflection. Repeat for at least three other angles of incidence.

Figure 6.2.9 *Station 2*

3. You will recall that wave speed, wavelength, and frequency are related by $v = \lambda f$. The frequency f is determined by the rate of vibration of the wave generator. It will not change during transmission of the waves. This means that the wave speed v is proportional to the wavelength λ. If you observe the wavelength changing, this means the wave speed is changing proportionally. Is there a change in wavelength between the incident and reflected waves?

Questions

1. When straight waves strike a straight barrier, how does the angle of incidence compare with the angle of reflection?

2. When the waves reflect from the barrier, does their speed change? Does their frequency change? Does their wavelength change?

Station 3: Reflection of Waves from a Curved "Mirror"

1. This time, instead of a straight barrier, you will use a piece of rubber tubing, which curls into a shape that is approximately parabolic. Set up the rubber tubing "mirror" so that it faces the straight-wave generator as in Figure 6.2.10(a).

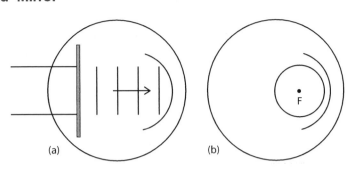

2. Observe what happens when the incident straight waves reflect from the parabolic mirror. What shape do the waves have after the reflection? Locate the point to which the waves appear to converge. This point is called the **focus** or **focal point** of the mirror. Sketch what you see.

Figure 6.2.10 *Station 3*

3. Turn off the straight-wave generator. Use the tip of your finger to generate circular waves at the focus of the mirror as in Figure 6.2.10(b). What shape do the reflected waves have this time? Sketch what you see.

Questions
1. Describe what happens to straight waves when they reflect from a parabolic reflector. Are parabolic reflectors ever used to reflect (a) light? (b) sound? Give examples.

2. Describe what happens when circular waves originating at the focus of a parabolic mirror reflect from the mirror. Name a device that does this with light waves.

Station 4: Refraction of Water Waves

A. The Effect of Water Depth on Wave Speed
1. To observe the effect of water depth on wave speed, arrange the wave tank so that there is a region of deep water and a region of shallow water over which water waves can pass. To do this, mount a rectangular sheet of transparent plastic in the tank using coins or washers to prop it up. Add water to the tank until the level is approximately 1–2 mm above the top of the plastic sheet. Figure 6.2.11 illustrates side and top views. The straight wave generator is used to provide the waves.

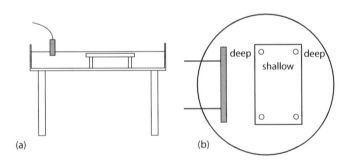

Figure 6.2.11 *Station 4A*

2. Generate continuous waves with the straight wave generator. Observe the wavelength of the waves in the deep water, and compare this with the wavelength in shallow water. Sketch what you observe. What happens when the waves re-enter the deep water? Measure the wavelengths in deep and shallow water and record them.

3. Calculate the ratio of the wavelength in shallow water to the wavelength in deep water. You can therefore calculate the ratio of the wave speed in shallow water to the wave speed in deep water.

B. Refraction of Water Waves

1. Arrange the shallow water region as in Figure 6.2.12, so that straight waves entering the shallow region meet its edge at an angle such as 30°. Adjust the generator frequency to obtain waves of long wavelength. Observe the waves as they pass into the shallow region.

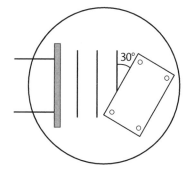

2. Make the following measurements on the water waves, as seen on your "screen."
   (a) What is the wavelength in the deep water? In the shallow water?
   (b) What is the ratio of the wavelength in shallow water to the wavelength in deep water?
   (c) What is the ratio of the wave speed in shallow water to the wave speed in deep water? Where does the change in speed actually occur?

   Figure 6.2.12 *Station 4B*

   (d) What angle does the incident wave make with the boundary between the deep water and the shallow water? This is the angle of incidence. What angle does the wave inside the shallow water make with the boundary? This is the angle of refraction.

3. Make a neat sketch illustrating what happens to water waves coming from deep water into shallow water. Show what happens to the waves when they again leave the shallow water.

4. Try different angles of incidence, such as 40° and 50°. Measure and record the angles at which the waves leave the boundary angles of refraction.

Questions

1. What happens to the speed of water waves when the waves pass from deeper water into shallower water?

2. You did not actually measure the wave speeds. How did you know the speeds had changed and by how much they had changed?

3. Why can you assume the wave frequency is constant as the waves proceed across the water in your wave tank?

4. When water waves enter shallow water in a direction such that the waves are parallel to the boundary, does the direction of the waves change?

5. When water waves enter shallow water from deep water in such a direction that the waves form an angle greater than 0° with the boundary, does their direction change? If so, in what way does it change? Is the angle of refraction greater than, equal to, or less than the angle of incidence?

6. When water waves leave shallow water and return to deep water, how does their direction change? For the water waves leaving the shallow water, how does the angle of refraction compare with the angle of incidence for the water waves that were coming into the shallow water in the first place?

Station 5: Diffraction of Water Waves

1. Set up a barrier (wall) near the middle of your wave tank using a block of paraffin wax or similar object. See Figure 6.2.13(a). Use the tip of your finger to generate waves on one side of the wall. Observe what happens to the waves as they spread past the edge of the barrier. Sketch what you observe. If these were sound waves, and you were standing at O, would you hear the sound?

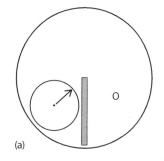
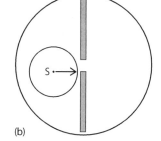

(a)

(b)

Figure 6.2.13 *Station 5*

2. Set up the arrangement in Figure 6.2.13(b) to simulate a doorway. Generate waves with the tip of your finger at S, and observe the waves as they pass through and beyond the door.
    Sketch what you observe. If these were sound waves, could you hear the sound in the adjacent room?

3. Change the width of the "doorway." Does this affect the amount of spreading of the waves as they pass through?

4. Remove the barriers from the tank and place a small object near the centre of the tank. Its shape is unimportant. A width of 2–3 cm would be appropriate. Generate waves on one side of the obstacle using the tip of your finger. Let the waves pass by the object. Sketch what you observe. Do they "cast a shadow" as they pass it, or do they seem to carry on unaffected by the obstacle? What happens if you use an obstacle that is (a) bigger? (b) smaller?

5. Set up your straight-wave generator and adjust the frequency so that the waves it produces have a wavelength of approximately 2 cm as seen on the screen on your table. By experimenting with different opening sizes and wavelengths, find out what the effect is of changing these two variables one at a time. Prepare a series of careful sketches showing how the waveforms look following diffraction.

6. Set up a small obstacle in the path of the straight waves. Experiment to see the effects of changing (a) wavelengths and (b) obstacle size. Sketch what you observe.

Questions

1. Is diffraction more noticeable with short wavelengths or long wavelengths?

2. Is diffraction more noticeable with small openings or large openings?

3. When straight waves pass through a small opening, what shape do the diffracted waves have? Sketch a diagram.

4. When straight waves pass by a small obstacle, what happens to the straight waves if the obstacle is (a) very small compared with the wavelength of the waves? (b) about the same size as the wavelength? (c) very large compared with the wavelength?

5. Describe at least three examples of situations you encounter daily that involve diffraction of waves of one sort or another. These might involve water waves, sound, or light.

Station 6: Interference

A. Interference in a Stretched Spring

1. To observe interference of waves in a Slinky, hold one end of the Slinky yourself and have your partner hold the other end of the stretched spring. Simultaneously, generate transverse disturbances in the same direction and with the same amplitude, as in Figure 6.2.14(a). Observe what happens when the two pulses pass through each other near the centre of the Slinky.

2. Repeat step 1, but this time, generate simultaneous disturbances that have the same magnitude but opposite amplitudes, as in Figure 6.2.14(b).

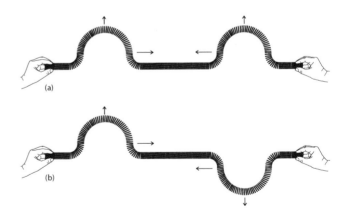

Figure 6.2.14 *Station 6A*

Questions

1. When the two pulses pass through each other such that a crest passes through a crest, as would happen in Figure 6.2.14(a), what happens to the amplitude of the combined waves?

2. When a crest arrives at the same point as a trough, as would happen in Figure 6.2.14(b), what happens to the amplitude of the combined waves?

B. Interference in Water Waves

1. Set up the arrangement in Figure 6.2.15. The generator generates straight waves, but as they pass through the twin slits, each slit causes diffraction and the two sets of circular waves are produced at the slits. Observe how the two sets of circular waves interfere with each other.

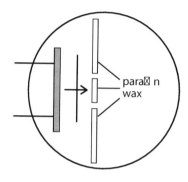

2. Each source of circular waves sends out successive crests and troughs, and the two sets of waves interfere with one another. Describe what you see on the screen where the troughs from one source of waves arrive simultaneously with the crests from the other source. What do you see in the areas where crests and troughs from one source arrive simultaneously with crests and troughs from the other source?

Figure 6.2.15 *Station 6B*

3. Replace the two-slit barrier with a twin point-source generator. Set up the twin point-source generator so that both vibrating point sources are in phase. This means that they both vibrate up and down in synchronization. If one point source vibrated upward while the other vibrated downward, they would be out of phase. This arrangement usually gives much better waves than the double slit arrangement.

Questions

1. When crests from one wave source arrive simultaneously with troughs from another wave source, what will you see on the screen at that point? Why?

2. When crests arrive with crests and troughs with troughs from two different wave sources, what will you see at that spot on the screen? Why?

3. Regions of zero disturbances on the screen appear as nearly straight lines called nodal lines. If a point on such a nodal line was a distance of $n\lambda$ from one point source of waves, where λ is the wavelength and n is an integer, how far would the same point be from the other point source? Is there more than one answer to this question?

4. Regions of maximum disturbance on the screen, sometimes called maxima, occur when the distance from one source is, for example, $m\lambda$, where m is an integer and λ is the wavelength. What is the distance to the other source? Is there more than one possible answer? Explain.

6.2 Review Questions

Complete these diagrams to show what happens to waves after they encounter the barrier or other obstacle. Name the phenomenon that occurs in each situation.

1.

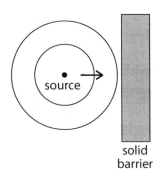

source →

solid
barrier

_____

phenomenon

2.

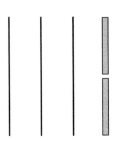

_____

phenomenon

3. If you look at streetlights through a fine mesh curtain, you will see a "starburst" effect. What phenomenon is involved in this situation?

_____

phenomenon

4. Use the following diagram to answer the questions below.

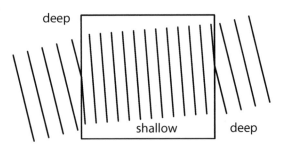

deep

shallow   deep

(a) The diagram shows water waves in a wave tank moving from deep water into shallow water and then back into deep water. What property of waves does this model illustrate?

(b) According to the diagram, what can you conclude happens to the waves when they enter the shallow water?

5. For the following situations, is there a point where the amplitude will be zero everywhere? If so, mark that point.

(a)

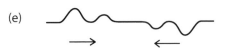

(b)

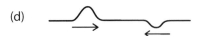

(c)

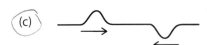

(d)

(e)

(f)

6. For which of the following waves can wave interference occur?

___✓___ sound

___✓___ light

___✓___ water

7. For which of the following waves can the Doppler effect occur?

___✓___ sound (most prominent for sound)

___✓___ light

___✓___ water

8. Does the Doppler effect occur if you are moving and the object making the noise is stationary? Explain your answer.

Yes, there is still a difference between source & observer

9. What can you conclude about the speed of an airplane overhead if you hear a sonic boom?

It is mach 1, supersonic (faster than speed of sound)

10. What is the difference between a sonic boom and the sound barrier?

Sound barrier is what's broken for a sonic boom to happen.

11. Draw two waves travelling toward each other that will create destructive interference when they meet.

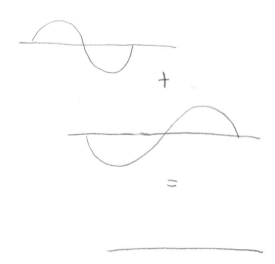

Chapter 6   Review Questions

1. What is the difference between a pulse and periodic waves?

2. Explain, with the help of a sketch, what each of these terms means with respect to waves:
   (a) crest

   (b) trough

   (c) wavelength

   (d) frequency

   (e) amplitude

3. What is a hertz?

4. How are frequency and period related?

5. A dog wags its tail 50 times in 20 s. What are (a) the frequency and (b) the period of vibration of the tail?

6. What is the difference between a transverse wave and a longitudinal wave?

7. For any kind of wave motion, how are wave speed, wavelength, and frequency related to one another?

8. Alternating current in power lines produces electromagnetic waves of frequency 60 Hz that travel outward at the speed of light, which is 3.0×10^8 m/s. What is the wavelength of these waves?

9. If the speed of sound is 330 m/s, what wavelength does a sound of frequency 512 Hz have?

11. Explain the difference between refraction and diffraction. Give an example of each phenomenon from everyday experience.

12. When waves slow down on entering a new medium, what happens to
    (a) their wavelength?

    changes (slows down)

    (b) their frequency?

    Stays the same

    (c) their direction?

    Changes

    (d) Under what conditions will the direction *not* change?

13. (a) What is constructive interference?

    (b) What is destructive interference?

14. In a wave tank, what causes a nodal line? A maximum?

    2 waves undergo constructive interference.

    when the waves cancel out (destructive interference).

15. The following diagram shows two parabolic reflectors. A small source of infrared heat is placed at the focus of one of the mirrors. Soon after, a match at the focus of the other reflector lights on fire. Draw a diagram showing how the wave model explains this.

f
source of infared radiation

f
matchhead

16. The sonar on a Canadian navy submarine produces ultrasonic waves at a frequency of 2.2 MHz and a wavelength of 5.10×10^{-4} m. If a sonar technician sends one wave pulse from underneath the submarine toward the bottom of the ocean floor and it takes 8.0 s to return, how deep is the ocean at this point?

Chapter 6   Extra Practice

1. Label the trough, crest, amplitude, and wavelength on the image below.

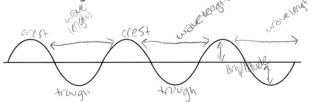

2. If a wave from trough to crest is 4.2 m high, what is the amplitude of the wave?

3. At room temperature, sound has a speed of 3.4×10^2 m/s. What is the wavelength of sound from a tuning fork that vibrates at 256 Hz?

4. Light travels with a speed of 3.00×10^8 m/s. What is the frequency of red light, if its wavelength is 610 nm? (1 nm = 1 nanometre = 10^{-9} m)

5. A rubber duck is floating in the waves and goes up and down three times in 1 s. If the wave travels an average distance of 4 m in a second, what is the wavelength?

6. What is the frequency of a wave that has a period of
    (a) 100 s?
    (b) 0.5 s?
    (c) $1.0 \times 10{-2}$ s?

7. In the diagram below, which wave has
    (a) the longest period?
    (b) the lowest frequency?
    (c) the highest frequency?

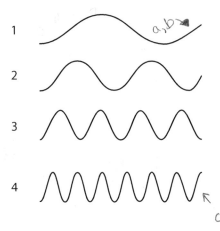

8. What is the period of the hour hand on a clock?

9. What is the period of the second hand on a clock?

10. An observer counts 36 waves arriving at the shore of a beach in a time of 3.00 min.
    (a) What is the frequency of the waves?
    (b) What is the period of the waves?

11. A small spider has became lost while looking for its web site. The spider is on the surface of an old phonograph record, which is spinning at 33 rpm (rotations per minute). It is trying to escape by jumping on the needle of the phonograph player. The spider misses the needle on the first try. How long will it have to wait for the next try?

12. If you increase the frequency of the wave generator in a wave tank, what happens to the wavelength of the waves?

13. What is the wavelength of a wave that has a frequency of 34 Hz and is travelling at 2.5 m/s?

14. What is the frequency of a wave that has a wavelength of 25 cm and is travelling at 5 km/h?

15. What is the speed of a sound wave with a frequency of 200 Hz and a wavelength of 35 m?

16. A helicopter pilot with nothing better to do counts 250 crests of water waves in a distance of 100 m on a lake below him. What is the wavelength of the waves?

17. The speed of light is 3.0×10^8 m/s. What is the frequency of light waves if their wavelength is 600 nm? (1 nm = 10^{-9} m) Consult a spectrum chart to see what colour of light this would be.

18. What measurable property of waves does not change as the waves move from one medium into another?

19. Draw two waves travelling toward each other that will create constructive interference when they meet.

7 Light and Geometric Optics

By the end of this chapter, you should be able to do the following:

➢ Use ray diagrams to analyse situations in which light reflects from plane and curved mirrors
  - state the law of reflection
  - identify the following on appropriate diagrams:
    - incident ray
    - reflected ray
    - angle of incidence
    - angle of reflection
    - normal
  - show how an image is produced by a plane mirror
  - describe the characteristics of an image produced by a plane mirror
  - identify a curved mirror as converging (concave) or diverging (convex)
  - identify the following on appropriate diagrams:
    - principal axis
    - centre and radius of curvature
    - image and object distance
    - focal point and focal length
  - draw accurate scale diagrams for both concave and convex mirrors to show how an image is produced
  - describe the characteristics of images produced by converging and diverging mirrors
  - conduct an experiment to determine the focal length of a concave mirror

➢ Analyse situations in which light is refracted
  - identify the following from appropriate diagrams:
    - incident ray
    - angle of incidence
    - refracted ray
    - angle of reflection
    - normal
  - use Snell's law to solve a range of problems involving:
    - index of refraction
    - angle of incidence
    - angle of reflection
  - define critical angle and total internal reflection
  - solve problems involving critical angles
  - identify a lens as converging (convex) or diverging (concave)
  - for a lens, identify the following from appropriate diagrams:
    - principal axis
    - focal point (primary and secondary)
    - focal length
    - image and object distance
  - draw accurate scale diagrams for both convex and concave lenses to show how an image is produced
  - describe the characteristics of images produced by converging and diverging lenses
  - conduct an experiment to determine the focal length of a convex lens

By the end of this chapter, you should know the meaning of these **key terms**:

- angle of incidence
- angle of reflection
- concave
- convex
- converging lens
- diverging lens
- electromagnetic radiation
- electromagnetic spectrum
- focal point
- image distance
- incident ray
- law of reflection lens
- mirror equation
- normal
- object distance
- polarization
- principal focus
- real image
- reflected ray
- refraction
- refractive index
- Snell's Law
- virtual image

By the end of the chapter, you should be able to use and know when to use the following formulae:

$$\frac{1}{d_i} + \frac{1}{d_o} = \frac{1}{f} \qquad n = \frac{c}{v} \qquad n_1 \sin(\theta_i) = n_2 \sin(\theta_r)$$

In this chapter you'll learn how lenses can help you see things differently.

7.1 Reflection

Warm Up

Make a pinhole camera with a Styrofoam or paper cup. Place a square of wax paper over the open end of the cup and hold it in place with a rubber band. With a pin, poke a small hole in the other end of the cup. In a dark room with a light bulb at one end, observe the image formed on the wax paper. Make sure the pinhole faces the light. Describe the image.

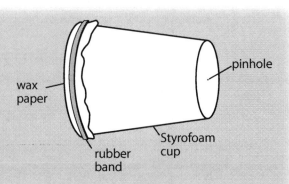

_____

_____

_____

_____

Properties of Light

Many useful devices have been developed because of growing knowledge of how light behaves. One can describe many of the properties of light without knowing exactly what light is, and one can invent many devices that use these properties. Cameras, eyeglasses, mirrors, microscopes, periscopes, magnifying glasses, spectroscopes and various kinds of projectors are some of the optical devices that use well-known properties of light. In this chapter, you will investigate some of the important properties of light.

The Electromagnetic Spectrum

Light is a form of **electromagnetic radiation**. Electromagnetic radiation is radiant energy that travels at the speed of light (300 000 km/s). Figure 7.1.1 shows the different forms of electromagnetic radiation that occur in nature. All the different forms together make up the **electromagnetic spectrum**. A key property of all forms of radiation is the wavelength-frequency-energy relationship. Figure 7.1.1 shows radiation such as AM radio having long wavelength, low frequency, and low energy. At the other end of the spectrum, X-rays have short wavelengths, high frequency, and high energy.

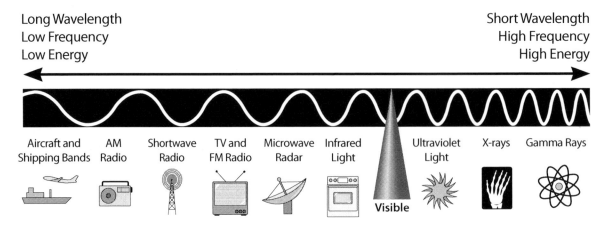

Figure 7.1.1 *The electromagnetic spectrum*

Table 7.1.1 outlines the major forms of radiation found in the electromagnetic spectrum. Within this whole spectrum of radiation, visible light is a tiny slice of all the possible forms of radiation.

Table 7.1.1 *Major Forms of Electromagnetic Radiation*

	Form	Frequency	Wavelength	Description	Example of Object of Similar Size
Long wavelength Low frequency Low energy	Aircraft and shipping bands	10^2–10^4 Hz	10^4–10^6 m	Long waves used for aircraft and shipping communications	Earth
	AM radio	10^6 Hz	1000 m	Radio waves used for sound broadcasting over short distances	kilometre
	Shortwave radio	10^7 Hz	100 m	Radio waves used for sound broadcasting over long distances (around the world)	soccer field
	TV and FM radio	10^8 Hz	1 m	Radio waves used for sound and image broadcasting	metre stick
	Microwave and radar	10^{12} Hz	0.01 m	Radio waves that can penetrate the Earth's atmosphere, making them ideal for satellite communication; short wavelengths so can be reflected off distant objects; also used in cooking.	centimetre
	Infrared light	10^{12}–10^{14} Hz	0.001 m	Radiation emitted from hot objects; the higher the temperature, the more infrared radiation emitted	millimetre
	Visible light	10^{15} Hz	10^{-6} m	Radiation observable by the human eye	dust particle
	Ultraviolet light	10^{15}–10^{17} Hz	10^{-7} m	Radiation from the Sun and human-made devices such as mercury vapour lamps; gives humans tans; stimulates vitamin D production in the skin	DNA molecule
Short wavelength High frequency High energy	X-rays	10^{17}–10^{21} Hz	10^{-9}–10^{-13} m	Two types used: long-wavelength X-rays used in medicine to penetrate skin (do not go through bone); short-wavelength X-rays used in industry to inspect metal for faults	atom
	Gamma rays	10^{19}–10^{21} Hz	10^{-10}–10^{-13} m	Produced when protons and neutrons in the nucleus of an atom are rearranged; used in medicine; kill bacteria in food	nucleus

Visible Light

Wavelengths of visible light range from 3.8×10^{-7} m for violet light to 7.6×10^{-7} m for red light. Wavelengths are often expressed in nanometres (nm), where 1 nm = 10^{-9} m. Table 7.1.2 lists some typical wavelengths in the visible range.

It is interesting to note that if your eye detects light in the range of wavelengths between 560 nm and 590 nm, it perceives the light as yellow. If, however, it sees a mix of colours, one in the range between 630 nm and 760 nm (red) and the other between 490 nm and 560 nm (green), it again perceives the light as being yellow!

Table 7.1.2 *Wavelengths of Visible Light*

Colour	Range of wavelengths
red	630–760 nm
orange	590–630 nm
yellow	560–590 nm
green	490–560 nm
blue	450–490 nm
violet	380–450 nm

Wavelengths We Use But Cannot See

If a beam of white light is dispersed with a prism, and the spectrum is viewed on screen, you will see all the colours from violet to red on the screen. In the early nineteenth century, the English astronomer William Herschel (1738–1822) was experimenting to see which colours of light gave the greatest heating effect when allowed to shine on the blackened bulb of a thermometer. He moved the thermometer bulb through the various parts of the visible spectrum and observed increases in temperature caused by the different colours of light. He discovered to his surprise that the greatest heating effect was observed if the bulb was placed *beyond* the red end of the visible spectrum! This is how **infrared radiation** was discovered.

Infrared radiation is extremely important to us. Infrared radiation from the Sun provides most of the thermal energy requirements of the planet. Scientists have developed infrared photographic techniques that permit satellite pictures of features on the Earth's surface, which can be taken through clouds, fog, or smoke. Objects can be photographed in the dark using infrared photography. Some auto focus cameras use infrared for focussing, which means they work in the dark. Infrared has many uses, including heat lamps, physiotherapy, and medical diagnostic photography. Astronomers are now making good use of infrared images of the stars and other objects in the universe.

Infrared wavelengths cover a wide range, the shortest wavelength beginning at the red end of the visible spectrum (760 nm) and the longest wavelength being approximately 300 000 nm. Beyond the infrared lies the radio part of the spectrum.

In 1801, the German physicist, Johann Wilhelm Ritter (1776–1810), was studying the effect of visible light on the chemical compound silver chloride, AgCl. When light falls on silver chloride, the white compound decomposes and forms silver, which appears black, and chlorine, which escapes into the atmosphere. This is similar to the chemical reaction for photographic film development where silver bromide is used.

Ritter knew that the effect was most noticeable at the violet end of the spectrum. He was surprised to find that if silver chloride was placed in a region beyond the violet end of the visible spectrum, the decomposition of the silver chloride was even more pronounced! Thus, **ultraviolet radiation** was discovered.

You cannot see ultraviolet, but it is wise to know about it anyway. It is ultraviolet light that gives you a suntan or sunburn. Too much exposure to the Sun or to ultraviolet-rich sunlamps can be dangerous. Ultraviolet can also damage parts of your retina, thus impairing your vision.

"Black lights," sold to make posters fluoresce, are actually sources of ultraviolet light. They also give off light in the violet part of the spectrum. Some black lights are essentially mercury vapour lamps, like fluorescent lamps used to light your classroom. Instead of having an inner coating of fluorescent chemicals, they have a violet-coloured glass tube that allows violet and ultraviolet light to pass through it.

Linear Propagation of Light

Light travels in straight lines — sometimes. Over short distances, in a given medium such as air or water, light travels in a straight path. If light encounters a different medium or a reflecting surface, its path will change. Gravity can also deflect light from a straight path. Einstein predicted this long ago, and experiments verified his prediction. In most situations you will encounter, however, you may assume that the path of light in a given medium is straight. You can predict the size and shape of shadows by assuming linear propagation of light.

When drawing pictures involving light, a straight arrow called a ray is used to represent the light. This type of diagram is called a ray diagram. Figure 7.1.2(a) shows a ray of light coming from the top of the candle and moving toward a mirror. For you to see the image of this candle in the mirror, the light needs to be reflected back to your eye. Another ray pointed in the other direction illustrates this situation. This completes the ray diagram (Figure 7.1.2(b)).

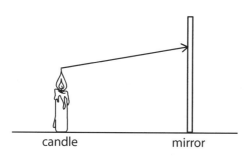

(a) *Draw the ray from the object to the mirror.*

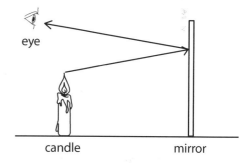

(b) *Draw the reflected ray back to the eye.*

Figure 7.1.2 *Drawing a ray diagram*

The Law of Reflection

If you look directly into a mirror and wink your left eye, which eye will your image wink? Now look at yourself in a wall mirror, note what fraction of your body you see in the mirror. Now walk back a few metres and look into the same mirror. Do you see more of your body, less, or the same fraction of your body? You are beginning to investigate the law of reflection and image formation in a plane mirror (Figure 7.1.3).

Figure 7.1.3 *A mirror reflects the image back to the observer.*

A ray approaching a mirror is called the **incident ray**. A **reflected ray** is the light that is reflected from the mirror. The dashed line that is perpendicular to the mirror is called the **normal**. The angle between the incident ray and normal is called the **angle of incidence**. The angle between the reflected ray and the normal is the **angle of reflection**. Figure 7.1.4 illustrates each of these terms.

The **law of reflection** states the angle of incidence is equal to the angle of reflection in the same plane. This means if $\theta_i = 45°$ then $\theta_r = 45°$.

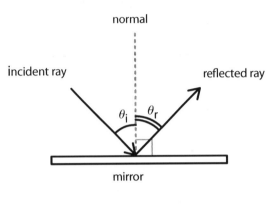

θ_i = angle of incidence

θ_r = angle of reflection

Figure 7.1.4 *In this diagram, the mirror is lying horizontally. The angles shown occur whatever position of the mirror.*

Image Formation in a Plane Mirror

A flat mirror is also called a plane mirror. When you look into a mirror you see an image that appears to be you, but there are several characteristics that make your mirror image different. An image that can be projected onto a screen is called a **real image**. Your mirror image cannot do this and is considered a **virtual image**. Figure 7.1.5 shows a ray diagram of the virtual image that forms "in" or behind the mirror. Note that the dotted lines represent an extension of the light ray.

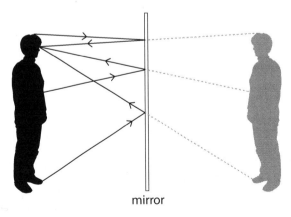

Figure 7.1.5 *A virtual image of the person or object appears in or behind the mirror.*

The virtual image is an exact reflection of the real person or object so it has these characteristics:

- The image is the same size as the original object.
- It is upright.
- It is the same distance from the surface of the mirror as the person or object is from the mirror.

The distance between the person and the mirror is called the **object distance**. The distance between the mirror and the image is the **image distance**. The image is also reversed. The right eye of the person is the left eye in the image. A common example of this is the word Ambulance printed in reverse on the front of the rescue vehicle. When drivers look in their rear view mirrors, they can read the word correctly. Table 7.1.3 summarizes the characteristics that can be used to describe an image.

Table 7.1.3 *Words to Use to Describe an Image*

Image Characteristic	Description
Type	real or virtual
Attitude	erect or inverted
Magnification	same size, smaller, larger
Position	distance from mirror surface

Quick Check

1. You are a basketball player, 2 m tall. What is the shortest mirror you need to see your whole self in it?

   1 m

2. At night, have you ever seen your image in your living room window? Why don't you see it during the daytime?

   The dark outside allows you to see reflection

3. (a) When you look into a mirror, where exactly *is* your image?

   Behind it (inside the mirror)

   (b) Is it on the mirror surface, in front of it, or behind it?

   Behind it

   (c) If you move closer to the mirror, what happens to your image?

   Becomes larger

Investigation 7-1A Looking into Mirrors

Part 1

Purpose
To locate the image in a plane mirror

Procedure
1. Mount a sheet of clear glass or Plexiglas vertically, as in Figure 7.1.3. The Plexiglas will serve as a mirror. Place a candle approximately 20 cm in front of the mirror. Light the candle and turn off the room lights. You should see an image of the candle in the mirror. Measure the distance from the candle to the mirror. This is called the object distance.
2. Obtain another unlit candle the same height as the burning candle. Place it behind the mirror, and move it around until it appears to be at the same location as the image of the candle. Measure the distance from the image location to the mirror. This is called the image distance.
3. Look very closely at the image in the mirror. Can you see a faint second image?

Concluding Questions
1. Where is the image in the mirror? How does the image distance compare with the object distance?
2. According to your observations, where does the reflection of light occur in the "mirror"?

Part 2

Purpose
To find out why the image in a plane mirror is "behind" the mirror

Procedure
1. Remove the light bulb section of your ray box. It will be your object for this investigation. Set up your light source approximately 10 cm in front of a plane mirror. A clothespin can be used to mount the mirror vertically.
2. Use the five-slit opening of the plastic baffle for your ray box to create five beams of light from the bulb, as shown in Figure 7.1.6(a). Use a sharp pencil to make a few marks to indicate the path of one of the beams (a) as it travels to the mirror and (b) as it leaves the mirror. See Figure 7.1.6(b). Don't move the mirror!
3. Repeat step 2 for another beam of light going and coming from the mirror. Before you move the mirror, draw a line along the silvered back edge of the mirror where the reflection occurs. Also, mark the position of the filament of the light bulb as accurately as you can.

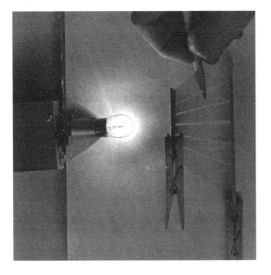

Figure 7.1.6(a)

Figure 7.1.6(b)

4. Use your pencil marks as a guide to draw a line to show the path of the first beam of light (a) as it travelled to the mirror and (b) as it travelled away from the mirror after being reflected. Repeat for the second beam. When you draw a line to show the path that light takes, the line is properly called a light ray.

5. Look carefully at one of the reflected rays. If you were looking directly into the mirror when the light bulb was in front of the mirror, from what point would this ray *appear* to have come?

6. With your ruler, draw a dashed line "behind" the mirror for about 12 cm beyond the end of the reflected ray as in Figure 7.1.6(c). Repeat with the other reflected ray. Where do the two dashed lines meet? Mark this point with an X. Is this the same location as that of the image you saw in the mirror? To find out, put the light bulb and the mirror back where they were before. Hold your pen where the X is as you look into the mirror. Is the image where the dashed lines meet?

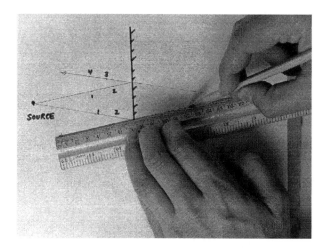

Figure 7.1.6(c)

7. At the point where one of the beams reflects from the mirror, construct a line perpendicular to the mirror. This line is called a normal to the mirror. Measure the angle between the incoming or incident ray and the normal. This is called the incident angle. Also measure the angle between the normal and the reflected ray. This is the angle of reflection. Repeat this procedure for the other beam of light.

Concluding Questions

1. Compare the distance from the object to the mirror with the distance from the image to the mirror. Explain any difference you observe.

2. The image in a plane mirror appears to be behind the mirror. Explain why this is so. Where does the light you see coming from the image really originate?

3. For each beam, how did the angle of incidence compare with the angle of reflection? Is this consistent with what you observed with waves reflecting from a plane surface?

Challenge

1. Imagine that you wish to photograph your image in a plane wall mirror. You are standing 2 m in front of the mirror. At what distance should you set your camera lens? Try this at school or at home with your cellphone.

Investigation 7-1B   Multiple Images

Purpose

To investigate multiple images in pairs of plane mirrors.

Figure 7.1.7 illustrates two pieces of Plexiglas arranged to give many images of a single candle. The Plexiglas acts as a mirror if the background is dark enough.

Figure 7.1.7 *Many images of a single object*

Procedure

1. Arrange two flat mirrors at an angle of 120°, as shown in Figure 7.1.8. Place a small object such as a golf tee or a rubber stopper approximately 10 cm in front of the mirrors. Look into the mirrors and count the number of images you can see. How many images do you see when the mirrors are at 180°? Gradually decrease the angle between the mirrors and watch what happens to the number of images.

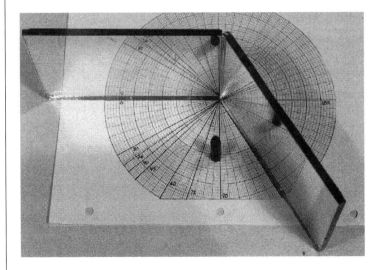

Figure 7.1.8 *Step 1*

2. To investigate the relationship between the number of images and the angle between the mirrors quantitatively, try setting your mirror at each of the angles in Table 7.1.4. In each trial, keep your head still (to avoid counting the same image twice by mistake) and count the number of images carefully. Copy the table into your notebook and record your results. Be sure to compare notes with other students.

3. Look at the data. Can you figure out a simple rule that will allow you to predict how many images you will see if the mirrors are set at any one of these angles? **Hint:** There are 360° in a circle!

4. If you think you have the rule figured out, predict how many images you will see if you set the mirrors at these angles: (a) 30° (b) 24° (c) 20° (d) 0°. (To check out your prediction for 0°, you will have to set the mirrors at 0° and then separate them, keeping them parallel with one another.)

Table 7.1.4 *Data Table*

Angle between Mirrors	Number of Images
180°	
120°	
90°	
72°	
60°	
45°	
40°	
36°	

Concluding Questions

1. What is the rule for predicting how many images you will see if you arrange two mirrors at an angle θ?

2. You wish to make a kaleidoscope toy with which you will see the same pattern repeated four times including the object. At what angle should you arrange the two long plane mirrors inside the tube of the kaleidoscope?

Challenges

1. Make an "infinity box." Use one mirror tile as the floor of the box and make walls out of four other mirror tiles. At the centre of the "infinity box," place an interesting object such as a flickering light bulb or a small moving toy.

2. Make a periscope on a large scale, using mirror tiles, so you can see down a hallway over the heads of students in the hall.

7.1 Review Questions

1. What is the relationship between frequency and wavelength in the electromagnetic spectrum?

$$C = f\,\lambda \leftarrow \text{wavelength}$$

speed   frequency

2. What is considered the visible spectrum in the electromagnetic spectrum?

wavelength →

360-780

3. Describe two forms of electromagnetic radiation that have wavelengths longer than visible light.

micro wave
infrared
radiowave

4. List three forms of electromagnetic radiation that have frequencies shorter than visible light.

UV
X Rays
gamma rays

5. Define the law of reflection and give one real-world example.

6. In your own words, describe how you can use a mirror to see around a corner. In your explanation use the terms reflecting ray, incident ray, normal line, and law of reflection.

7. What is the difference between image distance and object distance.

8. Why is the image you see in a plane mirror not considered a real image? (A real image is one formed by light arriving at a region in space, usually on a screen or film. The image in a plane mirror is called a virtual image.)

9. How many images of yourself will you see if you look into a pair of hinged mirrors forming these angles? (Assume you can fit!)

(a) 60°

(d) 10°

(b) 45°

(e) 1°

(c) 15°

10. Imagine you are 180 cm tall. What is the shortest mirror you can use if you want to see your whole body? Use a diagram to illustrate your answer. Will it matter how far from the mirror you stand?

11. Why is AMBULANCE written backwards on the front of the vehicle? Write your own name in such a way that it looks "right" when held up to a mirror. Draw a diagram to show why the letter "b" looks like a "d" in a mirror.

12. In the Warm Up you made a pinhole camera. Draw a diagram that illustrates why the image on the wax paper or screen was inverted. What are the other characteristics of the image?

13. Draw a diagram showing how you might use two prisms (45°–45°–90°) as "mirrors" in a periscope. Show how the prisms must be arranged to act as mirrors.

7.2 Curved Mirrors

Types of Curved Mirrors

You use many optical devices in your daily life, including eyeglasses, binoculars, cameras, microscopes, telescopes, and your own eyes. In this section, you will learn how some of these devices with mirrors work. Much use will be made of ray diagrams when explaining how light behaves when it passes through or into optical components such as plane and curved mirrors. You will recall that a ray is simply a line drawn to show the path that light takes. Remember: A ray is a mathematical convenience and *not* a physical reality!

The images you see in curved mirrors can be quite different from what you are accustomed to seeing in a plane mirror. If you stand close to a large concave mirror and look into it, you will see yourself "right side up" and "larger than life." A **concave mirror** has a shape that curves inward like a cave in a mountain. Some make-up or shaving mirrors are slightly concave. If you walk back from a concave mirror, you will find that at a certain distance your image is suddenly inverted and looks small (Figure 7.2.1(a)).

Convex mirrors always make you look smaller than real life, no matter what distance you are from them (Figure 7.2.1(b)). **Convex mirrors** curve outwards in the opposite direction of concave mirrors. You see convex mirrors in shops, where they are strategically placed so that the shop owner can obtain a wide-angle view of the store and the customers in it. Some rear view mirrors may have a small convex section on them so that the driver gets a wider angle of view of what is behind him.

Figure 7.2.1 (a) *A concave mirror;* **(b)** *A convex mirror*

Characteristics of a Concave or Converging Mirror

A good quality concave mirror is shaped so that rays of light incident on the mirror's surface will reflect predictably. Figure 7.2.2 describes the characteristics of a converging mirror. The **principal axis** (PA) is an imaginary line drawn through the **vertex** (V), perpendicular to surface of the curved mirror. Rays parallel to the principal axis will reflect through a single point, called the **focal point** (F). The distance between the vertex and the focal point is called the **focal length** (*f*). The point where parallel rays of light converge in front of a concave mirror is also called the principal focus, if the focussing occurs on the principal axis of the mirror.

PA = principal axis
V = vertex
F = focal point
f = focal length
C = centre of curvature
r = radius of curvature

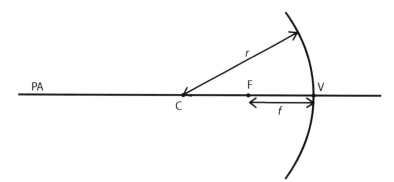

Figure 7.2.2 *Characteristics of a concave or converging mirror*

Reflection is reversible so light coming from the focal point will reflect parallel to the principal axis. Of course, any ray incident on the mirror will reflect in such a way that the angle of incidence equals the angle of reflection. This is illustrated in Figure 7.2.3 as ray 1 and ray 2. Ray 3 shows that any ray travelling through the focal point to the vertex will be reflected directly back along the same path.

The point C is called the **centre of curvature**. This is a point that represents the centre of the sphere from which the curved mirror was cut. The **radius of curvature** (*r*) is the distance from the centre of curvature to the mirror surface.

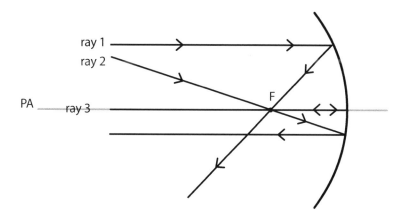

Figure 7.2.3 *Light rays reflecting on a concave mirror*

Diagrams used to illustrate concave mirrors are circular and two-dimensional. An inexpensive concave mirror is spherical in three dimensions. A top quality concave mirror is not quite spherical; the ideal mirror will be discussed later.

Predicting Where an Image Will Form

You can predict where a concave mirror will form an image if you simply keep in mind what the mirror was shaped to do and the behaviour of the two rays in Figure 7.2.3.

In Figure 7.2.4, two rays have been drawn coming from the top of the object (a candle). Ray 1 is parallel to the principal axis. It reflects from the mirror and passes through the focal point F. Ray 2 passes through the focal point, reflects off the mirror, and moves out parallel to the principal axis. An **image** of the top of the candle flame forms where these two rays converge.

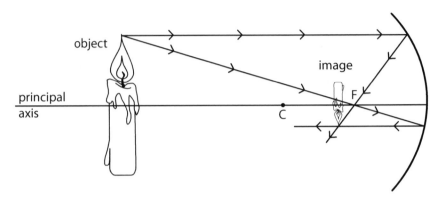

Figure 7.2.4 *The two rays from the top of the candle form an image after reflecting off the mirror.*

In Figure 7.2.5, a similar pair of rays has been drawn coming from a point at the bottom of the candle. These rays reflect and converge at a point in front of the mirror. The image of the bottom of the candle forms on a line just above the image of the top of the flame. Any number of pairs of rays might be drawn from points elsewhere on the candle. All of these pairs of rays will converge on a line the same distance from the mirror as the other image points.

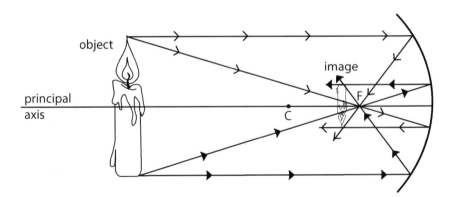

Figure 7.2.5 *With the addition of two rays from the bottom of the candle, a complete image forms.*

The object is located quite far from the mirror. It is at a distance greater than the focal length and also greater than the radius of curvature of the mirror. To summarize, the characteristics of the image are:

- Type: real
- Attitude: inverted
- Magnification: smaller than the object
- Position: closer to the mirror

Quick Check

1. Complete these ray diagrams to show where the image of the object will form and what its relative size will be. Draw at least two rays for each diagram.

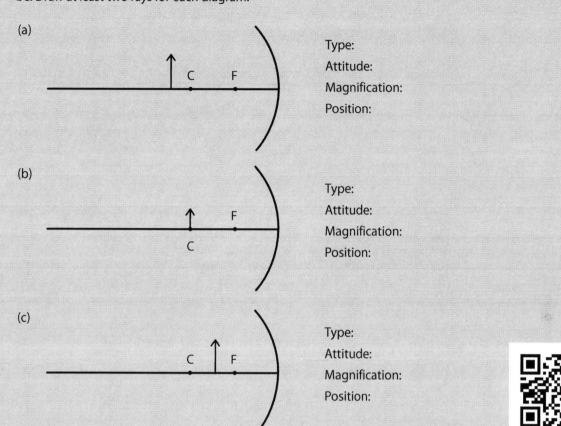

(a)

Type:

Attitude:

Magnification:

Position:

(b)

Type:

Attitude:

Magnification:

Position:

(c)

Type:

Attitude:

Magnification:

Position:

The Concave Mirror as a Magnifier

If you place your face very close to a concave mirror, so that you are closer than the principal focus, shown in Figure 7.2.6, you see an **enlarged virtual image** in the mirror. Unlike a real image from a concave mirror, the virtual image is right side up. The location of the image can be predicted using a ray diagram.

A ray coming from the top of the object in a direction parallel to the principal axis will reflect through the principal focus, as usual. To locate the image, a second ray is drawn in a direction such that it appears to have come from the principal focus. This ray will reflect out parallel to the principal axis. The reflected rays do not converge anywhere. In fact, they diverge and cannot possibly form part of a real image.

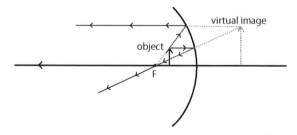

Figure 7.2.6 *When the object is between the principal focus and the mirror, the virtual image is larger than the object.*

Now, imagine you are looking into the mirror. From what point would the two reflected rays appear to come? If you extrapolate the two rays back behind the mirror, they appear to be coming from a point at the top of the virtual image in Figure 7.2.6. Similar pairs of rays might be drawn from other points on the object. Coinciding image points would then be found on the line representing the virtual image in the figure. This image is virtual, erect, and enlarged.

The Mirror Equation

Can the location of an image formed by a concave mirror be predicted by calculation? There is an equation for concave mirrors that permits you to do this quite easily. To show where the equation comes from, some simple geometry will be used. In Figure 7.2.7, a third ray has been drawn from the object to the mirror. This ray passes along a radius of the mirror. It therefore strikes the mirror perpendicularly and reflects right back on itself.

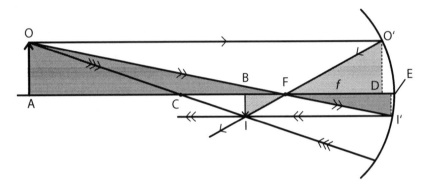

Figure 7.2.7 *Earlier diagrams only used two rays. In this diagram a third ray has been added.*

Several triangles are created in Figure 7.2.7. Notice that ΔIBF and ΔO'DF are similar. The height of the object is OA, which equals O'D. Distance FD is approximately equal to the focal length f of the mirror. The diagram exaggerates the difference between FE (f) and FD. You may assume that FD is very, very close to being equal to the focal length, f.

Since ΔIBF is similar to ΔO'DF, ∴ $\dfrac{IB}{O'D} = \dfrac{BF}{FD}$ **(1)**

Now O'D is the same as OA (the height of the object) and FD is almost equal to f, so

$$\frac{IB}{OA} = \frac{BF}{f}$$

Notice that ΔOAF is similar to Δ I'EF, so that

$$\frac{I'E}{OA} = \frac{EF}{AF}$$

Now I'E is the same as IB (height of the image) and EF is almost equal to f, so

$$\frac{IB}{OA} = \frac{f}{AF}$$ **(2)**

Combining equations (1) and (2),

$$\frac{BF}{f} = \frac{f}{AF}$$ **(3)**

Now image distance $d_i = BF + f$, and object distance $d_o = AF + f$, so we can rewrite equation (3) like this:

$$\frac{d_i - f}{f} = \frac{f}{d_o - f}$$

Therefore,

$$(d_i - f)(d_o - f) = f^2, \text{ or}$$

$$d_i d_o - f d_o - f d_i + f^2 = f^2, \text{ or}$$

$$d_i d_o - f d_o - f d_i = 0$$

Dividing through by $f d_i d_o$ gives

$$\frac{1}{f} - \frac{1}{d_i} - \frac{1}{d_o} = 0$$

This can be re-arranged to read

$$\frac{1}{d_o} + \frac{1}{d_i} = \frac{1}{f}$$

This equation will be referred to as the **mirror equation**.

Sample Problem 7.2.1 — Using the Mirror Equation

A concave mirror has a focal length of 20.0 cm. If an object is 1.00 m in front of the mirror, where will the image form?

What to Think About	How to Do It
1. Determine what is required.	Find image distance.
2. Select and rearrange formula.	$\frac{1}{d_o} + \frac{1}{d_i} = \frac{1}{f}$ so
	$\frac{1}{d_i} = \frac{1}{f} - \frac{1}{d_o}$
3. Solve for image location.	$\frac{1}{d_i} = \frac{1}{20.0 \text{ cm}} - \frac{1}{100.0 \text{ cm}}$
	$\frac{1}{d_i} = \frac{4}{100.0 \text{ cm}}$
	$d_i = 25.0 \text{ cm}$
	The image forms 25.0 cm in front of the mirror.

Practice Problems 7.2.1 — Using the Mirror Equation

1. A real image forms 25.0 cm in front of a concave mirror, which has a focal length of 20.0 cm. How far is the object from the mirror?

2. An image forms in front of a concave mirror at the same distance from the mirror as the object. Solve for the object or the image distance in terms of the focal length, f.

3. What is the focal length of a concave mirror that forms an image on a screen 40.0 cm away when an object is 20.0 cm in front of the mirror?

4. An object is placed 10.0 cm in front of a concave mirror of focal length 15.0 cm. Solve for d_i. Why is the answer negative?

The Ideal Shape for a Concave Mirror

The concave mirrors you have used so far have been either cylindrical (with the ray box) or spherical. These mirrors are relatively inexpensive to manufacture and are adequate for many uses. You probably noticed that they do not focus light precisely.

Parallel rays entering the mirror are converged to a narrow region, but not precisely to a point. There is some aberration. For precision work, as in quality telescopes, aberration must be avoided. The mirror must be shaped perfectly. What is the perfect shape for a concave mirror? In two dimensions, the name of the perfect curve for a concave mirror is a **parabola.** The three-dimensional equivalent of a parabola is called a paraboloid. To visualize what a parabola looks like, imagine a baseball being tossed into the air by a fielder to a catcher.

The path the ball takes is parabolic. Figure 7.2.8 shows what a parabola looks like. Reflecting telescopes use parabolic mirrors. Radio telescopes are also parabolic in shape, but they are much larger than optical telescopes.

Figure 7.2.8 *The shape of a parabola*

Convex or Diverging Mirrors

A convex mirror produces a virtual image that is erect and smaller than the object. Figure 7.2.9 illustrates the reflection of rays off a convex mirror. Note that the rays appear to be converging at the mirror's focal point.

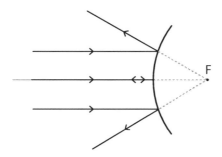

Figure 7.2.9 *Rays reflecting off a convex mirror*

Figure 7.2.10 shows how to find the virtual image in a diverging mirror. Ray 1 is parallel to the principal axis and the reflected ray appears to have come from the focal point. Ray 2 comes from a point on the object and travels toward the focal point. The reflected ray is parallel to the principal axis. The image forms where the rays appear to intersect.

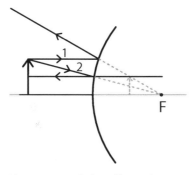

Figure 7.2.10 *A virtual image in a convex mirror*

Investigation 7-2A   An Introduction to Curved Mirrors

Purpose
To observe how light reflects from concave and convex mirrors

Part 1: Convex Mirrors

Procedure
1. Set up a ray box with a five-slit baffle. Adjust the position of the lens of the ray box so that all five beams are parallel. Aim the parallel beams at a cylindrical convex mirror, as shown in Figure 7.2.11.

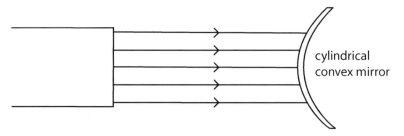

Figure 7.2.11 *Step 1— Convex mirror*

2. Carefully mark the position of one of the incident beams and the reflected beam corresponding to it. Trace the outline of the reflecting surface of the mirror. Remove the mirror. Draw a normal to the mirror at the point of reflection. Measure the angle of incidence and the angle of reflection. Does the reflection resemble what happened at a point on a plane mirror?
3. Obtain a spherical convex mirror from your teacher. Its shape is like a section of a sphere. Look into the mirror and describe the image you see. Is it right side up or inverted? Is it larger than your face, smaller, or the same size?

Concluding Questions
1. Why is a convex mirror called a diverging mirror?
2. Why does a convex mirror give a wide-angle view when you look at it?
3. Describe the nature of the image you see in a diverging mirror. Is it real or virtual? Enlarged or smaller? Erect or inverted?
4. What would *you* look like in a tall, vertical mirror shaped like a cylinder?

Part 2 Concave Mirrors

Procedure
1. Aim the five parallel beams from your ray box at a cylindrical concave mirror, as shown in Figure 7.2.12. Sketch the incident and reflected beams.

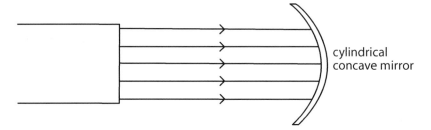

Figure 7.2.12 *Step 1 — Concave mirror*

2. Block the light from the outermost beams coming from the ray box, so that only the middle part of the cylindrical mirror is being used. Do you notice an improvement in the focussing? (Is the focussed light concentrated in a smaller area than before?) Sketch the incident and reflected beams again.
3. Measure the distance from the vertex or geometric centre of the concave mirror to the point where the light comes together on the axis of the mirror. This distance is called the focal length (*f*) of the mirror.

Concluding Questions
1. Why is a concave mirror called a converging mirror?
2. Why are concave mirrors used in some telescopes?
3. Does a cylindrical mirror focus *all* the incoming parallel beams of light to a single point? Discuss.

Part 3: Finding the Focal Length of a Spherical Concave Mirror

Procedure
1. Set up your spherical concave mirror on an optical bench so that it faces a small light source, such as the bulb from an opened ray box or a candle flame, which is at least 5 m away. See Figure 7.2.13. The rays of light coming from a small, distant source will be very close to being parallel. Wherever they converge in front of the mirror will be very, very close to being the focal point. If the focal point is on the principal axis of the mirror, it will be the principal focus. The distance from the vertex of the mirror to the principal focus is the focal length of your mirror.

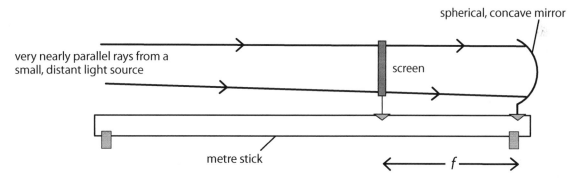

Figure 7.2.13 *Step 1 — Finding the focal length*

2. To see where the light from the distant source focuses, you will need a screen. Since you do not want to block the light coming into the mirror completely, cut a strip of file card about 1 cm wide and mount it in a screen holder in front of the concave mirror. Move the screen back and forth in front of the mirror until you see a sharply focussed, very small image of the distant light source. If the light source is sufficiently far away and small, the image you see will be, for practical purposes, a point. The distance from the vertex of the mirror to this point is the focal length of your mirror.
3. For future investigations, you will need to know the focal length of a spherical concave mirror. It is important to measure the focal length of your mirror carefully and label the mirror so that you use the same one later. Record the focal length on a small piece of masking tape on the side of the mirror.

Concluding Questions
1. If you placed the light source closer to the mirror (say 1.5 m), would the light from the source come to a focus? Would it converge at the principal focus? Discuss.
2. Why is it important to use a distant light source when you are trying to measure the focal length of a concave mirror?

Investigation 7-2B   Locating Images in Concave Mirrors

Purpose

To locate images formed by a concave mirror

Procedure

1. Mount your concave mirror at the far end of your optical bench or metre stick. Measure off a distance equal to the focal length of your mirror and mark the position of the principal focus on your metre stick with an F written on masking tape. At a distance equal to two focal lengths (2f), write a letter C on the tape.
2. Place a suitable object, such as a small candle or a miniature light bulb, at the other end of the metre stick or optical bench. The object distance d_o will be greater than 2f. Locate the image by moving a thin white card back and forth in front of the mirror until you see the image of the object in sharp focus. Measure the distance from the vertex of the mirror to (a) the object (d_o) and (b) the image (d_i). Record these distances.

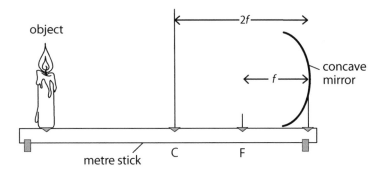

Figure 7.2.14 *Step 1 — Locating an image in a concave mirror*

3. Try a second object position at a distance greater than 2f. Locate the image and object and measure d_o and d_i.
4. Place the object at a distance of 2f from the mirror. Locate the image and measure d_o and d_i.
5. Place the object at a distance of approximately 1.5f from the mirror. Locate the image and measure d_o and d_i.
6. Place the object at the focal point F. Can you use this set-up to make a spotlight? If so, how would you do it?
7. Place the object at a distance less than f from the mirror. Can you form a real image? Look directly into the mirror. Can you see a virtual image? Describe the image.

Concluding Questions

1. Draw ray diagrams showing where and why the real images formed when the object was at these distances:
    (a) >2f,   (b) 2f,   (c) 1.5f,   (d) f.
2. If this concave mirror is being used as an astronomical telescope, where will the image form?
3. If the mirror is being used in an automobile headlight or in a spotlight, where will you place the object?
4. Why is it difficult to obtain a good image of the object when it is at F?
5. In general, what object distance range will give a real image?
6.   In general, what object distance range will give a virtual image?

7.2 Review Questions

1. What is the difference between a convex and concave mirror?

2. What is the difference between a diverging and converging mirror?

3. Which type of mirror makes the image smaller than real life?

4. Which type of mirror would you use for the following situations? Explain your answer.
   (a) make-up or shaving

   (b) security mirror in a store

   (c) clothes store

5. Match the following terms with the correct definition

   ___ Principal axis   A. The geometric centre of the curved mirror

   ___ Vertex   B. The point that represents the centre of the sphere from which the mirror was cut

   ___ Focal point   C. The distance between the focal point and the vertex

   ___ Centre of curvature   D. The distance between the centre of curvature and the mirror

   ___ Radius of curvature   E. An imaginary line drawn from the vertex and perpendicular to the curved mirror at that point

   ___ Focal length   F. Where light rays parallel to the principal axis converge after being reflected

6. For converging mirrors, describe the image characteristics for the following object positions.

Object Position	Image Characteristics
(a) Far away	
(b) Outside centre of curvature	
(c) At the centre of curvature	
(d) Between the focal point and centre of curvature	
(e) At the focal point	
(f) Between focal point and vertex	

7. Draw the ray diagrams for the following concave mirrors:
   (a) Object is more than two focal lengths away from the mirror

   (b) Object is between one and two focal lengths.

   (c) Object is at focal point.

   (d) Object is between mirror and focal point.

8. What shape of "trick" mirror would make:

   (a) A thin person look larger? _____

   (b) A large person look thinner? _____

   (c) A tall person look shorter? _____

   (d) A short person look taller? _____

9. On the diagram below, use two rays to show where the image of the arrow will be.

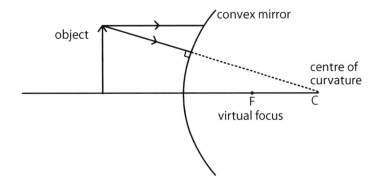

10. (a) Can a convex mirror form a real image? Explain your answer with a ray diagram.

(b) Can a convex mirror form an enlarged image? Explain your answer with a ray diagram.

Challenge

1. The commercially available double concave mirror shown here is called a Mirage. It creates a very realistic image at the opening of the top mirror. Is this image real or is it virtual? On a separate sheet of paper, draw a ray diagram to explain why the image forms where it does.

7.3 Refraction of Light

Refraction

A hand magnifier lens can make the Sun's rays converge to a small area on a piece of paper (Figure 7.3.1). It is possible to ignite paper this way. Why does the light converge or come together? The property of light involved here is called **refraction.** Refraction occurs when light travels from one medium such as air into another medium such as glass. The change in direction of the light at the boundary of the two media is called refraction. The bend is due to the change in the speed of light. Light travels slower through different materials or media. ("Media" is the plural of "medium.") The slower the light entering a medium, the greater the bend the light will make.

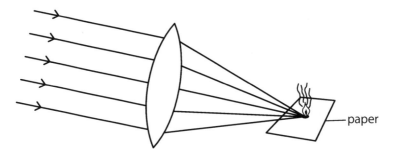

Figure 7.3.1 *Light refracted through a hand lens converges on a point that becomes so hot, it sets the paper on fire.*

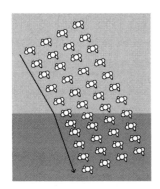

Figure 7.3.2 *Lines of soldiers bend as they move from one medium (pavement) to another (mud).*

To understand what causes refraction, imagine rows of soldiers marching side by side down a paved road. This is the first medium. There are many rows of soldiers one behind the other. Think of the first row of soldiers as a wavefront. The soldiers one behind the other form lines (Figure 7.3.2). The soldiers veer off the road at an angle toward a muddy field. This is the second medium. As soon as the first soldiers in the wavefront, reach the muddy field, each soldier in turn is slowed down, but tries to remain in step with adjacent soldiers. The wavefront is therefore refracted as it enters the slower medium. When the wavefront leaves the muddy field, the process is reversed, and the wavefront returns to its original direction.

Refractive Index

As the light enters a medium like glass it will bend. How much light bends depends on the **refractive index** of the medium in which the light travels. The refractive index of a medium is given the symbol n. It is calculated by dividing the speed of light in a vacuum by the speed of light in a medium:

$$n = \frac{\text{speed of light in a vacuum}}{\text{speed of light in a medium}} = \frac{c}{v}$$

Table 7.3.1 *Indices of Refraction*

Medium	Index of Refraction
Water at 20°C	1.333
Diamond	2.42
Glass	1.5–1.9 (depends on composition)
Air	1.00029
Quartz crystal	1.54

Table 7.3.1 lists some indices of refraction. For water, the index of refraction is 1.33, or approximately 4/3. For glass, the index of refraction is approximately 3/2. Different kinds of glass have slightly different indices of refraction. The index of refraction depends on the colour wavelength of light used and on the purity, temperature and composition of the material into which the light is travelling.

Notice that the index of refraction of air is very close to 1. In other words, there is very little refraction when light travels from a vacuum (as in space) into air. Also, this means that the indices of refraction for light travelling from air into other media will be essentially the same as for light travelling from a vacuum into the same media.

Generally, when light passes from a medium of low refractive index to one of higher refractive index, the light bends toward the normal. When light passes from a medium of higher refractive index to one of lower refractive index, the light bends away from the normal.

Snell's Law of Refraction

Figure 7.3.3 shows a ray of light travelling from a vacuum into a medium such as glass. The ray refracts toward the normal. The incident ray is labelled AO and the refracted ray is OC. In the diagram, AO and OC are radii of the same circle; therefore they are equal in length. AB is the distance of the incident ray from the normal, and CD is the distance of the refracted ray from the normal. The angle of incidence is θ_i; the angle of refraction is θ_r.

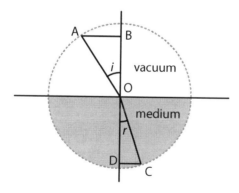

Figure 7.3.3 *A ray of light refracts as it moves from a vacuum to a medium (glass).*

The two triangles ABO and CDO are right-angled triangles. In these two triangles, trigonometry tells us that

$$\sin \theta_i = \frac{AB}{OA} \text{ and } \sin \theta_r = \frac{CD}{OC} = \frac{CD}{OA}$$

Dutch mathematician Willebrord Snell (1591–1626) discovered that there was an exact relationship between the angle of incidence and the angle of refraction for light travelling from one medium into another. Recall that for small angles, the angle of incidence was equal to the angle of refraction or vice versa. Snell was able to show that there was a relationship that was true for all angles greater than 0°.

In Figure 7.3.3, $\dfrac{\frac{AB}{OA}}{\frac{CD}{OC}} = \dfrac{\sin \theta_i}{\sin \theta_r} = n$ where n is a constant for a given medium.

It is called the index of refraction of the medium into which the light is moving from a vacuum.

Snell's law looks like this for light going from a vacuum into any medium:

$$\dfrac{\sin \theta_i}{\sin \theta_r} = n$$

where n is the index of refraction of the medium into which the light is moving. The general form of Snell's law accounts for two media where n_1 is the incident medium and n_2 is the refracting medium.

$$\dfrac{\sin \theta_i}{\sin \theta_r} = \dfrac{n_2}{n_1}$$

$$n_1 \sin \theta_i = n_2 \sin \theta_r$$

Quick Check

1. Light entering a block of glass at an angle of incidence of 18.5° leaves the boundary between the air and the glass at an angle of 12.0°. What is the index of refraction of this type of glass?

$$n_r = \frac{n_1 \sin \theta_i}{\sin \theta_r} = \frac{1 \sin 18.5}{\sin 12.0}$$
$$= \boxed{1.53}$$

2. Light is incident on a diamond at an angle of 10.0°. At what angle will it refract?

$$n_r \sin \theta_r = n_i \sin \theta_i$$
$$2.42 \sin \theta_r = 1 \sin 10°$$
$$= \frac{0.17}{2.42} = 0.071$$

3. A beam of light is incident on a sheet of glass in a window at an angle of 30°. Describe exactly what path the light beam will take
   (a) as it enters the glass.

   (b) as it leaves the other side of the glass. Assume $n = 1.500$.

4. What optical device is designed specifically to separate the colours in "white light" using the fact that different wavelengths (colours) have different indices of refraction in glass? Which colour refracts most?

Using Snell's Law to Calculate the Critical Angle

You can increase the angle of incidence of the light going from water into air until you can no longer observe refraction. The smallest angle at which you can observe no refraction and only reflection is called the critical angle (θ_{i_c}). At angles equal to or greater than the critical angle, the water-air boundary acts as a perfect mirror. At any angle equal to or greater than the critical angle, all light coming from the water will reflect back into the water. This is called total internal reflection. At incident angles less than the critical angle, refraction and weak reflection can both be observed.

In Figure 7.3.4, if a ray of light is coming from air into water, Snell's law might be applied:

$$\frac{\sin \theta_i}{\sin \theta_r} = n_w \text{ where } n_w \text{ is the index of refraction of water.}$$

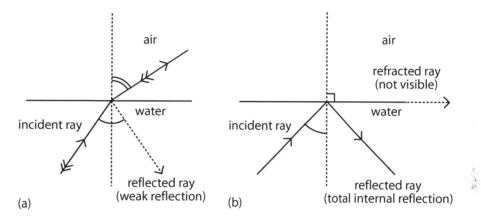

Figure 7.3.4 (a) *The incident ray reaches the water's surface at less than θ_{i_c} so it passes into the air;* **(b)** *The incident ray reaches the water's surface at the θ_{i_c} so it is reflected back.*

For angles less than the critical angle, the path of light is reversible. For a ray of light coming from water out into air, what was the incident angle now becomes the angle of refraction and vice versa. For light going from water out into air:

$$\frac{\sin \theta_i}{\sin \theta_r} = \frac{1}{n_w}$$

Consider what happens as the incident angle approaches the critical angle, θ_{i_c} (Figure 7.3.4). The angle of refraction approaches 90°. Just as the critical angle is approached, we can write:

$$\frac{\sin \theta_{i_c}}{\sin 90°} = \frac{1}{n_w}$$

where n_w is the index of refraction for light coming from air into water.

Solving for the critical angle, sin 90° = 1.0000 so:

$$\sin \theta_{i_c} = \frac{(1)(1.000)}{n_w} = \frac{1.000}{1.33} = 0.750$$

$$\text{and } \theta_{i_c} = 48.6°$$

The critical angle for water is therefore 48.6°.

Quick Check

1. Calculate the critical angle for diamond, which has an index of refraction of 2.42.

$$\sin \theta_{in} = \frac{1}{2.42}$$
$$= 0.413 \quad \sin^{-1}(0.413) = 24.4°$$

2. What is the critical angle for a glass that has an index of refraction of 1.500?

3. A certain material has a critical angle of 52.0°. What is its index of refraction?

The Rainbow — Dispersion by Raindrops

If you have ever looked at a rainbow carefully, you probably have noticed these conditions prevailed:

- The Sun was behind you.
- There were rain clouds in the sky in front of you.
- The rainbow forms an arc of a circle.
- In the primary bow (the brightest one), red is at the top and violet at the bottom.
- In the secondary bow, if it is visible, the colours are in reverse order.

Figure 7.3.5(a) illustrates what happens inside the raindrops. White light from the Sun refracts as it enters a drop. The white light is dispersed into component colours during the refraction. All colours of light experience internal reflection at the back of the drop. They are then refracted again and further dispersed as they leave the drop at the "front."

When you see a rainbow, you see the dispersive effects of millions of drops of water, not just one or two! You see red at the top of the primary bow with all the other rainbow colours below, ending in violet.

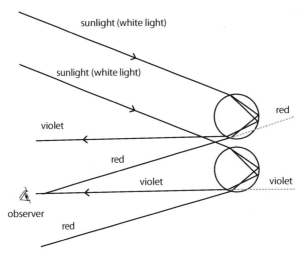

Figure 7.3.5 (a) *A primary rainbow: The red part of the rainbow is 42° from the "axis" of the bow; violet is 40° from the "axis."*

Sometimes a secondary, fainter rainbow may be seen above the primary rainbow. A secondary rainbow has the colours in reverse order. Figure 7.3.5(b) shows the double internal reflection that happens inside droplets producing a secondary rainbow.

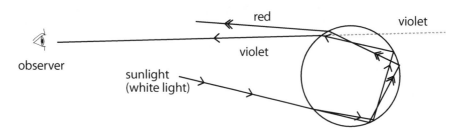

Figure 7.3.5 (b) *A secondary rainbow: The reversed colours of the secondary (higher) rainbow are due to double reflection of the Sun's light within the droplets.*

Wave Speed and Index of Refraction (Enrichment)

Proof That the Index of Refraction $n = \dfrac{v_1}{v_2}$

Consider a wavefront (labelled Aa in Figure 7.3.6) arriving at the boundary between two media. Medium 2 is one in which light slows down from speed v_1 to speed v_2. In the time t it takes for the wavefront at end A to reach the boundary B, the wavefront in medium 1 travels a distance AB, which equals $v_1 t$.

In the same time t, end a of the wavefront travels a distance ab inside medium 2. The distance ab equals $v_2 t$.

In Figure 7.3.6, you will notice that $\sin \theta_i = AB/aB$ and $\sin \theta_r = ab/aB$. Therefore the index of refraction, n, is equal to

$$n = \frac{\sin \theta_i}{\sin \theta_r} = \frac{AB/aB}{ab/aB} = \frac{AB}{ab} = \frac{v_1 t}{v_2 t} = \frac{v_1}{v_2}$$

Therefore, the index of refraction is equal to the ratio of the speeds of light in the two media:

$$n = \frac{v_1}{v_2}$$

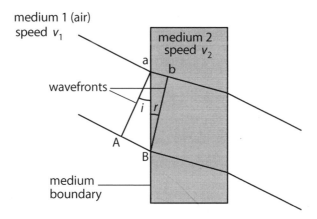

Figure 7.3.6 *As a wavefront moves from one medium to the next, it changes speed.*

When a beam of light of wavelength λ_1 enters a medium in which its speed is reduced from v_1 to v_2, its wavelength is reduced to λ_2 and the beam is refracted as in Figure 7.3.7. When the waves leave the "slow" medium, the speed is returned to the original v_1 and the wavelength is again λ_1. Refraction of a beam entering the second medium at an angle greater than 0° is caused by the change in speed of the waves.

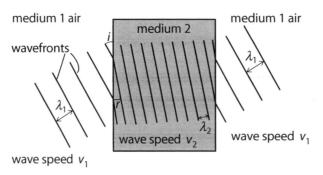

Figure 7.3.7 *Wavelength changes as the waves move through the different media.*

Recall that, for water, the index of refraction is 1.33. Snell's law applied to light entering water from a vacuum (or air) says that $\dfrac{\sin \theta_i}{\sin \theta_r} = 1.33$.

The speed of light in air is 3.00×10^8 m/s.
The speed of light in water is 2.25×10^8 m/s.
The *ratio* of the speed of light in air to the speed of light in water is

$$\frac{3.00 \times 10^8 \text{ m/s}}{2.25 \times 10^8 \text{ m/s}} = 1.33$$

Note that the ratio of the speeds is equal to the index of refraction for water. This relationship holds for other media as well. In general,

$$\frac{\sin \theta_i}{\sin \theta_r} = n = \frac{v_1}{v_2}$$

You will notice that the angle of incidence in Figure 7.3.7 is shown as the angle between the incident wavefront and the boundary between the two media. Also, the angle of refraction is shown as the angle between the refracted wavefront and the boundary between the media. When you do Investigation 7-3A, the angle of incidence will be taken as the angle between the incident ray and the normal. The angle of refraction will be defined as the angle between the refracted ray and the normal.

In Figure 7.3.8, lines have been drawn showing the paths taken by a single point on a wavefront as it moves into and out of the second medium. These lines, in effect, are identical with the incident ray and the refracted ray used in Investigation 7A. A little geometry will convince you that the incident angle (θ_i) in Figure 7.3.8 is equal to the incident angle i in Figure 7.3.7. Likewise, the angle of refraction (θ_r) is the same in both diagrams.

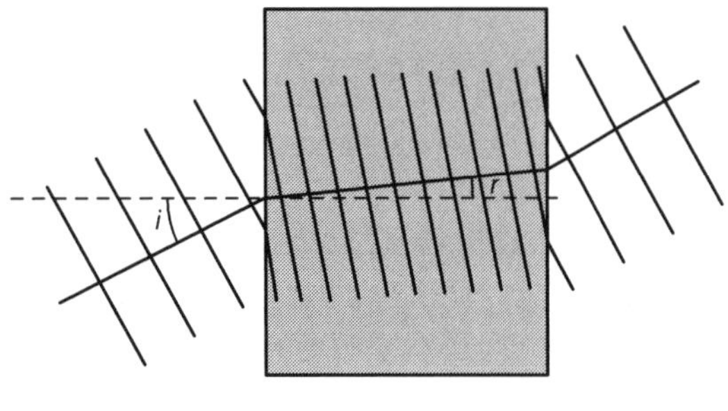

Figure 7.3.8 *The lines show the paths taken by a single point on a wavefront.*

Investigation 7-3A   Refraction of Light in Water

Purpose
To observe refraction of light travelling from air into water and glass or Plexiglas

Procedure

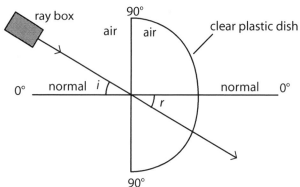

Figure 7.3.9 *Step 1 — Refraction of light in water*

1. Set up the clear plastic semi-cylindrical dish as in Figure 7.3.9. The centre of the flat side should be located on a normal drawn on a sheet of polar coordinate graph paper, as in the figure.
2. Turn off the room lights. Aim a narrow beam of light from a ray box along a line at an angle of 30° to the normal, so that it arrives at the centre of the flat side of the plastic dish. The beam should pass through the thin-walled dish without any noticeable deflection.
3. Pour approximately 100 mL of water into the dish. If available, use water that has a grain or two of Fluorescein dye in it to improve the visibility of the beam in the water. Observe the path of the beam of light now that there is water in the dish. Record the angle formed by the refracted beam and the normal. This is called the angle of refraction (θ_r). Also, record the angle of incidence (θ_i), which is the angle formed between the incident beam and the normal.
4. Experiment by slowly changing the angle of incidence from 0° to 90° in small steps. Is the angle of incidence larger or smaller than the angle of refraction? What happens at 0°? at 90°? Does light entering water from air bend toward the normal or away from the normal? Where does the bending occur?
5. You are now ready to do some serious measuring of angles of incidence and angles of refraction. For each angle of incidence in Table 7.3.2, measure as precisely as you can and record the corresponding angle of refraction.

Table 7.3.2 *Data for Investigation 7-3A*

Angle of Incidence (θ_i)	0°	10°	20°	30°	40°	50°	60°	70°
Angle of Refraction (θ_r)								

6. Plot a graph with the angle of incidence (θ_i) on the *y*-axis and the angle of refraction (θ_r) on the *x*-axis. These data will be used again later.
7. Repeat Procedure steps 1 to 6, but this time replace the dish of water with a Plexiglas or glass semi-cylinder.
8. Use your data from Part A to plot a graph of the sine of the angle of incidence against the sine of the angle of refraction for (a) water and (b) Plexiglas (glass). Determine the indices of refraction (*n*) of both materials from the slopes of the graphs.

Concluding Questions

1. Describe what happens to a beam of light when it enters water or Plexiglas from air.
2. Find the slope of the *straight* part of each graph. What units would this slope have? What relationship exists between the angles of incidence and the angles of refraction for the angles where the graph is straight? Which refracts light more, water or Plexiglas (glass)?
3. Is the refraction of light similar in any way(s) to the refraction of water waves? Discuss.

Investigation 7-3B   Internal Reflection and Critical Angle

Purpose
To observe what happens to light coming from a medium of higher index of refraction into a medium of lower index of refraction, and to find out the necessary condition for total internal reflection of light

Procedure
1. You will use the plastic dish full of water that you used in Investigation 7-3A, but this time you will observe what happens when the light travels from water out into the air. Set up the equipment as in Figure 7.3.10.

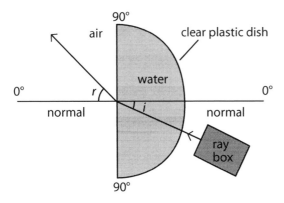

Figure 7.3.10 *Step 1 — Internal reflection and critical angle*

2. Examine your data table from Investigation 7-3A. Shine light through the round side of the dish so that it passes through the water. You want it to hit the centre of the flat side of the dish at angles of incidence that are the same as the angles of refraction in Investigation 7-3A. Is the path of light reversible for some of the angles? Is it reversible for all the angles?
3. Gradually increase the angle of incidence of the light going from water into air until you can no longer observe refraction. What is the smallest angle at which you can observe no refraction and only reflection? This angle is called the critical angle (θ_{i_c}) for water. Record this angle. At incident angles less than the critical angle, refraction and weak reflection can both be observed.
4. Repeat Procedure steps 1 to 3 using the Plexiglas (glass) semi-cylinder. What is the critical angle for Plexiglas (glass)?

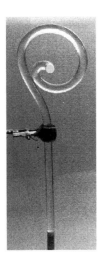

Concluding Questions
1. What is the critical angle for
    (a) water?
    (b) Plexiglas (glass)?
2. Sketch how light can be made to travel by total internal reflection through the curved plastic "optical pipe" in Figure 7.3.11.

Figure 7.3.11 *An optical pipe*

Investigation 7-3C Polarization

Purpose

To observe examples of polarized waves

Procedure

1. You can produce your own polarized waves quite easily. Have your lab partner hold one end of a long spring while you set it vibrating by moving it up and down until you get a wave pattern set up in the spring (Figure 7.3.12). The waves you are producing are vertically polarized. Notice that the waves are transverse waves. You can just as easily produce horizontally polarized waves by making the spring vibrate horizontally. **Polarized** waves all move in the same direction.

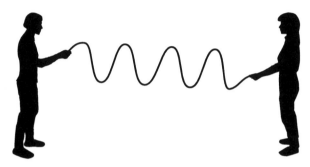

Figure 7.3.12 *Step 1 — Making polarized waves*

Light waves can be polarized. Light waves are electromagnetic waves, which means that electric and magnetic fields are involved. Details of the nature of polarized light must be left to later physics courses, but it is still possible to observe some of the *effects* of polarized light, using readily available materials.

Polarizing filters are specially made glass or plastic filters designed polarize light. For example, some sunglasses have polarized lenses. Figure 7.3.13 illustrates one model of how a polarizing filter works. In this case, the "filter" consists of the vertical posts on the back of a kitchen chair. These permit vertically polarized "waves" to go through, but not horizontally polarized waves.

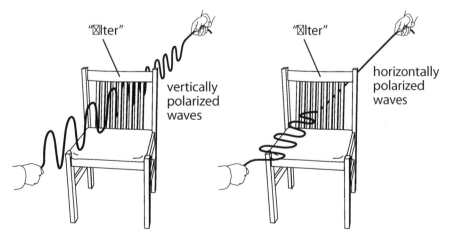

Figure 7.3.13 *A model of how a polarizing filter works*

2. (a) Place a small sheet of polarizing filter material on the overhead projector stage. The light that passes through this filter will be polarized one way or another.
    (b) Place a second sheet on the overhead projector stage, and let part of it overlap the first sheet (Figure 7.3.14). Rotate either one of the sheets slowly through a full circle. Sketch what you observe happening.

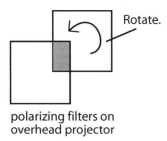

Rotate.

polarizing filters on overhead projector

Figure 7.3.14 *Step 2 — Polarization*

3. Look out the window at the sky through a polarizing filter. **Caution! Do not stare at the Sun!** Rotate the filter through a full circle. Can you find an alignment that makes the blue sky darker and the clouds whiter than usual? Can you find an alignment that makes a roadway seem to have less glare?

> Glass windows, water surfaces, and roadways produce a glare, due to the reflection of light from these surfaces. The light reflecting from roads, windows, and water surfaces is generally polarized *horizontally*. Sunglasses with polarized lenses have filtering material inserted so that it lets vertically polarized light through but *not* horizontally polarized light. This is why these sunglasses reduce glare from these surfaces.

4. Write the letter "e" on a sheet of plain white paper. Place a calcite crystal over the letter. The light passing through the calcite crystal is refracted in two different planes. This is called double refraction. Find out if the calcite crystal polarizes the light coming through the calcite. Hold a sheet of polarizing filter between the crystal and your eye. Rotate the filter slowly through a full circle. Observe what happens and record what you see.
5. Place a drop of copper (II) sulfate (bluestone) solution on a microscope slide. Allow the water to evaporate so that small crystals of copper (II) sulfate form. Place the slide on the stage of a microscope. Hold one sheet of polarizing filter below the objective lens and one piece of polarizing filter between the eyepiece lens and your eye. Slowly rotate one or the other of the filters. You should see some interesting colour effects. These are caused by a combination of polarization and interference of light waves.
6. Place a sheet of polarizing filter on the stage of an overhead projector. On top of it, place a tall jar or beaker of clear corn syrup. Look down at the corn syrup through a second sheet of polarizing filter. Rotate the second filter slowly through 90°.

Concluding Questions
1. Why is polarization considered good evidence that light consists of waves rather than particles?
2. Why are the polarizing filters in sunglasses arranged to transmit only vertically polarized light?
3. When photographing a water surface, a photographer may use a polarizing filter. Why would this improve the picture?
4. Does a calcite crystal act as a polarizing filter? Explain.

7.3   Review Questions

1. Why can't the fisher in the drawing below see the specific ray shown coming from the fish? Can she see the fish at all?

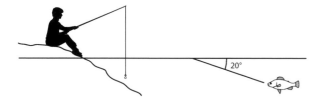

20°

2. (a) The fisher wants to spear the fish in the drawing below.

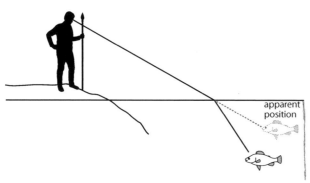

apparent position

Where should he aim? Circle one and use a diagram to explain your answer below.
(i)   at the apparent position of the fish
(ii)   above the fish
(iii) below the fish

(b) A high tech fisherman wants to zap the fish with a laser. Should she aim the laser at the fish, below the fish, or above the fish? Explain.

at the fish

3. Why can you see more than one image in a mirror made with very thick glass? Use a simple sketch to illustrate the effects of internal reflection within the glass of the mirror.

4. What is the critical angle of a glass, if its index of refraction is 1.58?

5. Light of frequency 5.00×10^{14} Hz is emitted by a laser. If light speed is 3.00×10^8 m/s, what is the wavelength of the light, in nanometres?

6. Light speed in a vacuum is 3.00×10^8 m/s. How fast does light travel in diamond, if the index of refraction of diamond is 2.42?

$$n = \frac{c}{v} \qquad 2.42 = \frac{3 \times 10^8}{v}$$

$$= 1.24 \times 10^8 \text{ m/s}$$

7. Show that, in general, for light travelling from a medium with index of refraction n_1 into a medium with index of refraction n_2, $n_1 \sin \theta_i = n_2 \sin \theta_r$.

8. When we say that the index of refraction of water is 1.33, what qualifiers should we add to this statement?

9. (a) What three phenomena are involved in the production of a rainbow?

   (b) Under what conditions will you see a rainbow?

   (c) What are the colours in the primary rainbow, listed from the top of the bow and going down?

10. In a vacuum, which colour of light travels fastest — red, blue, or green? Explain. Which colour travels fastest in a block of glass?

11. The index of refraction of a certain type of glass is 1.50. What is the speed of light in glass? (The speed of light is 3.0×10^8 m/s in air.)

12. Light travels with a speed of 1.95×10^8 m/s in a quartz crystal. What is the index of refraction of the quartz crystal?

13. Brain buster: A laser sends red light of wavelength 650 nm from air into water in a swimming pool. The index of refraction of the water is 1.33.
    (a) What wavelength will the light have in the water?

    (b) What colour would light of this wavelength appear if it were in air?

    (c) Why does a swimmer under the water see the light as red?

Brain Stretch
Use the Internet to find answers to the following questions.
1. Why do diamonds sparkle?
2. How is the science of fibre optics used to transmit telephone signals?
3. How does the refraction of light lengthen your day by several minutes?
4. What causes a mirage?
5. Why does a swimming pool never look as deep as it really is?
6. How can an expert quickly tell the difference between a real diamond and a fake diamond made of glass?
7. Why do some restaurants use thick-walled glasses to serve their soda pop drinks?

7.4 Optics

Warm Up

Your teacher will give you one or two lenses. Move them so this text becomes as clear as possible. Copy the image you observe through the lens and describe its characteristics. Why is it different from what you normally see?

Lenses

The word **lens** comes from a Latin word meaning *lentil,* perhaps because of the resemblance of the shape of a lens to the shape of that tiny bean.

Lenses are among the most common applications of physics you will encounter in everyday life. In addition to the lenses in your own eyes, you may wear glasses as well. Lenses are found in all kinds of projectors, in binoculars, telescopes, microscopes, photocopiers, and hand magnifiers.

Types of Lenses

Lenses come in various shapes and sizes. There are two basic types of lens, one concave and the other convex. A concave or diverging lens made of glass will cause incoming parallel rays of light to diverge or spread out. A convex or converging lens made of glass will cause incoming parallel rays to converge. Each of the lenses in Figure 7.4.1 can be given a descriptive name. See if you can figure out the reason behind each name. The prefix "plano" means flat.

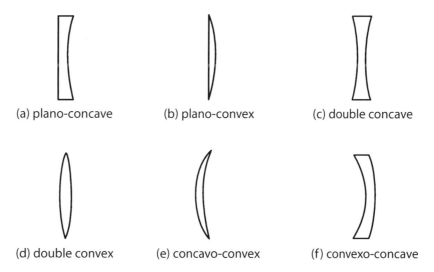

(a) plano-concave   (b) plano-convex   (c) double concave

(d) double convex   (e) concavo-convex   (f) convexo-concave

Figure 7.4.1 *The different shapes of lenses have different uses.*

The Terminology of Lenses

A **double convex lens**, like the one in the simple camera in Figure 7.4.2, has two spherical surfaces. For each surface, there is a **centre of curvature** (C_1 and C_2). For a symmetrical lens, the **radius of curvature** (OC_1 or OC_2) would be the same on both sides of the lens. The line passing through C_1, O, and C_2 is the **principal axis** of the lens.

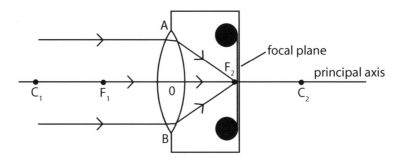

Figure 7.4.2 *A double convex lens*

The lens is shaped so that parallel rays from a very distant source will refract and converge to a **focal point**. If the focal point is on the principal axis, it is called the **principal focus**. The lens has two principal foci, labelled F_1 and F_2. Sometimes these foci are called the primary and secondary focus.

In Figure 7.4.2, film or digital sensor is located at the **focal plane** of the lens. A photograph of an object that is very far away will be in focus on the focal plane. For every point on the *object*, light will focus at a corresponding point on the *image* or photograph, which is on the focal plane.

The diameter of the lens is called the aperture. In adjustable cameras, the aperture can be changed to suit different lighting conditions or for special effects desired by the photographer. The size of the aperture is expressed as a fraction of the **focal length**, *f*, of the lens. The focal length is the distance from the middle of the lens (O) to the principal focus (F).

Typical apertures on an adjustable camera are: f/22, f/16, f/11, f/8, f/5.6, f/3.5, and so on. The smallest opening of this group is f/22. The aperture is only 1/22 times the focal length. On a dull day or in a low-light situation, the photographer might want to use an aperture of f/2.8, where the aperture is 1/2.8 times the focal length. In addition to varying the aperture of the lens, a photographer can control how much light reaches the film during an exposure by adjusting the shutter speed.

Predicting Where Images Will Form on Thin Lenses

You can predict where a lens will form an image if you know the focal length of the lens. In the diagrams in Table 7.4.1, F_2 is the principal focus and F_1 is the secondary focus. The three statements and their diagrams in the table are helpful in predicting where the image will form.

Table 7.4.1 *Information for Predicting the Formation of Images in Lenses*

Description	Converging Lens	Diverging Lens
1. Rays arriving at a converging lens parallel to the principal axis will converge at the principal focus of the lens. For a diverging lens, they will appear to come from the secondary focal point.	(a)	(d)
2. Rays passing through the secondary focus in a converging lens will be parallel to the principal axis after leaving the lens. For a diverging lens, the ray will appear to travel through the principal focus but will exit the lens parallel to the principal axis.	(b)	(e)
3. A ray passing through the centre of both types of thin lens will go through approximately straight.	(c)	(f)

Note that the rays in Table 7.4.1 are drawn as if they refracted at the centre of the lens. This is just a useful simplification. The refraction actually occurs at both the air-glass

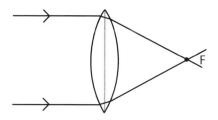

(a) *Refraction really occurs at the air-glass boundaries, like this.*

(b) *For simplicity, refracted rays are drawn as if refraction occurs at the middle of the lens.*

Figure 7.4.3 *Where refraction occurs*

Quick Check

1. Using the diagrams in all three rows of Table 7.4.1, determine where the image will form and the characteristics of the image for a converging lens.

2. Using the diagrams in all three rows of Table 7.4.1, determine where the image will form and the characteristics of the image for a diverging lens.

boundaries of the lens as in Figure 7.4.3(a).

The Lens Equation for Thin Lenses

When you need glasses, the optometrist takes careful measurements to determine the lenses you need to improve your vision. The same is true for when engineers are creating a lens for a camera. Important lens measurements include the distance from object to lens, the distance from image to lens, and the focal length of the lens. Figure 7.4.4 illustrates these measurements. AD is the distance from object to lens. DB is the distance

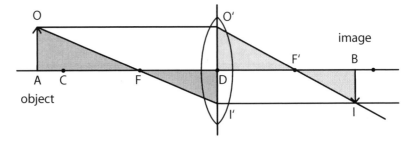

from image to lens. FD is the focal length.
Figure 7.4.4 *Lens measurements*

Sign conventions are used to describe the image formed by different lens. Table 7.4.2 summarizes these conventions.

Table 7.4.2 *Signs and Conventions for Describing images*

+	–
Focal length of converging lens	Focal length of diverging lens
Object and image distance for real objects and images	Object and image distance for virtual objects and images

The following proof gives the lens equation for thin lens. Recall that the location of an image formed by a concave mirror can be predicted using the mirror equation,

$$\frac{1}{d_o} + \frac{1}{d_i} = \frac{1}{f}$$

As you will see in the following proof, the same equation applies to lenses. In Figure 7.4.4, $\triangle IBF'$ is similar to $\triangle O'DF'$, therefore

$$\frac{IB}{O'D} = \frac{BF'}{FD}$$

but O'D = OA and F'D = f,

so

$$\frac{IB}{OA} = \frac{BF}{f} \qquad \textbf{(1)}$$

$\triangle I'DF$ is similar to $\triangle OAF$,

$$\therefore \frac{I'D}{OA} = \frac{DF}{AF}$$

but I'D = IB and DF = f,

so

$$\frac{IB}{OA} = \frac{f}{AF} \qquad \textbf{(2)}$$

Combining equations (1) and (2),

$$\frac{BF'}{FD} = \frac{f}{AF}$$

Therefore

$$\frac{d_i - f}{f} = \frac{f}{d_o - f}$$

$$(d_i - f)(d_o - f) = f^2 \text{, or}$$

$$\therefore d_i d_o - d_o f - d_i f + f^2 = f^2 \text{, or}$$

$$d_i d_o - d_o f - d_i f = 0$$

Dividing by $d_o d_i f$,

$$\frac{1}{f} - \frac{1}{d_i} - \frac{1}{d_o} = 0$$

Rearranging terms, the lens equation becomes

$$\frac{1}{d_o} + \frac{1}{d_i} = \frac{1}{f}$$

Quick Check

1. A convex lens has a focal length of 50.0 mm. How far from the lens will the image form of an object that is 5.00 m away?

$$\frac{1}{f} = \frac{1}{d_o} + \frac{1}{d}$$

$$\frac{1}{50.0 \times 10^{-3}} = \frac{1}{5} + \frac{1}{d} \quad = \quad 20 = 0.2 + \frac{1}{d} \quad \frac{1}{d_i} \boxed{19.8}$$

or $\frac{0.051}{m}$

2. An object is 100.0 mm away from a lens of focal length 50.0 mm. How far from the lens will the image form?

$f = 50.0\,mm$
$d_o = 100.0\,m$
$d_i = ?$

$$\frac{1}{50} = \frac{1}{100} + d \quad = \quad .02 = .01 + d$$

$$\boxed{d_i = 100\,mm}$$

3. A real image forms 60 mm away from a lens when the object is 30 mm from the lens. What is the focal length of the lens?

Optical Instruments

There are many kinds of devices that use lenses and mirrors to assist us to see things better. In this section, we'll look at several optical instruments: the human eye, magnifiers and microscopes, and telescopes and binoculars.

The Eye

The human eyeball is approximately spherical in shape and is kept firm by a jelly-like fluid called the vitreous humour. Light enters the eye through a transparent layer called the cornea (Figure 7.4.5). The cornea has no blood vessels in it and is transparent to light. Notice that the cornea has considerable curvature to it. The cornea is responsible for most of the refraction that produces the image in your eye. The eye lens does the fine focussing.

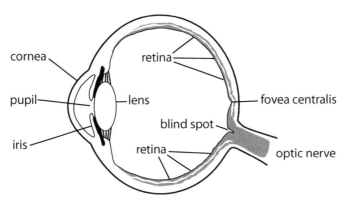

Figure 7.4.5 *Note that the image on the retina is inverted. The brain turns the image right side up.*

When you look into someone's eyes, the coloured portion you see is called the iris. The iris may be brown, green, hazel, blue, or other colours depending on the pigments in it. The colour of your eyes is inherited.

The iris serves a very important function. It contains one set of muscles, which can open the iris, and another set, which can close it. Inner muscles are circular, so when they contract, they make the opening smaller. Outer muscles are radial, so when they contract, they make the opening larger. The iris is very similar to the diaphragm of a variable aperture camera. Many quality cameras mimic the action of the eye, as they vary their aperture according to the amount of light arriving at the lens.

The opening in the iris, called the pupil, looks black but is actually transparent. Most of the light entering the eye is absorbed and does not reflect back out, so the pupil appears to be black. The size of the pupil varies according to how much light the iris detects. Look into your partner's eyes. Ask him or her to cover one eye with a hand. Watch how the pupil of the other eye becomes larger or dilates.

Light passing through the pupil then goes through the lens. The eye lens is not rigid like a camera lens. It is quite elastic and can change its shape! Under normal viewing conditions, the shape of the lens is disc-like and fairly flat, and the lens can easily focus images of distant objects on the retina. When you look at something close to you, the muscles surrounding the lens (ciliary muscles) relax, and the lens becomes more convex (bulged). This shortens its effective focal length and permits focussing of the image of a near object on the retina.

The Retina

The retina of the eye is the innermost layer of the eyeball. It lines the inside of the eyeball, and is made up of millions of light-sensitive nerve cells. One type of nerve cell, the rod, is sensitive to dim light. It is particularly sensitive to variations in intensity or brightness of light. Rods contain a chemical called rhodopsin, which requires vitamin A for its production. If someone suffers from night blindness, he or she will have difficulty adjusting to darkness after encountering the bright headlights of an approaching vehicle. Night blindness indicates a lack of vitamin A in the body.

Another type of nerve cell in the retina is the cone, which is capable of detecting colour. Three kinds of cones detect the three primary light colours (red, blue, and green). Collectively they somehow recognize all the various hues of objects around us. People who suffer from colour blindness have defective cones and cannot recognize all colours. The cones work best in brightly lit conditions. At night, it is very difficult to recognize colours accurately as most objects look grey in faint light.

Two locations on the retina are of special interest. These are shown in Figure 7.4.5. The fovea centralis has cones but no rods. This small, yellowish spot on the retina is especially sensitive to detail. When you read a map or a metre scale, for example, your eye tries to keep the critical detail focussed on the fovea centralis. At the other extreme is the blind spot. This is where the nerve fibres from all the nerve cells in the retina gather and leave the eye as the optic nerve, which transmits impulses to your brain. At this gathering point, there are no rods or cones. This is a blind spot.

For people with normal eyesight, that is how the eye functions. To see properly, light rays entering your eye must focus on the retina. For many people, some change happens to the eye that distorts their vision. This leads to a variety of possible conditions depending on what actually happened. Some common eye effects include farsightedness, nearsightedness, and astigmatism.

Farsightedness (Hypermetropia or Hyperopia)

If the eyeball is too short, rays will tend to focus *behind* the retina instead of on it. This causes farsightedness (Figure 7.4.6). Farsightedness can be corrected with eyeglasses having convex lenses.

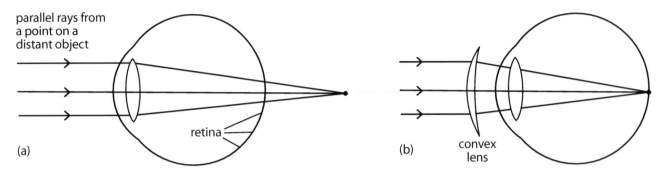

parallel rays from a point on a distant object

retina

(a)

(b) convex lens

Figure 7.4.6 (a) *If you are farsighted, light rays focus behind your retina.* **(b)** *Convex lenses are used to correct farsightedness.*

Nearsightedness (Myopia)

If the eyeball is too long, then light rays from a distant object tend to focus in front *of* the retina, and the image you get will be blurred (Figure 7.4.7). A concave lens can be used to correct this vision defect. The front of the lens is convex, but the back is concave to a degree that the overall effect is the same as a concave lens.

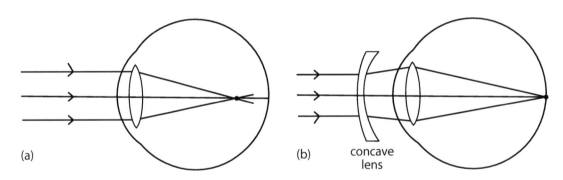

(a)

(b) concave lens

Figure 7.4.7 (a) *If you are nearsighted, light rays focus in front of your retina.* **(b)** *Concave lenses are used to correct nearsightedness.*

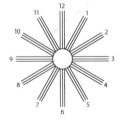

Figure 7.4.8 *This chart can be used to test for astigmatism.*

Astigmatism

If the cornea or the lens of your eye is unevenly curved, light passing through either of the cornea or the lens will be distorted. Part of the object you are looking at will be in focus, while other parts will not be. Eyeglasses can have lenses that correct for this defect. The lenses must be especially shaped to compensate for irregularities in the curvature of your cornea or lens. A chart like the one in Figure 7.4.8 is used to determine whether you have **astigmatism**. If you do, some lines will appear to be sharply in focus, while others are blurred.

The simplest kind of magnifier is a magnifying glass or hand lens, which is a single convex lens. Figure 7.4.9 shows how it works. The object is placed inside the principal focus. Rays from a point on the object diverge as they pass through the lens, so they cannot form a real image. A person looking into the lens, however, sees an enlarged, erect, virtual image of the object.

A crude magnifier can be made from either a drop of water or a rounded blob of glass made by melting some thin glass tubing and letting it solidify into a spherical shape.

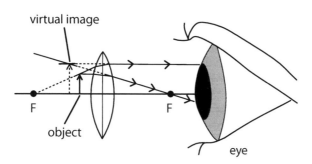

Figure 7.4.9 *A single lens can act as a simple magnifier.*

Compound Microscope

In a compound microscope, there are two lenses. As Figure 7.4.10 shows, the objective lens forms an enlarged real image just inside the principal focus of a second lens, called the eyepiece lens. The real image serves as an object for the eyepiece lens, which acts as a magnifier for the first image. The final image is a virtual image formed by the eyepiece lens of the real image formed by the objective lens. The final image is an inverted image of the object, because the real image was inverted by the objective lens.

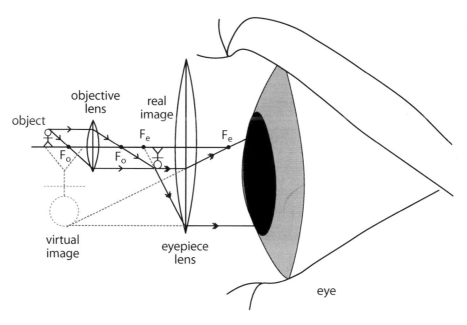

Figure 7.4.10 *In a compound microscope, two lenses work together to create the image you see.*

Telescopes and Binoculars

In the astronomical telescope, the objective lens produces an inverted image that is magnified further by the eyepiece lens (Figure 7.4.11). The final image is virtual and inverted, but in astronomical work this is unimportant.

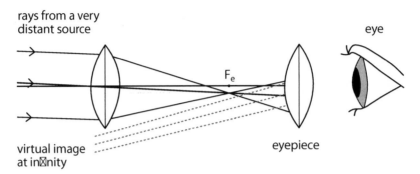

rays from a very distant source

eye

F_e

virtual image at infinity

eyepiece

Figure 7.4.11 *An astronomical telescope produces an inverted image with light from a very distant source.*

In a terrestrial telescope, as used by a birdwatcher or a sea captain, it is important to have an upright image. This can be accomplished by adding a third lens in between the objective and the eyepiece. The objective lens forms an inverted real image. The third lens forms another real image, which is an inverted image of an inverted image. The eyepiece lens then magnifies the second real image. The final image is a virtual, upright image. A pair of binoculars is really two terrestrial telescopes side by side, except that the image is made right side up by using a pair of prisms inside each "telescope" to invert the image laterally and vertically so that the final image is right side up.

Investigation 7-4A   Focussing on Lenses

Purpose

To observe how the property of refraction is used in lenses

Procedure

1. Place a dime in an empty test tube, as in Figure 7.4.12(a). Sketch a circle the size of the dime as you see it when you look straight down the test tube. Now add water to the test tube until it is partially full, as in Figure 7.4.12(b). Draw a circle showing the apparent size of the dime as you see it now. Add more water to the test tube until it is just about overflowing. The top surface will be convex as in Figure 7.4.12(c). Draw a circle to show the apparent size of the dime now.

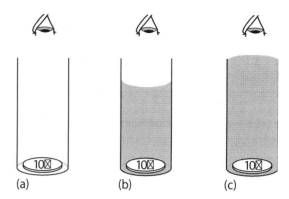

Figure 7.4.12 *Step 1 — Focussing on lenses*

2. Set up your ray box so that parallel beams of light pass through a concave cylindrical lens, as in Figure 7.4.13(a). Sketch how the light refracts as it travels through the concave lens. Do the same with a convex lens, as in Figure 7.4.13(b). Repeat with both lenses together, as in Figure 7.4.13(c). Try separating the two lenses by a centimetre or two.

3. (a) Fill a small Florence flask with water. Use the flask as a magnifying glass to read the writing on this page (Figure 7.4.14(a)).
    (b) Light a candle. Darken the room and use the Florence flask as a slide projector to project an image of the flame on the wall of your classroom (Figure 7.4.14(b)).

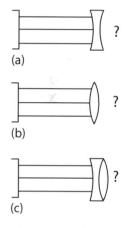

Figure 7.4.13 *Step 2 — Focussing on lenses*

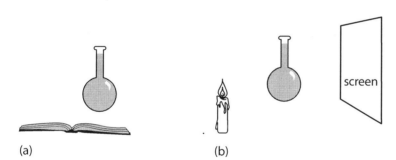

Figure 7.4.14 *Step 3 — Focussing on lenses*

4. Place a water-filled aquarium near a window. Push an empty Florence flask down into the aquarium, as in Figure 7.4.15. Look out the window through the empty flask. Describe the image you see. Now remove the empty flask, fill it with water and look at the same scene through the water-filled flask. Record what you saw in both situations.

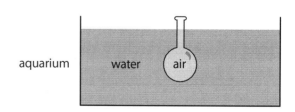

Figure 7.4.15 *Step 4 — Focussing on lenses*

Investigation 7-4B   Locating Images Formed by Convex Lenses

Purpose

Part 1: To predict where images will be formed by a thin convex lens when the object is at different positions on the principal axis

Part 2: To test each prediction by experimenting with a thin convex lens and an optical bench

Part 1

Procedure

1. Using Figures 7.4.16(a) to (e), draw at least two rays in each diagram to predict where the image will form for the object's location.

Concluding Questions

1. The arrangements in Figures 7.4.16(a), (b), and (c) are often used in photography. Which arrangement of object and lens would be used in:
    (a) a camera photographing a distant landscape?
    (b) an enlarger?
    (c) a slide or movie projector?
    (d) an overhead projector?
    (e) a camera that is capable of photographing a ladybug full size?

2. (a) Will you get a real image if you place an object at F, as in Figure 7.4.16(d)?
    (b   What would happen if you placed a small bright light source right at F?

3. (a) Will you get a real image if you place an object between F and the lens, as in Figure 7.4.16(e)?
    (b) Give an example of a situation where you would use this arrangement.

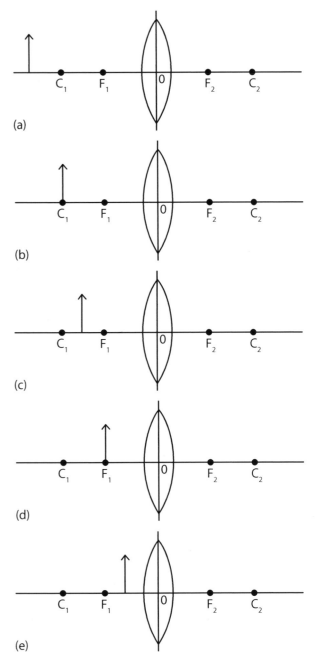

(a)

(b)

(c)

(d)

(e)

Figure 7.4.16 *Part 1: Step 1 — Locating images*

Part 2

You are given a convex lens, a small light source (bulb or candle), and an optical bench. Your job is to set up the apparatus the way it would be in each of the five diagrams in Figure 7.4.16, and to test the predictions you made with your ray diagrams.

Procedure

1. First, measure the focal length of your lens so that you know where to mount the lens in relation to the object. To do this, you need a distant light source so that the rays coming from it are essentially parallel as they arrive at the lens. Note that rays from a source too close will be diverging significantly and will not converge in the focal plane (Figure 7.4.17). Use a light source at least 5 m away. When you have measured the focal length, *f*, record it. The principal focus F of your lens will always be this distance from your lens. The centre of curvature C is twice as far from the lens as the principal focus F is. For example, if your focal length is 25 cm, then the radius of curvature will be 50 cm.

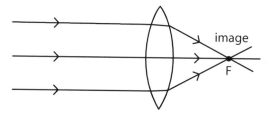 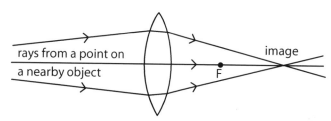

(a) *Parallel rays from a distant source converge at principal focus F.*

(b) *Diverging rays from a close source converge on an image point, but not at the principal focus F.*

Figure 7.4.17 *Part 2: Step 1 — Locating images*

2. In Figure 7.4.16(a) of your predictions, the object is at a distance, D_o, greater than the radius of curvature CO. Where did you predict the image would form? Move your lens to a position where it is a distance greater than 2*f* from the object. Locate the image by moving your screen around until you see a sharply focussed image on it. Was your prediction correct?

3. Test your prediction in Figure 7.4.16(b).

4. Test your predictions in Figures 7.4.16(c), (d), and (e). In Figure 7.4.16(e), try looking through the lens toward the object. Is this a real image or a virtual image?

5. Replace the convex lens with a concave lens. Can you produce a real image with it? Describe the image you can obtain with a concave lens.

Concluding Questions

1. You wish to project a slide on a screen. One of the letters on the slide is a p. When you place the slide in the projector, how must the letter look when you insert the slide (as seen from behind the projector)? (a) **p** (b) **d** (c) **b** (d) **q**. Explain.

2. When you use an overhead projector, why do you not have to write upside down to get an image right side up on the screen?

3. You wish to make a solar furnace using a very large convex lens. Where would the object that is to be heated be placed in relation to the lens?

4. You wish to photograph a spider life size. Where must (a) the spider and (b) the film or image sensor be located in relation to the lens of the camera? (Assume the lens is a simple convex lens.)

7.4 Review Questions

1. What type of lenses can be found on eyeglasses?

2. An object is 25 cm away from a lens of focal length 50 cm.
   (a) Where will the image form?

   (b) Will it be a real image or a virtual image?

3. A camera lens focussed at infinity forms a real image 50 mm from the lens. How far out from the film must the lens be moved to focus on a person standing 3.0 m in front of the lens?

4. The distance from the lens of someone's eye to the retina is 20.0 mm. If the image of a book held 40.0 cm in front of the eye is in sharp focus, what is the effective focal length of the lens?

5. A candle 5.0 cm high is located 80.0 cm in front of a convex lens of focal length 20.0 cm. How tall will the image of the candle appear to be on the screen?

6. A candle is placed 30.0 cm from a convex lens of focal length 20.0 cm. What will the magnification be? Will the image be real or virtual?

7. The magnification caused by a convex lens is represented by H_i / H_o, where H_i is the height of the image and H_o is the height of the object. Using that ratio, show that the magnification caused by a convex lens is equal to d_i / d_o (the ratio of the image distance to the object distance).

8. By convention, a concave (diverging) lens has a negative focal length. Draw an object, 5.0 cm high at a distance of 10.0 cm in front of a concave lens of focal length –6.0 cm. Describe the image by answering the questions below.

(a) How far from the lens will the image form?

(b) Will it be real or virtual?

(c) Enlarged or diminished in size?

(d) Right side up or inverted?

(e) How tall will it be?

(f) On which side of the lens will it be?

9. What causes "red eye" in photographs? How can a photographer avoid "red eye" in his or her photographs?

10. What is hypermetropia, and how is it corrected?

11. What is myopia, and how is it corrected?

12. You are looking through a microscope at a tiny bug crawling from the bottom left corner of your slide to the top right corner. In what direction will the bug be crawling when you look through the eyepiece lens?

13. Find out what a Fresnel lens is. (There is one in your classroom's overhead projector, and there may be one in the spotlights in your theatre.) What is the advantage of a Fresnel lens over a regular glass lens?

Chapter 7 Review

1. What is one advantage a pinhole camera has over a lens camera?

2. How was infrared light discovered?

3. Give an example of diffraction of light that you would experience in everyday life.

4. You are 1.6 m tall. What is the shortest wall mirror you need to see your whole body, while standing, in the mirror?

5. In a clothing store, a pair of large mirrors is hinged so that the angle between them can be changed. How many images will you see of yourself if you adjust the mirrors so that the angle between them is 45°?

6. Why do shopkeepers often place large convex mirrors at strategic locations in their stores?

7. You wish to form an enlarged real image of a light bulb filament using a concave mirror. Where should the light bulb filament be placed, in relation to the mirror's vertex?

8. If you use a concave mirror as a dressing or make-up mirror, where do you place your face in relation to the mirror?

9. An object is 2.5 m away from a concave mirror with a focal length of 1.0 m. Where will the image form? Will it be real or virtual?

10. What is the focal length of a concave mirror if a real image of an object 6.0 m away forms 3.0 m from the mirror?

11. A beam of light makes an angle of 35° with the normal as it approaches a flat glass block. If the index of refraction of the glass is 1.60, at what angle will the refracted beam enter the glass, relative to the normal? At what angle will the beam leave the other side of the block of glass if the walls are parallel?

12. What is the critical angle for a glass that has an index of refraction of 1.52?

13. Use a diagram to show why refraction causes a coin in the bottom of a swimming pool to look larger and closer than it really is.

14. The critical angle of a liquid is 45°. What is the index of refraction of the liquid?

15. Why does red light refract less than violet light?

16. At what speed would light travel in glass with an index of refraction of 2.0?

17. A student wishes to find the index of refraction of a block of glass. She shines light into the block at various angles of incidence (θ_i) and measures the angles of refraction (θ_r) for each incident beam of light. Here are her data:

angle of incidence	θ_i	0°	5.00°	10.00°	15.00°	20.00°	25.00°
sin θ_i							
angle of refraction	θ_r	0°	3.33°	6.65°	9.94°	13.20°	16.40°
sin θ_r							

(a) On a sheet of graph paper, use a suitable graph to determine the index of refraction of the glass. Use the most precise method, which involves Snell's Law.
(b) According to your graph, what is the index of refraction of the glass?
(c) What would the critical angle be for this type of glass?

18. In a movie, a nearsighted young boy is shown using the lenses from his eyeglasses to light a fire, by focussing the Sun's rays on some dried grass. What is wrong with this scene?

19. You wish to use a convex lens to achieve each of the following types of image. Where, in relation to the lens and the principal focus and/or centre of curvature, should you place the object?

(a) a small, real, inverted image

(b) a large, real inverted image

(c) a real image the same size as the object

(d) a large, erect virtual image

20. Complete the following ray diagram to show where the image of the candle will form and what its relative size will be.

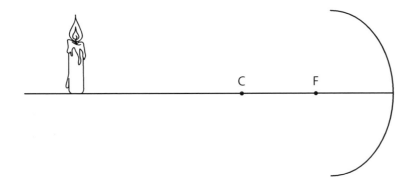

21. You wish to use a concave mirror (like the one in the diagram below) as a makeup mirror. You want your image to appear right side up and magnified larger than life. In relation to the mirror, where should your face be located if you are using the mirror for this purpose?

(a) at 1

(b) at 2

(c) at 3

(d) at 4

(e) at 5

22. What is the distance from a concave mirror to a real image, if the focal length of the mirror is 15.0 cm, and the object is 45.0 cm in front of the mirror?

23. Complete the following ray diagram to show where the image of the candle will form and what its relative size will be.

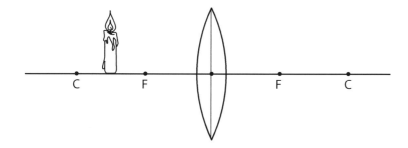

24. What is the focal length of a lens, if it forms a real image 20 mm away from one side of it, when a small lamp is placed on the other side, 30 mm from the lens?

25. What is the position of an image of an 8.3 cm toy superhero that is placed 0.8 m from a +60.0 mm focal length converging lens?

26. An object is placed 15.0 cm from a converging lens with a focal length of 20.5 cm. What is the image position?

Chapter 7 Extra Practice

1. What phenomena are primarily involved in the making of a rainbow?

2. What phenomena are mainly responsible for the blueness of the sky?

3. Why do sunsets appear red?

4. What property of light is used in lenses?

5. When white light enters glass from air, what colour is refracted most?

6. Sun tan and Sun burn are caused by what form of electromagnetic radiation?

7. Which colour of light travels fastest in a *vacuum*?

8. A spotlight photographed through a glass filter with thin grooves in it will appear to have a starburst effect around it. What phenomenon is primarily involved here?

9. Two plane mirrors are hinged and arranged to form an angle of 36° with each other. If you place a coin between them, how many images of the coin will you see when you look in the mirrors?

10. You are standing 2.0 m in front of a mirror, and you wish to take a picture of yourself. At what distance should you focus your camera?

11. If you run toward a mirror at 5.0 m/s, how fast does your image approach *you*?

12. A basketball player is 2.2 m tall. How tall a mirror does she need to see the entire length of her body?

13. When light of a certain pure colour enters a new medium at, say, 30°, what property of the light does *not* change?

14. Diamonds are noted for their brilliance and colour when viewed in a well-lit environment. What property or properties account for this?

15. A blue spotlight and a yellow spotlight are shone on the same area of a white screen. What colour will you see on the screen?

16. Look at the diagram below. Where should the fisherman aim his spear? (The fish is not moving.)

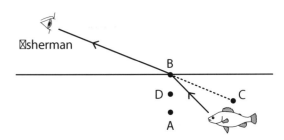

17. Two prisms are to be used to make a periscope. Which of the diagrams below shows the correct way to align the prisms inside the periscope?

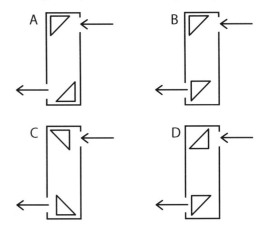

18. A beam of light enters a liquid at an incident angle of 35°. It refracts at 25° to the normal. What is the index of refraction of the liquid?

19. Diamond has an index of refraction of 2.42. If light enters the diamond at an angle of incidence of 63.0°, at what angle will the light refract?

20. The speed of light is 3.00×10^8 m/s in air. What is its speed in a plastic, whose index of refraction is 1.453?

8 Special Relativity

By the end of this chapter, you should be able to do the following:

- Explain the fundamental principles of special relativity

By the end of this chapter, you should know the meaning of these **key terms**:

- absolute reference frame
- length contraction
- momentum increase
- photons
- special theory of relativity
- speed of light
- time dilation

By the end of this chapter, you should be able to use and know when to use the following formulae:

$$t = \frac{t_0}{\sqrt{1 - \frac{v^2}{c^2}}}$$

$$l = l_0\sqrt{1 - \frac{v^2}{c^2}}$$

$$E = mc^2$$

$$p = \frac{mv}{\sqrt{1 - \frac{v^2}{c^2}}}$$

Albert Einstein discovered a new way of thinking about the universe.

8.1 Einstein's Theory of Special Relativity

Albert Einstein

Albert Einstein was one of the greatest, most creative thinkers in all recorded history. His ideas were truly revolutionary. For example, he suggested that mass and energy were equivalent. He predicted that mass could be converted into energy, and energy into mass. Einstein was a pacifist. He abhorred war and its destruction. Ironically, it was the application of his mass-energy equation that contributed to the development of the atomic and hydrogen bombs.

Einstein was born in Ulm, Germany, in 1879. He started his schooling in Germany and completed it in Zurich, Switzerland. After graduating in 1900, he worked in the Swiss patent office in Bern.

In 1905, he published several important scientific papers, which were to change the way scientists look at the universe. One of these explained that light comes in small particles of energy called **photons**. Einstein also described how light behaves not only as if it were a wave motion, but also as if it consisted of particles. In another paper he developed what is now called the **special theory of relativity**. That theory is the basis for this chapter.

In 1916 Einstein, working at the University of Berlin, published his general theory of relativity. In this theory, Einstein described gravity differently than the way Isaac Newton had. To Einstein, gravity was not a force but a curved field in space and time, created by the presence of mass. With his theory, he successfully predicted the amount of deflection of light from distant stars as it passed close to our own massive Sun. This deflection could only be measured during an eclipse. In 1929, Einstein's predictions were verified photographically during a total eclipse of the Sun and thus provided evidence for proving his theory.

In 1933, Albert Einstein left Germany and went to the United States, where he became a valued member of the Institute of Advanced Study at Princeton, New Jersey. Einstein died in 1955 in Princeton.

Frames of Reference

Before studying Einstein's theory of special relativity, you need to have an understanding of frames of reference. This concept is key to his theory. Luckily you already have had many different experiences with frames of reference. A frame of reference refers to the position from which an observer views a particular event.

Imagine you are rowing a boat downstream in a river where the water is moving with a velocity of 5.0 km/h (Figure 8.1.1). An observer tells you that your boat is travelling with a velocity of 10.0 km/h. You immediately realize there a problem here. Does the observer mean that you are travelling 10.0 km/h relative to Earth's surface (such as a point on the riverbank) or does the observer mean 10.0 km/h relative to the water?

If the observer means 10.0 km/h relative to the water, then your velocity relative to Earth's surface is 10.0 km/h + 5.0 km/h = 15.0 km/h. Or the observer's frame of reference is different from your frame of reference because, compared to the water, you think you're travelling at 5.0 km/h. It is important when dealing with velocities to specify the frame of reference in which the velocity was measured.

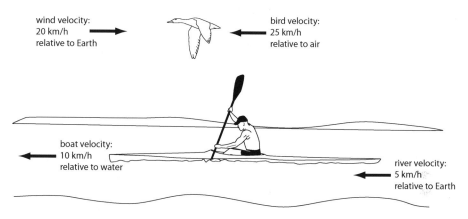

Figure 8.1.1 *Examples of frames of reference*

Quick Check

Look at Figure 8.1.1 to answer the following questions.

1. What is the velocity of the person in the boat relative to:
   (a) the water?   (b) Earth's surface?

   _____   _____

2. What is the velocity of the bird relative to:
   (a) the air?   (b) the water?   (c) Earth's surface?

   _____   _____   _____

3. What is the velocity of the water relative to the bird?

   _____

4. What is the velocity of the person in the boat relative to the bird?

   _____

5. What would all the velocities in Figure 8.1.1 appear to be relative to a camera in a spy satellite in geosynchronous orbit? Its position is "fixed" relative to a point on the rotating Earth.

   _____

Relative Motion

The Quick Check questions above have shown that an object can have two velocities at the same time, each one correct relative to a different frame of reference. To measure a velocity, we generally choose a frame of reference and use that frame of reference as absolutely still like in Figure 8.1.2. The two jets approach each other with a speed relative to the ground of 600km/h. Or put another way, if your speedometer says your car is travelling 80 km/h, then your speed relative to the ground below your car is 80 km/h. Relative to the centre of the planet, your car's speed might be several hundreds of kilometers per hour, since Earth is rotating on its axis and your car is moving with Earth's surface. Relative to the Sun, your speed is even greater. It would be over 100 000 km/h because Earth is revolving around the Sun that fast. And then there is always the centre of our galaxy to consider as a possible frame of reference.

Figure 8.1.2 *Two aerobatic jets approach each other "head-on" before doing a "level roll." Each aircraft is travelling approximately 600 km/h relative to the ground.*

The First Postulate of Relativity

Einstein's special theory of relativity is based on two fundamental assumptions that he made. These fundamental assumptions are called postulates. The first postulate is the **special relativity principle:**

> If two frames of reference move with constant velocity relative to each other, then the laws of physics will be the same in both frames of reference.

It is important to remember that the special theory of relativity deals only with frames of reference that are moving at constant velocity relative to each other. That means there is no acceleration involved. In relativity theory, there is no preferred frame of reference. For example, rather than saying your car is moving 80 km/h relative to the road below it, you could just as easily and correctly say the car is still and the road is moving 80 km/h relative to your car as in Figure 8.1.3. Your less informed friends may suggest an appointment with a psychiatrist, but relatively speaking, you would be correct.

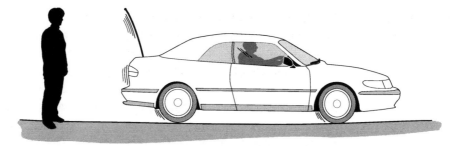

Figure 8.1.3 *The car is going 50 km/h relative to the person or the person is going 50 km/h relative to the car.*

Comparing Frames of Reference

Figure 8.1.4 shows two observers in two different frames of reference. Both are moving at constant velocity, and both would observe the same result for a simple experiment: throwing a ball into the air and catching it. If the person standing on the road and the person in the van both throw the same ball up in the same way, both will observe the same result. Also, an observer outside the van will find that the same laws of physics can be used to predict the path of the ball, even though the path of the ball will look different. In this situation it will be an elongated parabola because the van, and therefore the ball in the van, has a steady horizontal velocity.

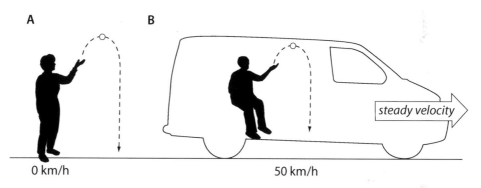

Figure 8.1.4 *The laws of physics are the same in both frames of reference.*

Quick Check

1. Both observers in Figure 8.1.4 are moving at constant velocity. What is the velocity of observer A relative to the road?

   _____

2. Sketch what the path of the ball thrown in the van would look like to an observer standing on the road looking into the van as it passes.

Is there any frame of reference that might be considered as truly "fixed" or unchanging? Such a frame of reference would be the **absolute reference frame**, relative to which all velocities might be measured. In ancient times, it was believed that Earth itself was at rest and that all other celestial bodies moved around Earth. If this were true, then Earth would be the absolute reference frame. When Copernicus showed that Earth actually orbited the Sun and not the other way around, the idea of using Earth as a fixed reference frame became outdated. The Sun cannot be used as an absolute reference frame because it is moving around the centre of the galaxy. And our galaxy itself moves relative to distant galaxies. It seems that everything in nature moves relative to something else.

The Michelson-Morley Experiment

In the late nineteenth century, two Americans A. A. Michelson and E. W. Morley conducted a vital experiment in search of the absolute frame of reference. Scottish physicist James Clerk Maxwell, in his theory of electromagnetic radiation, had predicted that the velocity of light would be 300 000 km/s.

The theory at the time was that light was a wave motion. The question that could not be answered was what was light travelling through in space? It was thought that there was a mysterious "something" called the **ether**, and that light waves were really vibrations in the ether. Perhaps the ether could serve as a fixed reference frame?

Michelson and Morley did numerous experiments, measuring the speed of light with the help of an instrument called an interferometer, which permitted detection of very tiny changes in the speed of light. Figure 8.1.5 shows one of the key experiments done by Michelson and Morley.

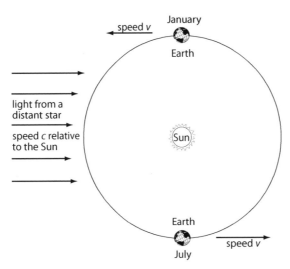

Figure 8.1.5 *Michelson and Morley used the light from a distant star in their experiment.*

In January of 1887, Michelson and Morley measured the speed of light coming from a distant star. In January, Earth was moving toward the star with a speed v relative to the Sun. The speed of light relative to the Sun was assumed to be c. The measured speed of light relative to Earth was predicted to be $c + v$. In July, Earth was moving away from the distant star and the predicted measurement for the speed of light was $c - v$. The careful measurements done by Michelson and Morley failed to detect any difference in the speed of light relative to Earth for the two situations. The measured speed of light relative to Earth was the same whether Earth or the observers' frame of reference was moving toward the source of light or away from it.

The result of the Michelson-Morley experiment and other follow-up experiments was quite surprising. Our everyday experience would not lead us to expect the speed of light to be independent of our frame of reference. Consider this example: You are driving north on a road, moving 70 km/h. A car approaches you travelling 80 km/h south. The speed of the other car relative to your car is:

$$80 \text{ km/h} + 70 \text{ km/h} = 150 \text{ km/h}$$

That is what you expect, and that is what really happens. Similarly, if you are travelling north at 70 km/h, and the faster car is travelling in the same direction at 80 km/h, the speed of the faster car relative to your car is:

$$80 \text{ km/h} - 70 \text{ km/h} = 10 \text{ km/h}$$

If, however, you replace the faster car by light, you find that the speed of light relative to your car is 300 000 km/s whether your car is moving toward the light or away from it.

The Michelson-Morley experiment is famous for its negative result or null result. It showed experimentally that the speed of light in space is the same for all observers regardless of their velocity or the velocity of the source of the light. The speed of light simply does not depend on your frame of reference at all. No evidence could be found that space, or the "ether" that some believed pervaded space, could be used as a fixed frame of reference. Recent new research suggests that some particles may be able to go faster than the speed of light. However, the general scientific community has not accepted these results as contradictory to anything proposed by Einstein.

Second Postulate of Relativity

The experimentally verified results of Michelson and Morley's work was predicted theoretically by Albert Einstein, who was not aware of their work. Einstein never did believe that there was such a thing as a fixed frame of reference or an ether. In fact, he summed up what he thought about the velocity of light in his second fundamental postulate of relativity.

> The speed of light in space is the same for any observer no matter what the velocity of the observer's frame of reference is, and no matter what the velocity of the source of the light is.

The two fundamental postulates of relativity were used by Einstein to derive some extremely interesting predictions related to time dilation and length contraction of objects travelling near the speed of light.

Time Dilation (Your Time ≠ My Time, Necessarily)

According to Einstein's special theory of relativity, a clock that is moving will run slow. This "stretching" of time by a moving object is called **time dilation**.

Is it possible that in two different frames of reference, identical clocks might run differently and that time might pass differently? In fact, this is one of the predictions of Albert Einstein's special theory of relativity.

Figure 8.1.6 on the next page shows an observer inside an imaginary glass-walled spaceship, made specially so that an outside observer can watch an experiment done by an inside observer. The inside observer is watching an event consisting of an imaginary oscillating light beam.

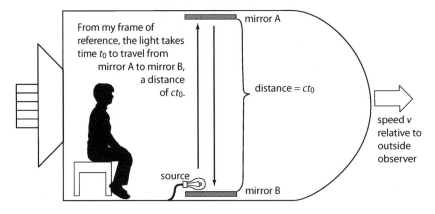

From my frame of reference, the light takes time t_0 to travel from mirror A to mirror B, a distance of ct_0.

mirror A

distance = ct_0

source

mirror B

speed v relative to outside observer

Figure 8.1.6 *This observer is inside a glass-walled spaceship watching a light beam.*

The oscillating light beam acts like a clock. The beam goes from the light source up to mirror A and back to mirror B. The inside observer measures the time for the light to travel from A to B and finds that the time is t_0. Since distance = speed × time, the distance that the inside observer sees the light beam travel is $d = ct_0$.

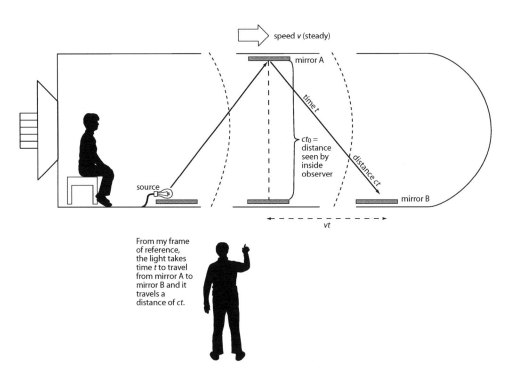

speed v (steady)

mirror A

time t

ct_0 = distance seen by inside observer

distance ct

source

mirror B

vt

From my frame of reference, the light takes time t to travel from mirror A to mirror B and it travels a distance of ct.

Figure 8.1.7 *The observer is outside the glass-walled spaceship watching a light beam.*

Figure 8.1.7 illustrates what an observer in a different frame of reference sees. The outside observer is not moving at speed v. He sees the spaceship going by at speed v, relative to him. To the outside observer, the light beam in the spaceship takes a time t to travel a distance ct while the spaceship moves forward a distance vt. A right-angled triangle is formed with sides ct_0, vt, and ct. According to Pythagoras' theorem:

$$(ct)^2 = (ct_0)^2 + (vt)^2$$

Therefore, $\quad (ct)^2 - (vt)^2 = (ct_0)^2$

and $\quad\quad c^2t^2 - v^2t^2 = c^2t_0^2$

or $\quad\quad\quad t^2(c^2 - v^2) = c^2t_0^2$

Dividing both sides of the equation by c^2:

$$t^2\left(1 - \frac{v^2}{c^2}\right) = t_0^2$$

Rearranging terms:

$$t^2 = \frac{t_0^2}{\left(1 - \frac{v^2}{c^2}\right)}$$

Taking the square root of both sides of the equation, we obtain an equation for t (as observed by the outside observer):

$$t = \frac{t_0}{\sqrt{1 - \frac{v^2}{c^2}}}$$

Now this may not seem to mean much, but let's look at it in a thought experiment.

Sample Problem 8.1.1 — Time Dilation

How much is time expanded or dilated from a fixed observer's point of view if the spaceship in Figure 8.1.7 is moving at one-half the speed of light? ($v = 1/2c$)

What to Think About	How to Do It
1. Choose the equation to use to determine time dilation.	$t = \dfrac{t_0}{\sqrt{1 - \dfrac{(0.5c)^2}{c^2}}}$
2. Identify what you know.	$= \dfrac{t_0}{\sqrt{1 - 0.25}}$
3. Decide if you have to rearrange the equation.	$= \dfrac{t_0}{\sqrt{0.75}}$
4. Solve.	$= 1.15 t_0$
	This means time is dilated by 15%. Or put another way, for each hour on the spaceship clock, the observer's clock is $1.15t_0$. This is time dilation. For every hour on the spaceship, the observer's clock reads an extra 9.0 min.

Practice Problems 8.11 — Time Dilation

An observer in a fixed frame of reference is watching an event that takes time t_0 to occur, according to an observer in a frame of reference moving at speed v relative to the fixed observer. Calculate the time the fixed observer will measure if t_0 is 5.0 s, and the speed of the moving frame of reference (a spaceship) is:

1. 0.65c

3. 0.995c

2. 0.866c

4. 0.999c

Experimental Evidence for Time Dilation

Elementary particles called mu-mesons (or muons) have an average "lifetime" of 2.0×10^{-6} s. Mu-mesons created about 6 to 8 km above Earth during collisions of cosmic rays with nuclei of atoms in air molecules have been observed to travel with a very high speed of 0.988c. The mu-mesons decay into electrons at the end of their short lifetime.

Consider a mu-meson formed at high altitude and travelling downward at a speed of 0.988c. How far will it travel during a lifetime of 2.0×10^{-6} s?

$$d = vt = (0.998 \times 3.0 \times 10^5 \text{ km/s})(2.0 \times 10^{-6} \text{ s}) = 0.60 \text{ km}$$

According to this calculation, none of the mu-mesons formed 6 to 8 km above the ground should reach the ground. The mu-mesons, however, are detected at ground level. To see why, consider the time of travel of the mu-mesons in the frame of reference of a stationary observer on Earth.

$$t = \frac{t_0}{\sqrt{1 - \frac{v^2}{c^2}}} = \frac{t_0}{\sqrt{1 - \frac{(0.998c)^2}{c^2}}} = \frac{2.0 \times 10^{-6} \text{ s}}{\sqrt{1 - 0.996}} = \frac{2.0 \times 10^{6} \text{ s}}{\sqrt{0.004}}$$

$$t = 3.2 \times 10^{-5} \text{ s}$$

In a time of 3.2×10^{-5} s, the mu-meson could travel a distance of:

$$d = vt = (0.998 \times 3.0 \times 10^5 \text{ km/s})(3.2 \times 10^{-5} \text{ s}) = 9.6 \text{ km}$$

Thus, when the effects of time dilation are taken into account, the mu-meson does have time to reach Earth's surface. This is why mu-mesons created 6 to 8 km above Earth can reach Earth during their average lifetime. The average lifetime is 2.0×10^{-6} s from the frame of reference of the mu-meson, but it is 3.2×10^{-5} s or 16 times as long from our frame of reference on a fixed Earth.

A Thought Experiment

Imagine your age is 30 a and that you have a daughter who is 6 a old, where "a" stands for year. You leave on a space trip in the year 2000 and travel at a speed of 0.99c for a time of 5.0 a (as measured by you in the spaceship). In other words, from the space traveller's frame of reference, $t_0 = 5.0$ a.

How much time will have elapsed when you return, from the frame of reference of your young daughter who was left behind on Earth? To find out, use the time dilation formula:

$$t = \frac{5.0 \text{ a}}{\sqrt{1 - \frac{(0.99c)^2}{c^2}}} = \frac{5.0 \text{ a}}{\sqrt{1 - 0.980}} = \frac{5.0 \text{ a}}{\sqrt{0.020}} = \frac{5.0 \text{ a}}{0.14} = 36 \text{ a}$$

What this means is: Having left Earth in the year 2000, you will return to Earth in the year 2036. Your daughter, whom you left at home, will be 6 a + 36 a = 42 a old.

You will be 30 a + 5a = 35 a old. Yes, your daughter will be older than you are. As a high-speed space traveller, you only age by 5 a, as measured from the spaceship frame of reference. To Earth observers, their clocks tell them that 36 a have gone by since you left on your journey.

Length Contraction

Einstein's special theory of relativity makes other predictions about objects moving at speeds greater than zero. Without going into mathematical detail, we shall simply state the prediction relating to the length of a moving object.

> The length of an object is measured to be shorter when it is moving than when it is at rest. This shortening is only seen in the dimension of its motion.

If the length of an object when it is standing still is l_0, the theory of relativity predicts that the object's length l when it is moving at speed v will be measured to be:

$$l = l_0\sqrt{1 - \frac{v^2}{c^2}}$$

Sample Problem 8.1.2 — Length Contraction

How long would a metre stick appear to be if it was moving past you with a speed of 0.995c?

What to Think About	How to Do It
1. Choose the equation to use to determine length contraction.	$l = l_0 \sqrt{1 - \dfrac{v^2}{c^2}}$
2. Identify what you know.	$= 1.00 \text{ m} \sqrt{1 - \dfrac{(0.0995c)^2}{c^2}}$
3. Decide if you have to rearrange the equation.	$= 1.00 \text{ m} \sqrt{1 - 0.990}$
4. Solve.	$= 1.00 \text{ m} \sqrt{0.010}$
	$= 0.10 \text{ m (or 10 cm)}$

Practice Problems 8.1.2 — Length Contraction

Calculate the apparent length of a 100 m futuristic spaceship when it is travelling at the speeds given below.

Note: If you are in the spaceship, you will perceive its length to be 100 m at all times at any speed.

1. 0.63c

2. 0.866c

3. 0.999c

Relativistic Momentum

The definition of momentum in earlier chapters ($p = mv$) does *not* apply to objects travelling at relativistic speeds. For lower speeds, as v approaches 0, the ratio v/c approaches 0, and momentum p approaches mv. In other words, the Newtonian definition of momentum works for lower speeds. Recall that Newton's second law can be written in terms of momentum: $F = \dfrac{p}{t}$. Newton's second law can be used at relativistic speeds, but only in this form, where p is **relativistic momentum.** The expression for relativistic momentum is:

$$p = \frac{mv}{\sqrt{1 - \dfrac{v^2}{c^2}}}$$

Mass-Energy Equivalence

Einstein was able to show mathematically that, as a consequence of his special theory of relativity, mass and energy are different aspects of the same thing. They are equivalent to one another. The total energy in a body is related to its mass by the following formula:

$$E = \frac{mc^2}{\sqrt{1 - \dfrac{v^2}{c^2}}}$$

When the body is at rest, $v = 0$ and the total energy equation reduces to:

$$E = mc^2$$

This is one of the most famous equations in physics. It says, for example, that a body at rest has energy because of its mass. Einstein predicted that mass could be changed into energy and that energy could be changed into mass. Both predictions have been verified experimentally. Mass is changed into energy during the nuclear processes that occur in reactors and in atomic and hydrogen bombs.

The first evidence that energy could be changed into mass was found in 1932. American physicist C.D. Anderson observed, in a photographic emulsion, evidence that a gamma photon, which is very high energy light, had changed into two particles: an electron and a positive electron, also called a positron. The positron is an anti-particle of an electron: it has the same mass as an electron but the opposite charge.

The mass-to-energy conversion results in the release of a huge amount of energy. For example, consider how much energy would be produced if 1 kg of mass were completely changed into energy.

$$E = mc^2 = (1.0 \text{ kg})(3.0 \times 10^8 \text{ m/s})^2 = 9.0 \times 10^{16} \text{ kg·m}^2/\text{s}^2$$

Note: 1 kg·m^2/s^2 = 1 N·m = 1 J. This means 1 kg of mass is equivalent to 9.0×10^{16} J or 90 000 000 000 000 000 J.

Quick Check

1. Let the mass of an electron be m. The speed of light is c. Calculate what the momentum of an electron would be at each of the following speeds, according to the Newtonian equation for momentum, $p = mv$.

    (a) 0.10c (b) 0.50c (c) 0.87c

    (d) 0.9999c (e) c

2. Calculate what the relativistic momentum of an electron would be at these speeds:

    (a) 0.10c (b) 0.50c (c) 0.87c

    (d) 0.9999c (e) c

3. Calculate the unbalanced force that would be needed to accelerate an electron from rest up to the speed of light, c, in a time t.

    $$P = \frac{mv}{\sqrt{1 - \frac{c^2}{c^2}}} = \frac{mv}{0} = \infty$$

Speed Limit for the Universe: The Speed of Light

Can a body be accelerated to the speed of light? Consider what would happen to the momentum (p) of an electron. The same argument applies to any object having mass. If the velocity v were in some way increased until it equaled c, then the momentum of the object would become:

$$p = \frac{mv}{\sqrt{1 - \frac{c^2}{c^2}}} = \frac{mv}{0} = \infty$$

The momentum of an object approaches infinity as the speed of an object approaches the speed of light. The unbalanced force needed to accelerate it to speed c would also be infinite. Therefore an object cannot be accelerated to the speed of light.

Could a particle have a velocity greater than c? If this were so, the magnitude of $(1 - v^2/c^2)$ would be less than zero, and the square root of a negative number does not exist in the real number system. The momentum would be imaginary.

It does appear, then, that the speed of light truly is the speed limit for the universe. A precise value for the speed of light is: $c = 2.99792458 \times 108$ m/s. For most applications, the speed of light is rounded off to 3.00×108 m/s. This is for light travelling through a vacuum. In air, the speed is only slightly lower.

8.1 Review Questions

1. On what two postulates is the special theory of relativity based?

2. You are approaching a star in a spaceship that is travelling at half the speed of light. How fast will the light from the star go past you?

3. An astronaut makes a trip in a spaceship travelling at a speed of 0.65c.
   (a) The astronaut's calendar and clocks indicate the trip lasts 10 a. How long does the trip last according to observers on a "fixed" Earth?

   (b) The spaceship is 50.0 m long when at rest. How long does it appear to be to an observer in a fixed position on a line parallel to the path of the spaceship?

4. An event takes t_0 seconds to occur, according to the occupants of a space bus that is moving at one-half the speed of light ($\frac{1}{2}c$). To a fixed observer outside the space bus, how long will the event take to occur?

6. From a fixed reference point, you observe a space bus pass by at a very high speed, v. The occupants say the space bus is 10 m long. If the space bus appears to be only 5 m long from *your* frame of reference, how fast is the space bus moving? Express your answer as a decimal fraction of the speed of light, c.

7. Circle the letter that you think best answers the question and than discuss the answer you chose in the space below.
   When you look at a distant star in the night sky, what are you seeing?
   (a) the star as it appears now
   (b) the star as it will look sometime in the future
   (c) the star as it looked sometime in the past

   Discussion:

5. How fast must a space bus travel in order for its length to appear to an outside observer that the bus contracts to one-half its full length?

8. A man is 25 a old. He expects to live to an age of 75 a. He plans to make a trip in a spaceship, leaving Earth in the year 2020. He would like to return to Earth in the year 2520. Is this possible? How fast would the spaceship have to travel?

9. If 1 mg of mass were converted into pure energy, how many joules of energy would be produced? (1 mg = 10^{-6} kg)

10. (a) If the mass of a golf ball (46 g) could be converted entirely into energy ($E = mc^2$), how much energy would be released?

(b) Imagine your home uses an average of 16 kW·h of electrical energy per day. If you could convert the energy from the mass of a golf ball directly into electrical energy (and store it), how many years supply would you be able to store away? (1 kW·h = 3.6×10^6 J)

11. Find out from your hydroelectric bill how many joules of electrical energy you use each month. If you could somehow convert 1 g of mass directly into electrical energy, how many months worth of electrical energy would this provide you with?

12. Discuss what happens to the momentum, p, of an electron, if it is accelerated to a speed approaching the speed of light. Discuss whether the electron can be made to travel at the speed of light.

13. The special theory of relativity deals only with frames of reference moving at uniform velocity. Find out how the general theory of relativity deals with gravity, space, and time.

Chapter 8   Extra Practice

Circle the letter for the correct answer to each question.

1. A 10 m long missile is test fired such that it moves with a speed of 0.1c. What is the apparent length of the missile at this speed?

   (a) 9.90 m
   (b) 9.95 m
   (c) 10.0 m
   (d) 10.1 m

2. Rajesh and Radha were Earthlings and twins, both 20 years old. That was when Rajesh went into space in a spaceship, moving at a constant speed of 0.8c, returning when he turned 25. How many years, according to Radha, did Rajesh spend in space?

   (a) 3 years
   (b) 5 years
   (c) 8 years and 4 months
   (d) 11 years, 2 months, and 5 days

3. What is the energy contained in an electron at rest in joules?

   (a) 0.0144 J
   (b) 1.14 × 10^{15} J
   (c) 4.10 × 10^{-15} J
   (d) 8.20 × 10^{-15} J

4. A source of light is at rest with respect to an observer. The observer then starts moving toward the light source with velocity v. If the initial velocity of light for the observer was c, what would be the new velocity?

   (a) c
   (b) v
   (c) $c - v$
   (d) $c + v$

5. Keelyn and Jon set their watches at 5:00 a.m. before Keelyn moves to space in a spaceship at a speed of 0.6c. What will be the time by Keelyn's watch if it is 5:20 a.m. by Jon's watch?

   (a) 5:12:64 a.m.
   (b) 5:16 a.m.
   (c) 5:17:70 a.m.
   (d) 5:25 a.m.

6. A spaceship is cruising with a speed of 0.7c and fires a missile with speed 0.5c. What will be the speed of the missile in the rest frame of reference?

   (a) 0.20c
   (b) 0.35c
   (c) 0.89c
   (d) 1.2c

9 Nuclear Fission and Fusion

By the end of this chapter, you should be able to do the following:

- compare fusion and fission reactions and give examples
- compare different types of nuclear reactors
- describe the advantages and disadvantages of using nuclear energy

By the end of this chapter, you should know the meaning of these key terms:

- alpha ray
- becquerel
- beta ray
- chain reaction
- critical mass
- fission
- fusion
- gamma radiation
- half-life
- isotope
- moderator
- radioactive series
- radioactivity
- radioisotope
- transmutation

A nuclear power station

9.1 The Discovery of Radioactivity

X-Rays, Fluorescence, and Becquerel Rays

In 1896, French physicist Antoine Henri Becquerel (1852–1908) was investigating fluorescent materials. Röntgen had recently discovered X-rays and Becquerel was curious to know whether fluorescent materials might give off these "new" rays as well as visible light. The phenomenon called **fluorescence** has interested physicists for many years. Fluorescence is the ability of some substances to absorb light of one wavelength, and then give off light at a longer wavelength. For example, the colouring on some posters is made of a fluorescent substance. This substance will absorb ultraviolet light from a "black light" and then emit bright colours in the visible range.

As fate would have it, one of the fluorescent compounds that Becquerel was working with was potassium uranyl sulphate $K_2UO_2(SO_4)_2$. Becquerel knew that if he exposed this compound to bright sunlight and then took it into a dark room, it would fluoresce. Delayed fluorescence like this is called **phosphorescence**. To find out if the fluorescence included X-rays, he placed the sample above a photographic plate, which was completely wrapped in black paper so that no visible light could reach the plate.

When the plate was developed, it was fogged, indicating that radiation was penetrating the black paper. Was it X-rays that were exposing the film? Becquerel made a very important observation. If the uranium compound was left sitting on the paper-covered photographic plate, the plate was exposed whether the compound was fluorescing or not. He concluded that the uranium compound was emitting the radiation that caused the plate to fog. This new radiation had nothing to do with fluorescence or phosphorescence. Its discovery was just good luck and good observation on the part of Becquerel.

No one knew what these new "rays" were, but they were called **Becquerel rays.** Whatever they were, scientists found out that they had several properties that were similar to X-rays:

1. They are very penetrating.
2. They expose photographic plates.
3. They are invisible to the eye.
4. They cause air molecules to become ions (i.e., they ionize the air).

The property that some substances have of emitting penetrating radiation, which ionizes the air, was called **radioactivity** by Marie Sklodowska Curie (1867–1934). Curie showed that all uranium compounds are radioactive and concluded that it was the uranium atom itself that was radioactive.

Other Radioactive Elements

Marie Curie made many extremely important contributions to the new science of radioactivity. She showed that the element thorium was also radioactive. She and her husband Pierre Curie (1859–1906) showed conclusively that the radioactivity of an element originated in the atoms of the element. It did not depend on any external factors or on compounds formed by the element.

In their search for other elements that might be radioactive, the Curies examined pitchblende ore, a mixture containing uranium oxide. They found that the degree of radioactivity, measured with apparatus invented by Pierre Curie, was many times greater than would be obtainable from uranium itself. It appeared there was an element in the ore that was even more radioactive than uranium. After carrying out lengthy chemical separations of the substances in pitchblende, they isolated a substance with 400 times the activity of uranium. They named the radioactive element in the isolated material polonium, after Marie Curie's native Poland. In the same year, 1898, they discovered another radioactive element in the pitchblende and called it radium. Radium was even more radioactive than polonium.

Pierre and Marie Curie were awarded the 1903 Nobel Prize for physics, along with co-winner Henri Becquerel. Marie Curie has the distinction of being the only scientist to win two Nobel Prizes for science achievements. She won her second prize in 1911 for chemistry, for her discoveries of polonium and radium. In addition to her own achievements, her daughter Irene Curie won the 1935 Nobel Prize for chemistry.

A Canadian Contribution

One of the truly great pioneers in atomic research did much of his important work while at McGill University in Montreal. Ernest Rutherford (1871–1937) was born in New Zealand. After earning his master's degree in physics there, Rutherford went to Cambridge, England, to work with J.J. Thomson, discoverer of the electron, from 1885 until 1898. In 1898, he accepted the position of physics professor at McGill University. He stayed at McGill University until 1907 and then returned to England.

Rutherford and Thomson studied the effect that X-rays have on air. The air is ionized, and thus rendered conducting by the passage of X-rays through it. When Becquerel rays were discovered, Rutherford was intensely interested in finding out more about them.

At McGill University, Rutherford and his graduate students investigated the penetrating ability of Becquerel rays. They let the rays from a sample of uranium metal pass through various thicknesses of aluminum foil and pass into a detector, which used the property of electrical conductivity of air. He found that the intensity of the radiation decreased as the thickness of the foil increased, but there was a "discontinuity" when the thickness reached a certain value. The discontinuity suggested to him that Becquerel rays were of at least two types. One of those types was far more penetrating than the other. The less-penetrating rays were labeled **alpha rays** and the more-penetrating rays were labeled **beta rays**. Alpha (α) and beta (β) are the first two letters of the Greek alphabet.

The identification of two types of Becquerel rays by Rutherford in 1899 was followed shortly after by the discovery of a third type of Becquerel ray by French physicist Paul Villard (1860–1934). In 1900, Villard found a form of radiation emitted by radium that was far more penetrating than either alpha or beta rays. This third form of radiation was labeled **gamma radiation**. (Gamma (γ) is another letter in the Greek alphabet.) Gamma radiation can pass through several centimetres of lead, or several metres of concrete, before being completely stopped. Gamma rays are more penetrating than X-rays. Figure 9.1.1 on the next page shows the relative penetration of the different types of radiation.

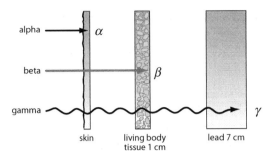

Figure 9.1.1 *Penetration of different substances by Becquerel rays*

Quick Check

1. What was Becquerel looking for when he discovered radioactivity by accident?

   _____

2. Who introduced the term *radioactivity*?

   _____

3. Who first identified alpha particles? beta particles? gamma radiation?

   _____

   _____

What Are α, β, and γ Radiation?

Many scientists, including Marie and Pierre Curie, Henri Becquerel, and Ernest Rutherford, took on the task of figuring out what *α*, *β*, and *γ* radiation are. One of the clever ways they used to study the behaviour of the different types of radiation was to pass a narrow beam of Becquerel rays through a magnetic field. If the magnetic field was strong enough, it separated the three kinds of radiation. Figure 9.1.2 is a simplified diagram of the apparatus used and the results observed.

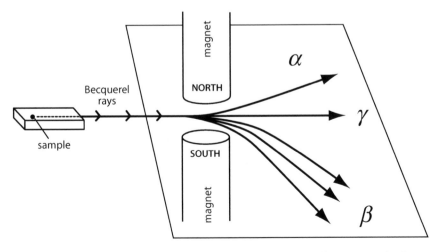

Figure 9.1.2 *A magnetic field can separate Becquerel rays into the different types of radiation.*

The alpha radiation was deflected in one direction, following a circular path while within the magnetic field. Beta radiation was deflected in the opposite direction, in circular paths of shorter radius. The gamma radiation was not affected by the magnetic field. Beta radiation was affected in the same way as cathode rays, which showed that beta radiation carried a negative charge. Since alpha radiation deflected in the opposite direction, it obviously carried a positive charge.

Becquerel used the technique of J.J. Thomson to measure the charge-to-mass ratio of beta radiation. The result he obtained was essentially the same as for electrons. Beta particles were electrons!

Experiments with alpha particles indicated they were much more massive than beta particles or electrons. The magnitude of their charge was equal to or twice that of the electron. The magnetic field experiments suggested that the alpha particle might be:
- a hydrogen molecule with a single positive charge (H^{2+}) or
- a helium atom with a double positive charge (He^{2+}).

Rutherford and T. S. Royds carried out an ingenious experiment to find out whether alpha particles were, in fact, helium atoms missing two electrons (He^{2+}). Rutherford and Royds knew that radon gas was radioactive and gave off alpha particles. They passed radon gas into a very thin-walled glass tube, as in the schematic diagram in Figure 9.1.3. An outer glass tube surrounding the radon-filled tube was evacuated with a vacuum pump. The outer tube had two electrodes built into it. After several days enough alpha particles from the radioactive radon had escaped through the thin-walled inner container into the outer container, and the contents of the outer container could be tested. A high voltage was applied to the two electrodes, and the discharge that occurred was examined with a spectroscope. The spectral lines observed were identical with the spectrum of helium gas. Alpha particles, Rutherford and Royd concluded, were helium atoms with two electrons missing (that is, helium ions with a double positive charge, He^{2+}).

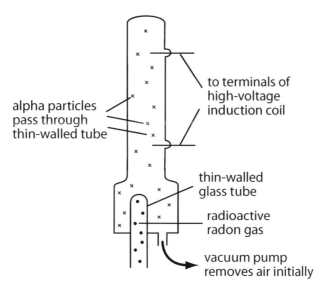

alpha particles pass through thin-walled tube

to terminals of high-voltage induction coil

thin-walled glass tube

radioactive radon gas

vacuum pump removes air initially

Figure 9.1.3 *Rutherford's and Royds' experiment*

Gamma radiation was very penetrating and was not deflected by magnetic or electric fields. Rutherford and a colleague, E. N. da C. Andrade, used a new technique involving diffraction by crystals to actually measure the wavelength of gamma radiation. This convinced Rutherford and Andrade that gamma radiation was similar to X-ray radiation. It was a form of electromagnetic radiation and travelled at the speed of light. Wavelengths of gamma radiation were shorter than the wavelengths of X-ray radiation. Thus, gamma rays, discovered in 1900 by Villard, were finally identified in 1914 by Rutherford and Andrade.

The work of many great scientists indicated that the atom could no longer be considered an indivisible particle with no internal structure. All the evidence gathered by Becquerel, the Curies, Thomson, and Rutherford and his colleagues suggested that radioactive atoms literally threw off fragments of themselves. Eventually it was shown that these fragments came from an inner core of the atoms, called its **nucleus**. It was Ernest Rutherford who demonstrated that the atom had a nucleus.

Quick Check

1. What effect does a magnetic field have on a beam of radiation containing a mixture of alpha particles, beta particles, and gamma rays?

   _____

2. Who showed that beta particles were actually electrons? How did he do it?

   _____

   _____

   _____

3. Who showed that gamma radiation was actually electromagnetic radiation like light and X-rays? What kind of experiment did this require?

   _____

   _____

   _____

What Happens to a Radioactive Atom?

Many scientists occupied themselves trying to figure out what actually happened during radioactive decay of atoms of elements such as uranium, thorium, polonium, and radium. In 1900, William Crookes made a surprising discovery. When a uranium sample was thoroughly purified, its radioactivity actually decreased! This was puzzling, and it was thought for a while that perhaps it was an impurity in uranium that was radioactive, rather than the uranium itself. Shortly after, however, Becquerel duplicated the experiment and obtained the same result. However, he found that if the originally pure sample was left standing for a while, it regained its activity. Eventually it became as radioactive as previous measurements of uranium had indicated.

In 1902, Rutherford and the English physicist Frederick Soddy (1877–1956) found that thorium showed the same behaviour as uranium. Purified, its activity initially became very low, but on standing for a while, the sample recovered its activity.

Rutherford and Soddy drew a startling conclusion from these observations. What was happening, they said, was that when a radioactive atom such as uranium gave off radioactive particles, the uranium atom changed into an atom of a different element altogether! This new atom gave off radioactive particles and became yet another element. The increasing radioactivity of the uranium sample was due to the growing concentration of these radioactive "daughter elements." The daughter elements were more radioactive than the parent uranium atoms, so the radioactivity increased from the time the pure uranium was left standing.

Natural Transmutations

The idea that one element could change into another element was revolutionary. The alchemists had tried unsuccessfully for centuries to find ways to change common metals into gold. Of course, there is still no chemical way to change one element into another, but radioactive decay is not a chemical reaction.

The process of changing one element into another through radioactive decay is called **transmutation.** The work by Rutherford and Soddy, which verified that transmutation did, in fact, occur when alpha and beta particles were given off by a radioactive element, was done at McGill University. The discovery resulted in Rutherford winning the Nobel Prize in chemistry in 1908. By that time, Rutherford had returned to England where he was associated with the University of Manchester.

Probing Atoms with Alpha Particles

Alpha particles were among Ernest Rutherford's favourite tools for his atomic research. While at McGill University, he had observed that beams of alpha particles, if made to pass through a thin metal foil, were scattered from their paths. Presumably, the deflection was caused by atoms in the foil. This scattering effect of atoms on alpha particles was explored further by two of Rutherford's physics students at the University of Manchester in England. Hans Geiger (1882–1945) and Ernest Marsden (1889–1970) used a zinc sulphide screen as a detector of alpha particles. Zinc sulphide phosphoresces when struck by alpha particles. Figure 9.1.4 is a schematic diagram of the apparatus, all of which was enclosed in an evacuated container so that air molecules would not be a factor in scattering the alpha particles.

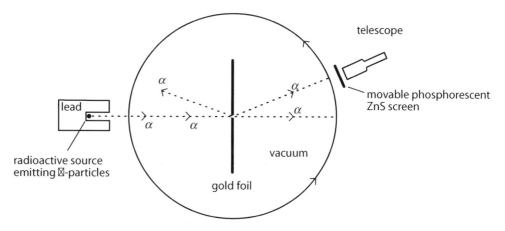

Figure 9.1.4 *Geiger's and Marsden's experiment*

Hans Geiger had earlier observed that the amount of scattering of the alpha particles by a metal foil increased if either (a) a thicker foil or (b) heavier atoms were used. However, most of the alpha particles went through the foil with little deflection, indicating that the atoms might be composed largely of empty space.

Rutherford suggested to Marsden, a young undergraduate student, that he find out whether any alpha particles were scattered through large angles. A few days later Geiger and Marsden reported to Rutherford that they had observed alpha particles coming backwards off the foil. This observation astounded Rutherford. After all, alpha particles, on the atomic scale, are very massive "bullets" with approximately 7000 times the mass of an electron!

Apparently, the fast-moving (10^7 m/s) alpha particles were being repelled by a powerful, highly centralized force within the atoms of the gold foil. The foil used initially by Geiger and Marsden was approximately 400 atoms thick. According to their observations, approximately 1 alpha particle in 8000 was turned back through an angle greater than 90°. What incredibly large force could turn around a massive alpha particle, travelling one-tenth the speed of light, and send it back the way it came?

The Rutherford Model of the Atom

The scattering of alpha particles by atoms could be explained by making the following assumptions:

(a) The atom is mostly empty space.
(b) Within the atom, most of the mass of the atom is concentrated in a tiny core carrying a positive charge. This core is the nucleus of the atom.
(c) Surrounding the nucleus are the negatively charged electrons. The mass of one electron is only 1/1836 times the mass of a normal hydrogen nucleus.

Figure 9.1.5 illustrates how Rutherford pictured the hydrogen atom: a dense core with a positive charge forming the nucleus. Around it, a negatively charged electron orbits the nucleus, much as a planet orbits the Sun. The atom as a whole is electrically neutral.

The nucleus of a hydrogen atom is simple. A single, positively charged particle carries most of the mass of the atom. In 1920, the nucleus of a hydrogen atom was given the name **proton**. By this time, it was becoming apparent that the proton might be a fundamental building block of all atoms. In fact, the number of protons in the atom of an element determines the number of electrons orbiting the nucleus. The number and arrangement of these electrons determines the chemical properties of the element. The number of protons in the nucleus of an element's atoms is the element's **atomic number**.

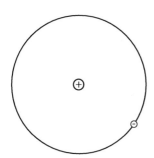

Figure 9.1.5 *Rutherford's model of the atom*

Discovery of the Neutron

In 1932, a third subatomic particle was discovered by the English physicist James Chadwick (1891–1947). Rutherford and others had predicted the existence of the neutron years before. The neutron has no charge and has nearly the same mass as a proton. The nucleus appeared to have two kinds of "building blocks": protons and neutrons. The protons and neutrons, called **nucleons**, together account for the mass of the nucleus of an atom. Protons alone account for the charge of the nucleus.

The proton-neutron model of the nucleus is still used. However, some questions naturally arise about this model. If there are no electrons in the nucleus, then where do beta particles, which are electrons, originate? They come from neutrons. Protons and electrons are **stable** particles, meaning they do not break down into other particle. Neutrons are **unstable**. Outside the nucleus, a neutron breaks down into a proton and an electron:

$$n^0 \ = \ p^+ \ + \ e^-$$

Within the nucleus, neutrons are stabilized in some atoms. But in radioactive atoms, neutrons are unstable. When the neutron breaks down, the electron leaves as a beta particle, but the proton stays in the nucleus. Notice that this raises the atomic number of the atom by one. It is no longer the same element.

Another question raised by the proton-neutron model of the nucleus is: What keeps the positively charged protons together? Positively charged particles should repel each other, especially when they are so close together. It turns out there is a force called the **strong force**. The nuclear strong force is only effective over very short ranges. However, the nuclear strong force alone cannot keep two isolated protons from flying apart. The presence of the electrically neutral neutrons seems to be necessary to keep nuclei with more than one proton together. The nuclear strong force acts equally between two neutrons as it does between two protons. It is only effective over a very short range (10^{-16} m). Having neutrons in the nucleus makes the strong force better able to compete with the electrostatic force trying to pull apart the nucleus.

Quick Check

1. What is natural transmutation?

   _____

   _____

2. Describe the Rutherford model of the hydrogen atom.

   _____

   _____

3. What is a proton? What is the atomic number of an element?

   _____

4. Is a neutron stable outside the nucleus? Explain.

   _____

   _____

Nuclear Reactions

Chemical reactions involve whole atoms, with some rearranging of electrons in the process. Nuclear reactions involve changes in the atomic nucleus. Radioactivity is due to nuclear reactions that involve the decay of a nucleus with the emission of particles or electromagnetic radiation. Radioactivity is beyond our control. It happens spontaneously and results in the formation of a new nucleus with a different atomic number. In other words, a new element forms. Natural transmutation occurs.

In order to write down what happens in nuclear reactions, certain symbols are used to represent subatomic particles. In the following chart, the subscript indicates the electric charge carried by the particle. The superscript indicates the number of nucleons (neutrons plus protons) in the particle (Table 9.1.1).

Table 9.1.1 *Subatomic Particles and Their Symbols*

Particle	Symbol
proton	$_{1}^{1}H$
neutron	$_{0}^{1}n$
electron (beta)	$_{-1}^{0}e$
helium nucleus (alpha)	$_{2}^{4}He$
gamma ray	γ

The charge and nucleon number system is also used for symbols of larger atomic nuclei. For example, the symbol for uranium-238 is $_{92}^{238}U$. The atomic number (nuclear charge) is 92. There are 238 nucleons in the nucleus. Since there are 92 protons, there must be 238 – 92 = 146 neutrons.

An example of a nuclear reaction is when uranium-238 undergoes radioactive decay and gives off an alpha particle. Here is how this nuclear reaction is written:

$$_{92}^{238}U \rightarrow\ _{90}^{234}Th +\ _{2}^{4}He$$

Because it ejected an alpha particle (helium nucleus), the atomic number of the new atom is two less (90). This is no longer uranium but thorium. The nucleon number is reduced to 234. Notice that there has been no overall loss of mass or charge! This reaction is an example of **alpha decay**.

The thorium formed from alpha decay of uranium-238 is also radioactive. It, however, undergoes **beta decay**. When thorium decays, one of its neutrons breaks down into a proton and a beta particle (electron). The proton stays in the nucleus and the beta particle is ejected. Here is how the net reaction is written:

$$_{90}^{234}Th \rightarrow\ _{91}^{234}Pa +\ _{-1}^{0}e$$

The *nuclear mass* has not been changed appreciably by the loss of an electron, but the *nuclear charge* has increased by one, and the new element is protactinium. Again, there is no overall loss of mass or charge.

The protactinium is also radioactive and undergoes beta decay as well:

$$_{91}^{234}Pa \rightarrow\ _{92}^{234}U +\ _{-1}^{0}e$$

As you can see, the series of radioactive decays has led us back to uranium. The atomic number of 92 tells us the element is uranium, but notice that the nucleon number is 234, not the original 238. This form of uranium has a different number of neutrons, 234 – 92 = 142 to be exact. There must be two forms of uranium! In fact, there are several forms of uranium. Different forms of the same element having different numbers of neutrons are called **isotopes.**

Isotopes

Isotopes of an element are chemically the same, but since the nuclei of the atoms have different numbers of neutrons, the atomic masses will differ. Three isotopes of hydrogen are illustrated in Figure 9.1.6.

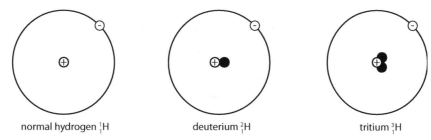

normal hydrogen $_1^1$H   deuterium $_1^2$H   tritium $_1^3$H

Figure 9.1.6 *Isotopes of hydrogen*

The most common isotope of hydrogen has one proton in the nucleus. This isotope is designated $_1^1$H. Hydrogen with a neutron in the nucleus also exists. Because it has two nucleons, this isotope, called **deuterium,** is designated $_1^2$H. A third isotope, **tritium**, has two neutrons in the nucleus along with the proton. Since it has three nucleons, it is designated $_1^3$H. The number of nucleons in the nucleus is called the **mass number**. The mass number of normal hydrogen is 1; of deuterium, 2; and of tritium, 3. Deuterium oxide is the "heavy water" used in nuclear reactors.

Isotopes exist of every chemical element. Some isotopes are stable and others are radioactive. Normal hydrogen and deuterium are stable, while tritium is radioactive, giving off beta particles as it decays and forms an isotope of helium.

$$_1^3H \rightarrow \ _2^3He + \ _{-1}^0e$$

$$_1^3H \rightarrow \ _2^3He + \ _{-1}^0e$$

Helium has three isotopes, designated $_2^3$He, $_2^4$He and $_2^5$He. The third element in the periodic table, lithium, has these isotopes: $_3^5$Li, $_3^6$Li, $_3^7$Li, $_3^8$Li and $_3^9$Li. Most naturally occurring lithium is Li-7 (92.5%) and Li-6 (7.5%). The other isotopes are artificially made **radioisotopes**. A radioisotope is an isotope that is unstable and therefore radioactive. Radioisotopes have many uses, such as in medicine, biology, nuclear reactors, pacemakers, geological dating, and weapons.

Most carbon in nature is the isotope carbon-12, $_6^{12}$C. Small amounts of the radioactive carbon-14, or $_6^{14}$C, are found wherever carbon is found, including the gas carbon dioxide (CO_2). Because the amount of carbon-14 in a given sample of carbon dioxide is well known, and the rate at which the C-14 decays is also well known, it is possible to estimate the date of ancient objects that contain carbon compounds, using the amount of carbon-14 remaining. The technique of radioactive dating has been used to determine the approximate age of the Dead Sea Scrolls and when previous ice ages occurred by sampling the trees knocked over by the glaciers.

Uranium has several isotopes, and all of them are radioactive. The most abundant isotope of uranium is $_{92}^{238}$U. Other isotopes of uranium include $_{92}^{233}$U, $_{92}^{234}$U and $_{92}^{235}$U.

Quick Check

1. What are isotopes? How are they the same? How are they different?

_____

_____

2. What is a radioisotope?

_____

3. Explain in detail what this symbol means: $^{238}_{92}$U.

_____

4. Complete these nuclear reactions:

(a) $^{226}_{88}$Ra $\rightarrow$ $^{222}_{88}$Rn +

(b) $^{214}_{82}$Pb $\rightarrow$ $^{214}_{83}$Bi +

(c) $^{218}_{84}$Po $\rightarrow$ _____ + $^{4}_{2}$He

(d) $^{210}_{83}$Bi $\rightarrow$ _____ + $^{0}_{-1}$e

The Half-Life of Radioisotopes

The rate at which a radioisotope decays can be measured. It is expressed in terms of the time it takes for half the radioactive atoms to decay. The time it takes for half the atoms in a radioactive sample to decay is called the **half-life** of the isotope. For example, uranium-238 has a half-life of 4.5 billion years. For example, if a sample of uranium-238 had 1000 atoms to begin with, then after 4.5 billion years, 500 of these atoms will have decayed to thorium-234. The thorium-234, in turn, decays into protactinium-234, which in turn decays into uranium-234, and so on.

Uranium-238 has an exceptionally long half-life. Uranium-235 has a half-life of 7.1×10^8 years, which is also very long. Uranium-237's half-life is only 6.63 days. Thorium-234, formed when U-238 decays, has a half-life of only 24.1 days. Protactinium-234 has a half-life of just over 1 minute! There are radioisotopes with half-lives of less than one millionth of a second.

The half-life of a sample of an element is determined by measuring the activity of the sample, in emissions per second, over a period of time. One emission per second is one **becquerel** (1 Bq). Higher activities are measured in kilobecquerels (kBq) and megabecquerels (MBq).

Figure 9.1.7 illustrates how an imaginary sample of 8000 carbon-14 atoms decays over a period of many years. Every half-life (5700 years), the number of carbon-14 atoms left is reduced by one-half the number that existed at the start of the half-life. Table 9.1.2 lists half-lives of some important radioisotopes.

Table 9.1.2 *Half-Lives of Selected Radioisotopes*

Isotope	Half-Life (a = year)
$^{3}_{1}H$ (tritium)	12.5 a
$^{14}_{6}C$	5700 a
$^{15}_{8}O$	2.1 min
$^{60}_{27}Co$	5.2 a
$^{131}_{63}I$	8.1 d
$^{90}_{43}Tc$	6.0 h
$^{235}_{92}U$	7.1×10^{8} a
$^{238}_{92}U$	4.5×10^{9} a

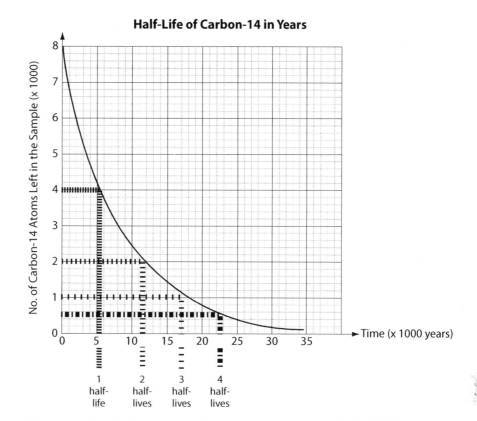

Figure 9.1.7 *Graph of the decay rate of carbon-14, a radioisotope with a half-life of approximately 5700 years.*

Sample Problem 9.1.1 — Calculating Half-Life

How long will it take for the number of radioactive $^{131}_{63}I$ atoms in a sample to be reduced to $\frac{1}{16}$ of the initial number?

What to Think About	How to Do It
1. Determine the half-life of I from Table 9.1.2.	8.1 days
2. Determine how many half-lives occur before 1/16 of sample is left.	$\frac{1}{16} = \frac{1}{2} \times \frac{1}{2} \times \frac{1}{2} \times \frac{1}{2}$ Therefore, 4 half-lives of iodine are required to get to $\frac{1}{16}$ of the original mass.
3. Multiply the number of half-lives by the length of one half-life.	Total time = 4 half-lives × 8.1 days = 32.4 days

Practice Problems 9.1.1 — Calculating Half-Life

1. Thorium-234 has a half-life of 24 d. How many atoms from a 4000 atom sample will still be thorium-234 after a period of 144 d?

2. After 26 a, the number of radioactive cobalt-60 atoms in a sample is reduced to $\frac{1}{32}$ of the initial count. What is the half-life of the isotope?

Radioactive Series

Recall that uranium-238 decays to thorium-234 and that thorium-234 decays to protactinium-234. In turn, protactinium decays to uranium-234. The series of decays does not end there. As Figure 9.1.8 illustrates, the series of decays results ultimately in stable lead-206. This is an example of a **radioactive series.** When an alpha particle is emitted during radioactive decay, atoms of a new element are formed, with an atomic number two less than the original element and a mass number four less. When a beta particle (electron) is emitted, the new element has the same mass number but an atomic number one higher. During radioactive decay, gamma rays are often emitted as well, but they do not affect either the atomic number or the mass number.

Quick Check

1. Write the nuclear reaction for the decay of radium into radon (Figure 9.1.8).

2. Write the nuclear reaction for the decay of Pb-214 into Bi-214.

3. How many different *elements* are involved in the radioactive series in Figure 9.1.8? How many different *isotopes* are involved?

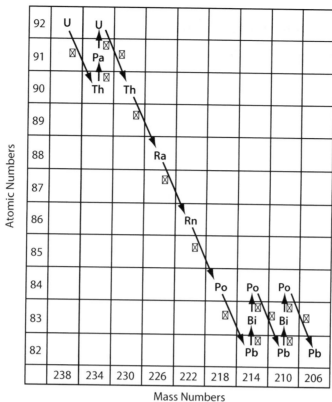

Figure 9.1.8 *A radioactive series of naturally occurring radioisotopes with* $^{238}_{92}$U *as the parent. Atomic numbers are on the left, and mass numbers are along the bottom of the chart.*

Artificial Transmutation of Elements

Artificial transmutation is a routine matter to modern-day physicists. The first physicist to succeed in changing one element into another element was Ernest Rutherford, who achieved this landmark reaction in 1919.

Rutherford filled a sealed container with pure nitrogen gas. He then bombarded the nitrogen with alpha particles. After the bombardment, he detected oxygen and hydrogen in the container. He explained this as being due to the transmutation of nitrogen into oxygen and hydrogen, according to this reaction:

$$^{14}_{7}\text{N} \quad + \quad ^{4}_{2}\text{He} \quad \rightarrow \quad ^{17}_{8}\text{O} \quad + \quad ^{1}_{1}\text{H}$$

nitrogen atom   alpha particle   oxygen atom   hydrogen atom (proton)

Since Rutherford's experiment, artificial transmutation has become a common procedure for today's nuclear physicists. In the early days, transmutation was achieved by bombarding atoms with particles from radioactive minerals. Later, physicists began to use particles accelerated by high-energy accelerators.

Investigation 9-1 Simulating Radioactive Decay

Purpose

To simulate radioactive decay and half-life

Procedure

1. Your instructor will provide you with 100 dice-size wooden cubes. One side of each one is coloured or marked in some way. The coloured side represents a decayed atom. (Dice can be used but you must choose one number to represent decayed atoms.)

2. Roll the cubes the way you would roll dice, each time recording the number of decayed atoms and the number of radioactive atoms still left after each roll. (The decayed atoms are removed from the set after each roll.) Do this until all the atoms have decayed.

3. Collect all class data, and prepare a master table listing combined class results. Plot a graph of radioactive atoms still left vs. number of rolls.

Concluding Question

1. From the graph, determine the half-life of your radioactive atoms, and express it in number or rolls.

9.1 Review Questions

1. What were the properties of the rays discovered by Henri Becquerel?

2. What was the significance of transmutation in developing an understanding of radioactivity?

3. How was the neutron discovered?

4. Why would you not expect alpha particles, on passing through gold foil, to be deflected significantly by electrons in the gold atoms?

5. What is meant by the half-life of an isotope?

6. Complete the following nuclear equations. Rewrite the equations and solve for *x*.

    (a) $^{14}_{6}\text{C} \rightarrow \, ^{x}_{x}\text{N} + \, ^{0}_{1}\text{e}$

    (b) $^{226}_{88}\text{Ra} \rightarrow \, ^{222}_{86}\text{Rn} + \, ^{x}_{x}\text{X}$

    (c) $^{x}_{x}\text{Ac} \rightarrow \, ^{221}_{87}\text{Fr} + \, ^{4}_{2}\text{He}$

    (d) $^{x}_{82}\text{X} \rightarrow \, ^{209}_{83}\text{Bi} + \, ^{x}_{-1}x$

7. After five half-lives, how much of a 4000 g sample of carbon-14 is left?

9.2 Nuclear Fission and Fusion

Warm Up

What is the difference between fission and fusion?

_____

_____

_____

Energy in the Atom

In 1932, English physicist John Douglas Cockcroft (1897–1967) and Irish physicist Ernest Thomas Sinton Walton (1903–1995) used a particle accelerator to produce high-speed protons. Because of their high speed, the protons also had high kinetic energy. These protons were made to collide with lithium nuclei. They were able to penetrate and disrupt the lithium nuclei, resulting in an artificially induced nuclear reaction:

$$^{7}_{3}\text{Li} + {}^{1}_{1}\text{H} \rightarrow {}^{4}_{2}\text{He} + {}^{4}_{2}\text{He}$$

In this nuclear reaction, caused by accelerated protons, the lithium nucleus was, in effect, "split." The result was two new nuclei, both helium. The newspapers reported that Cockcroft and Walton had "split the atom" for the first time.

An important observation from this experiment was that when the kinetic energies of the two helium nuclei (alpha particles) were added up, the total kinetic energy was greater than the kinetic energy of the proton that caused the reaction to occur.

However, the combined mass of the alpha particles was found to be less than the masses of the proton and lithium atom combined.

This experiment confirmed a prediction made by Albert Einstein (1879–1955) that mass could be changed into energy. He related mass to energy with his famous equation, $E = mc^2$.

What actually happened in the nuclear reaction induced by Cockcroft and Walton was that mass was converted into energy. Mass-energy, however, was conserved.

The same year as Cockcroft and Walton carried out the first artificial nuclear reaction, Chadwick bombarded beryllium with alpha particles that had been accelerated. The helium nucleus was absorbed by the beryllium nucleus, forming carbon atoms along with a "new" particle — the neutron. Energy was released in this reaction as well. This is how Chadwick discovered the neutron.

$$^{9}_{4}\text{Be} + {}^{4}_{2}\text{He} \rightarrow {}^{12}_{6}\text{C} + {}^{1}_{0}\text{n} + \text{energy}$$

This and other nuclear reactions can be used to produce free neutrons, which are now used as nuclear "bullets." Unfortunately, fast-moving neutrons are not very useful in nuclear bombardment experiments. Fast-moving neutrons go right through nuclei without having much effect.

Slow-moving neutrons are another matter! They can actually be absorbed by nuclei, with very important results. Fast-moving neutrons can be slowed down by passing them through deuterium oxide (called heavy water) or graphite (pure carbon). These substances slow down the neutrons enough to let them react with other nuclei. Heavy water and graphite used in this way are called **moderators**.

If a slow-moving neutron is captured by an atom of the most common isotope of uranium, uranium-238, here is what happens:

$$^{238}_{92}U + ^{1}_{0}n \rightarrow ^{239}_{92}U$$

The uranium-239 is unstable and emits a beta particle.

$$^{239}_{92}U \rightarrow ^{239}_{91}Np + ^{0}_{-1}e$$

Neptunium is radioactive, with a short half-life of only 2.3 days. It decays by emitting a beta particle to become plutonium-239.

$$^{239}_{93}Np \rightarrow ^{239}_{94}Pu + ^{0}_{-1}e$$

Both neptunium and plutonium are elements with atomic numbers higher than 92. They are just two of the many artificially produced elements beyond uranium in the periodic table. All are radioactive and have short half-lives. (Examine a periodic chart and see how many of these transuranium elements have been made by scientists.)

Nuclear Fission

A small fraction of natural uranium is the isotope uranium-235. When this atom absorbs a slow neutron, its nucleus undergoes an unusual transformation.

Recall that the strong nuclear force keeps the nucleus together, while electrical forces between like-charged protons tend to make it fly apart. In the uranium-235 nucleus, the balance between the normally dominant nuclear strong forces and the electrical forces is a fragile one. According to a nuclear model proposed by Neils Bohr (1885–1962) (called the liquid drop model), the addition to the nucleus of one more neutron might cause the nucleus to oscillate (Figure 9.2.1). If that happens and the electrical forces overcome the nuclear forces, the nucleus could break apart. This process can, in fact, occur. It is called nuclear **fission**, and it was discovered by two teams of scientists working independently, within days of each other. German chemists Otto Hahn and Fritz Strassman observed this reaction in 1939:

$$^{235}_{92}U + ^{1}_{0}n \rightarrow ^{144}_{56}Ba + ^{90}_{36}Kr + 2\,^{1}_{0}n + energy$$

Working in Denmark, two Austrian physicists made similar observations. Lise Meitner and Otto Frisch compared the process with the division of living cells and coined the label "fission" to describe what happened to the uranium nucleus. The most striking feature about nuclear fission is the release of very large amounts of nuclear energy due to the conversion of mass into energy, according to Einstein's equation, $E = mc^2$. The amount of energy released during fission is extremely large compared with normal chemical reactions. The source of the energy is the conversion of mass from the nuclei involved in the fission. Now, one nucleus undergoing fission may not be too significant, but keep in mind that for every fission that occurs, two or three neutrons are released. These neutrons can initiate more fissions, which, in turn, produce more neutrons and more fissions. The possibility of a **chain reaction** occurring is very real!

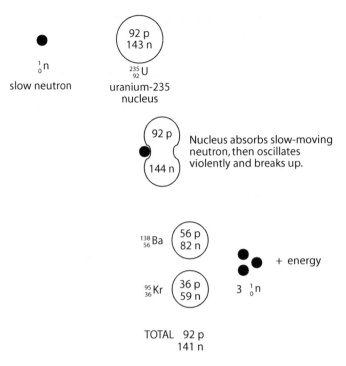

Figure 9.2.1 *The liquid drop model of one possible fission reaction*

A slow-moving neutron is absorbed by a uranium-235 nucleus. The nucleus, according to Bohr's liquid drop model, oscillates wildly then divides into two smaller "drops" — a barium-138 nucleus, and a krypton-95 nucleus. Three neutrons are also released!

Nuclear fission does not occur in naturally occurring uranium because uranium-235 makes up less than 1% of natural uranium metal. If fission did occur in a sample of naturally occurring uranium, neutrons from the uranium-235 would be safely absorbed by uranium-238 nuclei, which do not normally undergo fission. Even with pure uranium-235, a certain minimum mass called the **critical mass** is needed before a chain reaction can occur. If the needed critical mass is achieved, an explosion of incredible force will occur. In a nuclear bomb, two or more sub-critical masses of uranium-235 are forced together abruptly by a conventional explosive, and the bomb explodes.

Harnessing Nuclear Fission

Scientists realized that if the rate of the fission reaction could be controlled, it would be possible to harness the energy released in the reaction. The key to slowing the reaction is to control the rate of neutrons being produced from the fission reaction. If the rate of production can equal the rate of neutrons being used in the fission process, then a self-sustaining reaction occurs. To control the rate, scientists placed a moderator into the reaction. This is usually water, or it can be graphite or heavy water. Heavy water, also called deuterium oxide, is water in which the hydrogen atoms have two neutrons each. With the ability to control the reaction, nuclear reactors became a method of electrical generation for many countries including Canada. Other smaller nuclear reactors are used for medical and research purposes.

Nuclear reactors are currently based on the fission reaction. The energy release in the reaction is used to heat water into steam. The steam turns a turbine that generates the electricity.

There are six main components to nuclear reactors:
- Fuel — a material capable of undergoing fission; usually uranium oxide (UO_2)
- Moderator — a material for slowing down neutrons so the chain reaction can continue; usually water, but may be graphite or heavy water
- Control rods — a neutron-absorbing material designed to shut down reaction; usually cadmium or boron rods that can be added or withdrawn from the reaction as required
- Coolant — a liquid or gas to transfer the heat
- Pressure vessel — a steel container holding the fission reaction
- Steam generator — system to convert steam to electrical energy
- Containment — typically 1 m of concrete designed to protect the reactor

There are many different types of reactors. Each one is slightly different from the others and the main components may function in a slightly different manner. The three most common types of reactors are boiling water reactor (BWR), pressurized water reactor (PWR), and pressurized heavy water reactor (CANDU) (Table 9.2.1).

Table 9.2.1 *Top Three Types of Nuclear Power Plants in Commercial Operation*

Reactor Type	Main Countries	Number	Fuel	Coolant	Moderator
BWR	US, Japan, Sweden	94	enriched UO_2	water	water
PWR	US, France, Japan, Russia, China	265	enriched UO_2	water	water
CANDU	Canada	44	natural UO_2	heavy water	heavy water

Source: *Nuclear Engineering International Handbook 2010*

Boiling Water Reactor

The boiling water reactors consist of one loop (Figure 9.2.2). The pressure vessel contains the fission reaction. It is where steam is generated as well. The steam is then carried to the steam turbine to turn the generator. A condenser cools the steam back into water, and the water is pumped back into the pressure vessel. A major concern with this design is that all the liquid or steam in the system is radioactive. Any leaks would mean radioactivity would be released into the environment

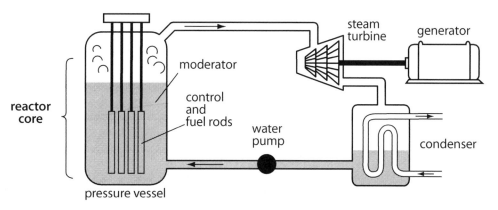

Figure 9.2.2 *Schematic diagram of a boiling water reactor*

Pressurized Water Reactor

A modified version of the boiling water reactor is the pressurized water reactor. The PWR is the most common type of nuclear reactor. In this design, the heated radioactive fluid from the primary loop does not come into contact with the steam and liquid used to turn the turbine in the secondary loop. The PWR is more efficient and safer than a BWR, but is more expensive to build.

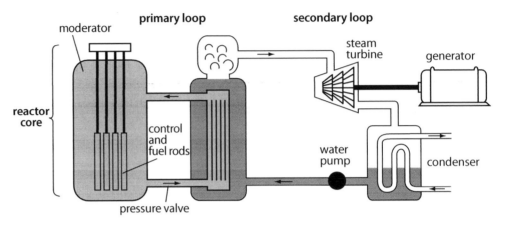

Figure 9.2.3 *Schematic diagram of a pressurized water reactor*

CANDU

The Canadian-designed CANDU (Canada Deuterium Uranium) nuclear reactor has a modified PWR design. The primary loop uses heavy water as the moderator rather than water. While this has a higher cost, the fuel a CANDU reactor uses requires a lower concentration of uranium. Other reactors use water as the moderator, but require an enriched form of uranium. New versions of the CANDU reactor can use regular water for the moderator if slightly enriched uranium is used. If a problem arises, the moderator is simply emptied from the reactor core and the reaction stops. In the CANDU reactor, the core and moderator are housed in the calandria.

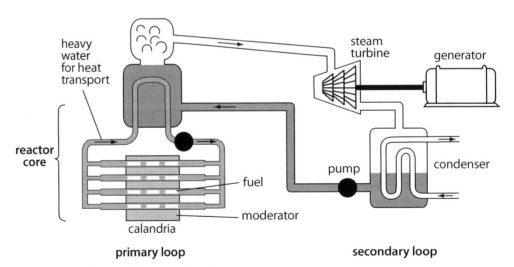

Figure 9.2.4 *Schematic diagram of a CANDU reactor*

Nuclear Fusion

Nuclear **fusion** is the opposite of fission. If light nuclei such as hydrogen, tritium, and deuterium are forced to within a distance of approximately 10^{-16} m of each other, the strong nuclear force exceeds the electrical repulsive force, and fusion may occur.

As you might imagine, if two like-charged nuclei are to get very, very close to one another without repelling, they must be moving at extremely high speeds. High speed means high kinetic energy, which, in turn, means very high temperatures — the sort of temperatures found near the centre of the sun and other stars. Fusion is the source of the Sun's energy.

Fusion occurring due to very high temperatures is called **thermonuclear fusion.** When light nuclei fuse, there is a loss of mass. This "lost" mass is converted into energy. (Remember $E = mc^2$.) The Sun actually loses millions of tonnes of mass every second. The energy produced from this mass leaves the Sun as electromagnetic radiation, including visible light, infrared, and so on.

Here is an example of a fusion reaction:

$$^2_1H + {}^2_1H \rightarrow {}^3_2He + {}^1_0n + \text{energy}$$

Two deuterium nuclei fuse to form helium-3, and a neutron is released in the process along with energy in the form of radiation.

The fusion process that takes place in the Sun involves a series of steps. The net reaction is believed to be:

$$^1_1 4H \rightarrow {}^4_2He + 2\,{}^0_{+1}e + \text{energy}$$

In the process, ordinary hydrogen nuclei are fused to helium with the emission of a **positive electron (positron)**. The positron is the **anti-particle** of an electron. It has the same mass as an electron, but the opposite charge. It is estimated that the loss of mass due to thermonuclear fusion in the Sun is at the rate of four billion kilograms every second! Fortunately, the Sun still has 2×10^{30} kg of mass left.

One of the great dreams of nuclear physicists is to master the process of fusion so that it can be controlled and used as a source of energy for humankind. Fusion is a "clean" process whose products are not radioactive. (Helium is one of these products. Helium is the harmless gas used in toy balloons.) Research is going on at the present time. Fusion has been achieved, but as yet, scientists have not obtained a sustained reaction that releases more energy than is put into the reaction to get it started. The fuel needed for a fusion reactor is simple hydrogen, which is available in plentiful supply from water (H_2O).

People have achieved fusion on a brief, horrendous scale in the development of the hydrogen bomb. The high temperatures needed are obtained by using a fission bomb (atom bomb) to force the reacting nuclei together. Research continues on finding a safe process for harnessing the energy in a fusion reaction.

9.2 Review Questions

1. (a) Describe the landmark achievement of Cockcroft and Walton.

   (b) What was the source of the excess energy in this reaction?

2. (a) What is nuclear fission?

   (b) What is the most important consequence of fission?

   (c) Why is a chain reaction feasible in nuclear fission of uranium-235?

3. What is it about the fission of U-235 that makes a chain reaction possible?

4. Compare and contrast three types of nuclear reactors.

5. Create a list of pros and cons of using nuclear power to generate electricity.

6. In a nuclear reactor, how is an explosion avoided when fission occurs?

Chapter 9 Review

1. How was radioactivity accidentally discovered?

2. What are the three properties of the Rutherford model of the atom?

3. What did early researchers such as Rutherford and the Curies know about the dangers of radioactivity?

4. What is the difference between a beta particle and gamma radiation?

5. What does the symbol $_{-1}^{0}e$ represent?

6. Describe the differences between $_{92}^{235}U$ and $_{92}^{238}U$?

7. Write the nuclear reactions for the following:
   (a) uranium-238 decaying to thorium-234

   (b) thorium-234 decaying to protactinium-234

8. What is meant by the half-life of a radioisotope?

9. Cobalt-60 has a half-life of 5.2 years. Describe what would happen to a sample of 1 million cobalt-60 atoms in a period of 52 years.

10. A solution containing a radioactive isotope is injected into your bloodstream just before you have a brain scan. Should the radioisotope used have a short half-life or long half-life? Explain.

11. Complete the following nuclear reactions.

    (a) $^{230}_{90}\text{Th} \rightarrow {}^{4}_{2}\text{He} +$ _____

    (b) $^{234}_{90}\text{Th} \rightarrow {}^{234}_{91}\text{Pa} +$ _____

    (c) $^{14}_{6}\text{C} \rightarrow {}^{0}_{-1}\text{e} +$ _____

    (d) $^{218}_{84}\text{Po} \rightarrow {}^{214}_{82}\text{Pb} +$ _____

12. Describe the main components of a nuclear reactor.

13. Identify and label the above nuclear reactor below.

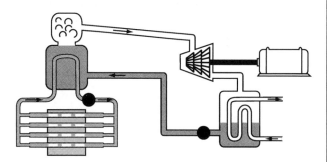

16. Why is fusion favoured over fission as a future source of energy for human use?

14. What is nuclear fusion? Give one example of a possible fusion reaction.

17. What kind of nuclei can undergo fusion? What conditions are needed?

15. Why is fusion difficult to achieve under controlled circumstances?

Chapter 9 Extra Practice

1. What evidence led to the identification of three types of Becquerel rays?

2. What is special about the nuclear strong force? Over what distance is it effective?

3. What is an alpha particle?

4. What does the symbol $^4_2$He represent?

5. For what research did Ernest Rutherford receive a Nobel Prize in chemistry?

6. Use this graph to answer the questions below.

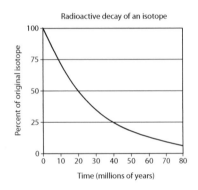

(a) What is the half-life of the element?
(b) How old would the element be after three half-lives?
(c) After 80 million years how many half-lives has the sample gone through?

7. Technetium-90 has a half-life of 6.0 h. If there are 64 atoms of technetium-90 in a sample to start with, how many atoms of this radioisotope will be left in their original state after one full 24-h day?

8. Complete the following nuclear reactions.

$$^{222}_{86}\text{Rn} \rightarrow {}^4_2\text{He} + \underline{\hspace{3cm}}$$

$$^{210}_{82}\text{Pb} \rightarrow {}^{210}_{83}\text{Bi} + \underline{\hspace{3cm}}$$

$$^{210}_{83}\text{Bi} \rightarrow {}^0_{-1}\text{e} + \underline{\hspace{3cm}}$$

9. Identify and label the nuclear reactor below.

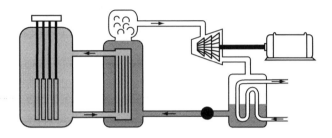

10. Identify and label the nuclear reactor below.

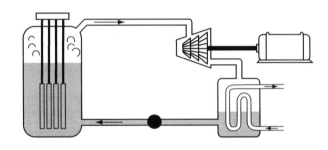

11. What happens when uranium-235 undergoes fission? Describe what starts the process, what happens during fission, and what the consequences are.

12. How is fusion different from fission?

13. What happens when a slow-moving neutron successfully encounters:
    (a) a uranium-238 nucleus?
    (b) a uranium-235 nucleus?

14. What is meant by critical mass? How is it achieved in an atomic bomb?

15. How is fusion initiated in a hydrogen bomb?

16. Why are scientists hopeful of achieving controlled fusion as a source of energy?

17. (a) What elements make up most of the stars?
    (b) What type of nuclear reaction occurs in stars?

10 Electric Circuits

By the end of this chapter, you should be able to do the following:

- Apply Ohm's law to a variety of direct current circuits
- Apply Kirchhoff's laws to a variety of direct current circuits
- Correctly use ammeters and voltmeters
- Solve a range of problems involving current, resistance, electric potential difference, electric power, and efficiency

By the end of this chapter, you should know the meaning of these **key terms**:

- ammeter
- ampere
- conventional electric current
- electric current
- electric power
- electromotive force (emf)
- equivalent resistance

- internal resistance
- parallel circuit
- resistance
- series circuit
- terminal voltage
- voltmeter

By the end of this chapter, you should be able to use and know when to use the following formulae:

$$I = \frac{\Delta Q}{t} \qquad V = IR \qquad P = IV \qquad V_{terminal} = \mathcal{E} \pm Ir$$

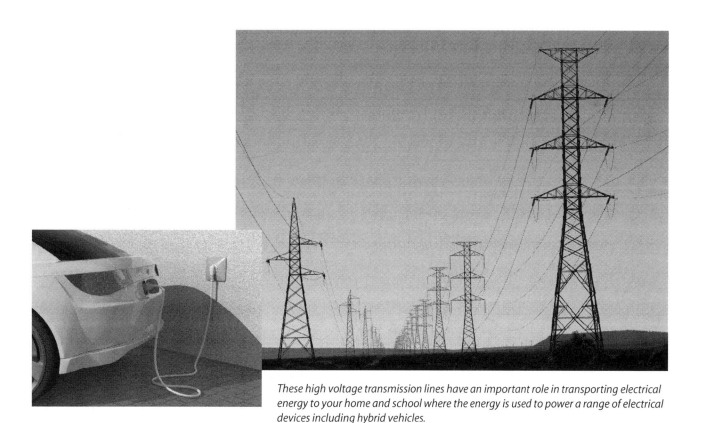

These high voltage transmission lines have an important role in transporting electrical energy to your home and school where the energy is used to power a range of electrical devices including hybrid vehicles.

10.1 Current Events in History

Galvani's and Volta's Experiments

Until 200 years ago, the idea of producing a steady current of electricity and putting it to use was nonexistent. The discovery of a way to produce a flow of electric charges was, in fact, accidental. In the year 1780, at the University of Bologna, Italian professor of anatomy Luigi Galvani (1737–1798) was dissecting a frog. First, he noticed that when a nearby static electricity generator made a spark while a metal knife was touching the frog's nerves, the frog's legs would jump as its muscles contracted! Galvani proceeded to look for the conditions that caused this behaviour. In the course of his investigations, Galvani discovered that if two different metal objects (such as a brass hook and an iron support) touched each other, while also touching the frog's exposed flesh, the same contractions of the frog's legs occurred. Galvani thought that the source of the electricity was in the frog itself, and he called the phenomenon "animal electricity."

Another Italian scientist, physics professor Alessandro Volta (1745–1827), of the University of Pavia, set about to test Galvani's "animal electricity" theory for himself. Before long, Volta discovered that the source of the electricity was in the contact of two different metals. The animal (frog) was incidental. If any two different metals are immersed in a conducting solution of acid, base, or salt, they will produce an electric current. Volta was able to show that some pairs of metals worked better than other pairs. Of course, no ammeters or voltmeters were available in those days to compare currents and voltages. One way that Volta compared currents was to observe the response of the muscle tissue of dead frogs.

Neither Galvani nor Volta could explain their observations. (There is no truth to the rumour that the frog's leg jumped because 1780 was a leap year.) Many years later, it was learned that radio waves generated by the sparking generator induced a current in the metal scalpel that was penetrating the frog, even though the scalpel was some distance from the generator!

Volta eventually invented the first practical electric battery. Zinc and silver disks, separated by paper pads soaked with salt water, acted as electric cells. Stacked one on top of another, these cells became a "battery" that yielded more current than a single cell.

Cells and Batteries

There are many types of electric cells in existence today. Usually when you purchase a "battery" in a store, you are actually buying a single **cell.** Strictly speaking, a battery consists of two or more cells connected together. Nine-volt batteries used in portable radios, tape recorders, calculators, and smoke alarms are true batteries. If you open up a discarded 9 V battery, you will see six small 1.5 V cells connected together, one after the other in what is called "a series."

Figure 10.1.1 shows one type of **voltaic cell** (named after Volta). The two rods, called **electrodes**, are made of carbon and zinc, as in the traditional **dry cell**, but they are immersed in a solution of ammonium chloride (NH_4Cl). In a real dry cell, a paste containing NH_4Cl, sawdust, and other ingredients is used. The chemistry of voltaic cells will be left to your chemistry courses. The reaction that occurs, however, has the effect of *removing electrons* from the carbon electrode (making it *positive*) and adding them to the zinc (making the zinc *negative*). In a real dry cell, the outer casing of the cell is made of zinc. The zinc is dissolved away as the cell is used, and may eventually leak its contents.

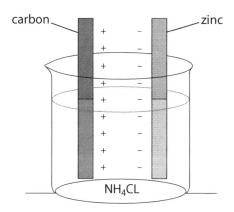

Figure 10.1.1 *A voltaic cell*

There are many kinds of cells and batteries. Rechargeable "batteries" may use nickel and cadmium, or molybdenum and lithium, or lead and lead oxide (as in the standard car battery). There are many kinds of cells on the market today, but they all produce electric current when connected to a conducting path.

Electromotive Force

In a carbon-zinc dry cell, forces resulting from the chemical reaction within the cell drive charges to the terminals, doing work to overcome the repulsive forces. The work done on the charges increases their potential energy. The difference in potential energy between the terminals amounts to 1.5 J for every coulomb of charge separated. We say the **potential difference** is 1.5 J/C, or 1.5 V. For a cell or battery that is not supplying current, the potential difference is at its peak value, which is called the **electromotive force (emf)**. It is given the symbol $\mathcal{E}$.

For a dry cell, the emf is 1.5 V. A nickel-cadmium cell is usually labelled 1.2 V or 1.25 V, but a freshly charged nickel-cadmium battery will have an even higher emf than its labelled rating. The cells in a lead storage battery have emfs of 2 V each. Six of these cells connected in series within the battery give a total emf of 12 V.

When electric charges *flow*, we say a current exists. A current will exist as long as a continuous conducting path is created for charges to flow from and back to a source of emf, as shown in Figure 10.1.2.

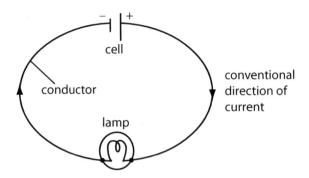

Figure 10.1.2 *Electric charges flow as a current through a conductor as long as there is no break in the path.*

Electric current is defined as the amount of electric charge that passes a point in a circuit in one second. If an amount of charge Q passes a point in a circuit in a time t, then the average current I through that point is $I = \dfrac{Q}{t}$.

Current could quite logically be measured in coulombs per second (C/s), but this unit is called the **ampere (A)** after André Ampère (1775–1836), a French physicist.

$$1\ A = 1\ C/s$$

One ampere is the sort of current that exists in a 100 W light bulb in a lamp in your home. (A 100 W lamp in a 110 V circuit would draw approximately 0.9 A.) In terms of electrons,

$$1\ A = 6.24 \times 10^{18}\ \text{electrons/s}$$

Current Direction

The direction of current was defined arbitrarily by André Ampère to be the direction that positive charges would move between two points where there is a difference of potential energy. In many simple circuits, we now know it is negative charges (electrons) that actually move. In solid conductors, the positive charges are locked in the nuclei of atoms, which are fixed in their location in the crystal. Loosely attached electrons can move through the conductor from atom to atom. In liquids and gases, however, the flow of charges may consist of positively charged ions as well as negatively charged ions and electrons.

Throughout this book, we shall use conventional current direction: the direction that positive charges would move between two points where there is a potential difference between the points.

Drift Velocity

How fast do electrons move in a wire carrying a current of, for example, 1 A? When a switch is closed in a circuit, the effect of the current can be detected immediately throughout the entire circuit. This might lead you to conclude that the electric charges (usually electrons) travel at very high velocity through the circuit. In fact, this is not so! The average **drift velocity** of electrons in a given set of circumstances can be calculated.

Within a length of metal wire, there are many, many loosely attached electrons (sometimes called "free electrons"). These electrons move about much like the molecules in a container of gas might move.

Let's consider the movement of electrons in a silver wire. Silver is an excellent conductor. Let's assume there is one free electron for every silver atom in a piece of wire. When the wire is connected to a source of emf, the potential difference (voltage) will cause electrons to move from the negative terminal of the source of emf toward the positive terminal. This movement is *superimposed* on the random motion of the electrons that is going on all the time with or without a source of emf.

The trip the electrons make from the negative to the positive terminal is not a smooth one (as it is, for example, in the vacuum of a CRT). Electrons in the metal wire collide with positive silver ions on the way, and transfer some of their kinetic energy to the silver ions. The increased thermal energy of the silver ions will show up as an increase in temperature of the silver conductor.

Assume the current in the silver wire in Figure 10.1.3 is 1.0 A. Then there are 6.24×10^{18} electrons passing the observer each second. This is because

$$1.0\ A = 1.0\ C/s = 6.24 \times 10^{18}\ e/s$$

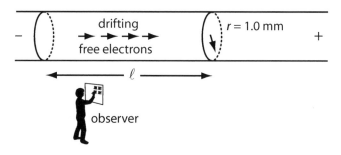

Figure 10.1.3 *Calculating the average drift velocity of electrons through a silver wire*

To calculate the average drift velocity of the electrons, we start by again assuming that there is *one free electron for every silver atom*, a reasonable assumption, since chemists tell us that silver usually forms ions with a charge of +1.

All we need to know is what length of the silver wire in Figure 10.1.3 would contain 6.24×10^{18} silver atoms (and therefore 6.24×10^{18} free electrons). We can find this out in three steps, as follows:

1. The mass of silver needed to have 6.24×10^{18} free electrons is

$$mass = \frac{6.24 \times 10^{18}\ atoms}{6.02 \times 10^{23}\ atoms/mole} \times 108\ g/mole = 1.12 \times 10^{-3}\ g$$

2. The volume of silver wire needed to have 6.24×10^{18} free electrons is

$$volume = \frac{mass}{density} = \frac{1.12 \times 10^{-3}\ g}{10.5\ g/cm^3} = 1.07 \times 10^{-4}\ cm$$

3. The radius of the silver wire in Figure 10.1.3 is 1.0 mm, or 1.0×10^{-1} cm. Its cross-sectional area is πr^2, so the length can be found as follows:

$$\text{length, } \ell = \frac{\text{volume}}{\text{area}} = \frac{1.07 \times 10^{-4} \text{ cm}^3}{\pi(1.0 \times 10^{-1} \text{ cm})^2} = 3.4 \times 10^{-3} \text{ cm}$$

Since a length of 3.4×10^{-3} cm contains 6.24×10^{18} electrons, and this many electrons pass the observer in 1 s, the average drift velocity of the conducting electrons is 3.4×10^{-3} cm/s, or 0.034 mm/s! This is true only for the stated conditions, of course. If the amount of current, the nature of the material in the conductor, or the dimensions of the conductor change, then the drift velocity will also change.

When you turn on a switch to light a lamp using a battery, the change in the electric field may travel at the speed of light, but the electrons themselves drift ever so slowly through the wire, under the influence of the electric field.

Representing Electric Circuits

Figure 10.1.4 shows a simple electric circuit. There is an energy source or battery, a device to use the electrical energy (such as a lamp), a switch or control, and wires to carry the energy.

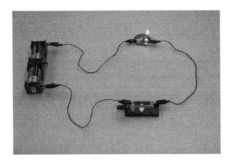

Figure 10.1.4 *A simple electric circuit*

Any circuit can be represented with a schematic diagram using a set of common symbols. Table 10.1.1 lists some of the more common symbols used for drawing electrical circuits. You will need to know each of these symbols so you can draw electrical circuits.

Table 10.1.1 *Common Symbols Used in Circuit Diagrams*

wire	————	power pack	
switch – open		ammeter	A
switch – closed		voltmeter	V
resistor		fuse	
single cell		light bulb	
battery			

The circuit in Figure 10.1.4 can be represented as shown in Figure 10.1.5.

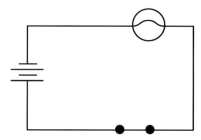

Figure 10.1.5 *A schematic drawing of the circuit shown in Figure 10.1.4*

Quick Check

1. Draw a circuit that has two light bulbs, a battery, a fuse, and closed switch.

2. Design a circuit that has a switch that can turn off two light bulbs at the same time.

3. Design a circuit that has two light bulbs and one switch that can turn one light bulb on and off while keeping the other light bulb on.

How to Read the Scale on an Ammeter

Figure 10.1.5 shows the face of a typical milliammeter. There are three scales printed on the face, but there are eight different ranges for this meter. When you connect the meter into a circuit, the terminal post labeled "C" is always connected to the negative terminal of the power source or to a part of the circuit that eventually leads to the negative terminal.

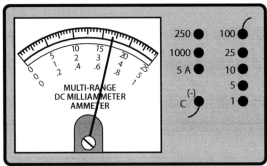

Figure 10.1.6 *An ammeter*

You must choose a suitable range for the current you have to measure. If you are not sure what range to use, try the red 5A terminal post first. This is the least sensitive range for the meter, so it can handle the most current safely. On this range, the milliammeter can handle up to 5 A.

What do the numbers on the terminal posts mean?

If you connect to the 5 A range, the meter reads anywhere from 0 A up to a maximum of 5 A. Read the middle scale of your meter. The markings mean exactly what they say: 0 A, 1 A, 2 A, 3 A, 4 A, and 5 A. On this range, the needle in Figure 6.1.6 is at 3.3 A.

If you connect to the 1000 range, the meter reads anywhere between 0 mA and 1000 mA. Read the bottom scale, but read the 1 on the scale as 1000 mA. Read 0.2 as 200 mA, 0.4 as 400 mA, 0.6 as 600 mA, and 0.8 as 800 mA. On this range, the needle in Figure 6.1.6 reads 660 mA.

If you connect to the 250 range, the meter reads anywhere from 0 mA up to 250 mA. Use the top scale but 25 reads as 250 mA. Read 5 as 50 mA, 10 as 100 mA, 15 as 150 mA, and 20 as 200 mA. On this range, the needle in Figure 6.1.6 reads 170 mA.

Quick Check

1. Look at the 100 scale on the meter in Figure 10.1.6.
   (a) What is the highest reading the scale will measure?

   (b) What is the needle reading in Figure 10.1.6?

2. What is the needle reading in Figure 10.1.6 for each of the following scales?
   (a) the 25 mA scale   (c) the 5 mA scale

   (b) the 10 mA scale   (d) the 1 mA scale

Investigation 10.1.1 Measuring Current Using Electroplating

Purpose

To measure current by counting copper atoms deposited on a carbon rod in a measured amount of time

Introduction

A solution of copper II sulfate contains two kinds of ions: Cu^{2+} ions, which give the solution its blue colour, and SO_4^{2-} ions, which are colourless (Figure 6.1.7). Two electrodes are immersed in the copper II sulfate solution and connected to a source of emf. The electrode connected to the positive terminal of the cell will attract SO_4^{2-} ions, and the electrode connected to the negative terminal of the cell will attract Cu^{2+} ions.

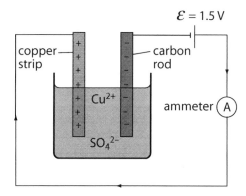

Figure 10.1.7

Cu^{2+} ions attracted to the negative electrode pick up two electrons, and deposit themselves on the negative electrode as copper atoms, Cu^0.

$$Cu^{2+} + 2e^- \rightarrow Cu^0$$

Meanwhile, at the positive electrode, which is made of copper, copper atoms *lose* two electrons and become copper ions, thus replenishing the Cu^{2+} ions in the solution.

$$Cu^0 \rightarrow Cu^{2+} + 2e^-$$

The two electrons return to the source of emf, the cell.

In this experiment, you allow the copper atoms to plate onto a negatively charged carbon electrode. If you measure the increase in mass of the carbon electrode after, say, 20 min of copper plating, you can calculate the mass of copper plated. This will give you the number of copper atoms plated, and from this, the number of electrons that were transferred in the 20 min. Finally you can calculate the current in amperes. You can also compare your calculated current with the current measured with an ammeter placed in the same circuit.

Procedure

1. Measure the mass of a dry, clean carbon rod as precisely as you can.
2. Set up the circuit shown in Figure 10.1.7. Make sure the carbon rod is connected to the negative terminal of the dry cell or other DC power source. The red binding post of the ammeter should be connected to the positive terminal of the cell, and an appropriate current range chosen as quickly as possible when the current is turned on. *Let the current run for a carefully measured time, such as 20 min.* Record current frequently, and *average* it.
3. As soon as the current is turned off, carefully remove the carbon electrode. Dip it in a beaker of methyl hydrate, and allow it time to dry. A heat lamp can be used to speed drying.

Caution! Methyl hydrate is both highly toxic and flammable!

4. Measure the mass of the plated carbon rod precisely, and calculate the amount of copper that has plated on its surface. Record the mass of copper.

5. To remove the copper, set up the circuit once more, but *reverse the connections* to the cell so that the copper plates back onto the copper strip.

Concluding Questions

1. One mole of copper atoms (63.5 g) contains 6.02×10^{23} atoms. Using this information and the mass of copper plated on the carbon rod, calculate
   (a) the number of copper atoms plated
   (b) the number of electrons transferred
   (c) the number of coulombs transferred in 20 min

2. If 1 A = 1 C/s, what was the current in amperes?

3. Compare your calculated current with the measured current by calculating the percent difference between the two currents.

10.1 Review Questions

1. If the current in a wire is 5.0 A, how many coulombs of charge pass a point in the wire in 1 min?

2. What is the current if 6.0×10^3 C pass a point in a circuit in 10.0 min?

3. If the current in a circuit is 12 A, how many electrons pass a point in 1 h?

4. The drift speed of electrons in a copper wire running from a battery to a light bulb and back is approximately 0.020 mm/s. The battery is at the front of a classroom and wires run around the perimeter of the room to the light bulb. The total length of wire is 40.0 m. How long would it take a single electron to drift from the negative terminal of the battery back to the positive terminal? Express your answer in days.

5. How much copper would be plated by a current of 1.5 A in a time of 1.0 h?

6. How much silver is deposited by a current of 1.000 A in 1.000 h? The mass of one mole of silver atoms is 107.9 g.

$$Ag^+ + 1e^- \rightarrow Ag^0$$

7. Draw a circuit with three light bulbs and two switches, and show the different combinations where one, two, and three light bulbs are lit.

8. What is the reading of the milliammeter below?

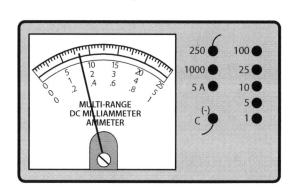

10.2 Ohm's Law

Resistance

Georg Simon Ohm (1787–1854) experimented with current in wires using variations in voltage to produce different currents. He found that for metal conductors at a given temperature, the current was directly proportional to the voltage between the ends of the wire.

$$I \propto V$$

Therefore, $\dfrac{V}{I}$ = constant.

For example, the potential difference (voltage) between the ends of a wire is 1.50 V and the current is 2.00 A. If the potential difference is increased to 3.00 V, the current will also double to 4.00 A.

The constant of proportionality is called the **resistance (R)** of the length of wire. The relationship among current, voltage, and resistance is written:

$$\frac{V}{I} = R$$

where R is the resistance, in **ohms (Ω).** This is called **Ohm's law.** Ohm's law can be written in two other forms, but all three forms are equivalent.

$$\frac{V}{I} = R \qquad V = IR \qquad \frac{V}{R} = I$$

Sample Problem 10.2.1 — Ohm's Law

The current in a portable stove's heating element is 12.0 A when the potential difference between the ends of the element is 120 V. What is the resistance of the stove element?

What to Think About	How to Do It
1. Determine what you know from the problem.	$I = 12.0 \text{ A}$ $V = 120 \text{ V}$
2. Determine the appropriate formula.	$R = \dfrac{V}{I}$
3. Solve.	$R = \dfrac{120 \text{ V}}{12.0 \text{ A}} = 1.0 \times 10^{1}\,\Omega$

Practice Problems 10.2.1 — Ohm's Law

1. A resistor allows 1.0 mA to exist within it when a potential difference of 1.5 V is applied to its ends. What is the resistance of the resistor, in kilohms? (1 kΩ = 10^3 Ω)

2. If a 10.0 Ω kettle element is plugged into a 120 V outlet, how much current will it draw?

3. A current of 1.25 mA exists in a 20.0 kΩ resistor. What is the potential difference between the ends of the resistor?

Resistors

Under normal circumstances, every conductor of electricity offers some resistance to the flow of electric charges and is therefore a **resistor**. However, when we use the term "resistors," we are usually referring to devices manufactured specifically to control the amount of current in a circuit.

There are two main kinds of resistor: (1) wire-wound resistors, made of a coil of insulated, tightly wound fine wire and (2) carbon resistor (Figure 10.2.1). Carbon resistors consist of a cylinder of carbon, with impurities added to control the amount of resistance. Metal wire leads are attached to each end of the carbon cylinder, and the whole assembly is enclosed in an insulating capsule.

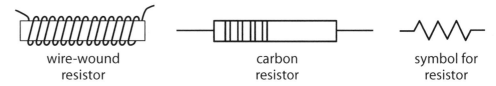

wire-wound resistor   carbon resistor   symbol for resistor

Figure 10.2.1 *Types of resistors and the symbol for resistors used in circuit diagrams*

In any resistor, electrical energy is transformed into thermal energy. There are some materials which, if cooled to temperatures approaching 0 K, offer no resistance to the flow of charges. These materials are called **superconductors**.

Resistor Colour Code

Resistors are either labelled with their resistance or colour-coded with four coloured bands, each of which has significance. The first coloured band gives the *first digit*. The second coloured band gives the *second digit*. The third coloured band gives the *power-of-10 multiplier (the number of zeros following the first two digits)*. Table 10.2.1 lists the colours and their codes. If there is no fourth coloured band, the manufacturer's tolerance is 20%. If the fourth band is gold, the tolerance is 5%. If the fourth band is silver, the tolerance is 10%. Think of tolerance as a range for the value of the resistor. No resistor is exactly the value indicated — the value is plus or minus the tolerance percentage given.

Table 10.2.1 *Resistor Colour Codes*

Band Colour	Number	Multiplier	Tolerance
black	0	10^0	
brown	1	10^1	
red	2	10^2	
orange	3	10^3	
yellow	4	10^4	
green	5	10^5	
blue	6	10^6	
violet	7	10^7	
gray	8	10^8	
white	9	10^9	
gold			5%
silver			10%
(no colour)			20%

Sample Problem 10.2.2 — Resistor Colour Codes

What is the value of a resistor that has the colours gray, blue, red, and silver?

What to Think About	How to Do It
1. Use Table 6.2.1 to interpret the colour code.	First colour: gray = 8 Second colour: blue = 6 Third colour: red = 2 Resistor rating: 8600 Ω
2. Determine the tolerance of the resistor.	Tolerance: silver (10%) 10% of 8600 Ω ± 860 Ω
3. Summarize the result.	Resistor's value is 8600 Ω ± 860 Ω.

Practice Problems 10.2.2 — Resistor Colour Codes

Use Table 10.2.1 to figure out the resistance rating of the following colour-coded resistors:

1. Red, red, red, silver

2. Brown, black, orange, gold

$$10^1, 10^0, 10^3 \quad 5\%$$
$$= 500$$

3. Brown, green, green, silver

$$1 \times 10^1$$
$$5 \times 10^5 \qquad 10\%$$
$$5 \times 10^5$$

4. Yellow, violet, yellow

Limitations of Ohm's Law

Ohm's law applies to metal resistors and metal-like resistors such as those made of compressed carbon. The ratio of potential difference to current, which is resistance, is constant for this class of material, providing that the temperature of the material remains constant.

Ohm's law only applies to metallic or metal-like conductors at a specific temperature. It does *not* apply to just any conductor in a circuit. For example, Ohm's law would not apply to a conducting solution or to a gas discharge tube.

Joule's Law

The English physicist James Prescott Joule (1818–1889) did experiments to measure the amount of heat released by various resistors under different conditions. He found that, for a particular resistor, the amount of thermal energy released in a unit of time by a resistor is proportional to the square of the current. The rate at which energy is released with respect to time is called **power**, so Joule's results can be expressed as follows:

$$P \propto I^2$$

$$\text{or } P = \text{constant} \cdot I^2$$

The constant in this equation will have units with the dimensions W/A^2, since constant $= P/I^2$. Consider the following simplification of these measuring units (W/A^2):

$$1\frac{W}{A^2} = 1\frac{\frac{J}{s}}{\frac{C^2}{s^2}} = 1\frac{\frac{J}{C}}{\frac{C}{s}} = 1\frac{V}{A} = 1\,\Omega$$

The ohm (Ω) is the unit for resistance. In fact, the constant of proportionality in the relationship discovered by Joule is the same constant of proportionality that is in Ohm's law. The ratio P/I^2 is the resistance of the resistor.

Joule's law can be written as follows: $P = RI^2$. By combining Joule's law with Ohm's law for resistors, other expressions for electrical power can be derived:

$$P = RI^2 = \frac{V}{I}I^2 = VI$$

$$\text{And } P = VI = V \times \frac{V}{R} = \frac{V^2}{R}$$

In summary, $$P = RI^2 = VI = \frac{V^2}{R}$$

Quick Check

1. What is the resistance of a 60.0 W lamp, if the current in it is 0.50 A?

$$P = RI^2$$

$$60.0 W = R (0.50 A)^2$$

$$R = 240 \,\Omega$$

$$\Omega = ohms$$

2. A 600 W coffee percolator is operated at 120 V.
   (a) What is the resistance of the heating element of the percolator?

   $$P = \frac{V^2}{R}$$

   $$600 W = \frac{120^2}{R} \qquad R = 24 \,\Omega$$

   (b) How much thermal energy does it produce in 6.0 min?

   $$P = \frac{E}{T}$$

   $$E = R \times T$$

   $$= 600 W \times 6.0 \times 60$$

   $$E = 2.16 \times 10^5 J$$

3. How much thermal energy is released by a 1500 W kettle in 5.0 min?

   $$E = 1500 \times 5.0 \times 60$$

   $$E = 4.5 \times 10^5 J$$

EMF, Terminal Voltage, and Internal Resistance

In Figure 10.2.2, the dry cell has a rated emf of 1.50 V. Assume you are using a high quality voltmeter to measure the potential difference between the terminals A and B of the cell, when essentially no current is being drawn from the cell other than a tiny amount going through the voltmeter itself. In that case, the voltage between the terminals will be nearly equal to the ideal value of the emf. That is, with no current, the terminal voltage of the battery, V_{AB}, will equal the emf, ε

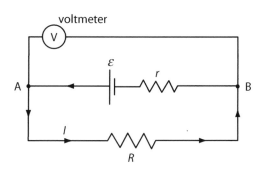

Figure 10.2.2 *The dry cell in this circuit has a rated emf of 1.50 V.*

If, however, the cell is connected to a resistor R so that a current I exists in the simple circuit including in the cell itself, then the terminal voltage is *less than* the cell emf.

$$V_{AB} < \varepsilon$$

This is because the cell itself has an internal resistance of its own, symbolized by r. According to Ohm's law, the loss of potential energy per coulomb between the terminals is Ir. The measured terminal voltage of the cell will be less than the ideal emf by an amount equal to Ir.

$$V_{AB} = \varepsilon - Ir$$

Sample Problem 10.2.3 — Terminal Voltage and Internal Resistance

A dry cell with an emf of 1.50 V has an internal resistance of 0.050 Ω. What is the terminal voltage of the cell when it is connected to a 2.00 Ω resistor?

What to Think About	How to Do It
1. Determine what you know from the problem.	$\varepsilon = 1.50 \text{ V}$ $R = 2.00 \text{ } \Omega$ $r = 0.050 \text{ } \Omega$
2. To solve, apply Ohm's law to the circuit as a whole, and consider the internal resistance r to be in series with the external resistance R. This means you will solve for the current in the circuit.	$I = \dfrac{\varepsilon}{R + r} = \dfrac{1.50 \text{ V}}{2.05 \text{ } \Omega} = 0.732 \text{ A}$
3. Now find the terminal voltage.	$V_{AB} = \varepsilon - Ir$ $V_{AB} = 1.50 \text{ V} - (0.732 \text{ A})(0.050 \text{ } \Omega)$ $V_{AB} = 1.50 \text{ V} - 0.037 \text{ V}$ $V_{AB} = 1.46 \text{ V}$

Practice Problems 10.2.3 — Terminal Voltage and Internal Resistance

1. A dry cell with an emf of 1.50 V and an internal resistance of 0.050 Ω is "shorted out" with a piece of wire with a resistance of only 0.20 Ω. What will a voltmeter read if it is connected to the terminals of the dry cell at this time?

2. A battery has an emf of 12.50 V. When a current of 35 A is drawn from it, its terminal voltage is 11.45 V. What is the internal resistance of the battery?

Investigation 10.2.1 Ohm's Law

Purpose

To investigate the relationship between the voltage applied to a resistor and the current in the resistor

Procedure

1. Set up the circuit shown in Figure 10.2.3. Start with one cell, an ammeter, and a carbon resistor. These are all in series as they form one path. A voltmeter is connected in parallel with the resistor, as there are two paths for the current to travel.

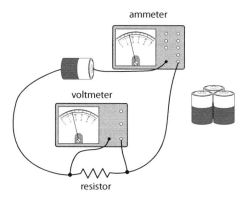

Figure 10.2.3

2. Prepare a copy of Table 10.2.2.

Table 10.2.2 Data Table

Number of Cells Used	Voltage across Resistor (V)	Current in Resistor (A)	Calculated Resistance (Ω)
1			
2			
3			
4			

Resistor rating: _____

3. With one cell in the circuit, measure the current in milliamperes (mA) and the voltage in volts (V). Convert the current from mA to A by dividing by 1000. (Move the decimal three places to the left. For example, 2.4 mA is equal to 0.0024 A.) Enter the current and voltage in your copy of Table 10.2.2.
4. Add a second cell in series with the first cell. Record the current and the voltage in your copy of Table 10.2.2.
5. Repeat with three cells, then with four cells. Enter your results in your copy of Table 10.2.2.
6. Complete the final column of your copy of Table 10.2.2. Divide voltage (*V*) by current (*I*) for each trial. This ratio, *V*/*I*, is the resistance (*R*) of the resistor, measured in ohms.
7. Replace the resistor with one of a different colour and repeat Procedure steps 1 to 6.

Concluding Questions

1. What happens to the voltage across a resistor when the number of cells in series with it is
   (a) doubled? (b) tripled? (c) quadrupled?
2. What happens to the current across a resistor when the number of cells in series with it is
   (a) doubled? (b) tripled? (c) quadrupled?
3. What happens to the resistance ($R = V/I$) across a resistor when the number of cells in series with it is
   (a) doubled? (b) tripled? (c) quadrupled?
4. What is the resistance in ohms (Ω) of (a) the first resistor you used? (b) the second resistor you used?
5. Consult Table 10.2.1 to see the manufacturer's rating of your resistors. Record these resistances in your notes. Why is the measured value different from the manufacturer's rating?

10.2 Review Questions

1. A current of 1.2 mA exists in a resistor when a potential difference of 4.8 V is applied to its ends. What is the resistance of the resistor? Express your answer in kilohms (1 kΩ = 1000 Ω).

2. A current of 3.0 mA exists in a 2.0 kΩ resistor. What is the voltage between the ends of the resistor?

3. What current will exist in a 30 Ω resistor if a 120 V voltage is applied to its ends?

4. A 3.0 V battery is connected to a carbon resistor.
   (a) If the current is 3.0 mA, what is the resistance of the resistor?

   (b) If a 6.0 V battery is connected to the same resistor, what will the current be?

   (c) What is the resistance of the resistor when the 6.0 V battery replaces the 3.0 V battery?

5. A 12 V battery sends a current of 2.0 A through a car's circuit to the headlights. What is the resistance of the filament in a headlight?

6. What voltage is needed to send 0.5 A through a 220 Ω light bulb filament?

7. What current exists in a 120 V coffee percolator, if the resistance of its heating element is 24 Ω?

8. A resistor has the following coloured bands: brown, black, red, gold. What is the manufacturer's rating of this resistor (see Table 10.2.1)?

9. Use Table 10.2.1 to figure out the resistance rating of the following colour-coded resistors:
   (a) Orange, red, brown, silver

   (b) Red, black, black, gold

   (c) Gray, green, blue, silver

   (d) White, violet, red

10. What colour code would you find on the following resistors?

(a) 500 Ω ± 20%

(b) 37 000 Ω ± 5%

(c) 10 Ω ± 10%

(d) 8600 Ω ± 20%

11. What is the resistance of the element of a 1500 W kettle if it draws 12.5 A?

12. A 1500 W kettle is connected to a 110 V source. What is the resistance of the kettle element?

13. When you pay your electricity bill, you are charged not for power but for the energy used. The unit for measuring the energy used is the kilowatt·hour (kW·h).

(a) How many joules are there in one kW·h?

(b) How much energy, in kW·h, does a 400-W TV set use in a month (30 days), if it is used an average of 6.0 h each day?

(c) If electrical energy costs $0.06/kW·h, what will it cost you to operate the TV set for one month?

14. How many kW·h of energy does a 900 W toaster use in 3.0 min?

15. A 1.0 kΩ resistor is rated ½ W. This rating means the resistor will be destroyed if more than ½ W passes through it. What is the maximum voltage you can apply to this resistor without risking damage to it?

16. A battery with an emf of 6.00 V has an internal resistance of 0.20 Ω. What current does the battery deliver when the terminal voltage reads only 5.00 V?

10.3 Kirchhoff's Laws

Resistors in Series

In Figure 10.3.1, four resistors are connected end-to-end so that there is one continuous conducting path for electrons coming from the source of emf, through the resistors, and back to the source. Electrons move through the resistors, one after the other. The same current exists in each resistor. Resistors arranged like this are said to be "in **series**" with each other. Figure 10.3.1 shows a typical series circuit.

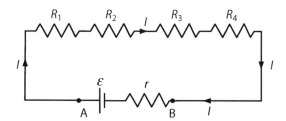

Figure 10.3.1 *A series circuit*

Within the cell, the gain in potential energy per unit charge is equal to the emf, ε. When a current I exists, energy will be lost in resistors R_1, R_2, R_3, R_4, and r. The loss of potential energy per unit charge in each resistor is the voltage V across that resistor. From Ohm's law, we know that $V = IR$. The law of conservation of energy requires that the total gain in energy in the cell(s) must equal the total loss of energy in the resistors in the circuit. It follows that the total gain in energy per unit charge (E) must equal the total loss of energy per unit charge in the circuit.

$$E = Ir + IR_1 + IR_2 + IR_3 + IR_4$$
$$\therefore\ E - Ir = IR_1 + IR_2 + IR_3 + IR_4$$

Recalling that terminal voltage $V_{AB} = E - Ir,$

$$V_{AB} = IR_1 + IR_2 + IR_3 + IR_4 = V_S$$

where V_S is the sum of voltages across the resistors in the external part of the circuit.

Another way of writing this is: $V_{AB} = V_1 + V_2 + V_3 + V_4 = V_S$

What is the total resistance of a series circuit like the one in Figure 10.3.1? In other words, what single resistance, called the **equivalent resistance** R_s, could be used to replace R_1, R_2, R_3, and R_4 without changing current I?

If $V_s = IR_s$ and $V_s = IR_1 + IR_2 + IR_3 + IR_4$, then

$$IR_s = IR_1 + IR_2 + IR_3 + IR_4$$

$$\therefore R_s = R_1 + R_2 + R_3 + R_4$$

Summary: For a Series Circuit

1. Current (I) is the same everywhere throughout the circuit.
2. The net gain in potential energy per coulomb in the circuit equals the net loss of potential energy per coulomb in the circuit. That is, for a circuit like the one in Figure 6.3.1, with a single source of emf,
$$V_{AB} = V_1 + V_2 + V_3 + V_4 + ... + V_n$$
3. The equivalent resistance of all the resistors in series with each other is equal to the sum of all their resistances.
$$R_S = R_1 + R_2 + R_3 + R_4 + ... + R_n$$

The resistors in Figure 10.3.2 are connected in **parallel**. The current divides into three branches. Electrons coming from the cell take one of three paths, which meet at a junction where the electrons all converge to one path again and return to the battery.

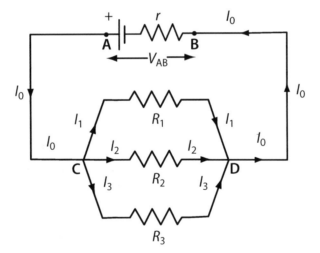

Figure 10.3.2 *Resistors R_1, R_2, and R_3 are placed in parallel in this circuit.*

Electric charge is a conserved quantity. The electrons are not "created" or "lost" during their journey through the parallel network of resistors. The number of electrons entering a junction (such as D) per second will equal the number of electrons leaving that junction per second. Likewise, the number of electrons entering junction C per second will equal the number of electrons leaving C per second. (The actual direction of electron flow is opposite to the conventional current direction shown in Figure 10.3.2.) If we express current in C/s or in A, as is normally the case,

$$I_0 = I_1 + I_2 + I_3$$

The net gain in potential energy per unit charge in the cell, which is V_{AB}, is equal to the loss in potential energy per unit charge between C and D. If you think of C as an extension of terminal A and D as an extension of terminal B of the cell, you can see that the difference in potential between C and D is the same no matter which of the three paths the electrons take to get from one terminal to the other. In fact,

$$V_{AB} = V_1 = V_2 = V_3$$

where V_{AB} is the terminal voltage of the cell, and V_1, V_2, and V_3 are the voltages across resistors R_1, R_2, and R_3 respectively.

Since the voltages are the same in each branch, we shall use the label V_p for the voltage in *any* branch of the parallel network.

Equivalent Resistance

What single resistance could be used in place of the parallel network of resistors, and draw the same total current? Call this the **equivalent resistance** R_p.

If the voltage across the parallel network is V_p, and the equivalent single resistance is R_p, we can apply Ohm's law as follows to find the total current I_0 entering the network:

$$I_0 = \frac{V_p}{R_p}$$

However, $I_0 = I_1 + I_2 + I_3$

Using Ohm's law again:

$$\frac{V_p}{R_p} = \frac{V_p}{R_1} + \frac{V_p}{R_2} + \frac{V_p}{R_3}$$

Eliminating V_p:

$$\frac{1}{R_p} = \frac{1}{R_1} + \frac{1}{R_2} + \frac{1}{R_3}$$

Summary: For a Parallel Circuit Network

1. Voltage is the same between the ends of each branch of a parallel network.
2. The total current entering a junction of a parallel network is equal to the total current leaving the same junction. As a result, the total current entering a parallel network of resistors or leaving the same network is equal to the sum of the currents in the branches.
3. The reciprocal of the single equivalent resistance that will replace all the resistance in a parallel network, and draw the same current, is equal to the sum of the reciprocals of the resistances in the branches.

$$\frac{1}{R_p} = \frac{1}{R_1} + \frac{1}{R_2} + \frac{1}{R_3} + ... + \frac{1}{R_n}$$

Combined Series and Parallel Circuits

Figure 10.3.3 shows a combined **series-parallel circuit**. The rules you have learned for series and parallel circuits can be applied to this problem. A logical approach for finding the equivalent resistance and current for the circuit in Figure 10.3.3 is to first reduce the parallel network to a single equivalent resistance, then treat the circuit as a series circuit.

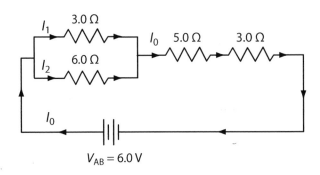

Figure 10.3.3 *A combined series-parallel circuit*

Sample Problem 10.3.1 — Resistors in Parallel

(a) What is the equivalent resistance of the circuit in Figure 10.3.3?
(b) What is the voltage across the 6.0 Ω resistor?

What to Think About	How to Do It
(a)	
1. First, reduce the parallel network to an equivalent single resistance.	$\dfrac{1}{R_p} = \dfrac{1}{3.0\ \Omega} + \dfrac{1}{6.0\ \Omega} = \dfrac{2+1}{6.0\ \Omega} = \dfrac{3}{6.0\ \Omega} = \dfrac{1}{2.0\ \Omega}$ $R_p = 2.0\ \Omega$
2. Next, add the three resistances that are in series with one another.	$R_s = 2.0\ \Omega + 5.0\ \Omega + 3.0\ \Omega = 10.0\ \Omega$
3. Then, find the current using Ohm's law with the total equivalent resistance and the battery terminal voltage.	$I_0 = \dfrac{V_{AB}}{R_s} = \dfrac{6.0\ V}{10.0\ \Omega} = 0.60\ A$
(b)	
1. Find the voltage across the parallel network by using Ohm's law on the parallel network by itself.	$V_p = I_0 R_p = (0.60\ A)(2.0\ \Omega) = 1.2\ V$

Practice Problems 10.3.1 — Resistors in Parallel

1. (a) Draw a circuit showing a 6.0 V battery with an internal resistance of 0.50 Ω connected to a parallel network consisting of a 25.0 Ω resistor in parallel with a 6.25 Ω resistor.

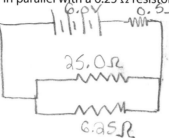

$$\frac{1}{R} = \frac{1}{25} + \frac{1}{6.25}$$

$$R = 5.0\ \Omega$$

$$R = 5.0\ \Omega + 0.50 = 5.5\ \Omega$$
$$V = 6.0$$
$$I = ?$$

(b) Calculate the current in the battery.

$$I = \frac{V}{R}$$

$$= \frac{6.0}{5.5} \qquad \boxed{I = 1.1\ A}$$

2. Calculate the equivalent resistance of each of the networks of resistors in Figure 10.3.4.

(a)
$$\frac{1}{R} = \frac{1}{6.0} + \frac{1}{12.0}$$
$$R = 4 + 3.0\ \Omega$$
$$\boxed{R = 7.0\ \Omega}$$

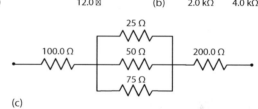

(a) 3.0 Ω   6.0 Ω   12.0 Ω

(b) 1.0 kΩ   2.0 kΩ   2.0 kΩ   4.0 kΩ

(c) 100.0 Ω   25 Ω   50 Ω   75 Ω   200.0 Ω

Figure 10.3.4

(b)
$$\frac{1}{R} = \frac{1}{3.0} + \frac{1}{6.0}$$
$$\boxed{R = 2.0\ \Omega}$$

(c)
$$\frac{1}{R} = \frac{1}{25} + \frac{1}{50} + \frac{1}{75} \qquad R = 13.7\ \Omega + 100.0 + 200.0$$
$$\boxed{= 313.7\ \Omega}$$

Kirchhoff's Laws for Electric Circuits

So far, we have looked at series and parallel circuits from the points of view of (a) conservation of energy, (b) conservation of charge, and (c) Ohm's law. Most simple circuits can be analyzed using the rules worked out for series and parallel circuits in this section. For more complicated circuits, a pair of rules called **Kirchhoff's rules** or **Kirchhoff's laws** can be applied.

Kirchhoff's Current Rule

At any junction in a circuit, the sum of all the currents entering that junction equals the sum of all the currents leaving that junction.

Kirchhoff's current rule follows from the law of conservation of electric charge. Charged particles are not "lost" or "created" in a circuit. The number of charged particles (usually electrons) that enter a junction point equals the number that leave that junction point.

Kirchhoff's Voltage Rule

The algebraic sum of all the changes in potential around a closed path in a circuit is zero.

Kirchhoff's voltage rule is really a restatement of the law of conservation of energy. In Investigation 10.3.1, you will examine several circuits from the point of view of Kirchhoff's laws.

Quick Check

1. Calculate the current in the cell in the circuit in Figure 10.3.5.

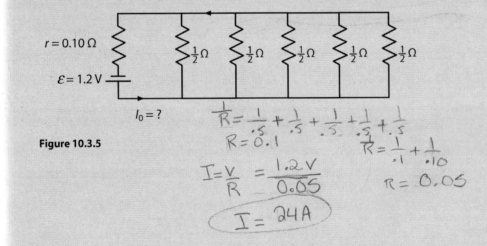

Figure 10.3.5

$$\frac{1}{R} = \frac{1}{.5} + \frac{1}{.5} + \frac{1}{.5} + \frac{1}{.5} + \frac{1}{.5}$$
$$R = 0.1$$

$$I = \frac{V}{R} = \frac{1.2\,V}{0.05}$$

$$\boxed{I = 24\,A}$$

$$\frac{1}{R} = \frac{1}{.1} + \frac{1}{.10}$$
$$R = 0.05$$

Quick Check continues

2. A wire has length ℓ and resistance R. It is cut into four identical pieces, and these pieces are arranged in parallel. What will be the resistance of this parallel network?

3. Four identical resistors are connected in parallel, as shown in Figure 10.3.6. The current is 2.0 A with all four resistors in the circuit. What will be the current if the wire at X is cut?

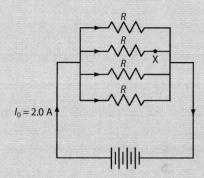

Figure 10.3.6

4. (a) What is the equivalent resistance of the network of resistors in Figure 10.3.7?

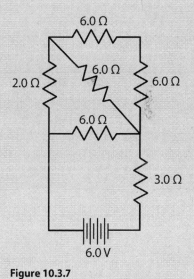

(b) What current exists in the 3.0 Ω resistor?

Figure 10.3.7

Investigation 10.3.1 Kirchhoff's Laws for Circuits

Purpose
To examine several circuits from the point of view of Kirchhoff's laws

Part 1 — A Series Circuit

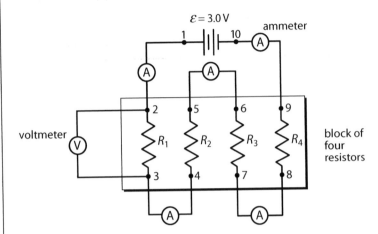

Figure 10.3.8

Procedure
1. To check Kirchhoff's current law, wire a series circuit like the one in Figure 10.3.8, and insert your ammeter in *each* of the locations, in turn, where the symbol A for ammeter is shown in the diagram. Record each current in your notebook (possibly on a diagram like Figure 6.3.8).

    $I_{1-2} = $ _____ $I_{3-4} = $ _____ $I_{5-6} = $ _____ $I_{7-8} = $ _____ $I_{9-10} = $ _____

2. To check Kirchhoff's voltage law, measure the terminal voltage of the battery or power supply, V_{1-10}. Then measure the voltages between the ends of each resistor. Remember that the voltmeter is not in the same conducting path as the circuit. An example is shown in Figure 6.3.8, where the voltmeter is connected correctly across the ends of resistor R_1. The symbol for the voltmeter is V. Record all the voltages in your notebook.

    $V_{1-10} = $ _____ $V_{2-3} = $ _____ $V_{4-5} = $ _____ $V_{6-7} = $ _____ $V_{8-9} = $ _____

Concluding Questions
1. Do your current readings support Kirchhoff's current law? How would you describe the current at various junctions in your series circuit?
2. Compare the potential gain in the battery (terminal voltage) with the potential drop in the resistors in the circuit. Do your results suggest that $\sum V = 0$?
3. What are some sources of error in this investigation? For example, how might the ammeter itself affect the results for current, and how might the voltmeter affect the results for voltage?
4. Calculate the resistance of each resistor using Ohm's law and the current and voltage readings for each individual resistor. Compare your calculated resistances with the manufacturer's ratings. (See Table 10.2.1 for resistor colour codes.) Organize your results in a table like Table 10.3.1 below.

Table 10.3.1 *Data Table*

	R_1	R_2	R_3	R_4
Measured Voltage, *V*	V	V	V	V
Measured Current, *I*	A	A	A	A
Calculated Resistance, *R*	Ω	Ω	Ω	Ω
Colour Code Rating, *R*	Ω	Ω	Ω	Ω

5. Calculate the equivalent resistance R_s of the whole series circuit by using Ohm's law and dividing the terminal voltage of the battery or power supply by the current in the battery. Compare this value with the sum of the individual calculated resistances.

6. What is the percent difference between R_s and $\sum [R_1 + R_2 + R_3 + R_4]$?

Part 2 — A Parallel Circuit

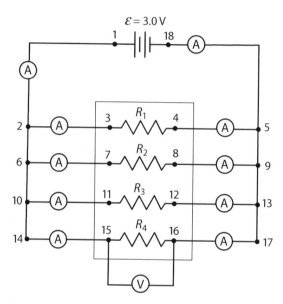

Figure 10.3.9

Procedure

1. Set up the circuit shown in Figure 10.3.9. To simplify recording your data, copy the diagram into your notebook. When you measure the current at each point labeled A, record the current right on the diagram in the ammeter circle.

2. Measure the voltage of the battery (V_{1-18}) and also the voltage across each resistor. Record the voltages in your notebook.

$$V_{1-18} = \underline{\quad} \quad V_{3-4} = \underline{\quad} \quad V_{7-8} = \underline{\quad} \quad V_{11-12} = \underline{\quad} \quad V_{15-16} = \underline{\quad}$$

Concluding Questions

1. Examine the currents at each of the eight junctions of the parallel network of resistors. Do your results confirm Kirchhoff's current law?

2. Compare the potential gain in the battery (terminal voltage) with the potential drop across each branch of the circuit, in turn. Do your measurements seem to confirm Kirchhoff's voltage law?

3. What are some sources of error in this experiment?

4. Use the measured voltage across each resistor, and the measured current in each resistor, to calculate $R_1, R_2, R_3,$ and R_4. Calculate the resistance of the parallel network:

$$\frac{1}{R_p} = \frac{1}{R_1} + \frac{1}{R_2} + \frac{1}{R_3} + \frac{1}{R_4}$$

Organize your data in a table like Table 10.3.2 below.

Table 10.3.2 *Data Table*

	R_1	R_2	R_3	R_4
Measured Voltage, V	V	V	V	V
Measured Current, I	A	A	A	A
Calculated Resistance, R	Ω	Ω	Ω	Ω

(a) R_p calculated in Concluding Question 4 =	Ω
(b) R_p calculated from $\dfrac{V_{1-18}}{I_0}$ =	Ω
Percent difference between (a) and (b) =	%

5. Calculate the equivalent resistance of the parallel network by dividing the terminal voltage of the battery by the current in the battery. What is the percent difference between this R_p and the result from Procedure step 4?

Challenge

1. Set up a series-parallel circuit like the one in Figure 10.3.10. Test Kirchhoff's two laws for this circuit.

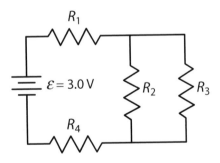

Figure 10.3.10

10.3 Review Questions

1. The current through A is 0.50 A when the switch S is open. What will the current be through A when the switch S is closed?

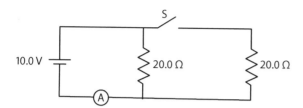

2. Which one of the following arrangements of four identical resistors will have the least resistance?

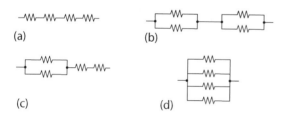

3. Use this circuit diagram to answer the questions below.

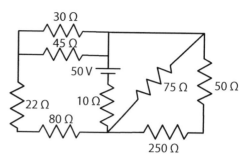

(a) What is the equivalent resistance of the entire circuit?

(b) What current is drawn from the battery?

(c) What is the current in the 50 Ω resistor?

(d) What is the voltage across the 22 Ω resistor?

4. What is the current in the ammeter A in this circuit?

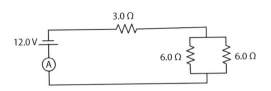

3.0 Ω

12.0 V

6.0 Ω   6.0 Ω

5. What is the emf of the battery if the current in A is 1.2 A and the internal resistance of the battery is 0.0833 Ω in this circuit?

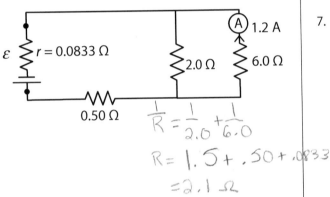

$\mathcal{E}$ $r = 0.0833\,\Omega$

(A) 1.2 A

2.0 Ω   6.0 Ω

0.50 Ω

$$\frac{1}{R} = \frac{1}{2.0} + \frac{1}{6.0}$$

$$R = 1.5 + .50 + .0833$$

$$= 2.1\,\Omega$$

$$V = IR$$
$$1.2 \times 6.0 = I_1 \times 2.0$$
$$I = \frac{1.2 \times 6.0}{2}$$
$$I = 3.6\,A$$

3.6 A +
1.2 A = 4.8 A

$$R = 2.1\,\Omega$$
$$I = 4.8\,A$$
$$V = 4.8 \times 2.1$$
$$= 10\,V$$

6. What is the voltage V of the power supply in the circuit below?

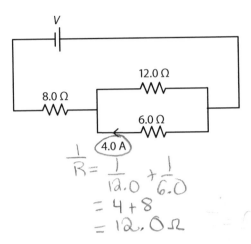

V

12.0 Ω

8.0 Ω

6.0 Ω

4.0 A

$$\frac{1}{R} = \frac{1}{12.0} + \frac{1}{6.0}$$
$$= 4 + 8$$
$$= 12.0\,\Omega$$

$$V = IR$$
$$12.0 \times A = 6.0 \times 4.0$$
$$I = 2.0\,A$$

$$R = 12.0\,\Omega$$
$$I = 6.0\,A$$
$$V = IR$$
$$= 72.0\,V$$

7. What is the internal resistance of the battery shown here?

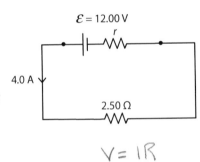

$\mathcal{E} = 12.00\,V$

r

4.0 A

2.50 Ω

$$V = IR$$
$$12.00 = 4.0\,(R)$$
$$R = 3.0$$

$$3.0 - 2.50$$
$$= 0.5\ \text{internal}\ \Omega$$

8. Use this circuit diagram to answer the questions below.

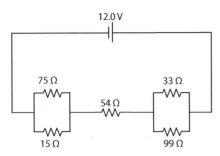

12.0 V

75 Ω

54 Ω

15 Ω

33 Ω

99 Ω

(a) What is the equivalent resistance of this circuit?

(b) What is the current through the 54 Ω resistor?

(c) How much power is dissipated in the 54 Ω resistor?

9. Use this circuit diagram to answer the questions below.

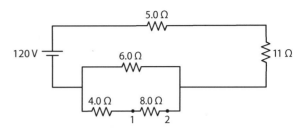

120 V

5.0 Ω

6.0 Ω

11 Ω

4.0 Ω

8.0 Ω

1   2

(a) What is the voltage across the 8.0 Ω resistor (between 1 and 2)?

(b) How much power is dissipated in the 5.0 Ω resistor?

Chapter 10 Review Questions

1. What is the difference between the terminal voltage of a battery and its emf?

2. What current exists in a wire if 2.4×10^3 C of charge pass through a point in the wire in a time of 6.0×10^1 s?

3. The current through an ammeter is 5.0 A. In one day, how many electrons will pass through the ammeter?

4. How much silver will be electroplated by a current of 0.255 A in one day?

5. A mercury cell has an emf of 1.35 V and an internal resistance of 0.041 Ω. If it is used in a circuit that draws 1.50 A, what will its terminal voltage be?

6. A set of eight decorative light bulbs is plugged into a 120 V wall receptacle. What is the potential difference across each light bulb filament, if the eight light bulbs are connected:

   (a) in series?

   (b) in parallel?

7. What is the resistance of a resistor if a potential difference of 36 V between its ends results in a current of 1.20 mA?

8. What is the potential difference (voltage) between the ends of a resistor if 24.0 J of work must be done to drive 0.30 C of charge through the resistor?

9. A resistor has the following coloured bands: brown, black, yellow, and gold. What is the manufacturer's rating of the resistance of this resistor?

10. You need a 4.7 MΩ resistor from a box of miscellaneous resistors. What coloured bands should you look for in your collection?

11. A 2.2 kΩ resistor is rated at ½ W. What is the highest voltage you could safely apply to the resistor without risking damage to it from overheating?

12. What current will a 1500 W kettle draw from a 120 V source?

13. A toaster draws 8.0 A on a 120 V circuit. What is its power rating?

14. A 60.0 W light bulb and a 40.0 W light bulb are connected in parallel in a 120 V circuit. What is the equivalent resistance of the two light bulbs?

15. A circuit in your house has the following appliances plugged into it: a 1500 W kettle, a 150 W light, and a 900 W toaster. The circuit is protected by a 20 A circuit breaker. If the house voltage is 120 V, will the circuit breaker be activated? Explain your answer.

16. How many kW·h of energy will a 400 W television set use in one month, if it is turned on for an average of 5.0 h per day? What will it cost you at $0.06/kW·h?

17. The cell in the diagram below is short-circuited with a wire of resistance 0.10 Ω. What is the terminal voltage under these conditions

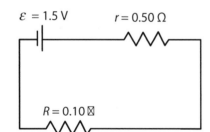

$\varepsilon = 1.5$ V $r = 0.50$ Ω

$R = 0.10$ Ω

18. A storage battery has an emf of 12.0 V. What is the terminal voltage if a current of 150 A is drawn just as the starter motor is turned on? The internal resistance is 0.030 Ω.

19. What is the equivalent resistance of resistors of 8.0 Ω, 12.0 Ω and 24.0 Ω if they are connected

   (a) in series?

   (b) in parallel?

20. A resistor is intended to have a resistance of 60.00 Ω, but when checked it is found to be 60.07 Ω. What resistance might you put in parallel with it to obtain an equivalent resistance of 60.00 Ω?

21. A 12.0 Ω resistor and a 6.0 Ω resistor are connected in series with a 9.0 V battery. What is the voltage across the 6.0 Ω resistor?

22. What is the resistance R in diagram below, if the current through the battery is 5.0 A?

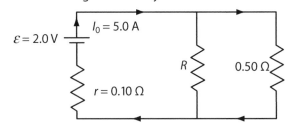

23. You have three 6.0 kΩ resistors. By combining these three resistors in different combinations, how many different equivalent resistances can you obtain with them? (All three must be used.)

24. For each circuit, find
    (i) the equivalent resistance of the entire circuit, and
    (ii) the current at the point marked I.

(a)

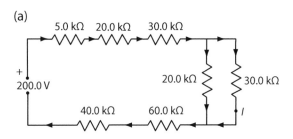

(b)

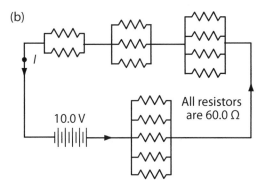

(c)

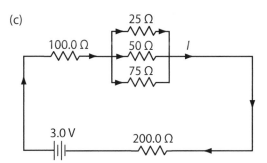

25. What is the voltage across the 6.0 Ω resistor in the diagram below?

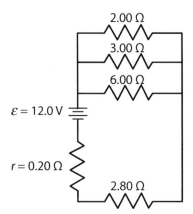

$2.00 \ \Omega$

$3.00 \ \Omega$

$6.00 \ \Omega$

$\varepsilon = 12.0 \ V$

$r = 0.20 \ \Omega$

$2.80 \ \Omega$

26. Twelve identical pieces of resistance wire, each of resistance 1.0 Ω, are formed into a cubical resistance network, shown in the diagram below. If a current of 12 A enters one corner of the cube and leaves at the other corner, what is the equivalent resistance of the cube between the opposite corners? Use Kirchhoff's laws.

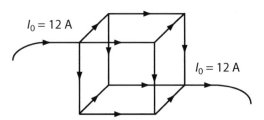

$I_0 = 12 \ A$

$I_0 = 12 \ A$

Chapter 6 Extra Practice

1. What are appropriate units for current?

2. How do the readings on voltmeters 1 and 2 change when the resistor R is added to the circuit as shown in circuit 2?

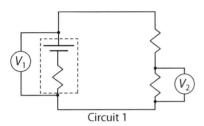
Circuit 1

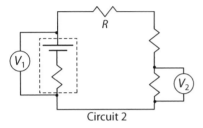
Circuit 2

3. What is the total resistance of this circuit?

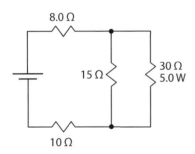

4. What is the current through the 20 Ω resistor?

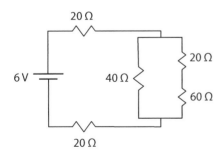

5. What is the current through R_2?

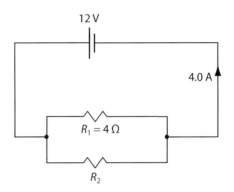

6. In what combination and how many 160 Ω resistors can be connected to draw a current of 6.0 A from a 120 V source? (Use the fewest number of resistors possible.)

7. A 12.0 Ω resistor is connected to a 24 V battery. What is the total charge that flows through the resistor in 1 min?

8. Given that the potential difference across the 5.0 Ω resistor is 2.0 V, find the current through the battery.

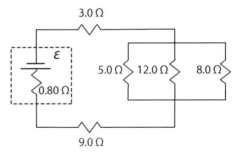

9. Given that the current through the battery is 1.2 A, what is the value of the unknown resistor R?

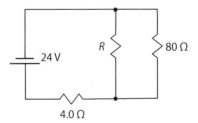

10. What happens to the terminal voltage of the cell when the switch is changed from closed (as shown) to open?

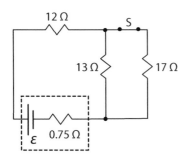

11. Where is the current in this circuit the lowest magnitude?

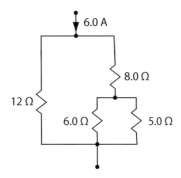

12. Where should you place a voltmeter(s) to calculate the potential difference of the voltage source?

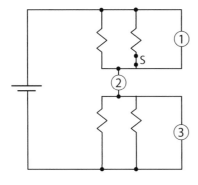

13. A battery has an internal resistance of 0.50 Ω. A voltmeter is hooked up to the terminals of the battery and reads 9.0 V when there is no current. What does the voltmeter read when there is a current of 1.2 A flowing through the battery?

14. What is the potential difference across the 15 Ω resistor?

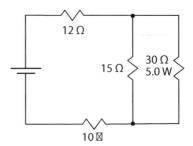

15. What is the power dissipated in this entire circuit?

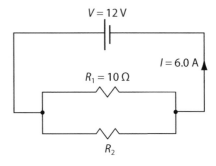

Answer Key

Page 4 – Quick Check
1. A law is a general statement of fact
2. Observation - Hypothesis - Experimentation
– Statement of Theory
3a. Quantitative   b. Qualitative
 c. Quantitative   d. Qualitative
 e. Qualitative   f. Quantitative
 g. Quantitative
4.

Page 6 – Quick Check
1. 0.5
2. 19^0
3. 1156
4. 800 or 8.00×10^2
5. 2.64159265358979 – a good point to discuss sig figs

Page 12 – Quick Check
1. 1 and 3 - low precision, points are spread apart; 2 and 4 - high precision, points are close together within a close range.
2. 1 and 2 – low accuracy; 3 and 4 high accuracy
3. 1 and 2
4. 3 and 4

Page 14 – Practice Problems 1.3.1
1. 12.93 mm
2. 48.1 m^3
3. 12.01 ml
4. 0.9 mm
5. 12.5 g
6. 16.767 kg

Page 16 – Practice Problems 1.3.2
1. 0.31 m^2
2. 5.2 cm^2
3. 6.7 cm
4. 76.8 g
5. 4.1×10^2 g/ml

Page 17 – Quick Check

1. (a) 0.00572 kg = 5.72×10^{-3} kg
(b) 520 000 000 000 km = 5.2×10^{11} km
(c) 300 000 000 m/s = 3.0×10^8 m/s
(d) 0.00000000000000000016 C = 1.6×10^{-19}C
(e) 118.70004 g = 1.1870004×10^2 g
2. (a) $10^{3+7+12} = 10^{22}$
(b) $10^{23-5} = 10^{18}$
(c) $10^{12 +(-13)} = 10^{-1}$
(d) $10^{-8+(-12)} = 10^{-20}$

(e) $10^{5-(-7)} = 10^{12}$
(f) $10^{-2-(-9)} = 10^7$
3. (a) 2.5×10^{-10}
(b) 6.2×10^{-11}
(c) 4.69×10^7
(d) 4.501×10^{-3}
4. 358 m^3 = 3.58×10^2 m^3
5. 11 g/ml

Page 23 - Practice Problems 1.4.1
1. 1.6×10^{-2} ks
2. 75 L
3. 4.57×10^8 m/s
4. 5600 dm

Page 24 – Practice Problems 1.4.2
1. 2.67 kg/L
2. 8.9994×10^{-7} kg/L
3. 16 m/s

Page 25 – Practice Problems 1.4.3
1. 34 000 g Hg
2. 1.47 L Pb
3. 1.5×10^8 km

Page 26 – Practice Problems 1.4.4
1. 4300 cm^3
2. 1030 g/cm^2
3. 0.51 lb/ft^3

Page 29 – Practice Problems 1.4.5
1a. Exponential
1b. Inverse
1c. Linear
2a. Linear
2b. 4 ^{0}C/min
2c. 42 ^{0}C
2d. Temp = (4 ^{0}C/min)t + 22 ^{0}C
2e. 14.5 min
2f. Temperature of water in beaker at START
2g. Uneven heating

Page 39 Practice Problems 2.1.1
1a. 1100 m
1b. 500 m
2a. 503 m
2b. 209 m
3. Total Distance = 38 m.
Displacement = 10.0 m 53° E of N

Page 41 Quick Check
1a. Average speed is total distance over total time. Instantaneous speed is speed at a give point in time.

1b. When an object is moving at a constant speed.
2. 89 km/h
3. 0.76 h or 46 min
4. 460 km

Page 44 Practice Problems 2.1.3
1a. Object at rest.
1b. Object moving away from origin at constant velocity.
1c. Object moving towards origin at a constant velocity.

2a.

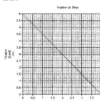

2b.

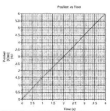

2c. Person moving with ball so graph line horizontal
3a.

Time (s)	1.0	2.0	3.0	4.0
Distance (m)	8.3	16.6	24.9	33.2

Time (s)	5.0	6.0	7.0	8.0
Distance (m)	41.5	49.8	58.1	66.4

3b.

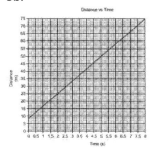

Page 46 2.1 Review Questions
1. Yes, when the direction is different
2. Right and left. Compass directions – north, south, east, west
3. 0.64 km
4. 2.3 h
5a. 1.3×10^2 s
5b. 2.2 min
6. 114 km/h
7a. 95 km
7b. 88 km/h
8a. G = 120m/min [S]

8b. B = 90 m/min [N] [S]

Page 49 Practice Problems 2.2.1
1a. 20km/h/s
1b. 3 m/s^2
2. 2.00 km/h/s or 0.56 m/s^2
3. -15 km/h/s

Page 52 2.2 Review Questions
1a. 16.7 m/s
1b. 25.6 m/s; 92.1 km/h
2. 3.0 s
3a. $v_f = 20m/s + 14.0m/s^2 t$
3b. 14.0 m/s^{2}t
3c. 14.0 m/s^2
3d. 14.0 m/s^2
3e. Observers were at different locations. The aircraft was already moving when observer (a) recorded data.
4. 5.0 m/s
5. -2.5 m/s^2
6a. 10 m/s^2
6b. 0
6c. -7.5 m/s^2

Page 56 Practice Problems 2.3.1
1a. 15.0 m/s
1b. 4.00 m/s^2
1c. Acceleration
1d. $v_f = 15m/s + (4.00m/s^2)t$
2a. 5.0 m/s
2b. 9.8 m/s^2
2c. 17 m/s

Page 58 Quick Check
1. 10 m/s [E]
2. 64.0 m
3. 41.6 m

Page 62 2.3 Review Questions
1a. 5.5 m/s
1b. -7.9 m/s^2
1c. $v_f = 5.5m/s - (7.90m/s^2)t$
2a.6.6 m/s
2b. -2.2 m/s^2
2c. 3.0 s
3. -1.23 m/s^2
4a. 4.0 m/s
4b. 10 m
5a. 3.00 m/s^2
5b. 45.0 m/s
5c. 3.38 x 10^2 m

6.167 m or 1.7×10^2 m
7. 1.0×10^1 s
8. 9.0×10^{15} m/s^2

Page 65 Practice Problems 2.4.1
1a. 1.0×10^2 m/s
1b. Air resistance slows the ball down
2. 62.6 m
3a. 18.6 m/s
3b. 17.6 m
4. 2.4×10^2 m

Page 67 Quick Check
1a. 49 m/s^2
1b. -9.8 m/s^2
1c. 49 m/s^2
2. (1.2, 0); at time 1.2 s, the ball reaches the highest point of its motion and comes to rest before falling back down.
3. 4.9 m form release, or 5.88 m from ground

Page 68 2.4 Review Questions
1. 0.40 m/s^2
2a. 196 m/s^2
2b. -9.8 m/s^2
2c. 196 m/s
2d. At B, because $v_y=0$ at peak of flight
2e. As soon as the ball leaves the pitcher's hand, the only force is gravity, which means $a = g$ = -9.8 m/s^2
2f. Direction is as important, as well as speed
2g. 82.3 m
2h. 82.3
2i. 0 – ball returns to original place
3a. 4.9 m
3b. 14.7 m

Page 69 Chapter 2 Review Questions
1. Velocity is speed and direction
2. 79 km/h
3a. 20.8 m
3b. 55.13 s
3c. 0.38 m/s
4. 2.56 s
5. When acceleration constant
6. 70 m/s or 252 km/h or 2.5×10^2 km/h
7a. 8.00 m/s^2
7b. 40.0 m/s^2
7c. 2.00×10^2 m
7d. $v_f = 20.0 \text{m/s} + (8.0 \text{m/s}^2)t$
8. 4.0 m/s
9. 77.3 s
10. 66 m/s

11. 49 m
12a. 16 m/s
12b. 6.8 s
12c. 6.4 s
13. 0.10 s to pass window
14a. 4.00 m/s^2
14b. 9.00 s
15. 121 m/s
16a. 3.1 m/s
16b. 0.64 s
17a. Graph of d vs t is a parabola
17b. Graph of d vs t^2 is a straight line
17c. A slope of 2.5 cm/s^2. So d = kt^2. Since
$d = \dfrac{1}{2}at^2$, the slope must equal $\dfrac{1}{2}a$. Therefore,
$a = 2k = 5.0 \text{cm/s}^2$

Page 77 Quick Check
1. 8.8×10^2 N
2. 64.9 kg
3. 1.7 N/kg

Page 80 Quick Check
1a. $\dfrac{1}{4}F_g$
1b. $\dfrac{1}{9}F_g$
1c. $4F_g$
1d. $9F_g$
2a. 9.80×10^2 N
2b. 1.62×10^2 N
2c. 1.4×10^{-11} N

Page 83 3.1 Review Questions
1. 600 N
2. $F \, \alpha \, m$
  $\therefore \; 3m = 3F$
3a. 7.8×10^2 N
3b. 1.4×10^2 N
4. 80.5 kg
5. 3.61 m/s^2; 37%
6. 143.9 N
7a. $2F_g$
7b. $2F_g$
7c. $4F_g$
7d. F_g

8. 6.86×10^2 N and F = mg gives 6.86×10^2 N

9a. 7.5×10^{-8} N

9b. 3.00×10^{-7} N

10. 2.5×10^2 N

11. 1.72×10^3 N

Page 88 Practice Problems 3.2.1
1. 30 N
2a. 29.4 N
2b. 24.5 N
3. 0.801

Page 92 3.2 Review Questions
1a. Steering, axles, chain, sprocket, lubricant
1b. Brakes, tires/road

2a. $\mu = \dfrac{F_{fr}}{F_N}$

2b. The units cancel
3. 0.480

4. 2.45×10^3 N

5. Friction force is independent of surface area of contact. The force remains the same.
6. 0.88

Page 94 Quick Check
1. 0.64 N
2. 1.33 N/cm
3. 20 cm

Page 97 3.3 Review Questions
1. N/cm or N/m
2. Note: question refers to Figure 3.3.1.
   $F = 1.33x$
3a. 2.7 cm
3b. 0.03 N
4. k is constant, 1.3 N/cm
5a. k = 20.5 N/cm
5b. $F_g = (20.5 \text{ N/cm}) x$
5c. 3.9 cm
5d. 61.5 N

Page 98 Chapter 3 Review Questions
1. 6.86×10^2 N and F = mg gives 6.86×10^2 N
2. 100 N
3. G is the same everywhere in the universe.
4a. Moon = 0.16g
   Mercury = 0.34g
   Ganymede = 0.15g
   Sun = 27.9g
4b. Mercury

5. 1.13×10^2 N

6. 1.8×10^2 N
7. 0.105
8a. If F_N (which is equal to F_g) is doubled, then the F_{fr} will double
8b. If stacks side by side, F_{fr} will stay the say as friction force is independent of surface area of contact.
9. 5.0×10^1 N
10a. Slope = 4.15 N/cm
   $F_g = (4.15 \text{ N/cm})x$
10b. $F_g = 6.23$ N
10c. x = 1.57 cm

Page 103 Quick Check
1. Rock has more inertial (and gravitational) mass
2. ISS astronaut has same inertial mass both on the station and on earth.

Page 104 Quick Check
1. The car will keep going straight.
2. As bus quickly stops all unsecured objects move forward (or in the direction of the motion) rather than backwards. Suitcase could not have moved backwards.
3. The lid prevents spills when car quickly stops or starts. During these moments, drink will not experience force while the cup the person holding will. Moving the cup, but not the drink could cause a spill without lid.

Page 108 4.1 Review Questions
1. Objects on table want to stay where they are. Pulling the tablecloth does not exert a force on the cup. The cup stays in place.
2. Twice as much apples have twice the inertia
3. The resting pen has the force of gravity and the force of the desk acting on it even though it is not moving. The forces are balanced
4. If the forces are balanced, the pen could be in uniform motion.
5. Backwards as the ball wants to stay where it is while the wagon is being pulled forward
6. Headrest prevents head from snapping back over seat during rapid accelerations.
7. The puck slows down due to a small amount of friction between ice and puck. Newton's Law still applies.
8. You feel your body moving forward. If you were wearing a seatbelt, you would feel your body pressing against seatbelt.

9. Zigzag because the inertia of the elephant would make it hard to make the quick direction changes.

Page 110 Quick Check
1. 600 N
2. 12 500 kg
3. 0.2000 m/s^2

Page 112 Practice Problems 4.2.1
1. 2.7 kg
2. 450 N each
3. 75 kg
4a. 20 N
  b. 0.41

Page 114 4.2 Review Questions
1. 25 N
2a. 2.5 m/s^2
2b. 5.1×10^3 m/s
3a. 5.0×10^1 m/s^2
3b. 6.0 N
3c. 7.2 N
4. 6.0×10^1 kg
5a. 1.3 m/s^2
5b. As fuel is expelled, mass decrease, so acceleration will increase. Also, gravitational field strength g decreases with altitude.
6. 0.11

Page 117 Quick Check
1a. Action Force: Foot pushing on stair; Reaction Force: Stair pushing on foot
1b. Action Force: Arm pushing on water; Reaction Force: Water pushing on arm
1c. Action Force: Oar paddle on water; Reaction Force: Water pushing on oar paddle
1d. Action Force: Wheels pushing on road; Reaction Force: Road pushing on wheels
2. Reaction force is ground pushing back on feet.
3. The log will move a bit to the left, but not as much as dog since log is heavier.

Page 120 4.3 Review Questions

1. Glove on ball
2. The club hitting the ball is the action force
3. 100 N
4. Each exert the same force
5. Both cars experience the same force
6. -2000 N

7. Throw one of your tools in the other direction

Page 122 Quick Check
1. 1.0×10^3 kgm/s
2. 1.98×10^4 kg
3. 25 m/s or 90 km/hr. Too fast for a bug!

Page 123 Quick Check
1a. 4.0×10^2 kgm/s
1b. -4.0×10^2 Ns
1c. -5.0×10^2 N
1d. Force opposes motion of player

Page 125 – Practice Problems 4.4.1.
1. 4.0 m/s
2. 1.5 kgm/s
3. 6.1 kg

Page 126 – 4.4 Review Questions
1. 0.20 kgm/s
2. 5.5×10^{-2} Ns
3. -12 m/s
4. 0.88 m/s
5. 25.8 N
6. 18 m/s
7a. -13.1 Ns
7b. -1.31×10^4 N

Page 127 Chapter 4 Review Questions
1. If the car stops suddenly, and you are not 'attached' to it, your inertia will cause you to keep moving at the same speed and in the same direction, until you collide with the windshield and/or steering wheel. A seatbelt attaches you to the vehicle, and you accelerate at the same rate as the vehicle.
2. In an inertial frame of reference (sum of forces equal zero), if there are no unbalanced forces acting on a mass, it will not accelerate. It will continue moving at the same speed and in the same direction. If F = 0, then a = 0.
3. 3.0×10^3 N
4. 2.0×10^{-2} m/s^2
5. 5.0×10^2 kg
6. 2.0 m/s^2
7. Newton's Third Law tells you that the force exerted along the rope is 500 N. The rope will not break.

8. Answers will vary, but example should clearly identify both action and reaction force.
9. The mutual force between the ground and the feet of the competitors is what wins the match.
10a. Momentum is a measure of the product of an objects mass and velocity
10b. Momentum in a closed system is conserved. This is an important property when studying motion.
11a. Impulse is the force exerted on an object for a period of time.
11b. 2.8 Ns
11c. 5.6×10^{3} N
12. The reaction force on the rifle accelerates it into one's shoulder.
13. – 3.6 m/s
14. 3.4 m/s
15. 3.0 m/s

Page 133 Practice Problems 5.1.1

1. 1.1×10^{2} J
2. 1.72×10^{4} J, or 17.2 kJ
3. W = F × 0 = 0

Page 134 Practice Problems 5.1.2
1. 73 W
2. 5.4×10^{5} J/h
3. Useable work: 2.7×10^{11} J; Heat: 8.1×10^{11} J

Page 139 5.1 Review Questions

1. 4.9×10^{2} J
2. 1.30×10^{3} J
3a. 1.2×10^{2} J
3b. 0
4. 8.6×10^{4} J
5. 375 J
6. Effort force (b) will only be 1/8th of the load
7. With the following pulley arrangement, mechanical advantage is ½. The load is ½ the effort. So, the effort is twice the load.

Effort

Load

8. 4.9×10^{3} W

9a. 6.9×10^{3} W
9b. 9.3 HP
10. 4.32×10^{6} J

Page 143 Quick Check
1. Doubling mass will double kinetic energy, but doubling speed will *quadruple* kinetic energy.
2. 4.19×10^{4} J
3. 7.2×10^{-2} J

Page 144 Quick Check
1. Potential energy doubles
2. 25.3 kg
3. 6.12 m

Page 147 Practice Problems 5.2.1

1. 7.67 m/s
2. 31.9 m
3. 5.10 m

Page 148 5.2 Review Questions

1. 3.14×10^{4} J
2a. 4.4×10^{5} J
2b. 750 m
3. 1.63 m/s²
4a. (-)5.2 m/s
4b. (-)7.41 m/s
5a. 2.0×10^{2} J
5b. 0.32 m
6a. 20% lost
6b. Heat, sound, friction energy loses account for energy lost
7. 3.8×10^{3} J
8a. 5.2 J
8b. Force is not constant as spring compresses. Average force identifies the assumption of constant force is being used.

Page 151 Quick Check
1a. Temperature is the average translational kinetic energy of all molecules in a material. Thermal energy is the total energy of all molecules in an amount of material. Heat is the amount of thermal energy transferred between one material to another.
1b. Heat refers to transfer of thermal energy. A body contains thermal energy.
2a. 293 K
2b. 586 K; 313°C

3a. Water
3b. Nail
3c. Nail loses heat to water
3d. Water; neither

Page 154 Quick Check
1. Convection
2a. Breeze toward shore
2b. Breeze away from shore
2c. Early morning breeze goes out to sea
3. Vacuum stops conduction, convection. Silvered walls reflect radiant heat back into the bottle. Rubber or plastic stopper slows heat transfer by all three methods.
4. Dirty snow absorbs more radiant heat.

Page 159 5.3 Review Questions
1. Translational, rotational and vibrational
2. 303 K
3. Radiation
4. From 2 to 1, and from 3 to 4
5. Body heat is reflected back to the body. Hypothermia victims require warming from the outside, and the suit prevents this.
6. Radiation
7. Convection
8. Metal blades conduct thermal energy away faster.

Page 161 Practice Problems 5.4.1
1. 2.3×10^7 J
2. $39\,^{\circ}$C
3. 4.0×10^6 J
4. Water has a very high specific heat capacity
5. $c = 3.9 \times 10^2$ J/kg/C

Page 163 Practice Problems 5.4.2
1. 90%
2. 960 W
3. 3.0 W
4. 12% efficient. Examples of waste are heat, sound and friction

Page 165 5.4 Review Questions
1. 5.0×10^4 J
2. 1.5×10^5 J
3. 1.6×10^6 J
4. 14.7 MJ
5. 200 J/kg/C
6a. 0.04 C/s
6b. 84 W

6c. 100 W
7. Higher specific heat capacity of water means ocean water helps moderates temperature
8. Three times as much light is emitted by the fluorescent light bulb
9. 90%

Page 167 Chapter 5 Review Questions
1a. 9.85 J
1b. 0
2. 126 J
3. Same amount of work both ways
4a. 4
4b. 60 N
4c. 11.2
4d. 4.2×10^2 W
5a. 12
5b. 2.40 m
5c. 168 J
5d. 168 J
6. 3.6×10^6 J/s
7. 20 kJ
8. $3E_k$
9. 17 cm
10. 20 cm
11. 9.9 m/s
12. 523 K
13. 323 $^{\circ}$C
14. Metal a good conductor of thermal energy
15a. Convection
15b. Conduction
15c. Radiation/conduction
16. Convection. Warm water is less dense than cold water
17. Water gives off 10 times as much heat.
18. Approximately 36 $^{\circ}$C
19. 720 kJ
20. 93%

Page 176 Quick Check
1a. 1.25 Hz
1b. 0.800 s
2a. 256 Hz
2b. 3.91×10^{-3} s
3. 0.25 Hz

Page 178 Practice Problems 6.1.1
1a. If f doubles, λ is halved
1b. If f halves, λ is doubles
2. 200 Hz
3. 1.5 m

Page 181 6.1 Review Questions

1. Energy
2. Pulse
3. 107 300 000 Hz
4. 0.04 s
5. 0.5 Hz
6. 4 m as captain is looking at whole wave from the trough
7. 1/60 Hz
8. 1/43200 Hz
9. 1/3 T
10. 10 Hz
11. 1.0×10^{-2} m
12. 2 m/s

Page 194 6.2 Review Questions

1. Reflection
2. Diffraction
3. Diffraction
4a. Refraction
4b. Wavelength shortens, direction changes and frequency is constant
5. Images 'c' and 'f' will produce a flat rope when the two wave meet in the middle.
6. Sound, light, water
7. Sound, light (red shift); water (e.g. insect on skimming on water surface)
8. Yes, it will occur because you are moving relative to the source; same as vice versa
9. The plane is going faster than the speed of sound
11. A sonic boom occurs when something moves faster than the speed of sound, which is also called the sound barrier.

Page 196 Chapter 6 Review Questions

1. A pulse in a non-repeating wave. A periodic wave is repeating waves
2. See page 175 in work text
3. Hertz is the measure of frequency and refers to how many times per second.
4. Frequency and period are reciprocals of each other.
5a. 2.5 Hz
5b. 0.40 s
6. Transverse waves are produced by a vibration or disturbance that is at right angles to the motion. Longitudinal waves travel in the direction of the pulse.
7. Wave speed is the product of wave frequency and wavelength
8. 5.0×10^{6} m

9. 0.645 m
11. Refraction is the bending of a wave like when a water wave enters a shallower body of water. Diffraction is when a wave spreads out as it passes through narrow openings, around corners or small obstacles. For example, the rainbow you observe when you move a DVD disc in the light.
12a. Decrease
12b. Frequency stays the same
12c. Change if wave enters at an angle
12d. No change if wave does not enter at an angle
13a. Constructive interference is when waves add together when they meet
13b. Destructive interference is when wave cancel each other when they meet
14. Nodal lines are destructive interference and maximum is constructive interference
15. Circular waves, originating at the focus, reflect from the first mirror as straight, parallel waves that travel to the second mirror, reflect as circular waves with a center at the focus of the second mirror, where the match is.

16. 4.5×10^{3} m

Page 205 Quick Check

1. 1 m
2. The dark outside allows you to see reflection from glass
3a. Same distance, but image in the mirror
3b. Behind
3c. Less of your image is viewable

Page 210 7.1 Review Questions

1. As f increases; λ decreases
2. Radiation that is detected by the human eye. 10^{15} Hz; 380-760 nm
3. Radio; Micro; Infrared
4. Ultraviolet light, X-rays and gamma rays
5. $\angle$ of incidence = $\angle$ of reflection in same plane
6. Answers will vary, but placing a mirror at an angle to the corner in such a way the normal line is pointing directly at the corner will cause the incident ray to reach the mirror and the reflecting ray to reach your eye as stated in the law of reflection.
7. Object distance = object to mirror distance
   Image distance = image to mirror distance
8. No light reaches the location of the image
9a. 5
9b. 7

9c. 23
9d. 35
9e. 359
10. You need a mirror half your height (90 cm)
11.

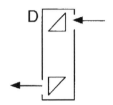

AMBULANCE

12. Image on screen was inverted, real and smaller
13.

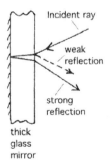

Page 215 Quick Check
1a. Real, inverted, smaller between C and F
1b. Real, inverted, same size, at C
1c. Image is found beyond C

Page 218 Practice Problems 7.2.1
1. 100 cm
2. D = 2f
3. 13.3 cm
4. d_i = -30.0 cm The image is virtual and appears behind the mirror

Page 223 7.2 Review Questions
1. Convex = diverging; concave = coverging
2. Converging focus rays; diverging spreading rays
3. Converging
4a. Concave
4b. Convex
4c. Plane
5. E, A, F, B, D, C
6a. Far away: Inverted, real, smaller, between C and F
6b. Outside C: Inverted, real, smaller, between C and F
6c. At C: Inverted, real, same size and at C
6d. Between C and F: Inverted, real, larger, beyond C
6e. At focal point: No image formed
6f. Between focal point and vertex: Upright, virtual, larger, behind mirror
7a. See worked solution video
8a. Concave
8b. Convex

8c. Convex
8d. Concave
9. Image will be upright, virtual, smaller and behind the mirror.
10a. No, all convex mirror images are virtual
10b. No, an image gets larger as an object gets closer to the mirror, but the image is never larger.

Page 228 Quick Check
1. 1.53
2. $\angle r = 4.11°$
3a. $\angle r = 19.5°$
3b. Light enters the glass at 30° from the normal, then refracts within the glass at 20° from the normal. When it leaves the glass it goes back into air, it will be at 30° from the normal again.
4. Prism, Violet refracts most.

Page 230 Quick Check
1. $i_c = 24.4°$
2. $i_c = 41.8°$
3. n = 1.27

Page 237 7.3 Review Questions
1. Incident angle is 70°, which is greater than the critical angle, so this particular ray will reflect back into the water. Some rays will refract out at other angle and reach the fisher's eyes.
2a. Below
2b. Aim at what you see. The laser refracts light too
3.

4. 39.3°
5. 600 nm
6. 1.24×10^8 m/s

7.

medium 1
vacuum (or air)
medium 2

Snell's Law: For the situation above, where light travels from medium1 into a vacuum and then into medium 2.

$\frac{\sin\theta}{\sin\theta_1} = n_1$ and $\frac{\sin\theta}{\sin\theta_2} = n_2$

$\frac{n_1}{n_2} = \frac{\sin\theta_2}{\sin\theta_1} \times \frac{\sin\theta_2}{\sin\theta} = \frac{\sin\theta_2}{\sin\theta_1}$

or, $n_1\sin\theta_1 = n_2\sin\theta_2$

8. Water is pure, light is coming from a vacuum or air, and the frequency is for 'average' visible light.

9a. Refraction, dispersion and total internal reflection

9b. Sun behind you and rainclouds in front of you

9c. Red, orange, yellow, green, blue, indigo, violet.

10. All the same speed in a vacuum. Red is fastest in glass.

11. 2.0×10^8 m/s

12. 1.54

13a. 489 nm

13b. Blue

13c. Frequency determines colour

Page 242 Quick Check

1. See Extra Help section of Chapter 7.0 in the online study guide (www.edvantageinteractive.com/sciencemoodle)

2. The images formed by a diverging lens are always virtual, erect and smaller than the object.

Page 244 Quick Check

1. 50.5 mm

2. 100 mm or 10.0 cm

3. 20 mm

Page 252 7.4 Review

2a. -50.0 cm

2b. Virtual image

4. 1.90 cm

3. $d_i = 0.05$m

5. $H_i = 1.7$ cm

6. Magnification is 2.00. The image is real because $D_o > f$

7. To come

8.

$\frac{1}{D_i} = \frac{1}{f} - \frac{1}{D_o} = \frac{1}{-6.0cm} - \frac{1}{10.0cm} = \frac{-16}{60.0cm}$

$D_i = -60.0$ cm/16 = -3.75 cm (virtual image)

$\frac{H_i}{H_o} = \frac{D_i}{D_o} = \frac{3.75cm}{10.00cm} = 0.375$

(Image is diminished.)

$H_i = 0.375 \times H_o = 0.375 \times 5.0$ cm = 1.9 cm.

Image is on the same side of the lens as object.

9. Red eye is the flash reflecting off the retina. Most cameras flash twice. The first flash causes the pupil to contract and the second flash takes the picture. The smaller pupil reduces 'red eye'.

Page 254 Chapter 7 Review Questions

4. 0.8 mm

5. 7

6. To get a wide-angle view

7. Place the filament between f and $2f$

8. Between the focus and the mirror

9. 1.7 m (real image)

10. 2.0 m

11.
$\angle r = 21°$
The beam will lave the glass at $35°$

12. $\angle i_c = 41.1°$

13. n=1/sin45°=1.41

14. To come

15. The shorter the wavelength (violet) the more the ray bends

16. 1.5×10^8 m/s

17a. The graph is a straight line through 0,0

17b. Slope is 1.50 (n=1.50)

17c. 41.8°

18. Wrong lens to focus light

19a. D_o is greater than $2f$

19b. D_o is between f and $2f$

19c. $D_o = 2f$

19d. D_o is much less than f

20. Inverted, smaller, real image forms between C and F

21. E

22. 22.5 cm

23. Inverted, enlarged, real image forms beyond C

24. 12 mm

25. 6.5 cm

26. -55.9 cm

Page 261 Quick Check

1a. 10 km/h

1b. 15 km/h

2a. 25 km/h
2b. 0 km/h
2c. 5 km/h
3. 0 km/h
4. 10 km/h
5. Assigning a positive value to velocities to the right in the figure.
Wind: +20 km/h
Bird: -5km/h
Boat: -15 km/h
Earth: 0 km/h
River: -5km/h

Page 263 Quick Check
1. Zero, which is constant!
2. Same as Figure 8.1.4, but the parabola is elongated

Page 270 Practice Problems 8.1.1
1. 6.6 s
2. 10 s
3. 50 s
4. 1.1×10^{2} s

Page 268 Practice Problems 8.1.2
1. 78 m
2. 50 m
3. 4.5 m

Page 272 Quick Check
1a. 0.10 mc
1b. 0.50 mc
1c. 0.87 mc
1d. 0.9999 mc
1e. mc
2a. Approximately 0.10 mc
2b. 0.58 mc
2c. 1.8 mc
2d. 71 mc
2e. p approaches infinity

3.
$$F = \Delta p / \Delta t$$
$$F \to \infty \text{ since } \Delta p \to \infty$$

Page 274 8.1 Review Questions
2. Speed = c
3a. 13 a
3b. 38.0 m
4. $1.15t_o$
5. $v = 0.87c$
6. $0.866c$ or approximately $0.9c$
7. c, light from a star takes time to reach our eyes on earth.

8. $v = 0.995c$
9. 9×10^{10} J
10a. 4.1×10^{15} J
10b. 2.0×10^{5} years!

Page 287
1. Radioactive decay
2. + nucleus with orbiting e$^-$
3. In nucleus with + charge; number of protons = atomic number
4. No, it splits into a proton and an electron

Page 290 Quick Check
1. Same number of protons, different number of neutrons
2. Artificially made isotopes or natural isotopes that are unstable
3. 238 = mass number (protons and neutrons); 92 = atomic number (protons only)

4a. $_{2}^{4}\text{He}$

4b. $_{-1}^{0}e$

4c. $_{82}^{214}\text{Pb}$

4d. $_{84}^{210}\text{Po}$

Page 292 Practice Problems 9.1.1
1. 62 atoms
2. 5.2 years. 1/32 is five half-lives.

Page 292 Quick Check
1. $_{88}^{226}\text{Ra} \to \ _{86}^{222}\text{Rn} + \ _{2}^{4}\text{He}$
2. $_{82}^{214}\text{Pb} \to \ _{83}^{214}\text{Bi} + \ _{-1}^{0}e$
3. 8 elements and 15 isotopes

Page 295 9.1 Review Questions
6a. $_{5}^{14}\text{N}$

6c. $_{89}^{225}\text{Ac}$

6d. $_{82}^{209}\text{X}$ and $_{-1}^{0}x$

7. 125 g

Page 303 Review Questions
9. 1.9×10^{3} atoms

11a. $_{88}^{226}\text{Ra}$

11b. $_{-1}^{0}e$

11c. $_{7}^{14}\text{N}$

11d. $_{2}^{4}\text{He}$

Chapter 10

Page 313, Quick Check

1.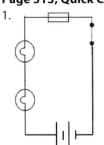

2.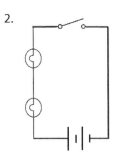

3.

Page 314, Quick Check
1.   (a) 100 mA
       (b) 67 mA
2.   (a) 16.7 mA
       (b) 6.7 mA
       (c) 3.5 mA
       (d) 0.67 mA

Page 317, 10.1 Review
1. 3.0×10^2 C
2. 1.0×10^1 A
3. 2.7×10^{23} electrons
4. 23 days
5. 1.8 g
6. 4.02 g
8. 80 mA

Page 319, Practice Problems 10.2.1
1. 1.5 kΩ
2. 12 A
3. 25 V

Page 321, Practice Problems 10.2.2
1. 2200Ω ± 220 Ω
2. 10 000 Ω ± 500 Ω
3. 1 500 000 Ω ± 150 000 Ω
4. 470 000 Ω ± 94 000 Ω

Page 322, Quick Check
1. 240 Ω
2.   (a) 24 Ω
       (b) 24 Ω, 2.2×10^5 J
3. 4.5×10^5 J

Page 324, Practice Problems 10.2.3
1. 1.20 V
2. 0.030 Ω

Page 327 10.2 Review
1. 5.8 Ω
2. 6.0 V
3. 4.0 A
4.   (a) 1.0×10^3 Ω
       (b) 6.0×10^3 A
       (c) 2.0×10^3 Ω
5. 6.0 Ω
6. 110 V
7. 5.0 A
8. 1000 Ω ±5%
9.   (a) 320 Ω ±10%
       (b) 20 Ω ±5%
       (c) 85 000 000 Ω ±10%
       (d) 9700 Ω ±20%
10   (a) green black brown
       (b) orange purple orange gold
       (c) brown black black silver
       (d) grey blue red
11. 0.104 Ω
12. 8.1 Ω
13.   (a) 3.6×10^6 J
      (b) 72 kWh
      (c) $4.32
14. 0.045 kWh
15. 22 V
16. 5.0 A

Page 333, Practice Problems 10.3.1
1.   (b) 1.1 A
2.   (a) 9.0 Ω
       (b) 2.0 kΩ
       (c) 314 Ω

Page 334, Quick Check
1. 6.0 A
2. R/16
3. 1.5 A
4.   (a) 6.0 Ω
       (b) 1.0 A

Page 339, 10.3 Review
1. 1.0 A
2. D
3.   (a) 50 Ω
       (b) 1.0 A
       (c) 0.13 A
       (d) 7.3 V
4. 2.0 A
5. 10 V
6. 72 V
7. 0.50 Ω
8.   (a) 91Ω
       (b) 0.13 A
       (c)).93 W

9.   (a) 16 V
          (b) 1.8×10^2 W

Page 342, Chapter 10 Review
2. 4.0×10^1 A
3. 2.7×10^{24} electrons
4. 24.7 g
5. 1.29 V
6.   (a) 15 V
          (b) 120 V
7. 30 kΩ
8. 80 V
9. 100 000 Ω ± 5 000 Ω
10. yellow, violet, green
11. 33 V
12. 12.5 A
13. 960 W
14. 144 Ω
15. I = 21.3 A; breaker is activated
16. 60 kWh, $3.60
17. 0.25 V
18. 7.5 V
19.   (a) 44 Ω
          (b) 4.0 Ω
20. 51.28 Ω
21. 3.0 V
22. 0.75 V
23. 18 kΩ, 9.0 kΩ, 2,0 kΩ, 4.0 kΩ
24.   (a) 167 kΩ, 0.48 mA
          (b) 77 Ω, 0.13 A
          (c) 314 Ω, 5.2 mA
25. 3.0 V
26. 0.83 Ω

Glossary

A

absolute reference frame (8.1) a frame of reference that is truly fixed and unchanging

absolute zero (5.3) temperature at which all the atoms stop moving; just under –273°C

acceleration (2.2) the rate at which velocity is changing; the change may be in magnitude, direction, or both

acceleration of gravity (2.4) constant acceleration of an object falling near Earth's surface

action force (4.3) the first force in the equation:

$$F_{A \text{ on } B} = -F_{B \text{ on } A}$$

alpha decay (9.1) when an unstable nucleus releases a helium nucleus (alpha particle)

alpha rays (9.1) less-penetrating Becquerel rays discovered by Rutherford

amplitude (6.1) the height of a wave

angle of incidence (6.2, 7.1) the angle between an incident ray and the normal to a surface

angle of reflection (6.2, 7.1) the angle between a reflected ray and the normal to a surface

artificial transmutation (9.1) changing one element into another under lab conditions

astigmatism (7.4) irregularities in the curvature of a cornea or lens

atomic number (9.1) the number of protons in the nucleus of an element's atom

average speed (2.1) total distance divided by total time

B

Becquerel (Bq) (9.1) a measurement of emissions per second, in reference to unstable isotopes

Becquerel rays (9.1) rays first discovered by Henri Becquerel and later found to be X-rays

beta decay (9.1) nuclear decay involving emission of an electron

C

Celsius (5.3) a temperature scale where water freezes at 0° and boils at 100° at one atmosphere of pressure

centre of curvature (7.2, 7.4) point in space representing the centre of the sphere from which a curved mirror was cut

chain reaction (9.2) continuous nuclear fission, accompanied by a large release of energy

coefficient of kinetic friction (3.2) the proportionality between kinetic friction and normal force; denoted by μ

concave mirror (7.2) a mirror that is curved inward

conduction (5.3) the ability of a material to transfer heat and electricity from one molecule to another

conductor (5.3) material in which electrons in the outermost regions of the atoms are free to move

constructive interference (6.2) when two or more waves combine to form a stronger wave

convection (5.3) a means of heat transfer by movement of the heated substance itself

convection current (5.3) the movement of molecules within fluids

conversion factor (1.4) a fraction or factor written so that the denominator and numerator are equivalent values with different units

convex mirror (7.2) a mirror that is curved outwards

crest (6.1) the highest point on a wave

critical mass (9.2) the mass required to start a nuclear chain reaction

cycle (1.2) a complete back and forth movement

D

degrees (5.3) on the Celsius scale, 100 equal divisions between 0°C and 100°C

dependent variable (1.4) a variable whose value depends on the independent variable

derived unit (1.4) a unit composed of one or more units

destructive interference (6.2) combination of waves where the crest of one wave overlaps with the trough of another to produce a wave of decreased amplitude

deuterium (9.1) an isotope of hydrogen with one neutron

diffraction (6.2) the spreading out of a wave as it passes through a narrow opening, around a corner, or around a small object

displacement (1.5, 2.1) straight line between the starting and final positions; a vector measurement

Doppler effect (6.2) apparent changed in frequency and wavelength of a wave that is perceived by an observer moving relative to the source of the wave

double convex lens (7.4) a lens that has two spherical surfaces

E

efficiency (5.4) for any energy-converting device, the ratio of useful energy output from the device to the amount of useful energy put into the device

effort distance (5.1) the distance through which the force was exerted

effort force (5.1) force exerted

electromagnetic radiation (7.1) radiant energy that travels at the speed of sound

electromagnetic spectrum (7.1) all the different forms of electromagnetic radiation

enlarged virtual image (7.2) a larger image that is "right side up"

experimentation (1.1) a process to determine whether or not the hypothesis was accurate in explaining the observations

F

fluorescence (9.1) the ability for a material to absorb the light of one wavelength and to release the light at a different wavelength

focal length (f) (7.2, 7.4) distance between the vertex and either focal point

focal plane (7.4) a plane centralized around the focal point; location of sensors/film in cameras

focal point (6.2, 7.2, 7.4) for a convex lens, the point at which a beam of light parallel to the principal axis converges. For a concave lens, the point from which a similar beam appears to come.

focus (6.2) the point where waves converge

force (3.1) a change exerted on an object; a push or a pull

free fall (2.4) motion under the influence of the gravitational force only

free-body diagram (1.5) a diagram showing all the forces acting on a body

frequency (1.2) the number of cycles completed in a given space of time

frequency (6.1) how often the waves pass a given point

friction (3.2) force opposing the motion of an object

G

gamma rays (9.1) emission of a high-energy photon

gravitational mass (4.1) mass measurement based on comparing the known weight of one object to the unknown weight of another object

gravitational potential energy (5.2) energy of an object due to its position above the surface of Earth

H

half-life (9.1) the time it takes for half a sample of a radioactive isotope to decay

heat (5.3) thermal energy transferred from one material to another

hertz (Hz) (1.2, 6.1) a frequency of one cycle per second

horsepower (5.1) Imperial measurement of power; 1 horsepower = 550 foot-pounds/second

hypothesis (1.1) an "if…then…" statement that explains the observations

I

image distance (7.1) distance between the mirror and the image

Imperial system of measurement (1.4) a system of units of measurement originally developed in Britain

impulse (4.4) the product of the force and the time interval during which it acts

incident ray (7.1) a ray approaching a mirror

independent variable (1.4) a variable whose value influences the dependent variable

inertia (4.1) the tendency for all objects to resist change in their states of motion

inertial mass (4.1) mass measurement based on the ratio of a known net force on an object to the acceleration of the object

infrared radiation (7.1) radiation that has a slightly shorter wavelength than visible light

instantaneous speed (2.1) the speed at a given instant in time

isotope (9.1) an atom that has the same number of protons as an element, but a different number of neutrons

J

joule (5.1) the SI unit for work and all forms of energy

K

kelvin (5.3) the SI unit for temperature

kilowatt (5.1) a measurement of power; used for large amounts of power

kinematics (2.1) the study of motion of all objects

kinetic energy (5.2) the total energy of a moving object

kinetic friction (3.2) the force opposing motion between two flat objects when one surface slides over another

kinetic molecular theory (5.3) all matter is made up of tiny particles that are constantly moving

L

law (1.1) a general statement of fact, without an accompanying set of explanations

law of action and reaction (4.3) [see Newton's third law of motion]

law of conservation of energy (5.2) law stating that the total energy of a mechanical system is constant. Energy can be transformed from one form into another, but the total amount of energy is unchanged.

law of conservation of momentum (4.4) law stating that within an isolated system, the total change in momentum is zero

law of inertia (4.1) law stating that every body continues in its state of rest, or motion in a straight line at a constant speed, unless a net force is exerted upon it; also known as Newton's first law

lens (7.4) a medium for bending light

linear function (1.4) an equation that, when graphed, results in a straight line

longitudinal wave (6.1) a wave with the motion of the medium being parallel to the motion of the wave

M

mass number (9.1) the number of nucleons in the nucleus

mechanical advantage (MA) (5.1) the ratio of output force to input force for a machine

mirror equation (7.2) equation relating the focal length of a curved mirror to the image and object distances; $1/d_o + 1/d_i = 1/f$

model (1.1) simplified description or representation of a theory

moderator (9.2) substance that slows down neutrons long enough for them to react with other nuclei

momentum (4.4) mass × velocity; given the symbol p

N

newton (N) (3.1, 4.2) a measurement of force

Newton's first law of motion (4.1) law stating that a body will continue to move at the same speed and in the same direction for as long as there are no unbalanced forces acting on it

Newton's law of universal gravitation (4.4) law stating that every body in the universe attracts every other body with a force that (a) is directly proportional to the product of the masses of the two bodies, and (b) is inversely proportional to the square of the distance between the centres of mass of the two objects

Newton's second law of motion (4.2) law stating that if an unbalanced force acts on a body, the body will accelerate. The rate at which it accelerates depends directly on the unbalanced force and inversely on the mass of the body; $a = F/m$.

Newton's third law of motion (4.3) law stating that if two bodies interact, the force the first body exerts on the second body will equal the force the second body exerts on the first body. The two forces will be opposite in direction and will act simultaneously over the same interval of time.

nodal lines (6.2) dark bands indicating a point where destructive interference occurs in a standing light wave

normal (7.1) an imaginary line that is perpendicular to a surface, such as a mirror, or to another line

normal force (3.2) for an object resting on a horizontal surface, the upward force that balances the weight of the object

nuclear fission (9.2) when a nucleus breaks apart into two different nuclei

nuclear fusion (9.2) when two nuclei are forced together, they have the chance to form a single, new nucleus

nucleons (9.1) protons and neutrons; subatomic particles that account for the mass of the nucleus of an atom

nucleus (9.1) the dense centre of an atom

O

object distance (7.1) distance between the person and the object

observation (1.1) collection of data through the use of human senses

P

parabola (7.2) a perfect curve for a concave mirror

period (1.2) the time in which a single cycle is completed

period (6.1) time interval between vibrations

periodic wave (6.1) a regularly repeating wave; wave that occurs at regular intervals

phosphorescence (9.1) delayed fluorescence; collects sunlight during the day, and releases it during the night at a different wavelength

photons (8.1) small particles of energy, usually light

position (2.1) the shortest distance between the origin and the location

positron (9.2) the anti-particle of an electron

potential energy (5.3) energy of position, usually related to the relative position of two things

power (5.1) the measurement of how much work a machine can do in one second

precision (1.3) describes the closeness, or reproducibility, of a set of measurements taken under the same conditions

principal axis (PA) (7.2, 7.4) a line joining the centres of curvature of the surfaces of a lens

proton (9.1) positively charged subatomic particle

pulse (6.1) a non-repeating wave

Q

qualitative observation (1.1) observation that describes qualities or changes in the quality of matter

quantitative observation (1.1) observation that has numbers or quantities associated with it

R

radiant energy (5.3) energy transmitted by radiation

radiation (5.3) any form of energy transmitted in the form of electromagnetic waves

radioactive series (9.1) a series of decays to get from one element to another

radioactivity (9.1) property of some rays to ionize the air, and to be very penetrating

radioisotope (9.1) isotope that is unstable and therefore radioactive

radius of curvature (7.2, 7.4) distance from the centre of curvature to the mirror surface

reaction force (4.3) the second force in the equation:
$$F_{A\,on\,B} = -F_{B\,on\,A}$$

reflection (6.1) occurs when a wave bounces off an object or other boundary

reflection ray (7.1) the ray that bounces off a mirror

refraction (6.1, 7.3) the bending of a wave; occurs when a wave hits an object at an angle or when a wave enters a new medium

refractive index (7.3) defines how much light will bend in a medium

relativistic momentum (8.1) how momentum changes based on the reference frame

resultant displacement (1.5) the vector sum of the individual displacement vectors

rotational kinetic energy (5.3) energy due to circular motion

S

scalar quantities (1.5) a measurement with a magnitude but no direction

scientific method (1.1) a method of drawing conclusions from observations

scientific notation (1.3) a way of expressing measurements; in the form $X \times 10^y$

slope (1.4) the relationship between x and y defined by the equation; the slope of a line describes its steepness

Snell's law (7.3) law stating that for any angle greater than zero, the ratio $\sin \theta_i / \sin \theta_r$ is constant for any light ray passing through the boundary between two media

sonic boom (6.2) when an aircraft exceeds the speed of sound, the shape of the waves behind it changes. These waves make a booming sound to an observer.

sound barrier (6.2) the increase in aerodynamic resistance as an aircraft approaches the speed of sound

source of error (1.1) anything that could contribute to inaccuracy and error during experimentation

special relativity principle (8.1) principle stating that if two frames of reference move with constant velocity relative to each other, then the laws of physics will be the same in both frames of reference

special theory of relativity (8.1) theory that describes how time affected by motion in space at a constant velocity and how mass and energy are related

specific heat capacity (5.4) the amount of heat required to raise the temperature of a given amount of a substance a given unit of temperature

speed (2.1) the distance an object travels in a given amount of time

spring constant (3.2) constant of proportionality k that appears in Hooke's law for springs; represents the slope of the line and is measured in units of force per unit length; amount of stiffness of a spring

stable (9.1) subatomic particles that do not decay; protons and electrons

static friction (3.2) acting force between two objects at rest that prevents them from sliding

strong force (9.1) a nuclear force that holds the nucleus of an atom together

T

temperature (5.3) a measure of the average kinetic energy of all the particles in a sample of matter

theory (1.1) explanation for the hypothesis being investigated

thermal energy (5.3) the total energy of all the molecules in an amount of material

thermonuclear fusion (9.2) nuclear fusion occurring due to very high temperatures

time dilation (8.1) the "stretching" of time by a moving object

total kinetic energy (5.3) all the kinetic energy in a material

translational kinetic energy (5.3) energy due to motion in straight lines

transmutation (9.1) the process of changing one atom to another via radioactive decay

transverse wave (6.1) a wave with the motion of the medium being perpendicular to the motion of the wave

tritium (9.1) an isotope of hydrogen with two neutrons

trough (6.1) the lowest point on a wave

U

ultraviolet radiation (7.1) radiation that has a slightly higher wavelength than visible light

universal gravitation constant (G) (3.1) constant used in the equation for Newton's law of universal gravitation; 6.67×10^{-11} N^{-11}m^2/kg^2

unstable (9.1) a subatomic particle that decays; neutrons decay into a proton and an electron when outside the nucleus

V

vector (1.5) measurement that includes both a magnitude and a direction

velocity (2.1) a vector measurement of speed and direction

vertex (V) (7.2) geometric centre of a curved mirror surface

vibrational kinetic energy (5.3) energy due to vibrations; "back and forth" movement

W

watt (W) (5.1) a measurement of power

wavelength (λ) (6.1) the distance between two successive crests or two successive troughs

weight (3.1) the gravitational force acting on an object

work (5.1) defined as two things that must happen: (1) a force must act on the object and (2) the object must move through a distance in the direction of the force

Y

y-intercept (1.4) where the line crosses the y-axis on a graph

Index

Electromagnetic spectrum, 200–201
Electrons
    beta particles as, 283, 286, 287
    free, 153
    gamma photons and, 271
    positive. *See* Positrons
Elements
    artificially produced, 297
    as isotopes, 288
    transmutation of, 285, 287, 293
Energy
    about, 132
    within atom, 296–297
    as capacity to do work, 132
    forms of, 132
    kinetic, 142–143
    mass and, 260, 271–272, 296, 297, 301
    mechanical, 142–149
    nuclear fission and, 298
    nuclear fusion and, 301
    radiant, 153
    as scalar quantity, 35
    thermal, 150, 151, 202
    total, 150
Energy transfer
    and power, 162
    temperature and, 150
    waves and, 174
Enlarged virtual image, 215
Equipment essentials, 6–7
Error(s)
    experimental, 11–12
    random, 11
    sources of, 3
    systematic, 11
Experimentation
    defined, 3
    error in, 11–12
Eye, 244–246

F
Farsightedness, 246
Fission
    bombs, 301
    defined, 297
Fluorescence
    defined, 280
    delayed, 280
Focal length, 213, 214, 240, 242–243, 245
Focal plane, 240
Focal point, 213, 240
Force(s), 75–100
    action, 117
    defined, 76
    of gravity. *See* Gravitational force
    and impulse, 122
    measuring unit for, 109
    multiple, 110
    mutuality of, 116–117
    net, 109, 142

normal, 86
nuclear strong, 287
reaction, 117
unbalanced, 109, 110, 121, 145, 273
as vector quantity, 35–36
Frames of reference
    about, 260–261
    absolute, 264
    comparing, 263
    of mu-mesons, 269
    and special relativity theory, 260–261, 262
    and speed of light, 264–265
    and time dilation, 265–267
    velocity measurement and, 262
Free body diagrams, 35–36
Free fall, 64, 145
Frequencies
    defined, 6–7, 175
    periods and, 175
Fresnel lens, 153
Friction, 85–87
    about, 85
    coefficient of kinetic, 86–87
    kinetic, 86
    and Newton's first law of motion, 104
    static, 85–86
Frisch, Otto, 297
Fusion, 301

G
Galileo Galilei, 3, 85, 103, 104
Gamma photons, 271
Gamma radiation, 281, 282–284
Gamma rays, 281–282, 292
Geiger, Hans, 285–286
Graphic relationships, 28
Graphite, 297, 298
Graphs, 27–32
    acceleration, 50–51, 54
    gravitational force and spring balance, 94
    position-time, 42
    of projectiles, 66–67
    speed-time, 50–51, 54, 57
    velocity-time, 66–67
Gravitational fields, 76, 80
Gravitational force
    about, 76–80
    and mass, 80
    and motion of planets around Sun, 78
    and spring balance, 78, 94
    unbalanced force and, 145
    and weight, 78
Gravitational mass, 103
Gravitational potential energy, 143–144, 145
Gravity
    acceleration of, 64–66
    deflection of light, 203
    Einstein and, 260
    as mutual force, 78

Newton and, 3
    as universal force, 78

H
Hahn, Otto, 297
Half-lives, 290–292
    of artificially produced elements, 297
Heat
    defined, 150
    measurement of, 160
Heat transfer
    by conduction, 152–153
    by convection, 153
    kinetic energy and, 152, 153
    power and, 162
Helium, 151–152, 301
Herschel, William, 202
Hertz, 7, 175
Hertz, Heinrich, 175
Hooke, Robert, 94
Hooke's law, 93–94
Horsepower, 134
Hydrogen bomb, 301
Hypermetropia, 246
Hyperopia, 246
Hypothesis, statement of, 3

I
Ideal conditions, 104
"Ideal" gas, 151–152
Image distance, 205
Image formation
    in plane mirror, 203, 204–205
    predicting, 214, 240–242
Imperial system of measurement, 19
    conversion from metric to, 20–21
Impulse, 122–123
Incidence, angles of, 204, 213, 229, 232
Incident ray, 204
Independent variable, 27
Inertia, 102–104
Inertial mass, 103
Infrared photography, 202
Infrared radiation, 153, 202
Instantaneous speed, 41, 50
Inter-disciplinary studies, 5
Interferometer, 264
International Bureau of Weights and
    Measures (BIPM), 20
International System of Units, 20
Isotopes, 288, 289–290

J
Joule, James, 132, 160
Joules, 132, 160

K
Kelvin, William Thomson, Lord, 151
Kelvin scale, 151

Kepler, Johannes, 78
Kepler's laws, 78
Kilowatts, 133, 134
Kinematics, 37–74
Kinetic energy
    about, 142–143
    accelerated protons and, 296
    acceleration and, 142
    average translational, 151
    defined, 142
    gravitational potential energy and, 145
    heat transfer and, 152, 153
    mechanical energy and, 145
    of nuclear fusion, 301
    rotational, 150
    speed and, 144
    total, 151
    translational, 150, 151, 153
    vibrational, 150
    work and, 144
Kinetic friction, 86
Kinetic molecular theory
    about, 150–151
    defined, 150

L

Laws
    action and reaction, 116–117
    conservation of energy, 145
    conservation of momentum, 123–124
    defined, 3
    inertia, 103, 104
    Kepler's, 78
    Newton's laws of motion, 3, 103.
        See also Newton's first law of motion;
        Newton's second law of motion;
        Newton's third law of motion
    planetary motion, 78
    reflection, 203–204
    Snell's law of refraction, 227–229
    universal gravitation, 3, 78–79, 80
Length contraction, 269
Lens
    defined, 239
    double convex, 240
    of eye, 245
Lens equation, 242–244
Lenses
    in compound microscope, 247
    concave, 246
    convex, 246, 247
    eyepiece, 247
    measurement of, 242–243
    objective, 247, 248
    terminology of, 240
    types of, 239
Light
    gravity deflection of, 203
    linear propagation of, 203
    properties of, 200

refraction of, 226–232
speed of, 200, 226, 227, 264–265, 273, 284
visible, 201, 202
Linear function, 27
Liquid drop model, 297, 298
Longitudinal waves, 176, 178

M

Magnetic fields
    about, 76
    and electromagnetic radiation, 174
    and separation of Becquerel rays, 282–284
Magnifying glass, 247
Magnitude
    and acceleration, 66
    defined, 38
    and displacement, 38
Marsden, Ernest, 285, 286
Mass
    acceleration and, 77
    and energy, 260, 271–272, 296, 297, 301
    exact, 10
    gravitational, 103
    gravitational force and, 80
    inertial, 103
    measurement, 77
    and momentum, 121, 122, 123
    in Newton's second law of motion, 109
    relativity and, 271
    as scalar quantity, 35
    and thermal energy, 160
    weight and, 77
Mass number, 289
Maxwell, James Clerk, 264
Measurement
    accuracy of, 9
    English units of, 19
    history of, 19–20
    Imperial system of, 19
    precision of, 9
    units of, 19
Measurements
    adding or subtracting, 13
    combining, 13–15
    multiplying or dividing, 15
Mechanical energy, 142–149
    as potential or kinetic, 145
Megahertz, 7, 175
Megawatts, 133
Meitner, Lise, 297
Metric system, 19–21
Michelson, A. A., 264
Michelson-Morley experiment, 264–265
Micrometer, 10
Microscope, compound, 247
Mirror equation, 216–217
Mirrors
    concave, 212, 213–215, 218–219

converging, 213
convex, 212, 219
curved, 212–225
diverging, 219
plane, 203, 204–205, 212
Models, theories and, 3
Moderators, 297, 298
Molecules
    and kinetic molecular theory, 150
    total energy of, 150
Momentum
    change in, 122
    conservation of, 123–124
    defined, 121
    and impulse, 122–123
    and infinity, 273
    measurement units, 122
    relativistic, 272
    as vector quantity, 35
Morley, E. W., 264
Motion
    kinematics and, 38
    laws of, 3
    Newton's first law, 103–104
    Newton's laws, 3, 103
    Newton's second law, 109–110, 121, 122
    Newton's third law, 116–117
    probe, 7
    projectile, 66
    relative, 262
    wave, 174
Mouton, Gabriel, 19
Mu-mesons (muons), 268–269
Myopia, 246

N

Nanometres, 175, 202
Nearsightedness, 246
Net force, 109, 142
Neutrons
    and beta particles, 286–287
    discovery of, 286–287, 296
    and isotopes, 288
    speed of, 296–297
Newcomen, Thomas, 134
Newton, Sir Isaac, 3, 76, 78, 79, 103–104, 260
Newton-metres, 132
Newtons, 76, 77, 109
Newton's first law of motion, 103–104
Newton's law of universal gravitation, 3, 78–79
Newton's second law of motion, 109–110, 121, 122, 145, 272
Newton's third law of motion, 116–117
    conservation of momentum and, 123–124
Nodal lines, 185
Normal
    angle of incidence and, 232
    defined, 204

Static friction, 85–86
Stevin, Simon, 19
Strassman, Fritz, 297
Strong force, 287
Sun
    Earth's revolution around, 3, 264
    exposure to, 202
    and thermal energy, 202

T

Telescopes
    astronomical, 248
    terrestrial, 248
Temperature
    about, 151
    and thermal energy, 160
    and transfer of energy, 150
    and translational kinetic energy, 151
Theory, statement of, 3
Thermal energy
    amount of, 160
    convection and, 153
    defined, 150
    infrared radiation and, 202
    mass and, 160
    materials and, 160
    measurement of, 160–170
    temperature and, 160
    and water, 160
Thermonuclear fusion, 301
Thomson, J. J., 281
Time
    dilation, 265–269
    and impulse, 122
    measurement, 6–7
    as scalar quantity, 35
Total energy, 150
Total kinetic energy, 151
Translational kinetic energy
    average, 151
    defined, 150
    radiant energy and, 153
Transmutations
    artificial, 293
    defined, 285
    natural, 285, 287
Transverse waves, 176, 178
Trigonometric ratios, 34, 186
Troughs, 175, 178, 183, 184

U

Ultraviolet radiation, 202–203
Unbalanced force, 109, 110, 121, 145, 273
Uncertainty, degree of, 10
Universal gravitation constant, 79
Unstable particles, 286
Uranium
    different forms of, 288
    isotopes of, 289–290
    nuclear fission and, 298

radioactive decay, 284–285, 288, 292
radioactivity and, 280–281
Uranium-235, and nuclear fission, 297–298

V

Variables
    dependent, 28
    independent, 28
Vectors, 33–36
    adding, 35
    defined, 33
    direction of, 33
    displacement, 34
    quantities, 35
    scalars and, 35
Velocity
    and acceleration, 50
    changing, 48
    defined, 42
    frames of reference and, 262
    graphic representation of, 42
    measurement of, 262, 264
    and momentum, 121, 122, 123
    and projectiles, 66–67
    speed and, 42, 48
    as vector quantity, 35
Velocity-time graphs, 66–67
Vertex, 213
Vibrational kinetic energy, 150
Vibrations
    periods of, 175
    and regularly repeating waves, 174
Villard, Paul, 281
Virtual image
    about, 204–205
    enlarged, 215
    in optical instruments, 247, 248
Visible light, 201, 202
Volume, as scalar quantity, 35

W

Walton, Ernest Thomas Sinton, 296
Water
    heavy, 297, 298
    thermal energy and, 160
    waves, 174, 178
Watt, James, 133, 134
Watts, 133, 134
Wave equation, 177, 183
Wavelengths
    about, 175
    of gamma radiation, 284
    infrared, 202
    measurement of, 175
    of X-ray radiation, 284
    Young's experiment, 184–186
Waves
    amplitude of, 175, 183
    constructive interference of, 183, 184–
        185

destructive interference of, 183, 185
diffraction of, 186
interference of, 183–186
longitudinal, 176, 178
motion, 174
periodic, 174
properties of, 174–182, 183
reflection, 177
refraction, 177
shock, 188
sound, 187
speed of, 177
tanks, 178
transverse, 176, 178
types of, 174
water, 174, 178
Weight
    and acceleration of gravity, 77
    defined, 77
    gravitational force and, 78
    mass and, 77
    measurement, 77
Work
    defined, 132
    energy as capacity to do, 132
    and kinetic energy, 144
    measurement of, 132
    moving objects and, 142
    and power, 162
Work-energy theorem, 144

X

X-rays, 200, 280, 281, 284

Y

Y-intercept, 27
Young, Thomas, 184

Z

Zeros, as significant digits, 9, 10

65633028R00208

Made in the USA
Charleston, SC
28 December 2016